While You Were Sleeping:
Pearls of Wisdom from the U.S. Army Command and
General Staff College's Guest Speaker Program

While You Were Sleeping:

Pearls of Wisdom from the U.S. Army Command and General Staff College's Guest Speaker Program

By Eric Hollister, Lieutenant Colonel, U.S. Army, Retired

Leavenworth, Kansas 2015

Acknowledgements

There are many people I need to thank for helping this project come together. I want to express my gratitude to Colonel Kenneth Evans Jr. and Mr. Willis F. Jackson Jr. of the Department of Logistics and Resource Operations at CGSC for fostering a command climate that afforded me the opportunity to conduct this research. I would like to thank Mr. Marv Nickels of the Command and General Staff School for seeing the value of these resources and green-lighting this project. I need to thank the CARL Archive librarians, Elizabeth Dubuisson and Kathy Bunker for their assistance and for putting up with me. Elizabeth especially spent a lot of time helping me track down all these recordings. Thanks also to Mary Kay Menard of the Leavenworth Public Library for helping to find some historic photos. Many thanks to Colonel (Retired) Kevin C.M. Benson and Major General (Retired) Larry Lust for their invaluable feedback on the project and for reading the first drafts of every chapter. Finally, I want to thank my beautiful daughters Natalie and Rebecca for being the greatest kids anyone could ask for, and my wonderful wife Carrie for being so supportive of all of my distractions, and for making my life a great place to be.

About the Author

Lieutenant Colonel Eric Hollister retired from the U.S. Army in 2013 after 21 years of service. He was commissioned as an Air Defense Artillery Officer in 1991, and served with the 2nd Armored Cavalry Regiment at Fort Polk Louisiana, the 1st Infantry Division in Germany, and the 25th Infantry Division in Hawaii. His deployments included duty in Haiti, Bosnia, and a 15-month tour in Iraq. His final assignment was as a curriculum developer and instructor at the Command and General Staff College at Fort Leavenworth, Kansas. He is currently the Senior Army Instructor for the Leavenworth High School JROTC program.

LTC Hollister has a BA in Music from UCLA, and an MA in Humanities from California State University, Dominguez Hills. His publications include *Ike Warned Us About This: The MICC's Stranglehold on Responsible Acquisition* (published in Joint Forces Quarterly); *A Shot in the Dark: The Futility of Long-Range Modernization Planning* and *The Professional Military Ethic and Political Dissent: Has the Line Moved?* (both published in AUSA's Land Warfare Papers); and *The Buck Stops at Fort Leavenworth: Harry S. Truman at the Command and General Staff College* (published in Army magazine).

LTC Hollister, his wife Carrie, and their children Natalie and Rebecca reside in Leavenworth, Kansas.

Table of Contents

Introduction

BACKGROUND

The U.S. Army's Command and General Staff College (CGSC) at Fort Leavenworth, Kansas is one of the most important institutions of higher learning for Army officers, and has been for well over 100 years. Here, mid-career officers obtain the knowledge and tools to assume higher levels of responsibility, culminating in senior Army leadership roles. Since its inception, guest speakers have regularly addressed this important body of officers.

Several years ago, as I was doing research on another project in the archives of the Combined Arms Research Library (CARL) at Fort Leavenworth, I discovered that there were hundreds of recordings of guest speakers who had appeared before students of the Command and General Staff College (CGSC). As I am a fan of all things old and dusty, I filed the information away for another time. I revisited the tapes several years later, wondering what treasures were hidden inside such an incredible collection. As they were in outdated formats (mostly open-reel tape), and were restricted for use by CGSC students and faculty, most had been untouched for decades and many not since their original recording. It was a gold mine of original source material. I approached the college with the idea for a book compiling the best of these speeches, and was given permission to use the tapes.

The task was daunting. After looking through the electronic catalog and physically culling through all the tapes (which I would eventually do three times), I came up with a list that would produce the most interesting material. Because of the sheer number of recordings, I generally limited my selections to Army Chiefs of Staff or Vice Chiefs (and their sister service equivalents), Army and Defense Secretaries, significant politicians, and well-known individuals whose comments would be of interest to most readers. The resulting list reads like a military history honor roll: Bradley, Montgomery, Ridgway, Taylor, Johnson, Abrams, and DePuy, not to mention three visits by President Harry Truman himself.

THE TAPES

Then began the process of listening to all of the tapes, which was simultaneously fascinating and tedious. By my rough count I listened to over 135 hours of remarks contained in over 125 tapes. Notes were taken in longhand, with scribbled stars highlighting the most interesting passages for later transcription. While I listened, I digitized the tapes for the future preservation and enjoyment of this priceless collection and so I could review the recordings, getting accurate transcriptions of the selected remarks. Obviously my own background and interests colored what I determined would be included in the book, but hopefully my selections will be interesting to all.

As I listened, I was struck by how there seemed to be no problems that the military faced in 2012 that hadn't happened previously. All of the guest speakers discussed issues they were confronting, issues that would recur in the remarks of future speakers: Shortage of resources, post-war drawdowns, personnel turbulence, societal changes and rifts, civil-military relations—in many cases the same speeches could be delivered today and would still be relevant. To highlight this, General Omar Bradley's speech to the graduating class of 1949 is the *Prologue* to this book. Another constant refrain was the ever-present allusion to an increasing rate of change, a realization that events were moving faster than ever before. Current and former service members and military historians alike will be fascinated by the comments the military leadership made at the time, without the benefit of hindsight. Finally, the frequency with which the Army Chiefs and

Secretaries and other high-level officials made appearances at CGSC is startling. By his own count, Harold K. Johnson spoke at the college 13 times. As Army Chief of Staff, Johnson spoke at the college three times in 1966 alone. In a three-month period, the class of 1974 heard General William DePuy, General Creighton Abrams, Secretary of Defense James Schlesinger, and Secretary of the Army Harold Callaway.

As opposed to presenting these remarks chronologically, they are organized into categories in order to better show trends over time within a certain aspect of the military. In most cases only a year is provided in the text to denote when the speaker appeared, as most speakers don't appear more than once in any given year. When the speaker appeared more frequently, the month is also provided. Appendix A, which lists all the speakers researched for this book, also provides specific dates of their appearances. I have also presented the remarks exactly as they were delivered, only inserting editorial comments where the speaker clearly meant the opposite of what they actually said.

More than one speaker alluded to the fact that a student in the audience would end up on the CGSC stage in 10-20 years giving his own speech. It is interesting to track the lineage and pedigree, if you will, of various CGSC alums who became guest speakers themselves. For example, it is very likely that both Abrams and Johnson were in the audience when General Bradley delivered the 1949 commencement address. Appendix B shows some examples (limited to those individuals used for this book) of some speakers and who they heard during their time at CGSC, as well as some contemporary leadership of the Army to demonstrate that the cycle continues unabated, linking our past to our present and future.

Finally, the original title of this book was *While You Were Sleeping: Pearls of Wisdom in the Command and General Staff College's Blue Bedroom.* The "Blue Bedroom" was the nickname given to Eisenhower Auditorium, where a majority of the following remarks took place. It was pointed out to me that not only would this title not lend itself to web searches, but only a small number of individuals would have any idea what the blue bedroom was or what took place there. Logic dictated a change.

Prologue

Speech delivered by Army Chief of Staff Omar Bradley to the CGSC graduating class of 1949

General Eddy, members of the class and their friends, it's a great pleasure to be back here again. And as I look around the outskirts of this assemblage, I see that things have not changed too much in 20 years. When I went to my graduation exercise some 20 years ago, I know there were some cars outside, packed, with the motors running. I notice the same thing today. And I'm sure it's not because you people have not enjoyed the course. I hope you have enjoyed it as much as I did. I think, however, it is not from some desire to hurriedly get away from what you've been doing, but it shows enthusiasm which still exists in you. You're school boys, school is over, and you're anxious to get home and on to other tasks. I'm sure it's not from any hurry to get away from your pleasant surroundings here.

If we Americans are to forge a long-range military policy which will endure, it must be internationally astute, and nationally within our means. Strategic plans for future defense can only be as valid as the peacetime preparations we can afford. Soldiers, sailors and airman must provide the United States with the sturdiest defense available within the price we can pay. That this is a very real and limiting factor no one can deny.

For we cannot afford to maintain over a long period of time the established forces that can assure a quick victory. However, we can afford, and must afford, sufficient forces in being, including the mobilization base and necessary reinforcements, to avert disaster in event we are attacked. In four years we demobilized an Army, a Navy, and an Air Force, until they were little more than occupation forces in foreign lands.

For the cycle of reestablishing a planned and ready military stature, we have reacted jerkily, spasmodically, to the stress and the tension from outside sources. In this atmosphere a truly long-range policy was only a conversation piece. Today in our armed forces, we have reached a stability which in my opinion can be the basis for the combat readiness which will avert disaster. With additional effort and a little more time, we can build the forces now planned into reliable guardians of defense.

Militarily speaking, the situation is as stable as it is going to be for some time to come. In the four years since V-J Day, I think the advantage has swung to our side. And that the aggressor, who was once a friend, is now on the defensive. Rather than expect a long period of friendly cooperation, however, we must anticipate a long period of tension, with day-to-day alternating improvements or setbacks, which must not be allowed to unstabilize the long-range plans for security. The American citizen must evidence a resoluteness and constancy that will signal our new stand for protected, secure freedoms. He will draw courage and strength for his own progress, and will reinforce the faith of our friends in Western Europe. The U.S. security dollar will be invested in long-term bonds, which are found to pay off in defense dividends and decreased cost. Better plans can be made, greater economies affected, and our allies can confidently chart their courses.

Since you are students of American foreign policy as well as military preparedness, you are interested in the consideration of the basic ingredients of a sound long-range military policy in support of the United States, which is an integrated plan of our peaceful intention and our military potential. First, in our present conditions, it must cost much less than we are spending now. Second, considering the enemies we may sometimes face, our combined forces must be much more effective than they are today. And speaking of effectiveness, or combat readiness as a military man would term it, our greatest danger is that we will be caught up in the fancy of futurism, and commit ourselves to unbalanced forces that will not match the forces which might oppose us. When I speak of balance I don't mean the dividing of funds equally among the three services. Nor do I mean an equation of so many ships equals so many soldiers equals so many air groups to create a pattern on a chart. When I speak of balance I mean effective forces equal to the tasks that modern warfare may thrust upon us. And in striking this balance we must include that which can be reliably contributed by our allies.

We can upset this equilibrium by committing ourselves not strategically nor numerically, but financially to plans which on the surface seem proper, but tomorrow tower over us in burdensome upkeep. So as a third ingredient I consider balanced forces, as I understand balance, as most essential. This guiding principle of economy, effectiveness, and balanced preparedness applies equally in my judgment to all three of the armed forces. We cannot afford to spend more money than is absolutely necessary on any one of the services merely to satisfy an emotional appeal. Every dollar spent must be strategically productive, for either national bankruptcy or a lack of preparedness will satisfy a lurking aggressor.

Long-range policy must be accompanied by long-range budget plans. Piecemeal attacks cannot be mounted forever. And in our year to year consideration of the budget we must look ahead at least 4 or 5 years. We cannot afford to spend $6 billion in the enlargement of a particular service that may require $7 billion to maintain the next year and perhaps $8 billion to maintain and improve in the succeeding years unless we realize and fully intend the long-range effect that this will have on our future capabilities.

For example, and as only a hypothetical picture, if we decide in fiscal year 1953 that we can afford only $12 billion in funds for the armed forces, and in the present fiscal year we launched a long-range program for one service that will in three years demand $8 billion of a $12 billion budget, then we would end up with a national military establishment entirely out of balance to meet an emergency. We would have nullified our effectiveness and decidedly compromised our security.

Long-range military policy must ultimately be interpreted by men with missions, trained and equipped to perform them. Civilians must set the policy. But they will continue to rely on their trusted military advisors for the practical applications.

Without sacrificing any of the economies or progress which can be opened by modern research and invention, some down-to-earth readiness must be the foundation of our present plans. This is our most pressing military problem. American ingenuity has been admired and respected by men everywhere. With the American soldier, the field expedient has often created sterling success from foredoomed impossibility. With inventive genius, he has often provided abundance from scarcity.

Nationally we are faced with a similar problem, and today every planner must put this ingenuity to work on the big picture scale. The American people are anxious for the first sign that we can positively win the victory in any future war. However, our plans can best provide for victory by preventing another war. Many soldiers, and even more statesmen, have worked towards the goal of winning the war without firing a shot. I believe that we can contribute greatly to this possibility for the United States. Success in the effort would be the ultimate in economy: Economy of lives, of resources, of American standards of living.

You are all familiar with the precept that another way to prevent war is to be so strong that no one will dare attack us. In this day and age however, this method of war prevention is too expensive. We must seek a better solution.

Another method would be to reestablish through the coalition of friendly nations the military power to back our peaceful intentions if challenged. In concert with the other signers of the Atlantic Pact, we may ultimately achieve this. In that event smaller forces, readily available, and readily capable of expansion might be relied upon. Our strength would lie in collective action and political combination backed by efficient, expandable forces. These forces must be ready and capable of keeping a toe-hold on any continent which may ultimately become the battlefield.

Our economy is thus linked to theirs, our foreign policy to their international ways and means.

As graduate students in the art and science of war, it is not necessary that I discuss with you the nature of modern warfare which will dictate our fundamental forces. We all recognize that we must have first and foremost a strategic Air Force, second to none, equipped with the ultimate in weapons that our research and development can provide. And our plans must be so complete that we know the application of this force will help carry us to the position we nationally wish to achieve when the war is over. With me you undoubtedly plan for a Navy, with its air arm and its essential Marine units for the fulfillment of the Navy's offensive and defensive mission, including the assistance that the Army and the Air Force must have to project the battle as far from our shores as possible. We must have a tactical Air Force. For every soldier knows that the fighter/bomber combination with the infantry, artillery, and tanks is the only practical battlefield force in modern war. Before presenting the detailed problem I would like to have you consider, I would add one more thought on modern warfare: It is essential for all of us to realize that successful modern war demands that the victor put continuous pressure on the enemy. For modern battle is a unified and continuing effort. To win we must pour on a series of continuing blows, rising to a crescendo of intensity and fierceness until the enemy and his war making potential crumbles. It is essential that no phase should fall off in intensity and thus allowing him to catch his breath and recuperate from the latest blow, to prepare for the next. If he is a strong foe, he may seize this opportunity if there is a lag, to strike a cunning blow back.

With economy our yardstick and preparedness our pattern, then let us estimate the size and composition of the American Army that fits the pattern. Smaller, less expensive defense forces for the nation, which [are] a member of a coalition. In analyzing the requirements, we must provide an answer to the question "What size Army must we and shall we maintain for the long run?" To meet the modern warfare requirements, we must maintain as a ready, mobile force, the smallest, self-contained organization capable of major battle accomplishments. And we must have, to go with it, the reinforcements, the mobilization base, the special mission units for bases we must seize and hold.

This is not nearly so large an Army as some might imagine. This ready force must have good soldiers trained to assume greater positions of responsibility. In an extreme perhaps, every private should be a potential first sergeant. These men must be trained not in just one type of warfare, but in many, and from many climates, and many strange conditions.

I think this is the place to put in a necessary caution. Too many planners, failing to consider our national dearth of manpower in comparison to other nations, think in terms of large, special forces: divisions capable of only amphibious work, or divisions capable of only airborne work. This is short-sighted. In the American armed forces we must have every division, in fact every combat soldier, trained to fight as infantry, and with the infantry, on the ground. That this force must be mobile, tactically and strategically, is a foregone conclusion. And if it is to be committed overseas, the necessary shipping must be readily available in the exact numbers and types of ships we need. Ports and port battalions must exist as transportation support in being.

Trained men and waiting ships are not enough. This force in being, which must be our minimum fighting establishment should have the best in modern equipment. Caught in the fascination of scientific development and research promise, the practical soldier may be misled in his thinking toward atomic warheads and guided missile long-range firepower to the exclusion of a very practical objective. Even with our generous industrial production, any future American Army must leave an absolutely clean battlefield. We cannot expect industry to provide, nor a Soldier to carry, any item he does not use. This applies to every other soldier who must support the advance of the ground Army. To save ourselves in order to win the battle, the American G.I. must be the best equipped, the best protected, and the man with the lightest load. This includes his rifle, his ammunition, his clothing, and his food. I don't believe that American ingenuity has been completely applied to this ultimate "economy plus effectiveness" problem. Lighten the soldier's load and at the same time decrease the weight of his supporting guns and their ammunition and we may in the sum total provide through research and development an airborne Army. By affecting this helpful economy, and by constant effort to use less of the strategically critical raw materials in our arms, we may be able to lower the steel and munitions requirements to the point we can provide a victory in lower cost in living standards as well as in lives.

Finally in general objective, this ready force must know its mission, and more than that, must like it. It cannot be a one-shot task force for a suicide attempt. Plans made for its employment must include a realistic concept of the logistical support and the reinforcements needed for sustained missions. And as we work out its speedy transportation with the Navy and the Air, we must provide the tactical air groups to push the divisions forward, and to maintain air superiority wherever possible. If this force is available, and we provide in our Army the schooling system, the depots and storage plants, the necessary Reserve and National Guard training assistance, we can meet the first requirement of a modern war at the same time Strategic Air launches the retaliatory attack. These are unusual and most difficult requirements. However they are not beyond the capabilities of good planning, forward thinking soldiers. And I urge you in the months to come to apply your minds and your education to this problem.

As a basis of discussion, I suggest one possible solution. Can the United States afford an Army Striking Force of any less than a completely ready reinforced corps balanced in division types, capable of sustained action, for the backbone of its long-range modern Army? This is not a time for classroom problems. After all, you've completed a year of rigorous study in a limited professional field. American military success has been founded on similar study by soldiers before you. Each of them had the capability of envisioning greater problems, and at the same time inventing more practical answers than their predecessors.

A review of World War II and its outcome has confirmed in my own mind the belief that the Army's system of professional education, which was revitalized and expanded after World War I, was one of the greatest contributions to the winning of World War II. For it provided us and our small nucleus of Regular Army officers, and our larger compliment of National Guard and Reserve officers, with skilled leadership as well as staff procedures which competently faced the tough tactical and strategic problems thrust upon us. Today as you graduate from the Command and General Staff College, you join the ranks of those soldiers who have a common professional education aimed toward the solution of higher staff and command problems. Your selection to attend this school is evidence of the Army's faith in your potential for assuming greater responsibility in the case of war. It is especially appropriate that we have discussed future plans and policies and necessary economies with you here today.

One final word to the future commanders and staff officers in the American Army: Keep within these possibilities as you plan. That is, the American Army can be no different than the American people. If our national aptitudes are mechanization, initiative, ingenuity, individuality, we must never attempt to suppress them. A man's religion and his politics are his own affair and must always continue to be. And if a man's respect for his superiors is based on appreciation of intelligence and ability of his leaders, then the leaders we offer them must have these better talents.

In your future military careers, I wish you and your families continued success and much happiness. As American citizens, you are expected to be outstanding.

1. The Army

Given the fact that the Command and General Staff College is an Army school, and most of the speakers in the time period studied were Army officers, at some point all of them discussed some aspect of the Army itself. Most of these remarks fell into several broad categories: the Army's mission, an officer's duty, Army history, Army life and the profession of arms, training, and the CGSC itself.

THE ARMY'S MISSION

Many of the speakers discussed the reason for the Army's existence and what its mission was (or should be). When he was the Commander of Forces Command (FORSCOM), future Army Chief of Staff Dennis Reimer summed it up nicely during an appearance in 1994.

> I think [author T.R.] Fehrenbach said it best in "This Kind of War" when he said "If you desire to defend a land, protect it and keep it from civilization, you must do this on the ground, the way the Roman Legions did, by putting your young men in the mud." That was true in the Korean War, it's true now, Desert Storm, and it's probably going to be true in the 21st century.

Atomic Weapons and President Eisenhower's "New Look" strategy left the Army of the 1950s and 1960s with an identity crisis, requiring their Chiefs of Staff to continually define and defend the reason for their existence. George H. Decker did this admirably during the December, 1960 graduation ceremonies of the Associate Course.

> We soldiers also share a conviction as to the future: a deeply rooted faith in the indispensability and in the permanency of the land combat function. We realize that the means to perform that function will change in the future as they have in the past. But we have an unshakable faith, that as long as there is land and people on the land, the land combat function itself will remain a decisive element in any future conflict.

> …We might consider doctrine as an Army creed, which spells out the way we view our purpose in life and our relations to others. I'd like to list some of the specific beliefs of this creed. First among our beliefs is a principle stated in General Order 100 of the War Department, dated 24th April, 1863. "Modern wars are not internecine war in which the killing of the enemy is the object. The destruction of the enemy in modern war, and indeed modern war itself, are means to obtain that object of a belligerent which lies beyond the war." The philosophy expressed in that statement permeates all our strategic thinking.

> …We believe that Army forces play a vital role in any form of war, from the outset of a general thermo-nuclear war to its conclusion, in the wide range of war short of the ultimate all-out form, and in the lower levels of violence such as counterinsurgency and guerrilla actions which are becoming increasingly important. We cannot be sure where Army forces may be employed, or under what conditions. However, to look at the trouble spots around the world, from Berlin to Laos, from Korea to deepest Africa, is enough for us to be sure that forces to operate in the land environment must be ready at a moment's notice for any kind of war, any place, and at any time. I'd like to emphasize that a static doctrine in today's dynamic world environment could result in military and national suicide. This is especially true during a period such as the present when our

strategic nuclear capabilities and those of the enemy appear to be approaching a state of parity. Such a situation has tended to produce the equivalent of a strategic nuclear disarmament. In this world environment, dual-capable land forces, an essential element needed to fight in wars below the general nuclear war level, assume an ever-increasing importance.

Harold K. Johnson, who would become Chief of Staff during the Vietnam War, spent a lot of time thinking and talking about the role of the Army, especially as the commandant of the college and as the Deputy Chief of Staff for Operations (DCSOPS). It was in this capacity that he spoke to the college in December, 1963.

> In our world, land is the prime focal point. Land is the basis of man's existence. Regardless of compensating advantages in other media, a nation's power from the air or on the sea stems directly from the quantity and the quality of the land that it controls. The practical aspect of this is that man fights most stubbornly for land, particularly when the disputed land is his home, and I think many of you have seen that in practice. Because always and everywhere men attach themselves more tenaciously to land than to almost any other material object. The Army's capability to establish control is a unique characteristic, since it means defeating an enemy without destroying it. It is this capability that so admirably serves the underlying purpose of American military power, which as I indicated at the outset, is to preserve stability. And this is a good theme, wherever you go, to preach, because it is the distinction between all of the elements of power. Power and destruction do not equate directly.

> How does the Army maintain stability? First, it prevents instability by maintaining control and fostering nation building, because we are the nation building force. This requires law and order. The maintenance of law and order presupposes the establishment of some measure of control, the second method to restore stability if an unstable situation develops within the free world. The effort necessary to restore stability is exemplified almost daily in Vietnam. A third method, and another continuing task of the Army, is to be prepared to fight if necessary to restore control or to establish control. And this is sometimes something we forget.

> The dividing line between methods of restoring control is never clear, because we are always dealing in some shade of grey. And to attempt to treat our problems as absolutes is one of the things that get us into difficulty from time to time. Because the issues are rarely clear. Nevertheless, each level of action is essential to our national strategy of Flexible Response. As we want to preserve the territorial integrity of the free world while keeping any level of conflict at the lowest level within the spectrum. We also share a conviction as to the future: A deeply rooted faith in the indispensability of the land combat function. We realize that the ways this function will be performed in the future will change, as they have in the past. But we should, each of us, have an unshakeable faith that as long as there is land, and people on the land, the land combat function will remain THE decisive element in a future conflict. Because somebody has to be around to establish control.

In March, 1966 Johnson, as Army Chief of Staff, elaborated on this point:

How do you establish control? And here you fall back to the mission of the infantry, modified just a little bit: To close with and defeat the enemy. Now note that I substitute the word "defeat" for "destroy." We still have to teach our platoon leaders, and our company commanders, and our battalion commanders to destroy, because that's their job, and this is step one in establishing control in the end where combat becomes so personal. But as you move yourself a little bit, we've got to recognize the world in which we live. There are few absolutes in this world, and we're always operating somewhere in the great grey areas between absolutes. And I'll touch on absolutes in a moment. So our purpose then is to defeat.

Now how do you close with and defeat the enemy? You do this through a process of fire and maneuver. Then you get into an argument which still, I shouldn't use the world "rages" because it doesn't rage, but still is prevalent within the Army and between and among the services. Which is the more important, maneuver or firepower? Well you have to go back and ask yourself the question "What's the purpose?" And if your purpose is control, you do this through maneuver, because what does firepower do? Firepower destroys, and that's not your purpose. You maneuver, and you employ your firepower for the basic purpose of permitting this maneuver force to close to establish control. Now this can be argued and will continue to be argued, I'm sure, ad infinitum. But it, I think in my view, still is a very persuasive argument with regard to the importance of the two. Now it doesn't mean that you can dismiss one, and place your full reliance on another. Because here again we come in this area of absolutes.

What is the nation's maneuver force? Easy answer: The United States Army. So we've always got a job in this business of accomplishing our nation's purpose in maintaining, establishing, or creating an environment of order. Always something to do.

Regarding what that "something to do" would entail, Johnson offered this in December, 1967:

Well, I've been a great believer that by concentrating on scouting and patrolling, what we term "minor tactics," that the structures we have can be adjusted to do almost anything. Question: How much of that structure aren't we using? Now every one of us, every one of us is deeply conservative. We've got to have a cushion. Always have a little bit tucked away in case the need arises. I can cite quite a few examples of this. And a degree of conservatism I think that we must maintain. Why? Because for us, on the ground, at the end of the line, a human life is at stake. Everything that we do, we do to support that rifleman, because he's the fellow that closes, and it's he who loses his life first. So we've got to be conservative, and we've got to continue to be conservative.

Johnson, at this point retired, added this in 1970:

While the question has been posed a great number of times, and it's sort of a rhetorical question, "Are we going to be the world's policeman?" The people who are asking the question are asking the wrong question. The question is "Does the world need a policeman?" How many of you have read *The Lessons of History* by Will and Ariel Durant? Not very many. It's only 102 pages long and it's a remarkable little book.

…They had examined 3,421 years of recorded history, and in that time there have been only 268 years without conflict somewhere. Does the world need a policeman? Somebody's got to be prepared to pick up the share. Now I'm not saying that we should do this alone, I don't think we should. But we've got to continue to contribute to maintain the stability throughout the world where we can logically do so. Now there are going to be ups and downs as to the popularity of doing it, and there are going to be ups and downs in the areas of international relations. We happen to be down now, whether we're all the way down at the bottom of the curve I don't know, before we start an upswing. I would hope that we're nearly there, if we're not there. But it means that we've got to disengage somewhat. We've got to be just a little bit looser at the plate so that we've got resources that we can go in a number of directions rather than resources that are committed to a single job. What does this mean? Over time, and probably not very much time, I think something less in Europe, something less firm on "Yes, we're coming fast." Hopefully something more firm on "If there's trouble, we'll certainly be in there among the first discussing what we can do about it." Hopefully not limited always to talk, talk, talk.

In 1973, former Chairman of the Joint Chiefs of Staff (CJCS) Maxwell Taylor offered up his version of a national security strategy and how the Army could support it.

What do I mean by Rational National Security? If I have to give a definition I would have to say that what I'm speaking about is a master national program integrating all forms of relevant national power to provide a level of protection to these national valuables—the assets, interests, sources of power that I mentioned [previously]. Valuables at home and valuables abroad. And furthermore a program…that rational citizens will consider reasonable and worthy of the price they are required to pay…

So I'm getting to the point where, perhaps I'm combat weary, where I'm going to give up on [previous models used to justify force structure], and I suggest going about it a different way. First is just to cite the kinds of things the general purpose forces may be called upon to do: Requirements to protect our citizens and their assets abroad, the defense against piracy and terrorism and international crime, examples of which we're seeing in all sides, the need to keep our sea lanes open, our air lanes open, electronic communications intact, the possible requirements for peacekeeping in conjunction with the United Nations and other regional pacts. And then, always to have a big stick, not a big stick as Theodore Roosevelt meant, but at least a stick of moderate size in the closet to help the president when he appears at international councils to argue the interests of the United States. So there's a package of things that obviously must be done, the question then comes up again, how much is enough? Well I would answer it this way. The actual dollar budget for national security every year in the long run is the visceral feeling of the President of the United States after listening to many, many advisors as to how much the country can afford to spend for national security. And that's the way it's going to continue to be, I think, for a long as we have our present form of government.

So now that being the case let's agree to set to one side the funds necessary for this limited, maximized deterrent that I've described at the outset, and we'll pay that bill, put it to one side, and that's that. We won't touch that. Then we have to see what we have left. Then I think that gives us our answer. We would take whatever funds we have left for the general purpose forces and build our force based upon the money available and the volunteers of quality that we can get—I'm assuming a continuation of the all-volunteer force. I don't think we should want to have volunteers, have any man in the Army uniform who is not a good man: Excellence first, quality first. And certainly limited numbers, how many I don't know, of young men that will meet that standard in this country in any given year. I would want to be able to "hire" that man, so to speak, if he's willing to present himself. If he doesn't, I won't take a second-rater. And that will fix pretty well the size of my force, as will the dollar figure affect the size because I will have to take into account modernization of equipment at the same time. So the impact of the cost of volunteers and modern equipment I think will set the ceiling on the general purpose forces, justified in the general way by the vast number of incidents and episodes that may arise requiring their intervention.

Howard H. Callaway was the Secretary of the Army as the nation emerged from the Vietnam War. Always an entertaining speaker, he appeared at CGSC twice in 1974 and offered his thoughts on the post-war Army. In May of that year, he told the students about the challenges they would face after graduation:

> I think you are going to find quite a different Army from the time you came in here. I think you're going to find that the Army of today is more upbeat. I think you'll find stabilized tours have given, to a large extent, the kind of leadership I'm talking about. And I think when you go out you can be extremely challenged by what you'll find. I happen to believe that no one can do a good job without a challenge. I happen to believe that the problem the Israelis had at the beginning of the last war was because the six-day war was too easy. It was so easy they really didn't think they had a challenge out there. They thought they could, you know, "What about that? It's just Arabs, no problem." If that's true, if I'm right, we ought to have the finest Army we've ever had in the history of the world. [Laughter] Because the challenge you're going to get to go out there and to have an Army with a major global mission, one of the two super powers of the world, maintaining this generation of peace, with a well-trained Army, training, knowing every minute that the higher their state of training the less chance they'll have to use it. Getting that kind of motivated Army to lead this nation forward in this generation of peace and doing it all without a draft is going to be a challenge worthy of everything you've got. And because of that challenge I think it's going to make the Army a whole lot better. And if any of you any night wake up and you haven't got anything to do the next morning, give me a call, we've got a few challenges left we can put you on.

In December he spoke to a different group of students about the deterrent quality needed at that particular time.

> I'll close by saying what I said to a group of businessmen in New York last week. I'm not sure I meant for it to come out this way, but anyway it's the way it came out: That timing is the most important thing that there is in life. Timing is always the most important thing. And right now timing is perfect, because the Army is moving towards becoming an outstanding Army, and I sincerely believe the finest Army that we've ever had in our 200 years...And that's happening all at the time when the world is falling apart. You know, that's when you need a good Army. I really think that the world situation is such now that we need the Army now, it needs to be ready. And if it's good enough, and if it's

as good as you and I want it to be, well we're not going to have to use it. And I think that's the challenge that we've got. To be good enough, strong enough, and be *clearly* strong enough so that at this time when the world is falling apart, when the tensions are enormous, that our Army's good enough sitting there that everybody knows its capability, and knowing it they don't want to try. And therefore, we preserve the peace without any casualties on our part, just by being that good, that well-trained, that well-disciplined.

The Vice Chief of Staff, General Walter T. Kerwin, Jr., continued this line of thinking at the graduation ceremony in 1976.

You know many people also fail to understand that when we do become embroiled in a war we have failed. It essentially means that we have failed as a nation to convince our enemy that we have both the will, and I stress the will, as well as the means to protect and defend our own interests. And you recall back in 1962, [Soviet Premier Nikita] Khrushchev would never have risked introducing the Soviet missiles into Cuba had he not misperceived the resoluteness, the will, and the willingness of the President of the United States and the people of the United States to defend their interests in the Western Hemisphere. So the key to deterrence is perception. If the American people don't want war, they must maintain a sufficient deterrent, both strategic and general purpose.

Many speakers addressed deterrence, specifically being ready to go at a moment's notice to accomplish whatever the Army was asked to do. Army Chief of Staff Fred Weyand talked to the students about readiness in 1975.

The one thing that we have been embarked on as a course is that this Army must be ready, and it must be balanced. Readiness first, because the strategic equation has changed over what it was 20 or 30 years ago. And [the Korean War] was a watershed in that, like the [1973-74] oil embargo in another area. Korea showed us that if we were going to be a world power in a military sense and could influence events we had to be ready now. Not six months from now, not a year from now. There's no one around to take up the slack while we get ready. And we've got commitments that if unfulfilled, destroy our credibility and ultimately will destroy us. Readiness is important, even more important than numbers. And General [Creighton] Abrams and myself made a commitment to each other: We didn't know how many divisions we'd have. We knew how many we wanted, how many we needed, but the Congress and administration would dictate what that number would be. But whatever that number, they'd be ready.

In 1979, Army Chief Edward "Shy" Meyer put this readiness into historical perspective.

I would say that if you ran through the halls of the Pentagon, you could still hear the echoes of past Chiefs of Staff saying the same thing about having an Army that goes to war. That's not something new. That's something all of us have to attempt to focus on. But the need for an Army that can go to war is something that's absolutely paramount at this particular time in our history. As you take a look at what's happened, both strategically and in the tactical nuclear arena, the conventional arena, you realize the one thing that's going to deter war is an Army, an armed force, that is truly capable of going to war. You'll recall the words of [Former Secretary of War] Elihu Root, "Not to promote war, but to preserve peace." And that's the purpose of our Army. If we can have an Army that's good enough, if that other son-of-a-gun across the border realizes that we are good enough, then it's less likely that we're going to have to go to war. So the key is to be able to create an Army that can do that... Now some of the key areas that we're focusing on today as we take a look at this Army are basically what I call force readiness. You'll recall in the past we had focused on unit readiness, today we have to truly focus on total force readiness. Because the ability of the United States Army to go to war is controlled by three basic factors for effectiveness: One is our geography. That's what helps us project power. Two is the capability of our forces, and three, it's the will of our society, of our national leaders, to be able to project that power.

The end of the Cold War saw the Army once again trying to define its mission, moving from Soviet containment to something much more fluid and difficult to pin down. Many speakers spent time trying to bring clarity to this problem, including Chief of Staff Gordon R. Sullivan in 1992.

I want you to think about these things this year: What is the role of the Army in the post-Cold War era? What does ethnicity mean to the Unites States Army? You want to know what ethnicity means, read about Afghanistan. What is the role of the Unites States Army with our allies? With the people you will go to class with, you need to think about some of these roles. Social issues. I'll talk about those, there are lots of them out there that will impact on the Army.

As a former lawyer, Secretary of the Army Togo West was a very eloquent speaker. In 1994 he laid out the role of the Army in the new national security environment that existed in the post-Cold War era.

This Army—and we say this to ourselves, I think sometimes we are not as eager to say it outside— this Army exists to wage war. That is why we put uniforms on our citizens. That is why they take the constitutional oath. That is why they put themselves at risk. Because when all else fails our nation needs men and women, NCOs and officers who are prepared to go to war. It exists, then, as an instrument of compulsion for our nation, when all else fails, when diplomacy has taken its last shot, and when we have no choice as a nation but to seek to cause another nation, or some other entity, to submit to the will of the United States. In short, the first way in which this Army fits that new scenario is in its ultimate role to "compel." It's had to do that, from time to time. We expected, when I flew down to the aircraft carrier to see the 10th Mountain Division [en route to Haiti for Operation Uphold Democracy], that they were about to go into a situation in which they were asked to compel. We know during [Operation] Desert Storm that that is precisely what our armed forces did, and we thought they might have to do it again in the recent involvement in Kuwait and in Saudi Arabia.

The second role in which our Army is used in this new national security environment is to "deter," as a deterrent. To serve as a deterrent, to be able to fulfill this role, three conditions must exist: First of all, the first condition that I described has to be true. You cannot deter if you are not able to compel. Secondly, you must be perceived as able to compel. And thirdly, we must be perceived as being willing to compel. And the deterrence... is often what we describe as a key role of our Army, and it is. And as a follow-on to the first [role] and has been used—again in Haiti—that's eventually what the force ended up being, a deterrent force. The authorities there finally said "Well fine, come on in, we won't resist." Certainly deterrence operated in Kuwait and in Saudi Arabia. And of course our forces in Europe and on the Korean Peninsula continue to be there in a size and a strength to provide a significant deterrent to those who do not see their interests as aligned with those of the United States, or is antagonistic to those of our allies.

The third of the 'fits' for our Army with this national security strategy is to "reassure." When we are not present in sufficient number or do not wish to be present in sufficient number, but wish to show our commitment to our allies, we still need for the number one purpose of our Army to be true. That is that it can compel, it is perceived as able to compel, and we're perceived as willing to use it. But to provide reassurance. The best example of that is on the northern border of the former Yugoslav Republic of Macedonia.

And the final use of the Army in this environment…is one that has existed as long as there has been a republic, but is newly discovered by many commentators. They talk about it as if it's something new. And that is to support: Support our domestic authorities when events exceed their ability, with their domestic agencies, to carry out their responsibilities. Most notably the [1871] Chicago fire—some years back, I might add. Or the [1989] California earthquake, or fires in the northwest, floods wherever they may occur.

General Reimer, when he was Chief of Staff, put this more succinctly for the students in 1996.

A full spectrum force is something we have added [to the Army Vision] the past few months. It reflects the fact that we've changed our Army from a primarily threat-based force that was organized and equipped based on the Soviet threat, to a capabilities-based force that provides capabilities to the nation: The capabilities to reassure allies and friends, to be able to support the civilian authorities in terms of domestic crisis, and to be able to deter and compel an enemy. That's a major change, and the United States Army has made that during the past four years, and we're now a full-spectrum force and a capabilities-based force.

In the 1990s, missions in Haiti and Bosnia (among others) generated much debate within the Army about operations other than war (OOTW), and whether or not those types of missions were appropriate. Interestingly, the debate over alternate missions was not new, as the Commander of Training and Doctrine Command, William E. DePuy, demonstrated in March, 1974.

After the Korean War, we went through a period in which, well, when General Max Taylor was the Chief of Staff we had the limited war. A fad. And then we had the Pentomic Division—this all before your time. Nuclear Warfare. Then we got counterinsurgency. Now I'm not criticizing anybody, I was right in the middle of all these "fads" myself. I was just bright-eyed and eager and got right in the middle of all. But now that I think back on them, I can see what happened. Then we went off and fought the [Vietnam] war and everybody got kind of disenchanted with that so then we sort of went into management.

General Bernard Rogers, who would eventually become Chief of Staff, alluded to mission focus in remarks to National Guard commanders in 1976 when he was in command of FORSCOM.

> … I want to tick off these things we're trying to concentrate on in Forces Command and the total Army. First [Training areas needing focus]: Oriented towards Europe. Now that may not be the most likely area of the next war for us, but that's where we need to orient, because if we can satisfy the requirement for Europe, we can satisfy the requirements for the rest of the world.

Chief of Staff Carl Vuono addressed the students in 1990 shortly after the Operation Just Cause in Panama, and addressed future Army missions this way:

> There's a linkage between what we did in Panama and what we can do worldwide. People say "Is the future of the Army for Panamanian kind of actions?" The answer to that is no. It's wherever we're asked to do something. Whether it's the central region of Europe, Korea, Middle East, wherever it might be, or Latin America, we've got to make sure we've got the kind of force that can do something when it gets on the ground in support of whatever it is the National Command Authority asks us to do.

Future CJCS John Shalikashvili spoke in 1992 after his successful leadership of Operation Provide Comfort, a peacekeeping operation in Northern Iraq. During his remarks he stressed to the students the importance of mastering their wartime duties.

> I would be surprised if sooner or later some of you wouldn't get involved in something like [Provide Comfort] but remember no two are alike. What is it that you can do right now to prepare yourself for it? I have often been asked since then by some very responsible people how we ought to change our training program, our exercises, our procurement policies and so, to be more ready to do something like this. And my answer has been the same ever since I left [Northern Iraq], because I am convinced it's right. We ought to change nothing. That 18th Engineer soldier who fixed the runway in Sirsink [Iraq] did what he was trained to do for war. The medic who was working on an amputated leg of a Special Forces guy who had it blown off [by] a mine was doing that which he was trained to do in war. The Civil Affairs guys, the Special Forces guys, certainly all the security force guys, the engineers who were fixing roads and other—and the list just goes on and on and I can't think of anything, whether that's communications, or whether that's airdropping things, or whether that's flying fixed-wing aircraft with supply missions or attack birds to provide security. All of it is what you and your soldiers are trained to do. And all I'd ask you, all I'd tell you is to be prepared for this, is really kind of very simple thing. [Shows "Professional Competence" on the screen] And it always is important, but it's doubly important when you find yourself at the end of the world with not a chance to rehearse something or think it through, you need to perform on a moment's notice. And you might be a Lieutenant Colonel who arrives and tries to develop a communications system for something stretching hundreds of miles, and you've got to know your business. You can't turn to somebody and say "Tell me what I need to be doing." So I really ask you to not worry about what you need to do to get ready for this, other than to be as good a logistician, a medic, or infantryman or artilleryman that you possibly can be.

But the second one is, because these things are so unusual…what you really have to possess is a flexibility of the mind. You can't just walk out of here and feel comfortable that you understand how a division operates as part of a corps, and part of something or other. You've got to be flexible enough to take what you have learned here, to know the things that you have learned about your craft, and apply it to some very, very unorthodox things that no one had talked to you about. And to be able to grab here that which applies, disregard the others, and grab here that which applies, and apply it to the task at hand. So don't get yourself locked in to this one kind of a way of doing business. And think of that. Because I think in the days ahead, you and I will be called upon to use that an awful lot.

But finally having said all that I'll return to something I said at the very beginning. [Shows "WHEN ALL IS SAID AND DONE…OUR BUSINESS IS FIGHTING OUR NATION'S WARS" on screen] That yes, be aware that you might get involved in humanitarian operations and [Non-combatant Evacuation Operations], and disaster relief operations, all those things short of war. But ultimately, you and I are here to do this. [Points to screen]. That's what you've got to focus on. And if you do this well and you are comfortable that you know that well, the other stuff will come.

General Sullivan was the Army Chief when the explosion of peacekeeping operations began, and he constantly stressed where he felt the Army's attention should be focused, stating in 1992:

Can you keep a total force, Active Army, Army Guard, Army Reserve and civilians, trained and ready to fight? You can say lots of things about hurricanes, forest fires, [Civilian Conservation Corps] camps, rebuild the infrastructure of the United States. Forget it! [Points to the Army Flag on stage] Fight and win. That's what we get paid for. Fight and win. We can do all of that other stuff, but you must keep an organization which can fight and win. And that is not amateur sport.

And again in December of the next year:

Our mission is to fight and win the nation's wars. That's why we exist. We cannot forget that. I have a sign on my desk. If you were to call me, usually I'd be standing there, doing something, I'd look down: Don't Forget: Our mission is to fight and win the nation's wars. That's what that's all about right there [Points to the campaign streamers on the Army flag]. We can do the other stuff.

His successor, General Reimer, also stressed the Army's mission focus, while Reimer was still FORSCOM commander in 1994:

While there is a great deal of uncertainty in the future, I think there are also some trends that point out what's going to happen. First of all, as [CIA Director] Jim Woolsey said, the world is going to continue to be a complex, a dangerous and unpredictable place. And while it's changed dramatically since 1989, it's still dangerous out there, and a couple things I think to keep in mind. The operational tempo is going to remain busy. It's going to remain high. And you're going to find yourself responding to Operations Other than War, and the many, many other missions that we're given. But I think it's terribly important for all of you to keep in mind that the fundamental mission is, and the mission that we cannot fail in, is to be able to fight and win the nation's wars.

And as Chief of Staff in 1996:

> Trained and ready for victory, most important thing we do during peacetime. Keep up the focus on that. I tell all the commanders "Continue to focus on your most difficult mission." That most difficult mission is the conduct of high-intensity warfare. Don't get confused about these other things. When we do these other things that your people are going to have to do, they're going to get the time to train up for them. Don't lose the focus, the focus has got to be on winning the nation's wars.

> There have been a lot of discussions about should we do the Bosnias, should we do Somalia, should we do Haiti? Should we fight forest fires in the Northwest? The answer in my mind is if you're not willing to do that, you're going to become a very small Army. Because someone is going to ask the question "Why do we need all these people in the Army if we can never use them?" We've always done that, think back on our history. We helped settle the West, we helped develop the waterways, we helped put in the dams throughout our country. I think there is a valid need here. What we're doing right now is to try and reshape the global village. To try and prevent wars in the future so we don't have to fight them. They're easy to win if we can prevent them.

Special Operations officers have a unique viewpoint, and speakers at the college were no exception. The commander of U.S. Special Operations Command (USSOCOM), Wayne A. Downing, covered operations other than war (OOTW) in 1995.

> You know, it's interesting. Our special forces do a lot of work around the world with other countries' militaries. And in many of the developing nations of the world, the militaries are the most dominant element of the government. And we find the militaries of these countries being involved in a wide range of developmental-type projects, nation building-type projects. I think the interesting thing is when you look back on our history, our Army, and really our Navy did the same kind of thing. Our Navy was designed to protect commerce and encourage trade. Our Army was really created to expand this country. I mean we founded West Point, not for the military aspects of West Point, but to train engineers, who were going to go ahead and expand this country. You look at the pre-Civil War and post-Civil War army, and you will see armies that were involved in a wide range of activities that in many cases were not military at all. I'm not advocating that we're going to get involved in those types of things in the future, but I just think we've got to be very flexible as we look at what our role is going to be in the 21st century.

Another USSOCOM commander and future Chief of Staff, Peter Schoomaker, was asked in 1999 how changing environmental criteria altered the training and education of the leaders of the regular forces. Part of his answer addressed the OOTW debate.

> I think we need to be careful that we don't go beyond what I am really saying here. I'm not saying that we don't continue to have a responsibility to operate from the top end of the spectrum to the bottom. We must still be prepared to deal with and win our nations wars. So what we must not be is blind to…we cannot accept that if you're ready at the

top it kind of covers all of the bases—it doesn't. And what you end up with is you're going to have to be prepared to operate at that level and still understand that there are things that are happening in and around you short of [conventional war] that are equally as dangerous in terms of what it is.

In 1997, the Secretary of Defense, William S. Cohen, was asked if the peacetime engagements, conflict avoidance, and deterrence operations helped the military's ability to conduct warfighting.

I think you should get [CGSC Commandant Montgomery] "Monty" Meigs up here to answer that question for all of you right now because he's a prime example of someone who's been involved in peace efforts, of keeping the peace in Bosnia, of avoiding conflict. And utilizing those skills, and I know that sometimes there is some degradation overall in terms of unit operations that have to be upgraded, and we do that. But I would say that first of all what we have to do is to make sure we remind ourselves that our first obligation is to, in fact, be prepared for the wartime engagements. Those are the ones that help us maintain the peace. That from time to time we are going to be called upon to conduct peacekeeping operations. I hope, and I intend, to try to keep those to a minimum. We've got to be very selective when we use our uniformed military for operations that are humanitarian obviously in nature, that have a salutary and important interest, but do not affect our vital, national security interests. And then we have to go through the analysis. Is it vital national security interests? Is it just important? Or is it simply humanitarian? And what we have to do is make sure that we husband the resources that we have. That we not over-extend our military for the peacekeeping operations or the humanitarian operations, and we may have to do that from time to time. If there is a failed state. If there is a country that suddenly is so overwhelmed that they have no infrastructure, they have no water, they have no electricity, they have no food, and they're starving, and there's no means of helping them, obviously, the United States, given its high standards and sense of morality, we're going to help. On a temporary basis. And we do that.

But we have to be very selective in carrying that out because overall if we have too many deployments for the peacekeeping operations, then we're going to see a degradation of our military capability which we will have to call upon, or may have to call upon, to conduct major conflict. So it's something that we watch very closely, it depends a lot upon the political environment, it depends a lot upon [the 24-hour Cable News Network] CNN. The so-called CNN Curve. The CNN Curve is when they start to focus, and not just CNN, but the world television starts to focus upon human tragedy, our hearts start to beat in sympathy and empathy, and the pressure is on, we must do something. And then of course things start to go awry and people start dying and the curve starts to go down, saying "What were we doing there?" That's called the CNN Curve, and we have to be very careful about that. That we make a very studied analysis of what is in our interest, where can we be helpful, what are the risks, are the risks acceptable, and how do we get out of it once we get in? The so-called exit strategy.

Also in 1997, Secretary West recalled some of his remarks to 10th Mountain Division soldiers en route to Haiti.

I was asked to say a few words…I reminded them of this: At the time there was lots of talk about whether we should be there or not. That, I said, one senator had advised me they should not pay attention to it. Matters of war and peace are supposed to be debated in a democratic society, and we were debating it. They should consider that the joyful noise of democracy. What they should know is that, far from merely being representatives of the United States, that wherever one airman flies into foreign airspace or one sailor sails into foreign waters or a Marine storms ashore on a foreign beach, or a soldier is on foreign land, that there, too, is America. And that whenever that soldier stoops to give a helping hand to a citizen, to pick up a child, whenever that Marine falls there, wounded, America has stooped to help, and America has fallen.

During his 2001 appearance, Senator Pat Roberts (R - Kansas) spent a lot of time discussing how to determine what was really in the national interest, saying "It is one thing to have a cause to fight for. It is quite another to have a cause to fight and die for." This was a point driven home by General Vuono in 1990.

Freedom isn't free. We have 23 magnificent youngsters who aren't with us because of the Panamanian operation. Freedom isn't free. You and I know that. But we know also that we've got a responsibility not just for the United States, but around the world to preserve freedom. And those countries where there's not freedom, when they ask us, then we go. And we've got to be trained and ready to be able to accomplish what we've been asked to do. And that's what we did on [Operation] Just Cause. And so I think all of us, those who wear the uniform, regardless of service, and those who are part of the civilian force who support the various services, ought to be damn proud of what a great bunch of American troops did in a country called Panama, on an operation called Just Cause.

AN OFFICER'S DUTY

Many speakers impressed upon the students the importance, righteousness, and completeness of the oath they took and the duty to their nation. These comments are especially noteworthy when coming from those who played significant roles in the Vietnam War, given its outcome and the nature of civil-military relations during that particular conflict. Future head of Military Assistance Command, Vietnam and then Army Vice Chief of Staff Creighton Abrams was the keynote speaker at an Associate's Course Graduation in 1965, and had this to say about those who assume the responsibility for the Nation's defense:

Whatever we have in this country, with all its riches, with all its buildings and things, with all its pleasures and all its money, we have had throughout our history only because in times when it was dark and perilous, and when the future was uncertain, there were always enough men who felt this in their heart, and who could persevere skillfully and with determination through the periods of uncertainty, unwavering. And whatever we will have in the future depends always on whether there are still enough of this kind of man. At the moment I have no doubts that there are enough.

General Johnson spoke frequently about values during his many appearances on the CGSC stage. In 1962 he chose not to mince words when discussing a commander's duty on the nuclear battlefield.

I might raise one other point here, too. In one of the comments that has been made on the study [Tactical Dispersion on the Nuclear Battlefield], a rebuttal came back to us that said that a commander may have to choose between his mission and safeguarding his force. Now this isn't the way I was brought up. And this isn't the way I want you to be brought up. If you've got to die to fulfill your mission, too bad, you die. [Applause]

As Chief of Staff, Johnson explained the completeness of an officer's commitment to the students in December, 1967.

Every one of us raised his hand when he joined the army, and he said that he swore to defend and uphold the Constitution of the United States against all enemies, foreign and domestic. And when you took that obligation, you took on an unlimited commitment. Our commitment differs from any other kind of commitment that exists in our society, because that commitment goes so far as to lay down your life, when this is required. And that's a pretty extensive commitment. When you took that commitment, we didn't promise "See the world." We didn't promise "Keep your nose clean and you can retire after twenty years." We've been trying to say your job is the defense of your country. And this country won't be defended unless you do it. Now if you don't like it, the thing to do is leave, because it's not going to be easy. And you should know that. You should know that. The only thing I can say is that we're doing all that we humanly can to make this as equitable, and make the hardship as limited, as possible. But we can't remove it. We can't remove it. And as I said when I started out, it's a troubled world in which we live, and it's not getting any less troubled. And when people question what our country does, and if you look around and you ask the question: Who else? There's only one answer: No one. So, if you believe in freedom, and if you want to preserve what your family and friends enjoy, you have to pay the price. I have no doubt whatsoever, but that this price will be paid. None. And the reason I don't have any doubt, is because we have today the finest professional corps of officers that we have ever had. We're working hard on maintaining standards that we've had, and we think we can maintain them. But you're the Army. You're the defenders of this nation. And unless you do it, there's no one else. No one else.

Johnson's successor as Chief of Staff, William Westmoreland, discussed the oath to junior officers at Fort Leavenworth on June 4, 1970.

And although our job is to carry out our orders, to carry out national policy, and to be apolitical in that in accordance with the philosophy of the role of the military as provided in the Constitution, a man in uniform should not and cannot get involved in political activity, because his oath is not to any man or partisan cause. His oath is to support the Constitution of the United States and the Commander in Chief. So we have to take this on the chin, we cannot defend ourselves publicly, we cannot engage in political and public debate in this regard. We have to take the professional approach, fully understand the role that we play in society, and continue to march forward proudly in doing our duty, and performing the service required and provided for by the Constitution.

...When you go in the Army you give up certain rights. You subject yourself to a disciplinary situation that does not attain in civilian life, but is nevertheless absolutely essential if we're going to have the type of military force that we're required. An undisciplined force, a force made up of other than dedicated men, would be a menace to the society that they're trying to defend. Of course no thinking American would want that type of military organization defending their country. They would not want an organization that was not loyal to the Commander in Chief. An undisciplined organization, an organization that was rife with individuals who were addicted to drugs and narcotics, an organization that tolerated dissent. Where when an order was issued, well, people got up and objected to it and demonstrated against it. That type of organization would be a tremendous liability to the nation. They would not be able to provide the defenses required. They would not be responsive to the duly elected authority. And can you imagine that type of organization and having the lethal weapons that we have in our inventory? That type of organization would give some credence to [the military coup d'etas thriller] *Seven Days in May*. This is sheer fiction now, and I'm sure always will be. But if we ever tolerated, or ever got ourselves in the position where dissent was tolerated, where orders were not obeyed and could be accepted or ignored, or discipline was not enforced, or standards of conduct, and honesty, and loyalty, and dedication were not emphasized, our Army would be a menace to society.

Westmoreland spoke to graduating CGSC students on the subject of duty during the following day:

This is not a time for you to weaken your zeal, or succumb to any barrage of criticism. Our nation continues to need men with your dedication and your loyalty as never before. Today as in the past it takes more effort for man to pursue the right than the wrong, more strength to adhere to the proven traditional rather than yield to changing fad, more restraint to argue the logical than shout the emotional. Your course and performance of duty must be uncompromising, unyielding, unswerving. It includes an undivided loyalty to a cause that is just and right and proper. It includes perfection, and pride, and precision. It includes honor, integrity, and character, dedication to one's country. And it includes that additional effort that in many instances spells the difference between success and failure.

General Kerwin covered the subject of duty at the 1976 graduation ceremony.

Our military profession is unique. There is no other profession in this nation, on which the Nation's future hinges on a system of responsibility and absolute allegiance to a duty rather than to an individual. And you all recall in your commissioning oath which you took some number of years ago, that you pledged your allegiance not to a government, not to a monarch, not to any group of people, but to an idea. And that idea is written on our Constitution of the United States. The officer corps is the sacred custodian and the trustee of the means of violence which is available to this nation. And therefore it's also our perpetual responsibility to ensure that these implements of violence are used only in the execution of constitutional responsibilities. And you'll notice that in the 200 years of the existence of this government, never once has the United States Army been a threat to the Constitution, to the government, or to its people. And we Americans have come to expect that responsibility and reliability of the military as a matter of course. But I point out to you that such a history is almost unique in this world today. And this special trust and special responsibility requires a truly special code of standards and ethics.

At a graduation ceremony 20 years earlier, Lieutenant General James M. Gavin, then the Chief of Army Research and Development, took this historical example a bit further when he said:

> I would like to be sure, on a deep personal conviction, that the thought remains with you that our philosophy stems from one idea, and that is we are motivated by a driving and dynamic force, and we are for something, not against something. And this idea of Western Man, coming as it did from the continent of Europe, finding fertile soil here, is one that has inflamed the minds of men wherever it has come in contact with them. And it has until this day.

ARMY HISTORY

Much like Generals Kerwin and Gavin above, many speakers have invoked history to provide students some perspective of the Army. General Abrams, in 1965, was no exception.

> The courageous examples set by those who have fought on so many battlefields, those who have earned the 145 campaign streamers on the Army flag, have not been forgotten by our own generation. The help voluntarily given to us in our country's early struggle for freedom, the strength of purpose which emerged from the ensuing years, and which was forged and tempered on the battlefields of World War I and World War II and Korea, unite to compel us to assist those who fight for their freedom today. For those who complain about our country's motives in assisting other nations, let them read the record! Our performance in giving assistance will stand the scrutiny of history beside that of any nation. Our country's attitude in peace, or even in victory after war, has been one of enlightened humanity based on the principles of Christ. Handed down, and for which he died nearly 2000 years ago, on the cross at Calvary. The challenge to each of you and to the nation is clear: You set your course through life when you took your oath of office while over 190 years ago, 55 courageous men meeting in Philadelphia set our nation's course when they signed the document which ended with the following words: We therefore declare that the United Colonies are and of a right ought to be free and independent states. And for the support of this declaration, with a firm reliance on the protection of divine providence, we mutually pledge to each other our lives, our fortunes, and our sacred honor.

In 1975, on the eve of the Nation's Bicentennial, General Weyand discussed the promotion of freedom as a framework of the need for an army.

> ...going back to the Revolutionary days...it's interesting at the very least to realize how revolutionary those doctrines and concepts that our founding fathers came up with were in those times. And they continue to be revolutionary. And that Constitution they drafted has very great meaning, because in those days they were challenging, did challenge, the divine right of kings. And they were not at all sure that that would be permitted to continue. That those doctrines and principles of freedom and bringing the human being out of the deep degradation and morass of where he'd been and bringing him up to the light and making something of human beings and making something of human dignity, as opposed to the state and the institution. Would the world powers permit that to survive? And yet they were determined that it would survive. There was a great debate then about the Constitution, about those principles and how they'd defend

them and protect them. And they realized very quickly that they could not protect them in isolation. That they had to promote them. And they had to reach beyond the United States in promoting those. They had to, in order to ensure those principles and those values, they had to make them available for free men or men elsewhere in the world. And they, at the same time, realized how important strength was in all of this. And I suppose this dawned on them for a number of reasons.

These forefathers of ours even then realized that they couldn't hold this precious thing in isolation. They realized too that they needed strength. And it was then that one of them coined that phrase "Freedom is not free." And so this keeps coming back and coming back. And so there was this great debate about the Army. Why, now that the war was over, long and difficult though it had been, why did we need an army? And [James] Madison as a matter of fact engaged in a debate and the title of it was "Why an Army?" Sounds very modern as an issue. What's the political utility of an Army? And so they debated and discussed this. And they came to the same conclusion that we have come to that day, and that is that strength is necessary to protect our values. As [former Secretary of State] Dean Rusk said not too long ago: As you look back in history, and look for the causes of aggression, causes for our sometimes innocent involvement in conflicts, it was never our strength that got us involved, it was always weakness. And so Dean Rusk used to say that it was weakness that was provocation and temptation to the aggressor. And so this was a lesson that these founding fathers learned a long time ago.

We do try to do too much at the Washington level that we're not capable of doing. And fortunately too, through the 200 years that we can look back on this Army, it has shown a tremendous capacity to overcome the stupidity and errors of its leadership. It just kind of keeps moving on, and it gets the job done, and guys come and go, but that Army just hangs in there.

Secretary of the Army John O. Marsh continued along this constitutional vein in 1986, tracing the Army's heritage back to the birth of the Nation.

Of those 40 men who signed [the Constitution]…23 had served in the Army. 12 had been in the militia and 11 the Continental Line, the Regular Army of the United States. Now just because they had fought a war and drafted a Constitution didn't mean they had stopped serving their country. You see these individuals, because they were a majority, controlled that convention. Now they could have taken the life and death powers of the nation, to raise taxes, to raise armies and navies, to declare war, and vested them in the executive branch. But they didn't. They placed those in the Congress of the United States because it is the servant of the people. And under our sense of values the people are the supreme voice of this great country. Now, what did they do? They returned to civilian life, and of those 23, 11 went to the Senate, 8 became governors, 7 became members of the House, one would be Speaker of the House of Representatives, 3 would be judges, 2 would be ministers to foreign countries, 2 would be members of the cabinet, and one of them of course, we know, would become the President of the United States. And so you see we have a very important legacy that the American people need to know.

General Reimer referred to some more recent history in 1998.

Saving Private Ryan. It's a wonderful film for the story it tells. [My] favorite scene [is at the] end of film when Ryan is standing at Normandy, with all the crosses, his youth long gone, he turns to his wife and says "Tell me I'm a good man, tell me I did a good job." *Saving Private Ryan* was about a generation who saved our world. That is what all of us have inherited. That sacrifice they gave us. Are we worthy? That's what has to drive us.

ARMY LIFE AND THE PROFESSION OF ARMS

Another frequent topic covered by the guest speakers was the Army profession, the meaning of service, and some of the different aspects of Army life. During his graduation address in 1956, LTG Gavin warned the students against leaning too heavily on the past.

> We staff officers, and I am one too now, like to invoke the prophets of old. It's something to lean upon that's reassuring when you can't think of any other answer, and it's a source of confidence when you need it. And such clichés such as Napoleon's "God is on the side of the heaviest battalions," or, more recently, [Giulio] Douhet's "Nothing that has happened in the history of warfare [can] affect aerial action," vintage of 1921. Or, more recent than that, [Alexander de] Soversky in 1947 "He who commands the skies controls the land beneath." All a lot of nonsense, because no longer may we match the clichés of yesterday with the military technology of today and serve any useful need in creating weapon systems. And weapon systems exist only to serve a human need. Go not forth from these halls loaded with clichés that may prove useful, because they will prove exceedingly dangerous to lean upon, I can assure you. Now this is part of the dilemma but it stems from the more profound state of affairs. Death can be wrapped up in these very few words.

General Abrams, during his 1965 appearance, extolled the personal nature of the profession, and the importance of the pursuit of excellence.

> Of all the things we have…airplanes, or helicopters, or guns, or ships, or rifles, or money, the thing that determines everything that's done good or bad in the Army in the final analysis is people. They're you—as individuals, it's how you feel in your heart. It's not so much what it says in the book, although you need to know that. It's what you feel here that determines whether it's done well, whether it's done thoroughly, whether our country wins.

General DePuy sounded a similar chord in June, 1974, saying "There really is no such thing as the United States Army. Yes, you can talk to soldiers in it, you can belong to units within it, you can read the regulations about it, but there is no such thing. The United States Army, like the other services, or like other armies, is simply you, wherever you are, doing whatever you can do, and doing it the best way you can."

In late 1975 General Weyand related the difficulty in explaining the profession to those who hadn't served.

> The Army has to be appreciated by the American people. They've got to feel that this Army is their Army, and it's a good Army. And it's got a job to do. The political utility of force…they say "What is that?" Well, the question is the political utility of it is *having* it.

It's not using it, it's having it. But these things are kind of complex and they're difficult for them to understand. [The American people] also don't understand that the reason we've got a good Army, the reason I've got young men and women of the caliber of you, and you make up part of the finest, most experienced, professional officer corps this Army's ever had. I know that times now are tough, but generally speaking you could go outside and in a pure economic sense do much better than you are doing now. So we make a point when we talk to Congress or talk to the news media that you are not working for the government, you are serving the government, and there's a very, very important difference there. There's no such word in my vocabulary as comparable pay, because I don't believe there's such a thing. Competitive, yes. That's one of the six or seven programs I've got on my list when I talk to the president or whoever it is, I say we have to maintain competitive pay. And that involves a lot of things, including money, but more than that, because these guys are going to fight if they have to fight, and they'll be the ones that will do the dying and making the sacrifices. You're not going to be doing that for a standard of life, you'll be doing it for a way of life, and our people have got to understand that: That you haven't come in here to get rich. And you've probably read, or maybe you haven't, but you certainly understand that, what is it, then, that brings you into the Army and keeps you here? Part of it, a little part of it, inertia? Okay. But most of it is that feeling that you're with an institution that has integrity and takes care of its own. And that starts right down at the battlefield. We do not leave our wounded on the field of battle, we don't leave our dead on the field of battle, except under the most extreme circumstances.

General Meyer talked to students in 1979 about detours he perceived as distractions that kept officers from mastering their profession.

You have to take this period of time to be able to focus on becoming a professional, on becoming professional soldiers. We have had in the past a lot of what I call dallying around in other areas by our officer corps. We have had a period in which we have sent officers off to do different kinds of things in big, high office buildings and dealing with civilians and dealing with academicians and so on. In the kind of world that we're talking about in the future, we... need...professional...soldiers. [slowly, with emphasis on each word] Soldiers who have thought about how to go to war, soldiers who are thinking about how to go to war, and soldiers who know how to go to war. So when you come out next summer, I expect to have coming out of this class soldiers who are—and I'm sure the sailors, airmen and Marines, too...even the Marines, [chuckles] will be able to come out...as soldiers who are capable of applying yourself to the needs that we have. That's absolutely essential...If you're able to develop yourself so that when you go out you're able to be considered a professional, then you will have used this year, this opportunity, to its utmost. And then you and I have the opportunity of creating an army that we both want to serve in. And that's what it's all about.

In 1994 Secretary West warned the students against satisfaction and complacency in the profession.

Our issue is the fact that any human institution, once it becomes satisfied with itself, stops progressing, and inevitably begins to decline. And if that is true, then we must realize that even as we accept the greatness and the goodness, we can be better. Better not just in the ways that the occasional critics and the debators are talking about. Of course we will do something about training; we've already got that underway. Of course we will have to do something about our modernization, we know that. But better in the ways that are not often discussed, and even if they are, may not be enough highlighted. Oh, better, yes in the way that we treat our soldiers, because that has to be essential for us, the central part for us. And better, yes in the way that we worry about our families. Because without our families we have no soldiers, we have no enlisted, no service members, no Army, no Navy, no Air Force, no Marine Corps. The families are essential. Better, yes in the ways that we talk about ourselves, the ways in which we describe ourselves and envision ourselves in the eyes of others. And better in the ways that we hope for ourselves, in our aspirations for what this Army will be like in the next millennium, in our aspirations for how this Army will relate to the society around it.

Two years later, General Reimer evoked a legendary leader from the past to convey the importance of the profession to the survival of the nation.

Our profession is special. It's not a profession in which you are going to get rich, it's a profession in which you make a great contribution to the nation. Douglas MacArthur said it best in 1961, when he said "Yours is a profession of arms. The will to win, the sure knowledge that in war there is no substitute for victory. But if you fail, the nation will be destroyed." I can't say it any better. I can't emphasize the importance of what you're doing any better than that.

Many speakers spoke of the relationship between the Army profession and the nation it served. On June 5, 1970 General Westmoreland spoke to the class about the difficulties with this relationship during the Vietnam War.

Yet the recognition you so richly deserve has gone unnoticed by some. And your dedication to serve your country has met with deprecation by others. Some groups and individuals do not understand the role of the professional soldier in our society. Admittedly, they represent the minority. But part of this minority is vocal and bent on destroying an institution vital to the survival of the nation.

A part of your service life should be directed towards community relations. All too often military families tend to isolate themselves on military posts, to become a closed society because of the complete services offered: housing, commissary, military hospitals, [Post Exchange], and the like. Nowhere is this more true than when a serviceman is overseas with his dependents. Military personnel and their dependents should associate when they can with civilian contemporaries to strengthen the civil-military dialogue of mutual understanding. Tell civilians why you are in the service. Tell the Army story as often as you can. Tell them that your service on the international scene is as necessary as a policeman on the local scene. Tell them about the obligation of your oath of office. That the commissioning oath demands loyalty to the national cause that transcends personal desire. That your performance is rewarded by their appreciation of your role in carrying out, not making, national policy.

Secretary of Defense James R. Schlesinger amplified these points in 1974.

Why do we have an Army? I'm sure General Abrams ruminated with you on this subject. That question goes back to what is U.S. Policy? What is the U.S. society like? The army in any society, in particular a democratic society, will be a sensitive barometer of American life. It will reflect the good aspects of society, it will reflect many of the bad aspects. And we should recognize that at this stage in our nation's history, and indeed in this stage of the history of the western world, there are genuine and legitimate doubts about the moral stamina of the Western Democracies.

A year later, the 8th Army Commander Richard Stillwell summed up society's expectations for the current graduating class: "We know that however our Army may measure relatively in size, fourth, fifth, sixth, it is totally unacceptable for that army ever to be second best." In 1981 General John Vessey was able to paint a less gloomy picture about the relationship between society and its military.

For us in the United States the outcome has been the existing relationship between the society and its warriors, the armed services, or its guardians, as Plato calls them. And a part of the relationship is our own professional code of ethics and our concept of service. We don't work for the Army, we serve in it. We don't choose the missions for the Army or the wars it will fight, we accomplish those missions to win those wars. You are the nation's guardians, its warrior class for the '80s and '90s. You have chosen to serve, and you've demonstrated that choice of service by being here. And I would also say to you that the nation has chosen you to serve it, and it has demonstrated that by choosing you to come here. Or, as in the case of Socrates' guardians, the higher the duties, the more time and skill in art and application, the whole reason behind your year at the Command and General Staff College.

In 1997, Secretary Cohen was able sound much more positive about the relationship.

I don't think the story gets out enough how good we [the military] really are. Wherever I go, and I've been travelling all over the world, what I see are the best and the brightest people this country has to offer, being in uniform, who are out there on the front lines, who are dedicated, and well-trained, and well-led. Patriotic, enthused to be doing what they're doing, and serving our nation extraordinarily well. The American people should be as proud as they can possibly be that we have the best fighting force in the world today.

That same year, Secretary West described what being in the Army meant, and how those who have served are changed in ways those who haven't cannot understand.

Being a Soldier changes you in ways that can never be undone. That once you have done it, you will never be the same again. You will never be the same that you would have been had you never undergone it. To be a Soldier is to be changed in permanent ways. To be a Soldier is to bear almost insupportable burdens, whether they are the physical burdens of just pure, gut-wrenching hard work, or the emotional burdens of our relationships with our peers, or our family members, or the lonely burden of leadership. To be a Soldier is to have hidden wellsprings of strength unknown to our civilian society, deep within ourselves which we can reach into in moments of crisis, to find the strength to do what our duty requires, hidden wellsprings of strength all around us, in our fellow

31

soldiers, other members of our unit. And the additional strength of the surety of knowledge that the first two exist, should we need them.

When speaking about life in the Army, especially during graduation ceremonies, many acknowledged the contribution made by the officers' wives (the gender-neutral term 'spouse' doesn't appear until the mid-nineties). Some of the attempts were memorable, starting with Under Secretary of the Army Paul Ignatius in 1964.

One hears a great deal today about the plight of the modern woman: Educated beyond the intellectual demands associated with keeping house and raising children, and casting about for something useful to do with the time made available by automatic washing machines, dispose-alls, brown and serve rolls, and the just add water and stir way of life. I do not know the extent of which all this may be a problem for women in general, but I suspect it is less of a problem for the Army wife. Whether in this country or overseas, the Army wife has a job to perform, a duty to fulfill, and her husband's career is truly her career also. I can only speculate on the degree to which each officer's graduation today has been aided by the help of his wife, but I suspect the contribution has been a significant one, and I offer my congratulations to the wives of the members of the graduating class.

In 1965 General Abrams put it a little differently.

While we cannot say that they have enlisted, or been commissioned, in the armed forces of the United States, we must in the same breath say that they are truly members. They, changing the home, moving it from place to place, scullery maid, chef in the daytime and gracious lady at night, and at times like this, an equal and powerful partner. My hat is off to them.

General Westmoreland used humor to thank the wives during his graduation address of June 5, 1970.

Although seldom acknowledged, you also, you ladies, you Army Wives, serve your nation in the greatest tradition in the United States Army. Your patience under adversity and your loyalty are deeply appreciated. You wives can also play a vital role in keeping your husband from developing an exaggerated opinion of their own importance. [Audience laughter] From your reaction obviously they do. I remember a young officer who had enjoyed some early success, his name will be unmentioned, who was talking to his wife as he was adjusting his tie to go to his Command and General Staff School graduation exercise. He remarked to his wife as he proudly viewed himself in the mirror, he said "I wonder how many truly great men there are in the world today?" His wife ruefully replied "One less than you think." [Laughter and applause]

Many of the speakers gave impressions and stories about the Pentagon, and their lives and duties as they related to that venerable building. General Westmoreland did not have a high opinion of his new job as Chief of Staff in 1969, saying "Here in my new job I find life very dismal and sometimes discouraging in the Pentagon. So it's a great pleasure to be in the field and particularly here at Leavenworth, and to be among people that I have a rapport with." [Laughter and applause] Retired General Max Taylor addressed the fact that he no longer worked in the

Pentagon during his 1973 visit. "Well, let me explain to all present, if there's any doubt, that I'm speaking entirely for myself today. I'm often asked 'Do I represent the Pentagon, Army Generals?' and all of that, and I say 'No, my only capacity now is that of an indignant taxpayer!' Certainly an indignant taxpayer has had a hand in some of the suggestions which I'm going to put forward."

Secretary Callaway had good stories involving his duties, and his remarks in May, 1974, were no exception, as he took the stage wearing Army fatigues.

> I probably should start with [CGSC Commandant] General [John] Cushman's comments on these fatigues. I don't know if you ever get into any problems in your life, but I seem to get in problems all the time. I left the Army as a first lieutenant. I pretty well understood the Army as a first lieutenant and thought I'd do it. I knew how to salute and that sort of thing. And I get back now and everybody's saluting me and they tell me that I'm not allowed to salute back, so I'm sort of holding my hand down. And I started going out in the field and getting in tanks as we did yesterday, and I got a chance, the first chance I had to fire a missile in the M-60A2 and some of that to see what's going on, and I started out going in civilian clothes and going around and it just didn't make much sense getting in the tanks and fooling around with the weapons and that sort of thing. So when I'm on the road I wear fatigues. I'm not authorized to wear anything else—I'm probably not authorized to wear this, [laughter] but I do. I've been out of the Army quite a while and I had never seen all these belts that these guys are wearing, and I said "Gee, that's a nice looking belt, I'd like one." And General Barry said "That's a General Officer's belt." [Big laugh] I'd never seen one before, I didn't come in contact with general officers too much as a first lieutenant.

During his visit in December of that same year, he was asked if he had any personal surprises on the job. His answer probably didn't surprise too many in the audience. "You talk about one of the great things in life. Getting to know a guy like Abe, and getting to have him one door apart, and walk in ten times a day in his shirtsleeves and sit down and just talk about the Army. You know, not many people in life have had that experience, it's an enormous experience." General Abrams had died just three months prior to Callaway's visit. He continued. "And Fred [General Weyand], very different from Abe, but you've got a Chief of Staff now that is just outstanding." Another student asked him to discuss short war scenarios in some detail.

> I'm really getting out of my field if I go into this too much. You know, the Secretary of the Army is responsible for manning and equipping the Army and stuff and...you know I don't know any better than to ask things. I'd been Secretary of the Army for about six weeks and I was talking to Abe and I said "Abe what is it you do every Monday afternoon?" And he said "I go down to the Tank." I said "Hmm. What do you do down in the Tank?" And he said "Well, I talk to the other chiefs and we talk about strategy." I said "Hey, I'd like to go with you sometime." [Long pause before response, presumably from Abrams] "You didn't get the point?" [Laughter] You know Abe and I were so close, Abe would have taken me, but if I'd gotten in there the building would have exploded. It's just if the Secretary of the Army got to walk in the Tank—well, I got to walk in when it was closed and look at it—but to walk in while it was operating and to actually hear what was happening that would destroy the whole world. I'm being a little facetious in that, but the Joint Chiefs hold themselves very much in the strategy role and it's very clear in their minds that the Secretary of the Army is not in that net. [Laughter]

In 1979, just a few months into his new position, General Meyer relayed to the students the sequence of events that led to his appointment as Chief of Staff.

I'm excited by the opportunity, first of all to be the Chief of Staff of the Army, [Laughter] and second of all by the opportunity to speak to all of you. I won't put it in priority, troops. [More laughter] I will say as I start out that a funny thing happened to me on my way to Heidelberg. [Laughter] I got waylaid over at the White House. I got redirected. My wife had to somehow get untrenched from all the packing boxes that were already packed and on their way to Heidelberg [Germany]. And I went through sort of a traumatic period early in May trying to readjust speaking German to try and remember how to continue to speak Washington-ese and Pentagon-ese. And that's not always easy. I thought I'd tell you about my interview with [President Jimmy Carter] on a Saturday morning. I got a call late on Friday afternoon and it said—the Secretary of Defense told me nobody was supposed to know, I was to go and see the president tomorrow morning at 9:30. And I thought, well, he knows I'm going over to Europe—he didn't tell me what I was going for—well, I'm going to Europe. He wants to find out how I'm going to win the war over there if war starts and I'm ready to tell him. So I went over there and we talked about how I was going to win the war in Europe if it stated. "What are your ambitions?" Funny question to ask, here I thought I was doing pretty good as a three-star! [Big laugh] I was fifty years old, here I was a three-star general, I was going to be a four-star general, I was going over to command 7th Army, gee wilickers, that's a pretty good record. I said "Well, I'll tell ya...Mr. President," I was courteous. "When I was a young lieutenant of Infantry, down in Fort Benning, Georgia, my goal in life always was to be a colonel of Infantry, and to be able to live in one of those great big houses on Baltzell [Avenue], right across from the golf course, and to be able to work with young men right up until the day I retired." Well, I don't think he thought that was very funny because he asked again "Well, yeah, but what are your ambitions?"

I told him what my true ambitions always had been. I said "What do you mean?" And he said "Well after you've been in Europe, what are your ambitions?" And I said "Well I'd like to come back and have to opportunity to work at TRADOC or here in the building or something like that." And then he said "Well what about now?" Well I took a couple of deep gulps, and told him all the reasons I really wanted to go to Europe, and why I really thought I could be a better Chief of Staff if I had the opportunity to command over in Europe. I didn't tell him that I hated ticket punchers and I didn't want to get credit for having commanded in Europe just by getting put on orders to go there. [Laughter] But anyhow, I ended up telling him some of the reasons, and finally he said "Okay, I'll let you know what I'm going to do." Well, next Tuesday I got a call saying I was going to be Chief of Staff of the whole United States Army. And I want to tell you that's kind of an awesome responsibility. Particularly when you contemplate the kind of futures which we might have to face, the kind of obstacles we might have to face, the way General Thurman lined them up in his introduction in the start. But I really had an opportunity to go through a period where I really felt like I'd been pole-axed, and then I realized very quickly that first of all I can't do it myself. That I have to rely on great people that are in the Army, the Active, Reserves, and civilians that are there. And that I have to rely on them to do it. And two, that all I can do is the very best that I am capable of, and if that's not good enough I really like to hunt and fish and golf and do all those other things, and make money, I could go ahead and do that. So I didn't feel any compunction about it. So that's sort of how I got to be Chief of Staff of the Army. Assumed command on the 22d of June, and it's been a fast pace since then.

General Shalikashvili was asked a question about his future in 1992, based on rumors of his being named the head of U.S. Army Europe.

> I'm not in the running for CINC USAREUR. I have heard that I'm being considered to replace General [John] Galvin [as Commander in Chief, U.S. European Command]. I'm deeply honored by that. [Applause] If that is true I'm going to have to learn to be more regal and dignified as I stand before you the next time and I promise to work on that very hard. At least I'll wear a tie or something. But right now the emotion that's going through me with that as a prospect is a little scary and very humbling, and I know I have to rush home and study an awful lot to come even close to what General Galvin does. So I'll do that if you'll allow me.

President Clinton appointed him Chairman of the Joint Chiefs of Staff the following year. General Max Thurman, Vice Chief of Staff of the Army and a future commander of TRADOC, was a dynamic speaker and had some great stories to tell. In 1986 he told the students about visiting soldiers who had been wounded in the Grenada operation of 1983.

> I would remind you about the quality of young soldiers that are coming in the United States Army. And to do that let me sort of recount to you three little vignettes that sort of demonstrate that. The Chief of Staff asked me to go down and visit the wounded that were coming out of Grenada, because he was going down to the Rangers to welcome them back to Fort Stewart, so I said I'd be happy to do that...It was about 10:00 at night and I went up to see the kids on the wards [at Walter Reed Army Medical Center]. I walked in the first room and there's a kid sitting up in the middle of the bed, had a telephone in his ear, and he said "My God Granddad there's a four-star general standing in front of me, I'll hang up and call you back." I was standing there in my suit of lights [laughter] and I said "No, let me have that phone, I want to talk to your Granddaddy." And I said "Granddaddy, this is General Max Thurman, the Vice Chief of Staff of the U.S. Army." He said "Who is that?" [Laughter] Such is fame. So I said "Listen, I want to tell you that your grandson is doing fine, I want to pin a Purple Heart on him, he's perfectly okay. We'll give him some checks here and he'll probably be home by the end of the week." And I marched out of the room after giving the phone back to the youngster and pinning his purple heart on. Now what was that youngster reminding us about? He was reminding us about the power of family, and in the case of arduous service, either in peace or war, that one of the first things we all want to do is get back in touch with our family, we want to report to people that we're doing fine.
>
> I walked into the second room and there was a kid laying supine in the bed with his right leg propped up in the air and a big bandage on it, and I reached over to shake hands with [him] and he reached up and grabbed my hand and pulled me right square down on the bed and threw his arm around me. And he said "I want to tell you about how my buddy saved my life in Grenada." Well, I wasn't going anywhere [laughter] and I had not been hugged by a 24-year old Blackhawk crew chief in some time, so I listened. And he said "My buddy and I, we went through basic training together, we went through advanced

individual training together, Blackhawk crew chief school together, and we were both posted to Task Force 160 together." Now this is October of 1983, and he said "My buddy was killed off of Panama a month ago. And when I got in a jam in Grenada, my buddy went to see God and asked God to intervene and save my life." 24-year-old blackhawk crew chief. So I cried. And I pinned a little Purple Heart on him and I walked out of the room, and I said "Now what was that youngster telling us about?" He was telling us about two things, in my view. One, about the power of cohesion, which says that people who work together, train together, or have to go to combat together and they have to associate together for a substantial period of time if they are to build up the bonds of cohesion, which ultimately cause people to lay down their life for one another, or have enough spirit within them that they're willing to do that—lay down their life for one another. And the second thing he was reminding me about was that as a 24-year-old youngster in the United States Army, he had enough guts to witness to his God in his manner in front of a very senior officer of his service. So I was very touched by that.

Third youngster I went in to see was a Ranger, again he was supine in the bed, the right foot was parked up in the air, he'd been shot in the leg a couple of times. I said "Listen troop, I understand you're a Ranger." "Yes sir." "How many jumps have you got?" He said "45." "How long have you been in the airborne?" "Two and a half years." "Is it really true you came in there at 500 feet over the Grenada runway and jumped out of a perfectly good airplane with no reserve parachute?" He said "Yes, Sir, we did that." I said "Tell me about it." He said "Exciting, general, exciting." [Laughter] He said "We normally don't do that too often." I said "Look, tell me how you got wounded." He said "Well, I came around this corner and there were three guys there with AK-47s, and they shot me and I shot the three of them." He said "Three to one ain't bad, is it general?" I said "No, that's right on, troop, that's what you're supposed to be doing." I said "Now I'll pin this Purple Heart on you, and you get one other thing. You're an 11-Bush, aren't you?" [Army Military Specialty 11B, Infantryman] "Yes Sir." "You are an 11-Bush in combat?" "Right, Sir." I said "You get one of these things," And I held up a [Combat Infantry Badge], and with that he ripped of his pajamas and he said "Just punch it in there general, just punch it in there!" [Huge laugh and applause] And so I did, but I couldn't get these little grippers through the back side of his chest. Now I tell you those three stories, and they're all three true. And I tell you to give you some insight into the great young troopers who are presenting themselves, the men and women who are presenting themselves for service in our United States Army, Navy, Air Force, Marines and Coast Guard. And they're dynamite young soldiers and sailors, airmen, Marines, Coast Guardsmen who are coming to us, and they're looking for something.

TRAINING

Some of the speakers discussed training as well, especially during the post-Vietnam era, given the advent of the All-Volunteer Force and the dramatic changes to training that occurred in the mid-to late-seventies and early eighties. The man who is widely considered to be the founding father of modern training is the aforementioned General DePuy, who was the first commander of the Army's Training and Doctrine Command. His comments about the general state of training in the Army as he saw it in March, 1974, are remarkable.

A year ago yesterday, not as the commander, but knowing I would be, I started traveling around, hitting the schools, coming out here. And I have to tell you that some of the things that I found out there amazed me, and as a matter of fact, disappointed me. I'd been away from the school system, been away from that part of the Army for a long, long time. I'd never been assigned to a school, on the faculty or as an instructor. But what I found in visiting around was—and hopefully not stepping on the toes of any of the people that are over here on the right, your left front—I was disappointed to find certain things not happening in the schools. I was disappointed to find that they weren't digging holes at Fort Benning. I was disappointed to find that they weren't driving bulldozers at Fort Belvoir. I was disappointed to find that they didn't have any batteries of artillery out there camouflaged as demonstration. I was disappointed to find that 95% of the instruction at the Transportation school was above battalion level for the Advanced Course...Captains. Now, you know, the transportation function is above battalion level to some extent, but not 95 percent of it. Well this worried me and I began to wonder "Why?"

Because in each case the commandants pointed out that there was a terrible squeeze on time. There was too much to do. And there wasn't enough time to do it...we went off and fought the war [in Vietnam] and everybody got kind of disenchanted with that so then we sort of went into management. That became the fashion, the buzzwords were management. Before that ever really ran its course we were into alcohol, drug abuse, race, volunteer Army, behavioral science, and all that. Well when you look down in the curriculums of the service schools you see a kind of accretion, it's like the sediment on the bottom of the ocean. All that old stuff's still there, and then all that new stuff is layered on top. And what happened is that kind of squoze [sic] out soldiering. I mean that's what had to give. Soldiering had to give.

TRADOC is trying to get soldiering back into the curriculum. They're digging holes at Fort Benning and driving bulldozers at Fort Belvoir, all sorts of things. [Applause] Well, you know, we kind of felt like maybe we were alone in thinking that was right. And then along came the Arab-Israeli war and that jarred everybody. Because the first Arab-Israeli war was just kind of fun to talk about. The second Arab-Israeli war was serious. And when you talk to those Israeli officers and soldiers who have been over here training, and when we send visitors over there, and we send a lot, those people are down to fundamentals, or back to fundamentals. They're concerned with soldiering and fighting. They're not spending a lot of time on excursions from that. Now that war is trying to tell us something.

General Abrams discussed training and readiness a few months later.

I'm meeting Monday with General Kerwin and General DePuy about it. We're in a terrible shape, we're just on a damn treadmill. We've always been on a treadmill. You get these fellows out there, they get their units up, really got them—they can shoot, they can do things, they've got the spirit, they've got the skill, and about the time they get that done, we take half then and scatter them all over the world. And so he starts all over again. Well there's no way. We've got to make some changes, somehow. We've got to find a way to really develop a skilled and disciplined Army. Today the T-62 and M-60 series [tanks], each one of them have got some pluses and minuses, but in the main they're sort of a standoff. They're about equal. What's going to make the difference is the crews. [sic] Why shouldn't we do that? We should. How do you do it? You don't do it by scattering them every year.

Another Chief, General Vuono, had this to say about training in 1988.

And finally in the training arena, the importance of better, tougher, more exacting joint and combined training, that we don't just pass off joint and combined training. It's something we have to do, and I'll force them to do it. It's something we say we must do, and that we must plan it just as we plan our own internal training to get the most out of it, because if we don't do that, then we're going to short-change ourselves on the battlefield. And in my view, that's where the payoff on a trained unit, trained individual, and trained leader takes place, because you know in battle you lose lives. War is a nasty business and people get killed in war. But I don't want to be part of any Army that has one soldier get killed because he or she wasn't properly trained. Because if that happens, you see, we can't blame it on anyone else. You can't blame it on Congress, you can't blame it on the media, it's our fault. It's our fault. Because leaders train soldiers, leaders train units, and leaders train other leaders.

In 1999, future Chief of Staff General Schoomaker drove this point home even more starkly.

…Dealing with this whole issue of whether we're going to be able to fulfill our security functions as military forces in an era where people expect no casualties, because I don't think it's doable. I don't think it's doable…If you think you can train to the standard you need to and never take any risk, and that we're never going to put a soldier, sailor, airman, Marine's life on the line in training, you're missing it. And I think the institutions are missing it if they think that. There is not a statement I hate more than the statement that there is nothing in peacetime worth a soldier, sailor, airman, marine's life in training. Now some of you may object to that but I'm sorry. We're in a risky business. And if we don't train to standards that are higher than combat we'll pay on the battlefield. I lost 7 dead in Desert Shield/Desert Storm. We were operating 200 to 250 miles behind the lines. How do you think I lost them? Do you think the enemy had anything to do with it? No, it was one aircraft crash, one helo crash. The enemy was only capable of wounding one of my soldiers. The enemy is the least dangerous thing on the battlefield. The most dangerous thing is safety of flight. The second most dangerous thing is blue on blue. And you're not going to solve either one of those if you don't train. And if you go back and you take a look at any one of the conflicts we've been in and see where our casualties are from I think it will surprise you of how many of our own we have hurt, and that's an indictment of the way we train.

THE COMMAND AND GENERAL STAFF COLLEGE

Finally, many of the speakers felt compelled to say something about the school itself, its proud history, and the expectations of its graduates. Secretary of the Army Frank Pace expressed his envy of the students during the graduation ceremony in 1952.

I envy you the year that you've had here. One of the privileges that is not vouchsafed to those of us who serve in public positions in Washington is the privilege of thinking and reflecting on the problems of our times. Unfortunately for many years the great problems of government have revolved around the capacity to join the duelers and the thinkers. How do you get men who in the busy requirements of large governmental operations find the time to think about where the progress of government and nations move? And at the same time how do you ensure the fact that those who are charged with the 'doing' of things that must be done, likewise are the men who plot and plan the program and plan along which we travel? Unfortunately that problem has never been completely solved in the history of man. Certainly today, with the complicated problems of our world, and particularly the complicated problems of our nation, the need for tying the two together becomes even more imperative. And therefore you that have had the privilege of both thinking and receiving the ideas of others in the field of command and general staff are receiving the basic qualification for becoming both a doer and a thinker.

General Decker reminded the 1960 graduates of the Associate Course what they should take away from their time at the school.

You'll forget much of the factual information you've been taught here. And I suspect that such matters as stock levels at a field army ammunition supply point are already fading from your memory. [Laughter] However, the lasting benefits of this course stem from those exercises requiring you to use the information given you. Throughout your stay here you have been required again and again to analyze the situation, to weigh the alternatives, and to select a course of action. Thus you have been developing your ability to make military decisions both as a staff officer and as a commander.

Following one of President Harry Truman's visits to the college on December 15, 1961, General Johnson discussed a conversation he and the president had prior to his remarks.

The other observation occurred as we were coming up the stairs backstage or under the stage, when President Truman said "You know, this is a wonderful institution because it has provided us the leadership for our Armed Forces that has enabled us to win two world wars." And I think that this particular thought is one that you can take with you as you depart from here.

General DePuy seconded this observation in March, 1974:

World War II, in my memory and my understanding was a triumph for Fort Leavenworth. It wasn't the battalion commanders of World War II that were remembered after the war. It was the Eisenhowers and the Bradleys and the people who spent a couple years here. They were the managers of the war. They expanded an Army of 120,000 people into eight million. They did a magnificent job. And it was the staff officer who emerged as the hero of World War II, at least in the eyes of the public, and the kinds of people who had those jobs.

Famed military historian S.L.A. Marshall spoke of the spirit of the school in 1962.

There is too much to be done by those of us who understand that the strong stay free only so long as they exert their strength for freedom. About this school there is an aroma of high feeling, not to be found or lost in science or Greek, not to be fixed, but all-pervading. You have helped to make it that way for others, and this is part of their reward in being here. In time of difficulty, and it will come, my prayer is that some residue of the spirit of this school will steady you. Keep your hearts as open as your minds, for only those who do both are fit to lead men who serve their country in the hardest game of all. And if you wonder, at the end, why you have known a great comradeship here, then I would give it to you at the end in words of verse I learned when young, which set forth the objects of a soldier's dreaming: To put the cause above renown, to count the game above the prize, to honor as you strike him down the foe who waits with fearless eyes, to count the life of battle good, and dear the land that gave you birth, and dear yet the brotherhood that binds the brave of all the earth. [From *Clifton Chapel* by Sir Henry Newbolt]

General Johnson was even more somber in December, 1963, trying to demonstrate the importance of the students' experience at the college. These comments are all the more remarkable considering they were given at a graduation address with families present.

[CGSC] is a tremendously important institution in the scheme of the Army, and on top of that, in a time when the art that we must be prepared to perform at some time is being practiced in such a wide variety of ways. And I talk about training on the one hand, to perhaps dying in Vietnam on the other hand, which is a rather grim way to say it, you get an across the board look here that you can't get any other place. And over a period of thirty years, regardless of the number of assignments you have, you're not likely to get the spectrum of things that you get here.

Army Secretary Stephen Ailes highlighted the quality of the Army School system in 1965, championing its ability to produce officers who knew how to do their jobs.

American Industry made a great advance and volume production became a possibility with the development of the concept of interchangeable parts. If something goes wrong with the fuel system of your automobile, you can remove the carburetor and replace it with one just like the old one which you know will work… Now in many ways the Army itself is an organization of interchangeable parts, and continuity is maintained in combat organizations at installations and posts all over the world, because the new officer rotating in to replace the officer rotating out usually has a basic grasp of how to perform his job. He knows what the S-1 [personnel officer] or the G-3 [operations officer] is supposed to do and knows the procedures. And furthermore he knows what everybody else is supposed to do in the organization. And the receiving organization doesn't have to train a new man from scratch to fill a unique job. It must be very clear to you that the Army school system in general, but the Command and General Staff College here in particular is primarily responsible for that result.

In 1973 General Taylor gave the students a glimpse of his Leavenworth experience.

I mentioned the marked problems because I understand that is somewhat a thing of the past. I'm sure it is an outmoded concept, but we had it nonetheless. But we believed that if we had a stupid officer in the class, that that should be exposed. He should be exposed not to embarrass him, but hopefully to correct him. Our feeling in the long run that it is far better to discover stupidity at Leavenworth, than it was to discover it later in the battlefield. Nonetheless I understand that that is not the mode today. I'm sure you have a better one. [Laughter]

General DePuy related an indirect message from General Abrams to the graduating class in June of 1974, saying "When General Abrams came out and talked to you, all of you together and a few of you separately, he came back to Washington and told General Weyand and some of the rest of us that we could relax, go on leave, he had been with you and the future of the Army was well in hand." General Weyand told a terrific CGSC tale in 1975, relating a meeting of former Army Chiefs.

I had a good experience last month. I got the brilliant idea, since I wanted to share all these problems, of calling in the retired 4-star generals and sitting them down, briefing them for a day, and listening to what they had to say. And that was a good experience for me because I found I didn't even have to go back to George Washington, all I had to do was go back to those guys and they had same problems: unit rotation, Reserve readiness, lack of equipment, training problems, lack of understanding by the American people of what the Army's needs are and what it's all about, what its utility is and so on and so forth. And so it was a very healthy exchange. Best part I got out of it was listening to some of them talk about their time when they attended this college and how important it was to them. And in the process of doing that they'd tell all kinds of little stories. General [Lyman] Lemnitzer told me about—he was in this class, now in those days there were lieutenants here. And Lemnitzer's class was the first of the one-year classes. And they had a guy named Talley in their class, and they seated them alphabetically, and Talley was in the back, and he was also, well let's say relatively speaking, one of the dumbest people in the class, and so the instructor called on him. And Talley stood up and the instructor painted this scene for him of commander "A" going out faced with this situation, well "what did he do?" Well, the guys around Talley said [whispering] "Reconnaissance." And Talley said "Sir, he goes on reconnaissance." Oh very good. Then he painted another scene about what this commander saw on reconnaissance, and "What does he do now?" [whispering again] "Key staff officers." [Talley] "Calls the key staff officers, Sir." Yeah, he did that. He went through about two more questions, well, what did they decide there? And then he got into something complex about the—and each time Talley got the answer from this whispered group around him. Got into the commander's estimate, wanted him to describe that. And these guys around Talley were silent. And so the lieutenant says "Sir, that's all we know back here." [Big laugh]

Former Chief General J. Lawton Collins told the faculty in 1983 how he had *almost* become an instructor at the college.

General [Stuart] Heintzelman was the commandant here when I took the course, which incidentally was a two-year course, the second year being devoted to Corps and Army and larger units, and to the logistical problem, about which I knew very little prior to that time, and which is an extremely valuable two years. Heintzelman called me in at the beginning of the second year and said he's been observing my work and I was doing very well and all that sort of business, and he had a letter in his hand and he said "I'm going to put in for you as an instructor." He must have seen my face fall. It stopped him. And I said "Well, General, do you mind if I make a statement?" He said no. I said "I've been teaching or being taught now 15 or 16 consecutive years, and if I were to be stationed here at Leavenworth for another year, I think I'll lose all practical ability, if I ever had any." He said "By God, Collins, you're right." And so he let me go to troops, which is what I wanted, to go back to troops, which he permitted me to do. But nevertheless, despite the fact that I said no at that time, my judgment is, as I said earlier, that the thing that really made an Army for us was our school system. I said at one time I'd give up a division before I'd give up one of our schools. They are the crux of our system and I hope we will always support them, and I think you gentlemen, the instructors here, are lucky to have this job. I certainly learned a lot from you all—the instructor always learns more than the student does, and I certainly learned a lot at the various Army schools that I had the good fortune to attend.

Secretary West told the students what he expected of them in 1994.

The point, though, is that a year spent here that does not at some point in your lifetime involve thinking about how this Army, your service, these armed forces can be better, is a year that is not as fruitful as you may have hoped for. And it is not the responsibility of teachers and staff and faculty to make that happen. The standards by which you must judge yourselves in this aspect are the standards that you create and to which you hold yourselves accountable.

Three years later he was asked how the Army could achieve a common view of the battlefield and still avoid groupthink.

That's what Command and General Staff College is about. [muffled laughter] We get you here at a time in your careers where you 've been doing a lot of group think, you've been part of organizations, you've been doing what the unit does, thinking what the unit thought. And we say to you "You've got a year, go sit in seminars, ask hard questions, and think." And I say that only partially facetiously. Where does our spirit for original thinking, where does our emphasis come from, where does the push? From right here at Leavenworth. From the [Army War College at] Carlisle Barracks. From all the places where we say to you for a minute, put aside the responsibility to achieve a day-to-day, weekly objectives, cast off the need to meet some goal by the end of the month. And instead concentrate on ideas. And incidentally, your concentration doesn't have to be constructive. If you ever have a teacher, or instructor, just a supervisor or facilitator say to you "Let's have some constructive criticism, some constructive thought here," they're just trying to avoid the possibility that some thought, some principle, some cherished notion, may get attacked, and might be destroyed in the process. So destructive thinking isn't so bad either. The point is, you're right, we do need to avoid group think, although once you are out on the battlefield, as you know, there's not a lot of time for that. Somebody's got to be in charge, and someone's got to take the heat for making the decisions. But if here in your seminars, you are not attacking ideas just as often as you are generating them, if you here in your seminars, you're not examining virtually everything that's put before you…underneath the platform to see if there are really legs holding it up, then you're not doing what the taxpayers are contributing a year's worth of time for you to do.

Wesley Clark, Supreme Allied Commander, Europe, during the Kosovo operation, never imagined he would be executing a mission so closely related to his CGSC studies, an experience he related to the students in 1999.

> When I was a Captain here at Leavenworth in 1974/75 I wrote an [Masters of Military Art and Science] thesis. Some of you may have read this thesis. I went through and re-read it last night in preparation for coming to this presentation today. It's a pretty good thesis. [Laughter] I recommend it to you. But I never dreamed I'd have to live it. So be careful what you do in your year or your two years at this institution. Not just the greatest year of your life. It's the year in which if you don't lay the professional foundation for your military duties you won't be able to stand up to the pressures later on. Because you won't know enough, you won't have thought them through, and you won't, ultimately, be able to look yourself in the eye with the courage of your own convictions, and persuade others that you're right. So I hope you'll use this year to best advantage, I wish you all the best. Good luck.

A large focus of CGSC was the art of command and leadership. As the students were the future leaders of their respective military organizations, the guest speakers invariably covered this most important topic.

2. Leadership and Values

As CGSC was (and is) a school for the Army's Field Grade officers, the topic of leadership was one of the most discussed, as many speakers imparted their thoughts on the subject to the students. Some defined leadership, while others discussed traits that good leaders must possess. Many gave examples of leadership through personal or historical vignettes. Leader requirements were often outlined, and many speakers offered sage leadership advice to the mid-career officers. Values were often discussed, both as a subset of leadership, and as a topic in their own right.

In late-1995, Secretary West demonstrated the difficulty in pinning down a definition of leadership.

> Whatever [Leadership] is, it is certainly not something that is bestowed on you and me just because somebody says "Hey, you're a leader." I certainly don't bestow it, even though I can [provide instruction] for promotion boards and approve their recommendations. The president doesn't bestow it just because he sends the nominations over, and certainly the Senate Armed Services committee doesn't bestow it. And it's not something to be seized, even though the novelists tend to write it that way. They're always talking about somebody seizing leadership. Well, you don't just walk into a room or a unit and say "By golly, I'm in charge, here's your first order," although I think that a lot of us use that technique. [Audience chuckles] Nor, contrary to what a lot of people write, do I believe that leadership is something that's earned. I don't believe you earn your stripes just by sitting in that seat or staying around for ten years. I don't think leadership is the reward for sticking it out.
>
> Now maybe it's a bit of all three of those. Certainly it helps us if someone will put their hands on our brow and say "You're anointed." It's not a bad thing to have happen. And certainly not bad if we are willing to walk into a situation and seize the opportunity to do what has to be done. And surely, if we do go in there and demonstrate to our peers and those we expect to follow us that we know the job, that we're willing to stick it out and do the work, we do earn their respect. And that certainly aids leadership as well. There's no doubt that it's all of those things. I don't have the magic answer.
>
> I know it's an opportunity more than it is a privilege. I know that it's a challenge more than it is merely something good that happens to you. I know that I probably need to learn how to follow before I could ever be a good leader. And I know that I probably have a lot to learn before I'll be an effective one…We have lots to learn and we continue to learn for as long as we're alive. Leadership is an opportunity to serve. Leadership is a kind of yoke around our neck that hooks us to those we expect to follow us and makes us their servants just as much as they stand and are assigned to carry out our orders. Leadership is about taking responsibility—indeed let me cut off this discussion of leadership by giving you someone else's words that are better than mine.
>
> Years ago—I'm a lawyer by profession so you won't be surprised if I use the words of a former Supreme Court Justice. Oliver Wendell Holmes said this—and he wasn't just talking about leadership though I find it instructive. He said "I learned in the classroom and in the regiment how best I think I (we) can serve ourselves and our nation: To see so far as one may, to try to understand the forces at work behind the details, to hammer out as solid and compact a piece of work as one can, to try to make it first rate, and to leave it unpublished." Well, there's a prescription for leadership, in a way. The vision to look as

far out as we can, to try and see the big picture and at the same time feel how it is affected by the details. The willingness even as we leave others to the details, to care about them. To care about the work product, that it be the best we can produce from ourselves and those that we seek to energize. And then, the sense of self-confidence that leads us to leave the glory and the credit to someone else. Indeed, leadership is not about glory at all, is it? Although it is nice to have it. It's about taking responsibility. It's about getting the job done. It's about being there when we're needed, for our soldiers.

General Max Thurman had this to say about strategic leadership in 1992.

What is a strategic leader?…My view is it's a CEO or a general officer at the four-star rank, and some specific three-star generals. Not all, but some. [Deputy Chief of Staff for Operations] is a strategic leader…But every Tom, Dick and Harry three-star is not necessarily a strategic leader. [Laughter] And let me be first to tell you Brigadiers that you don't qualify either, okay? [Referring to new colonel-promotable directors recognized at beginning of session] Now, what is [the strategic leader] responsible for? Getting people to operate innovatively and creatively within limits.

LEADERSHIP TRAITS

The traits listed by the speakers over the years ran the gamut, starting in 1952 with remarks by Major General (Retired) Ernest Harmon, who was a division and corps commander during World War II.

Good leadership requires keen observation. Keep flexible in your mind. While you are becoming a specialist, don't forget to be a soldier. Don't dissipate yourself on liquor and in foolishness. You can have quite a few drinks in your life, I've been able to have a few, but I haven't allowed it to destroy my character or my stamina. I've seen so many fellas start out much smarter than I am, 'cause I'm not a smart man at all, but when they arrived at the time we could use them in war they were so dissipated in their character by excess drinking or whatnot, that they couldn't stand the strain. And you've got to stand the strain. If I had my choice between a brilliant man and a man with a strong back, the man with the strong back is the fellow that has to stay out here and make a decision, stay up all night, and have the courage and guts to stay with it! And that's what you must develop here as you are growing up. Don't sap your strength with foolishness along the way, or…your country can't use you at a time when you should be used.

Another Chief of Staff, Lyman Lemnitzer described the true test of leadership to the graduates of the 1961 class.

Anyone can be effective when working with ideal people under ideal conditions and under ideal circumstances. But people and circumstances are seldom ideal. In fact, they are never ideal. The real test of leadership, therefore, is the degree to which the commander, notwithstanding difficulties and hardships and deficiencies, rises to the challenge, makes the most of what aspects are available, and achieves the fullest capability that is attainable.

The following year S.L.A. Marshall was relating a conversation he had with a civilian about discussing decisions and orders with subordinates. The man he was speaking to didn't understand why orders weren't explained and discussed with subordinates.

> I said "The reasoning is simply this, that we've had the argument on the way up and they've lost it. And let me tell you if we go ahead and do what I propose to do and I fall flat on my face there isn't one of them that's going to feel sorry for me. They'll say 'We told the old so and so. And he didn't listen.' But on the other hand, if your dope works out, you put it over, this is your main chance to profit by what I call the Mystique of Command. He said "That's a good term, what do you mean?" I said "I want that they would be a little bit in awe of me, and think that I've got something that they haven't got, even though this may be an illusion." And I said "That's the extra something that you need if you're going to lead."

In 1964 Major General (Retired) William F. Dean, who became a POW and won the Medal of Honor leading the 24th Division during the Korean War, talked about his early impressions of general officers.

> Before World War II we didn't think we'd see a war...We used to talk, what does it take to be a general? One said the only characteristic is to be ruthless. I disagreed...I thought you had to be queer in some way or another. As I look back, when the chips are down, no matter how it hurts you, to save lives and to fulfill your mission, sometimes you have to relieve those you least want to relieve.

General Lemnitzer introduced the recurring topic in his 1961 graduation address, telling the students about the requirement for moral courage.

> Courage is probably the most fundamental attribute of a commander. It must be the kind of courage that endures, despite the stress of battle, and the dangers and reverses which are a part of all battlefield experience. Obviously the commander must have physical courage for he must set the example. But the commander, more than other men, and the higher the commander the more pronounced it is, there is a special requirement for moral courage & spiritual courage. This is the type of courage that enables a commander to do what he knows is right, regardless of the consequences to himself. This is the courage to accept criticism and blame in silence when it is in the best interest of the organization and the nation. Without such courage there can be no initiative. And any amount of knowledge or imagination will be sterile, for they in themselves produce nothing.

During General Dean's appearance in 1964, he brought up a different aspect of moral courage, that of loyalty.

> Loyalty up, oh, we're always loyal up. But are you loyal when you get an order from your superior headquarters, and in the presence of your contemporaries or subordinates, you say "What in the devil are they thinking up there? Are they going crazy? We'll try to do it, but..." The division commander gets an order from Corps, and in front of his Chief of Staff, or Regimental Commanders, or any of his staff he says "The damn Corps' going crazy. What do they think we can do?" Right then your subordinates have tabbed you as

being disloyal. You are disloyal if you get an order you do not feel will work and you do not go, unannounced, to your own outfit, and say "Sir, I feel this order will not work, for the following reasons." And after you superior hears you out, and he says "But that's the way I want it done nevertheless." Then you go back to your outfit and you implement that order as though it were your own idea. You don't have a chance of making a good show of it if you indicate in any way, by innuendo or intimation, that you think it's a lousy order. Your outfit's not going to put their weight behind it. But if they think you think it's a good one, they're going to do their damnedest. And that's loyalty up. I've had that experience where a regimental commander of mine came back, in France, said "General, I don't think this will work, I think it would be much better if we did it this way." We had time, we weren't going to jump off for three days. He hadn't announced to his outfit he was going back to set the general straight. He just came back, unannounced. I called my staff in, we thought it over, we rescinded the first order, we had time, we planned it according to his suggestions. As a result, we got a Corps commendation. I got the credit for his loyalty. He didn't go back to his outfit and say "I set the old man straight." That was loyalty. That was loyalty up. You have to expect that both ways.

In 1966 General Bradley also spoke about loyalty.

After a decision is made, everyone must be behind it 100%. I thought the British were admirable in that respect during World War II. No matter how much discussion there had been on the subject, as soon as a decision was made you never heard any doubts expressed. You had to believe everyone involved in making a decision had never entertained any ideas except those expressed in the decision. I'm afraid that we Americans sometimes had some second-guessers, and I don't mean later, but during the carrying out of that plan.

The next month former Army Chief of Staff General Matthew Ridgway also discussed aspects of loyalty and dissent, using some historical examples.

Now I do want to mention some examples of moral courage, for I think they are less well-known. They can be considered as proof of true greatness of soul, and where the individual has not measured up, he has generally failed fortune's bid to fame. To me such instances most frequently found in war are those where the career of the leader is at stake, and where his actions or decisions will determine a saving or slaughter of many of his men. History is full of these cases...the lure of glory, the fear of being thought afraid, of losing personal power and prestige, the mistaken idea that blind obedience to orders has no alternative, have been followed by tragic losses of lives with little to no gain. History often glosses over the countless thousands of lives which have been fruitlessly sacrificed for the pull of power, prestige, and publicity. [Sir Douglas] Haig's Flanders campaign in 1917 is a conspicuous example. 100,000 men sacrificed for the gain of 1,000 yards of almost bottomless morass. It is easy to gamble with other people's money, and sometimes easier still with other men's lives, particularly when your own is in no great danger. You remember the commander's conference prior to one of the big offensives in World War I, when a Corps commander who's CP was miles behind the front spoke out during a lull in the meeting, saying "I'd give ten thousand men to take that hill." And a liaison officer from a front line infantry unit, remarking to a brother officer standing beside him in the back of the room, "Generous old bastard, isn't he?" [Laughter] The military deals harshly, as it should, with failure to carry out orders in battle. The commander present on the scene is entitled to full and enthusiastic execution by subordinates.

Yet when faced with very different situations from those anticipated, as well as in the transition from plans to orders, there sometimes comes a challenge to one's conscience. The compelling urge to oppose foolhardy operations before it is too late. Before the order is issued, and lives are needlessly thrown away. Or the leader may be faced with a decision, "Shall I take the responsibility for discarding the original mission? Shall I take the initiative, and strive for success along different lines?" He'll have to put those questions to his conscience. "Blind obedience is due only to superiors present on the spot at the moment of action," said Napoleon, and I concur.

I find a statement of mine from some years ago which I still support. It was this: It has long seemed to me that the hard decisions are not the ones you make in the heat of battle. Far harder to make are those involved in speaking your mind about some hare-brained scheme that proposes committing troops to action under conditions where failure seems almost certain, and the only results will be the needless sacrifice of priceless lives. When all is said and done the most precious asset any nation has is its youth, and for a battle commander ever to condone the unnecessary sacrifice of his men is inexcusable. In any action you must balance the inevitable cost in lives against the objectives you seek to attain. Unless the result to be expected can reasonably justify the estimated loss of life the action involves, then for my part I want none of it.

General Ridgway talked about the trait of self-discipline in leaders during his 1966 visit.

Only those who discipline themselves can exact discipline from others. When the chips are down, when privation mounts, and the casualty rate rises, when the crisis is at hand, which commander, I ask, receives the better response? The one who has failed to share the rough going with his troops? Who is rarely seen in the zone of aimed fire? Who expects much and gives little? Or the one whose every thought is the welfare of his men consistent with the accomplishment of his mission? Who doesn't ask them to do what he himself has not already done, and stands ready to do again when necessary? Who with his men has shared short rations, the physical discomforts and rigors of campaign and will be found at the crises of action where the issues are to be decided? I know your answer: Self-disciplined, self-controlled, and so in control of others no matter how tough the going. Washington at the battle of Long Island and at Valley Forge, Grant at Shiloh, [Ranald S.] McKenzie of the Fourth Cavalry and his epic raid, which Colonel [Russell] "Red" Reeder has so well portrayed in one of his many fine books. The junior officer pursuing hostile Indians in sub-zero weather in our Western Plains, closing up at dark for a dawn attack with no fires permitted, and only cold rations, if any, before H-hour. Much the same many times in Korea, I might add, and I'm sure under equally arduous conditions in Vietnam today. The young ship commander named Kennedy, his PT boat sunk in action, his crew safely on the beach, then swimming out in shark-infested waters to try and intercept a friendly destroyer and rescue his men. The world's annals and our own are studded with the names of such men, of all services and all grades, always ready to assume responsibilities they could always assign to others, and know they would be willingly accepted. True to themselves and their conscience, their men sensed they would be true to them, giving them full credit, and frankly admitting mistakes and accepting responsibilities when they themselves are to blame.

In 1960, General Decker described a good decision maker. "In real life, the choice between courses of action is often narrow, perhaps even as narrow as in Leavenworth problems. Sometimes there are several acceptable courses of action. The real test of the military decision maker is to weed-out the trivia to go to the heart of the matter, to decide, and having decided, to execute." Regarding this execution, General Dean schooled the class of 1964 on the importance of timely decision-making, saying "I have seen instructors of mine here at Leavenworth that were outstanding as instructors, but unfortunately, when they had the opportunity, they didn't measure up. Why did they fail? Not because they lacked the qualities I am going to innumerate. In most cases it was because they couldn't make a decision in time. They were hunting for perfection." In 1967, Secretary of State Henry Kissinger spoke of this as well, but at the strategic level.

> I'm not saying that early action is always to be preferred to inaction. All I'm saying is that whether one acts or doesn't act depends on an assessment that cannot be proved at the time that it is made. And the most difficult problem for any policy maker is therefore a moral quality: The willingness to act on the basis of insufficient knowledge, and walk alone, until events either vindicate him, or prove him wrong, but in any event, to act on judgment, and not only on knowledge. Policy cannot be reduced simply to a science, and the attempt to do so reduces it to sterility. To wait until one knows all the facts is to become the prisoner of events. And therefore any assessment of foreign policy, inevitably, is dealing with an element of conjecture.

As stated earlier, General Harmon implored students to "keep flexible in your minds," and many speakers talked about the necessity for a leader to deal with ever more specialized areas of their craft. Omar Bradley offered a quote from industry to address this problem in 1966: "Specialties dominate almost every problem today. Leaders must understand without becoming specialists. Thomas Watson of IBM once said that 'Genius in an executive is the ability to deal successfully with matters he does not understand.'"

In 1973, General Ralph E. Haines Jr, the last Commanding General of Continental Army Command (which would soon be divided into Forces Command and Training and Doctrine Command), gave his thoughts on specialization to the faculty of the Leadership Department.

> So I think we…in the Army more than any service have to become deeply involved in people problems. You see, only the Marine Corps has the situation that we have, where an officer starting at the bottom of his profession immediately is responsible for 30 or 40 people. [In] What civilian job does an individual who is recruited on campus and starts at the bottom have that responsibility and the totality of that responsibility that we have and not just 8 hours a day, 5 days a week, but 24 hours a day 7 days a week? So that since that responsibility is such a strong one, they don't have that in the Navy or the Air Force as Second Lieutenants. They don't command at that point in time. And they don't get their first command until they've been in a significant period. So I think we have to be people oriented. And if an individual doesn't relate to people easily and without forcing it, I think he's in the wrong business, to be wearing the insignia of an officer. [If] He wants to be a specialist in some more abstract area, and he still wants to be in the defense department, then he'd better be a Department of the Army civilian, or even a warrant

officer who has the capability to deal in certain specialist areas, although the warrant officer's horizons are currently being broadened to include management of people. The individual that wants command only to get poop sheet credit is not the individual that we want in command in the first place. And I think that this situation is gradually changing.

General Sullivan told 1995's graduates that flexibility and adaptability were among the traits they needed to possess.

But the interesting thing about all this change is that today's Army requires the kind of leaders that we've always required: Adaptable, flexible, ready to participate and lead an organization in battle or an organization faced with the nation's crises. It requires leaders inculcated with our institutional values, selfless service to nation, quiet professionalism, competence, courage, character, duty, honor, country. The importance of those values, linked with an undying respect for the individual as an individual, men and women, enduring respect for the value of the individual, are not a luxury. These are not luxuries. They are part of this nation's soul. And they are what ensure victory in battle.

There was one trait General Sullivan was able to highlight in 1992, when one of his presentation slides came up backwards on the screen. "Look, if you think for one minute that slide coming up backwards bothered me, forget it! You've got to laugh at life, gang. 'Cause if you don't enjoy life, I'll tell you, someday you are going to regret that you haven't had a good time." Interestingly, this also occurred during his 1994 visit, making one wonder if it was a set-up to enable him to discuss the zero-defect perception.

LEADERSHIP IN EXECUTION

Many of the speakers discussed leadership through the recounting of their experiences or those of others, often with humorous results. General Bradley frequently used this technique during his appearances. In 1966, he related the importance of having self-confidence in order to instill confidence in one's subordinates.

Having self-confidence instills that confidence in his troops. Just before the Normandy invasion, all leaders were cautioned that they must never say anything, which when overheard, might indicate any doubt in the success of the operation. In spite of that, there was at least one division, and possibly two or three, that had word passed around them that none of them would live through the beach assault. There'd be 100% casualties. Well you can't let troops go into action under those conditions, so I took the time to go down and talk to the assembled officers of that division, and I talked to every unit of that division, pointing out that that wasn't so. Fortunately I had been through the invasion of Sicily, where the losses were much less than we'd all expected, and tried to convince them that sure, some of them would get killed. But it would not be anything like 100% losses. I heard afterwards it paid off a little bit because a correspondent told me he went over on an LST [landing ship, tank], and he saw a Sergeant reading a novel as they went across. And he said "Sergeant, aren't you scared, aren't you worried?" [The Sergeant replied] "No, General Bradley told us it would be alright, I'm not worried." [Laughter]

General DePuy also used the Normandy invasion to discuss leadership during the June 1974 commencement exercises.

> On Omaha beach, the more difficult of them all, for a while the landing troops were not able to get off the beach. And then as the day wore on, a few men, I think General Abe would probably put it this way, and maybe the Marines would too, but a few good men started to move. They saw what they had to do and they tried to do it. And General Montgomery couldn't do anything about that, or General Eisenhower, or General Huebner who commanded the First Division. But the sergeants and the privates, the lieutenants and the captains of the 16th Infantry, and on their right the 116th Infantry of the 29th Division, they had to do it. They did it. But a lot of men didn't go forward. It was my observation at the end of World War II that when fighting was really rough, that some 10% of the soldiers made it go. And now you're leaving here. And you're going out into what you probably think of as the United States Army. Now you're all supposed to be 10-percenters, and I hope you are.

In 1967, General Bradley was asked about leaders using distinctive items of apparel to help their subordinates identify them, an obvious allusion to General George Patton. "Like two pistols?" He replied, causing much laughter in the audience.

> Sometimes they play a very important part. When General Patton took over the Second Corps in...Western Tunisia...he had to impress himself on that corps. Discipline was a little bit run down. Men were wearing their stocking cap without helmets, and all sorts of things. And General Patton really made his impression on that corps and made it quickly. We were about to go into combat, so he felt he had to do something to make the men all the way down realize that something new had happened. I saw him one day stop a truck, the only thing wrong about it was a guy who had tied up the back of the truck had left a string of rope hanging down about that far, it wasn't bad. Goodness, you'd see any truck running around here today and the cover's probably got a loose end. But he gave that fella one of the damnedest cussings out I ever heard over that little thing. I was a little bit worried at the time, but then I stopped to realize this is one way that he's letting people know that he's here. Now that man went and told everybody what a raw deal he had, [laughter] but it wasn't but a few days 'til everybody knew there was a new corps commander. Now to that point he impressed himself on the men and let them know, he had issued orders that the men would wear helmets at all times, keep their shirt buttoned and their tie on. Wasn't too hot then, got hot later on. But he issued these orders and anybody that didn't do it was immediately grabbed up and fined. He went around with his two pistols, he went around with his flag flying on his command car. Every time he went down the road he made plenty of noise. He accomplished his purpose.

> Incidentally on that helmet business...After the first day of fighting in Northern Tunisia, after I had taken command and General Patton had gone back, I went into the evacuation hospital, and one of the nurses had a steel helmet on. And I was talking to some of the wounded, and she finally got up the courage and said "General, do we have to wear these steel helmets here in the hospital while we're attending to patients? It sort of falls off!" I looked up at her, I hadn't realized she'd been wearing a helmet, and I said

"Goodness, no." So I immediately issued orders that nurses didn't have to wear steel helmets. [Laughter] But he did impress on that Corps that things were different.

Bradley was also asked about any leadership problems he encountered when leading officers that had once been his superiors, in particular General Patton.

[Bradley clears throat...which elicits laughter] General Patton was six years my senior. Way back in 1925 we lived across the street from each other as majors. I got to know him pretty well. First time I really served under him was when I went to North Africa in late February and the first of March, 1943, and I was detailed as General Eisenhower's eyes and ears. I was supposed to go where I thought he'd go if he had time and look into training, weapons, a few other things. But when Patton became Corps commander on the 7th of March up in Tunisia, he told Ike "I don't want any goddamn spy around me, make Bradley my deputy." [Laughter] So I became Deputy Corps Commander, and we had a very close relationship. We alternated days, one day I'd go up in front and he'd stay at headquarters, and the next day he'd go up to the front and I'd stay at headquarters to take care of any emergency. And it worked out very well. Then when he went back to plan the invasion of Sicily he asked if my corps would be substituted for the one that had been slated, because he thought he liked to be with me. So I went into Sicily as his subordinate commander. Later I was ordered to England to organize the First Army headquarters and later the Army group headquarters, Patton was set up as an Army commander under me. I've had many people come to me and say they never heard Patton say one word against me. He'd talk about everyone else from the president down, [laughter] but he never said anything about me. And I think that was the mark of leader, who could step down from being the commander to become a subordinate of a man his junior, and never question it at all. And we got along very, very well together.

He was also asked to provide an example of a leadership problem he faced.

You must control your whole operations through channels. Only one time did I violate that principle. It was after we broke out through Avranches [France], I was down in that area, and I found a gap of twenty miles in our lines where there was not a single unit. I had to fill it in a hurry, it was just south of Mortain. I grabbed off the 35th Division, which belonged to Patton, and gave them orders to go into that gap. I immediately went to Patton's headquarters, he wasn't there, he was out on the peninsula, but I told his Chief of Staff what I'd done, and I apologized for ordering direct...But in a way I was sort of getting even with [Patton], he had done that to me in Sicily. [Laughter] He had moved one of my regiments while I was up visiting the front lines. I had a reserve to cover the gap, and he had moved it up front and left the gap, but nothing happened so it was alright!

A year earlier Bradley was asked about leadership techniques that he found most effective in getting the maximum effort from staff.

In the first place, I tried to pick as good officers for my staff as possible. When I first took over the 82d at Camp Claiborne, I was very fortunate that the man in the War Department who called me up to tell me that I had been selected to organize and activate this whole division happened to be a very efficient officer, and he asked me to name some staff for him, and I said I'd like to think it over for a half an hour and call him back. And I called him back and I said "Well, to start with for Chief of Staff, are you available?" And he said well, he thought he could arrange it, and being in the G1 section in the War Department I thought he ought to know some pretty good officers [laughter] so I said "You select a group." [Big laugh & applause] When he submitted his selection, he'd gone right after the best ones, I knew them all, and I said "That's okay with me," and he being in G1, he got 'em... When I took command of II Corps, General Patton had just released it, and he had required the staff to have breakfast at the same time as the enlisted men, I think it was 6 am. Well if you know anything about combat operations you know that your staff officers are up until one, two-o'clock every night, receiving the reports from the field of the operations of the previous day, and after a while you pretty much wear them out if you make them get up at six o'clock. So I immediately changed breakfast hours for the staff to 8:30. That didn't hurt me. [Laughter] But I got more efficiency out of the staff—they worked the hours that best suited the staff and we were lucky to have all that experience.

During his appearance in 1964, General Dean was asked how large unit commanders could project their influence down to subordinate units. He answered with a Patton story of his own.

I feel at division level at least, the most effective means was to get down and visit battalion CPs [command posts]...let yourself be seen. Let people know who you are at a distance. The enlisted man and junior officer will always magnify in the telling of what he sees. [Laughter] If he sees you up there, toward the front, by the time he gets through you're out front, leading the charge, after he tells about it. Well, that's not exactly accurate but it builds up the idea that the old man is up here with us. General Patton had that idea. He didn't wear two ivory-handled pistols because he wanted to look like a cowboy, or one of our TV shows. He did it so his troops would know 'that's the old man' no matter if they were 50 feet from him or a couple hundred yards.

When I reported [to Fort Leavenworth], 24th September, 1945, General O.P. Weyland was here as Assistant Commandant...He had had the 19th Tactical Group, which gave full support to Patton's Army. And he told me then that General Patton used to always drive forward in his car that was really decorated, so you could know it was his car. He had a very shiny helmet, and he had his two pistols. And you could see him from a great distance. So everybody saw him. But no one ever saw him driving back to the rear, back to his CP. Bacause when he got there, they covered the stars, and they put down a light plane, and he was flown back. So no one ever saw General Patton going to the rear. At least that's what General Weyland told me. Now that's a technique. He wasn't dishonest, he wasn't afraid of being shot at. But he couldn't run his Army and stay up there all the time. But he went up frequently enough so that his outfit would know he was up there with them. And that has a big effect. You project yourself that way. And another thing that you have to do, if you're going to do that, you're going to have a Chief of Staff, and a deputy, that can issue orders in your name if communications go out while you're there. You have to depend on them, and you have to give them that responsibility and be prepared to back them up. That's where loyalty both ways works.

Dean was also asked whether perhaps he had been too far forward or not careful enough when he was captured during the Korean War.

For three years as a guest of the communists, I had time to think about this. For those three years I was convinced I had been in there, I'll stay in there. I felt I hadn't accomplished a great deal. I hadn't accomplished anything, as I saw it. But when I came back and talked to some of the survivors who had been there, and talked to other commanders, they convinced me, that although it may have appeared dumb, the whole effect was good, because it generated a spirit in the 24th [Division] that endured throughout the Korean War. I was told that from subsequent commanders of the division. They felt that it built up in the minds of those Tarot Leafers [referring to the 24th Division unit patch] that if the old man could go up there and take a chance, they could too. So they convinced me that maybe it was alright. You want to know why I was up there? You see, in World War II we had time, for the most part, to get ready. Before you went overseas, you were exposed to these "Why we fight" series. Korea broke suddenly. We weren't as poorly trained as some of the historians have attempted to state we were, but we hadn't really thought we were going to fight tomorrow. I told every batch of recruits that came to the division, every batch of replacements, "We might be fighting any day." I'd been Military Governor of Korea. I been in Korea before I'd come to Japan. I had a feeling the North Koreans were going to attack before they did. I prophesized that they were going to attack at the end of the rice harvest in 1948. And I feel that that's [the way] some of the South Koreans felt because that's why they got our State Department to persuade our Department of Defense to leave the Fifth Combat Team over there until June of 1949. See, we were all going to pull out in December of 1948, [but] we did stay longer.

Deputy Chief of Staff for Logistics, Joseph M. Heiser, Jr, visited the college in 1971, and delivered surprisingly entertaining remarks related to logistics, about which he was understandably passionate.

The point I'm making is that we had a bad situation in the outfit I was in, and I was overnight ordered into that outfit…[7th Infantry Division] General [Claude] Ferenbaugh came in there and he was going to make a mark out of his logisitics people by saying "Where's that new ordnance officer?" And I stood up reluctantly in this tent, and he said "Where's that damn ordnance outfit" he had been told was 180 miles down behind the furthest back Regiment? Well, because I had been to Leavenworth and because I had some buddies that knew that wasn't the right thing to do, I had, just five minutes before that briefing that night, moved my outfit up five miles in front of General Ferenbaugh's advance CP! [Laughter] And you think I'm up here kidding but I'm not kidding. He asked "What about that outfit?" And I told him "Sir we're five miles in front of you"…This was his first night in the division, and he said—I can't tell you exactly what he said to start out—and then he said "If everybody will do the same damn thing we'll get along in this division!" And I have to tell you that General Ferenbaugh never questioned another thing I did for the whole time we were in Korea together, over a year in that division. Now the point I'm making is he's the first guy, when I was a lieutenant colonel, to be so—uh, is perspicuous a good word?—to be so farsighted, etcetera, that he could put down and recognize that this lieutenant colonel should have been a general officer! [Big laugh]

In 1983, a member of the faculty asked General Collins to compare the leadership styles and field command abilities of Generals MacArthur and Ridgway.

> Well in the first place, Matt Ridgway was a front line commander. He actually visited the front. MacArthur never visited the front. He was a rear area commander. His quality was strategic field, the other stuff was a little below him, maybe. He never really got up in combat that I knew of, in modern times. Now he had done a good job in World War I as a battalion commander in the [42nd] "Rainbow" Division. I understood that he did a good job. And he was competent at that stage of the game, but he never did pay too much attention to the troops, the fighting men up front. Never got out in the field. He was a lofty, theoretical commander up here, far removed from the dirt and the dust and mud and whatnot of a commander of front line troops. So I would say he was a fine strategic man up to a certain point, but one that lacked the knowledge of the fighting side of the Army, tried to do it from far distances. Here he was trying to coordinate the fighting in Korea between [Edward] "Ned" Almond [X Corps commander] on one side of the Taebaek Range and [Walton] "Johnnie" Walker [8th Army commander] on the other side with a practically impassable mountain chain in between. So at the end when things were looking bad all he did was issue an order. I never could believe that he really thought they could fight their way across those ranges that way. They couldn't with what they had available. Too formidable terrain.

During his March 1967 visit, General Johnson highlighted an unfortunate example of leadership in action that occurred regularly during the Vietnam War and was a by-product of the budding information age.

> We have held that you give a commander a job to do, you give him the resources, and then let him do his job. Well, the trouble with that is that first, communications have improved too much, we know too much, we know more really than it's desirable to know sometimes. Transportation has improved too much. Pity the poor company commander in Vietnam… I venture there were days the battalion commander was over your head, the brigade commander was over your head, your division commander was over your head, and your field commander was over your head, and maybe General Westmoreland was there for half an hour, every one of them listening to your channel, and every one of them at some time trying to come up on it. [Laughter] I was in Korea in 1951 as a regimental commander when my division commander visited me by helicopter one day. And I said "The good old days are gone." [Big laugh and applause]

Fresh from his command of the 4th Infantry Division, in 1971 General Rogers related some changes in leadership styles dictated by the times.

> We did away with the curfew. You see, how do you tell a soldier who has defended his country in Vietnam, correction has fought in Vietnam—and there is a distinction I believe—how do you tell that soldier "You don't have sense enough to know when to come in, so you've got to be in at midnight, and we're going to have a bed check for you."

REQUIREMENTS OF LEADERS

A discussion of leadership invariably led to thoughts on requirements for successful leaders. As CGSC Commandant, General Johnson had many opportunities to address the students, and in November 1961 he spoke about his time as a prisoner of war in World War II.

> For a man who wasn't going to make a career out of being a prisoner of war, I've done a pretty good job of it. I always hark back to experience as a prisoner and I must say, I don't recommend it, so take what I say with a grain of salt. But these POW camps, I don't care where they are, are probably the greatest laboratory of human behavior that it's possible to conceive. You can't duplicate them in an experimental project. And there's one thing you need to know about people, and I derive mine from my experience in a prisoner of war camp, and this is that the basic instinct in all of us is to survive—this is basic in, I guess, all animal life, not only in human beings on their two feet, but in four-legged animals as well—and then covering or sheltering or perhaps even concealing this instinct to survive there is a veneer. You might even call it a layer of fat in some cases. And this veneer varies in each of us, and there is a different boiling point, if you want to put it that way, or there's a different ability to reach through and penetrate this layer that covers the instinct to survive, so that when you start probing in at somebody, he may react quicker than his neighbor, because he's fighting back. When you consider your relationships with other people, you've got to figure that each of them is going to have a different "fight back" point. Some people are automatic fighters of the problem. There are a million ways to get a job done, and we've got to consider what we want to get done.

General Haines told the Leadership Faculty about differing leadership requirements as they related to the All-Volunteer Force in 1973.

> Leadership styles change—I don't think someone who stands up and says "This is what we are doing because I say so" is an effective leader. The American soldier since the earliest days of the republic has wanted to know "Why?" This isn't peculiar to the Army even today. We've always explained to our people before an attack the whys of the thing given in as much detail to the lowest levels as we could. Because the American soldier expects that, and he's a more effective soldier when he's a more informed soldier. So I'm convinced that when time is not of the essence, when time is not limiting, any effective leader gathers his people together to explain to them the rationale for decisions. We don't have to have a debating society in the Army, and I don't think we should ever allow ourselves to go in that direction. But leaders must feel it incumbent upon them to keep their people informed and to give them backgrounds for decisions that they make. Now if they do that, and if there is this loyalty down and this empathy and this understanding which I have previously alluded to, then when you are in a time-sensitive situation, he directs a man to do something, he does it instinctively as a knee-flex type of operation because he has that trust and confidence. He knows that leader is not going to order him into a situation where he himself is unwilling to share the dangers and the inconveniences that may be involved. He's not saying "Do like I tell you to do and not like I do." So yes, I think we must move away from the individual who feels that he can just tell people "That's the way to do it and don't bother me with any details, you're in the Army now and that's the way we do it." In many cases that was a defensive mechanism of an individual who either didn't know the rationale behind the decision or wasn't able to

articulate it. And as we get officers and noncommissioned officers with broader horizons, why I think they will operate more effectively. I tell a drill sergeant when a young trainee asks you "Say Sarge, tell me about that situation in the Middle East," they shouldn't have to drop the guy to do thirty. They should tell them about that situation in the Middle East, and then drop him to do thirty. [Laughter]

Haines was asked what he felt was the most important leadership problem today.

I think we must obliterate the last vestiges of the ticket-punching syndrome that we have in the Army. When an officer has been interested in his career to a point of making that his primary motivation, and he has given something less than the full loyalty to his subordinates that I believe he should. In other words there has not been the selflessness in the discharge of leadership that I think is perhaps the most important single attribute of leadership. I think that until we re-imbue our officer corps with the fact that well-being, the welfare and the security of the personnel that they're privileged to lead come first, and first every time, and their own well-being and their security and welfare second, and second every time, and that we lose some of the soul of the Army. Now this is a hard thing to inculcate in an individual but it goes right back to the oath of an officer, you know? And I think that that oath is a very solemn oath and we should repeat it every now and then to ourselves. But I think that oath is as solemn an oath as a priest or a minister takes to serve his God. And if you don't feel that very strongly, if you're not willing to put your responsibilities as an officer and your responsibilities to your country first ahead of your family even, and certainly ahead of your personal welfare, then I think that you're in the wrong profession. And I think this whole business of individuals seeking to further their career if necessary at the expense of their associates, seeking primarily to get into jobs where they have what they term 'high visibility' and hence are primarily at the Washington level, has been not in the best interests of the Army. And I would hope that we can break that down.

Along these same lines, in 1979 General Meyer laid out the requirement for leaders to set a proper command climate within their unit.

Now in the establishing of a climate of leadership that's necessary for us to be able to ensure that we're able to go to war, that we're able to maximize the capability of each individual, to me, that's one of the most difficult tasks that we face. Now I realize that where you were last assigned that you felt that in your capacity as a leader that you were the ultimate leader: The quintessential soldier, capable of passing on to each individual soldier the spirit, the morale, the desire to be able to expend himself to his total capability. But that's not true in all of our Army, I can just assure you of that. That wasn't true in the 3rd Division, even when I commanded it, and when General [Jeremiah] Brophy commanded a brigade, and when Johnny Jackson here was out there, that wasn't true at that particular point in time either, despite all the great leadership qualities and all those other kinds of things. The biggest obstacle to a climate of leadership, in my judgment, is what I call vertical discrimination. I think our Army has begun to be able handle—begun, we still have problems, but I say we have begun to be able to handle the horizontal discrimination. That's the discrimination among individuals as individuals based on race or sex and so on. I think we've done a reasonably good job in beginning to understand how to interact as individuals. Where we have not done a good job, in my view, is in what I call vertical discrimination. It's the discrimination that exists between the NCOs and the soldiers, between the officers and the NCOs. It's the discrimination that permits generals to have a wall built around them that does not make them accessible so they're able to hear the voice and the sounds of the soldiers. It's all of the obstacles to the free flow of data, the free flow of information, the free flow of ideas. The free flow of concerns, the free flow of needs, all of those free flows. Why is that? Well you'll find social scientists will say much of it is interest in self, interest in career, interest in a whole host of other things rather than interest in unit, interest in subordinates.

In 1998, 25 years after General Haines raised his concern about "ticket-punchers," Secretary of the Army Louis Caldera relayed a similar worry.

> The Sergeant Major of the Army [Robert E. Hall] and I were talking about [challenges because of high operations tempo] recently. I asked him "How are our officers doing?" And he said "There is a perception among some of our soldiers that the officers are looking toward their next job and not thinking about their current job." I don't want to indict our entire officer corps; I just want you to think about that, because I want you to think about that challenge of doing your current job well. That is the absolutely best thing that you can do for yourself, for our country. And taking care of your soldiers as part of doing that job is critical to your success, but it is critical to making sure that the role that you are currently playing, maintaining that high state of readiness, is a reality. And it will lead to success and the opportunity to fulfill other roles at other times. I'm convinced of that. But I urge you to think about those obligations and how you execute that requirement.

Not surprisingly, the officer corps present felt a bit indicted, and asked two follow-up questions regarding this remark during the question period (see end notes).

General DePuy had no shortage of requirements for future leaders, as in 1975 when he told them "I can tell you it's my conviction if you can't be audacious when it's proper to be audacious and cool and conservative and wise and sly and cunning when that's what you have to be, you're in the wrong business." During that same appearance he had spent a significant amount of time describing how lethal the modern battlefield would be. He realized later he might have gone a bit too far.

> I run a great risk of leaving the impression that battlefield is too dangerous to fight on! There are two things you can do about that. One is to ignore it on the premise that you might scare everybody, and thus be counter-productive. And the other is to talk about it before you go to war and not after. All soldiers love to tell stories. I just have to tell you that nobody told me what I should have known before World War II. And I was involved in 'present shock' at the beginning. It was a lot worse than I thought it would be. And it looked hopeless. And nobody had ever explained to me how you can operate under that situation that looks hopeless, that there are ways of actually getting the job done. That was in Normandy. I was in an outfit that was very unsuccessful. And the whole thing looked utterly hopeless to me. And it looked utterly hopeless to thousands of other people and they as a consequence did very, very badly. Now I needed to have thought about that ahead of time but nobody ever mentioned it. I was in a division in which I don't think a single man, oh there may have been one or two, but I doubt there

was anybody in my division who had ever fought. It was a people's army. So I have concluded that between the two dangers, the danger of 'future shock' and the danger of ignoring the problem I'll chance the 'future shock.' Because I believe you can operate on that battlefield. You're dealing with humans on both sides, and if you're the more skilled, the more determined, the wiser, and the cooler, you can not only win but you can win big. But you're not going to do it just through the courage of your soldiers. You know if you try and compensate for your own lack of tactical skill by relying on the courage of your soldiers, it sometimes works, but it's not very honorable. And we've all seen that happen too.

That same year General Vessey, who was then the DCSOPS, told the students what he expected from leaders with regard to quality training.

[Describes Beetle Bailey comic demonstrating boring training] We've trained the Army like that for years. As a private I always—we had a big fat guy in the outfit I was in. And we didn't have any classrooms in those days and we used to sit on the floor in day room, and I always got behind this guy, because I knew when Lieutenant Olson gave his lecture on the rules of land warfare that I wasn't going to make it through. And I didn't want to be caught, so I always sat behind that guy. And I say to you that the soldiers we've got today, and the techniques and tools that have come out of TRADOC, and the interesting and exciting things that are going on in the training development business, is if you've got any of that jazz going on in your outfit, you're in deep trouble and you ought to get it wiped out. And the philosophy you ought to establish is if you can't do anything better than that [sitting in the orderly room receiving training] with your soldiers, send them home. You know? Let them go play basketball or baseball, or something. But don't have them sit there listening to some dumb-brain NCO or officer tell them something about something that they can't even relate to the job that they're going to have to do on the battlefield. Have them do real things, or don't have them do anything.

He also covered the leadership versus management debate that is ever-present in the Army.

I put up [the slide] *Common Sense Personnel Management Business.* Your commandant and I were talking last night about the difference between leadership and management. And I get kind of repulsed when I read articles in Army magazine or Military Review or Parameters or whatever it happens to be about "Management is no good in the military services. What we need are leaders and not managers." And that's a lot of hooey! I say to you on the personnel management side of the house that you can stand up and tell soldiers about how you're fighting for their well-being, but these outside forces are making it difficult for you. But if the guy doesn't get paid on time, or orders for promotion from PFC to Spec-Four take about two-and-a-half, three months to get through the mill and for him to get his money, he's not really going to get much out of your speech. What you can do is influence this system, one to make sure the technicians do the technical part as well as they can, and you can give out some general policies.

Part of that mix between leadership and management involved mastery of logistics, a subject on the mind of the Army's Inspector General, Richard Trefrey, who spoke to the students in 1978.

When I was a battalion commander in Vietnam and when I was a [division artillery] commander at Hood, I probably spent 90% of my time on logistical problems…There is a great tendency for people out of here to think that life revolves around a turret, a pair of goggles and dust around the neck. That's true, only in so far as it's in pursuit of ammunition or food! [Laughter] Don't get captivated by all the goose eggs and all that stuff. [Logisitcs] is where the money is, and I just wish I'd learned more here than I did, as far as this aspect of life is concerned. You will always find people who consider themselves [German Field Marshall Erwin] Rommels and Pattons, but you'll find goddamn few who want to be Somervells [Brehon Somervell, Commanding General of Army Service Forces in World War II]. But your existence is going to be dependent on you taking a deep, personal abiding interest in what we're talking about this morning. And that's part of what's wrong, systemically, in the Army today. It's because nobody really wants to be a logistician. They think that's a dirty word, when in fact if you're combat arms, if you'll take my advice, you'll spend about 90% of your time learning about it. That's a systemic failure. We could show you some of the instruction that's provided at some of the service schools. For example, Military Intelligence: Military Intelligence has probably some of the highest priced equipment there is, and in their advanced class they teach one and a half hours of logistics, period. Jesus, it's a wonder we came out as well as we did, because you know you just don't inhale this stuff. This is very difficult, and it's complex, and it has to be learned.

During his visit in 1983, one of the instructors at the college asked General Collins to comment on the importance of a commander's understanding of logistics.

I was fortunate in going to more than one school. I went to Field Artillery school so I learned something about field artillery. We had a pretty good course in field artillery right down in Benning, but we concentrated on it there. Then I was later sent to the [Army] Industrial College [which became the Industrial College of the Armed Forces]. And that's not same thing as logistical support of a unit, it's at still a different higher level, it is the organization of the nation's supporting arrangement, an extremely valuable thing, and utterly important from a broad standpoint. But I think the officer that has a chance to learn something, either by being stationed at a large unit that has a good logistical support system, or to go to one of the supply colleges, is lucky. Because logistics—you can't move without a good logistical system, and unless you know how to handle logistics, you are going to be sunk. You're always going to be short on ammunition, so you're going to always have to pay close attention to getting enough ammunition up, and then your problem becomes the allocation of the artillery. You have to know something about logistics, and the capacity of artillery, and the capacity of air, those two things, to support the infantry.

In 1962, S.L.A. Marshall shared his views on officers and strategic thinking.

Why am I speaking on a detour here referring to strategy when this is a discussion of leadership problems under combat conditions? I'll tell you why. I thoroughly believe that officers at all levels should interest themselves in higher politics. On one occasion General Eisenhower said to me "I cannot understand the preoccupation of so many officers with strategy. After all, a theater requires thousands of tacticians, but has room for only one strategist." I replied "I do not agree. It is primarily out of becoming

61

fascinated with strategy that a young officer soon finds himself immersed in the whole art of war. It stirs his imagination. Once that interest is quickened, he can get back to tactics, with a keener appreciation and finally will become a real student of human nature, which is the basic study in generalship." And gentlemen never forget it.

This requirement to understand and operate within higher strategy was nothing new, as the graduating class of 1952 learned from Secretary Pace.

The Army today also needs ideas in an area of which on the surface may not seem tailored to the requirements of the battlefield. Today we must provide "Cold War soldiers" as well as battlefield commanders and planners. For in this half-peace, half-war, neither the soldier or the diplomat alone can lead the American people in a wise course of action. Military implications in capabilities figure in much of our national policy. This nation has been precipitately lifted into the role of world leadership. In effect that makes United States policy international policy. Nearly every international arrangement, political, economic, or diplomatic has its military implications. Our Army leaders must be statesmen as well as soldiers. As General Bradley has said, the soldier must have the education, the scope of imagination, and the background that allows him to perform his role in the military area of policy determination. These leaders must have advice on a variety of subjects. I feel very deeply that if all of us in the armed forces do not maintain our lead in the field of ideas, we are doing a disservice from the nation, and to the free world.

Many of the speakers covered the requirement for leaders to display candor, either as staff officers or commanders. General Johnson focused on the staff officer during his remarks in December 1963.

...there is a tremendous burden that falls on each individual staff officer. It's imperative that when he develops a paper, that he hasn't got a one-sided paper, that he's considered both sides. That he's put his prejudice back in the corner, and he's put his druthers in the other corner, and he sat down and has laid this thing out honestly. And he's researched, and he's gone in and tried to uncover every point that has a bearing on this particular problem. And then when he starts up the line with his paper, because frequently these days you're going to brief it. Don't brief one side. Brief the pros and cons. Now I think this is one of the places that we suffer as a service to an appreciable extent.

General Bradley approached this from the commander's point of view in 1966: "I would suggest to all commanders that they inform the members of their staffs that anyone who does not disagree once in a while with what is about to be done is of limited value and probably should be shifted to another job or other place where he might occasionally have an idea." In 1973, General Taylor was asked about self-criticism within the service, and had this to say about candor.

Well, in terms of in-house disagreement, absolutely we must disagree. God knows—is anyone saying we ought to be a corps of yes men, not disagreeing with your superior? If so, the Army has sure changed a hell of a lot. I never knew a senior officer worth his salt that didn't only respect, but he rewarded the vigorous independent thinker who was willing to stand up and be counted. I often tell a story—it's trivial but it is well on the point. When I was Deputy Chief of Staff, J. Lawton Collins was Chief of Staff, and he was rabid on what I'm talking about. [Quoting Collins] "We must never have an Army of yes men, I want to be damn sure this staff and the Pentagon—every man knows that they can come to my office anytime. He'd better have a good case, I might throw him out if it is stupid, but if he's got something he's willing to run that risk on, I want to see it." We were sitting getting ready for a JCS meeting, and the routine was the Chief sits at a little table, and General [Charles] Bolté, the deputy for operations, was explaining the issues in the book to prepare the Chief to face the battle down the hall. And I was there and the other deputies. And in the middle of one paper that General Bolté was going over with General Collins, a staff officer came in and passed General Bolté a little slip of paper. And Charlie read it, and laughed, and passed it to the Chief. "Read this, you'll like it." Well it said: "General Bolté: If General Collins shows any tendency to change the last line of paragraph three, resist him at all costs. Signed, Majors Miller and Mauch." [Laughter] It delighted us all. And I might say Majors Miller and Mauch didn't get marked down for that performance. Now I just can't understand it, I know I've heard it said "You can't go in and see your boss and tell him he's about to do something wrong." If that can't be done today we're really in trouble. And furthermore the boss won't be a boss very long, because he's going to stumble. If you don't get the best out of your advisors around you, to help you from making your blunders, boy, no matter how good an individual you are, you'll still make some real beauts.

In 1988, General Vuono was asked when a senior leader should resign rather than carry out orders or policies with which he disagrees.

Oh, I think it depends on the circumstances…I think it depends on what the particular issue is. I think in [Navy] Secretary [James] Webb's case he felt very strongly about a particular issue and he decided the way he could best express that opinion and also the fact that he felt inside him that he couldn't continue to carry out the policy based on his disagreement it was time to resign. I think all of us face that situation given whatever the event might be. And I think you approach it, one: Is it something that I can't live with and I can't continue to serve? In that case you've got to stand up and be counted. On the other hand, there's a hell of a lot of areas where there's disagreements on a particular issue, not necessarily when you're a general officer. It happens at other ranks. And what you've got to decide is it one that's so serious that you should resign or retire? Or is it one that you feel that you still can serve and make a contribution and continue to improve the organization? I think we've all been through that.

And I think this idea of saying "Well, so and so should have resigned on account of that." I think sometimes that's thrown around too flippantly. You know, a lot of people thought about that as a result of the Vietnam conflict. Said "Well, I don't know why the Joint Chiefs just didn't resign en masse when the president decided to increase the size of forces in Vietnam and didn't mobilize." And so we had to draw down around the world to support the Vietnam conflict, which is what we did. And why didn't the Joint Chiefs resign during that period of time? I was in Vietnam in a battalion during that period of time, and my sights were a lot different. But in reflection if you think about that, I'm sure that that went through their minds. I don't know that, but I'm sure it went through their minds. But I'm sure they determined, not for any—sometimes people think "Well, it's for self-serving when a guy won't resign. He compromises his integrity and he sticks around." That's not the case. I think in that case they felt legitimately that they could

63

continue to serve and continue to help that effort by staying on active duty as opposed to resigning, getting a little bit of press initially, and then not having any influence over the operation. I think it's purely depending on the circumstances and how you see that circumstance. There's no cookie cutter approach to that.

During the same visit Vuono was asked to describe the difference between the role of a major stepping into staff position as opposed to a leadership position. His answer quickly moved to the importance of enforcing standards.

No different in terms of what you should do. Know your business. Be a good listener. High standards—know and enforce. A great sergeant major that I served with a bunch of times, Bill Peters, used to say "The Army is an easy place to work. The only time we get in trouble is when we don't know what the standard is, or when we don't enforce it."

During his opening remarks at the June 16, 1961, graduation ceremony, General Johnson, at that time the CGSC Commandant, stressed standards one final time before the students left the school.

The caution that I would leave with you is this: Frequently we lose sight of the standards and principles by which we live and by which we work, as they become obscured by the mundane details of everyday living. Periodically fall back and take a look at those principles. Your own. Dust them off. Polish them. And reestablish them as a yardstick for your own conduct, and your own performance. This I would urge you to do.

A few months later in November of that same year, Johnson spoke to a different class about standards and how they related to officer efficiency reports, specifically when a person had to rate another officer.

The new [officer evaluation] system recognized not so much the man being rated, or it continues to recognize him, because I think, in terms of rating the person, it's a fair report, but it also introduces the factor of the rating officer. He's human, this report says. Because one of the most difficult things in the world to do, is to sit down, even in the privacy of your office, face to face with a subordinate, or someone who has almost the same date of rank that you do, and tell him what he's doing right, without gilding the lily too much perhaps, but much more difficult is to tell him what he's doing wrong and what you don't like about him. This is hard to do. And I think that virtually every one of you will agree with this. To call a spade a spade, and sometimes get your hands and your feet dirty in the process. And perhaps make an enemy. Because somehow, as Americans particularly, and I think to a lesser extent some of our allied officers, I think sometimes they're reasonably frank with us. But, we want to be liked, and we don't want to do anything that will upset this. So this report recognizes this.

Many years later, in 1974, General Abrams was still wrestling with this problem.

I think we still have quite a ways to go in getting established, universally, ethical, and if you will, moral standards in the officer corps that we have to have from the top down. It's a hard thing to tackle. You know, I sailed into the efficiency report thing at one point a little over a year ago. And that was not a good experience. [Laughter] It sounded sensible to me, and it was a thing about everyone trying to do their best to tell it like it is, and we all know that all the officers in the Army are not water-walkers. But what it is, fellows will take the view "That's right, they're not. But they're in somebody else's outfit, not in mine." And when everybody does that, well you haven't gotten anywhere. I'd have to say, I don't know if it should be surprising, but it's been a difficult pill for me to swallow. We have made selections for advancement in the senior field grades and into the general officer corps where there were serious deficiencies of character not reflected in any way, anywhere, in the total record. Now we know that they happened in retrospect, and looking into it after the fact, and finally leading to sort of catastrophic failure.

You know on the one hand you want to be compassionate in the handling of humans. It always seems unfair to hang a fellow or sort of ruin him for one thing. And I think that's right, I think it has to do with experience. If we could follow a philosophy which I think in itself is hard to do, that we were more compassionate and more understanding and more forgiving with lieutenants. Trying to follow the idea that good judgment comes from experience and experience comes from bad judgment. [Scattered laughter] No, it's right. In other words you've got to make—a fellow that never made a mistake is a guy that never did anything. Now, as you go up in years of service, well really all we're talking about is years of experience, then you should begin—that bad judgment stuff...well, it should get down out of the 70, 80 percent! [Laughter] You know it should get down to the lower part, and I think it's only reasonable to expect that. And finally when you get to the point of well, say, for the sake of argument, the rank of colonel and in command, the bad judgment should be pretty small. And out of that, you ought to get some generals that don't have very much of it at all.

We just have a problem in convincing and establishing and getting accepted as a way of life in the officer corps that that's the way you do it. And defects of character, depending somewhat on what they are, for the young man you can go through counseling and correction and so on. If it takes it takes, if it doesn't then you've got to bite the bullet then. As you go up the line it becomes less acceptable in any form and at any time. And you've got the fellows who are responsible have got to bite the bullet. And they haven't been, in the main. So I think that's the reason I feel this way is that if you push on something real hard in the Army today, you know, as a must, it'll bring to light some of the weaknesses. Because rather than admit they haven't achieved it, they'll find some way to get around it. And you get a misrepresentation, a false report if you will, of what the circumstances are. The officer corps really should be tough enough in spirit and character so that you can turn on the heat for good reason and you get an honest feedback from it. It's what you have to have, it's what you need. We've got that in some places. We haven't got it everywhere. Until we get it everywhere we're going to be struggling with it.

During the same visit he also talked about selection for schooling and promotion.

The most selective process we have got in the Army is selection to general officer, that's where the weir narrows down to its finest point. The next on is the selection for senior service college. And the next one is the selection to [CGSC]. The fact that you come here, it's a great opportunity, but it in itself, doesn't guarantee anything. The only thing that guarantees anything is sustained superior performance wherever you are, in each new job and each new task. It's a credit to everyone that's here that they got selected to come here. It was not only because of your performance in the past, but the Army is also bettin' on the coming. And that is the most significant part of the selection: It's a bettin' on the future, and bettin' on sustained superior performance. And the same thing happens in the selection for the senior service college. There's no reward in it, that's not it. The Army is bettin' on the future. And I'm talking to most of these selection boards now, both before and after, and I'm certainly making it clear to them, none of these things are rewards for past performance. If they can't feel as a board that there's a brilliant and promising future in this selection, don't put him on the list. We can't use him. Because not everybody can come here, and not everybody can go to the senior service college. So that's a sort of a long, rambling answer, but I think that's the way we really feel about it. One of the reasons I've taken to talking with them before and after—the after is really an educational think. Both General Weyand and I sit down with them. When they've been through the ringer of that board. You know that's really a traumatic experience sitting on one of those boards, and trying conscientiously to do the best thing you can for the Army. We learn a lot from it. One of the reasons we're doing it though, is that in my judgment and in General Weyand's judgment, we've had one or two boards since I've been there that, I don't know what the hell happened to them, we got sniffing that swamp gas in Washington or something. [Big laugh] I don't have any relatives that were trying to get promoted, I'm just talking about the Army and I think they made some bad mistakes. Well, we've got to live with that.

In 1992, General Max Thurman applied some humor and statistics to the problem of determining who the best officers were.

[Shows "Mary Kay" chart: *Top 10%: Self-actualize; Middle 80%: Stimulate to act like top 10%. Bottom 10%: Deselect*] Now the Mary Kay chart. I use this because when I took over as the Recruiting Commander, I called up Mary Kay [Ash, founder of the Mary Kay company]. She's doing house marketing out there, and I said "Mary Kay, how do you manage your workforce?" She said "It's fairly simple. The top 10% self-actualize; you don't have any problem with that. The middle 80% you have to stimulate to act like the top 10%. And the bottom 10% couldn't sell anything. So you get them off the rolls but you let them continue to buy the product. So we give Cadillacs to people." Pink Cadillacs or whatever it may be, in order to stimulate the 80% in the middle to act like the 10% at the top. You know I hate to say it, but half of the people are in the upper half. [Laughter] Now I did not know that for a very long time, but when I was in the Recruiting Command I went out to the Rand Corporation and I said to them "Could you tell me how many people are in the upper half?" And they said "Give me $300,000 and we'll give you the answer." And so I gave them $300,000 and three months later they came back and said "We want to report to you reliably, by analytical methodology, we can substantiate that half the people are in the upper half." [Laughter] Now I really hate to tell you this. You know, half the generals are in the upper half. Half the generals are in the lower half. Half the battalion commanders are in the upper half, half in the lower half. So you know we're dealing with this process all along, and in our process, you have to continue to select the good ones and de-select the bad ones.

He also emphasized the importance of standards.

If you only get one thing out of my presentation today, I'd like for you to get the notion about standards. And that notion goes like this: If you don't set the standards in your organization, somebody else subordinate to you will set them, and they may not be congruent with what you had in mind. I say again: If you don't set the standards, somebody under you will, whether it's a company commander, or it's a platoon leader, or it's a noncommissioned officer, or it's the squad leader, they'll set the standards for you. I found that out in spades in the Recruiting Command, when I took it over. There was a big scandal going on. The problem was the standards had eroded. Once we got the standards straight with everybody, everybody did right. People will make decisions on their own volition in the absence of instruction. Most people are 99.44% good. But they will make decisions on their own if you don't give them any standards, and the standards may not be what you had in mind, but you may be living with them.

Thurman continued and tied maintaining standards and providing honest evaluations to one final requirement for all leaders: to be competent. "If you have troops who are risking their lives with you, we owe you competent leadership. If you're one of my troops, I owe you good leadership. I will be intolerant of poor leadership. Why? Because you're liable to get killed with an incompetent leader, and we owe you good leadership. We have to train leaders, and we have to be ruthless about getting rid of incompetent leaders."

SAGE ADVICE

Many of these senior leaders also imparted some of their extensive experience in the form of advice for the students, such as in 1966 when General Ridgway spoke on the importance of understanding human nature in an answer to a question about moral courage.

I don't believe, gentlemen that, now to kingdom come, that you're going to change human nature much. And under the stress of battle, men react in different ways, particularly troops that are committed for the first time. And those human elements are still the most difficult, the most complex, the most varied, and they are the ones with which you must deal. And all these other things are very important in their own field, but I guess probably that you couldn't put it better than Napoleon did, that the moral [courage] is to the physical as three is to one and maybe fifty to one.

A few months earlier in March, General Johnson discussed a different aspect of human nature as it related to leadership, saying "You can whip people, and you can drive them, but you can only drive them as far as your whip reaches. And that's not the way to do it. There's a lot of it yet, I must say, but that's not the way to do it." In 1967, General Bradley elaborated on this point.

One who commands must project energizing power to marshal his subordinates. The test of a leader lies in the reaction and response of his followers…he should not have to "impose" authority. Bossiness, in itself, never made a leader. He must make his influence felt by example, and the instilling of confidence in his followers. The greatness of a leader is measured by the achievement of the led. This is the ultimate test of his effectiveness.

In answer to a question regarding admitting mistakes, Bradley had this to say in 1966: "We all make mistakes. Of course, before we make that mistake we should get all the advice we can from our staff, and so that when we make that mistake, they're partially responsible. [Big laugh and applause] But by all means, admit your mistake, because if you don't admit it when they know you are wrong, the next time they will have less confidence in you." In June, 1970, General Westmoreland implored the students not to lose what he called 'personal touch' as they rose higher in the ranks.

> Most of you here today will move to battalion command within the next few years. The old saying "There are no bad battalions, but just bad battalion commanders" must be your watchword. When you assume command, you will for the first time have a staff to assist you for meeting your very great task. From now on your exercise of command will be most often through subordinate commanders, not man to man with your troops, as it was as company grade officers. But as you move to higher levels of responsibility, you must never lose your personal touch. The ability and the will to see for yourself what is occurring within the units. The mission of your unit and the welfare of your men must always be your charge. All else is secondary. What you are and what you do in a unit are not lost on the men whom you command. They know the difference between real accomplishment and the facade of false achievement. They know the spirit of the unit perhaps better than you. They will be the first to perceive if there is a difference between what the unit is and what you say it is. What they expect is leadership from a commander who is interested in making a meaningful contribution to the unit and the Army, rather than using the unit as a stepping-stone for personal career advancement. What the Army expects from you is your best effort. And only you know what that is.

General Abrams prescribed an "appetite suppressant" to students in 1974.

> From the top you've got to be careful that you don't get into the proscription of too much detail. If you can get acceptance and practice of the philosophy, of the general direction, and then depend on the intelligence and wisdom of those who are there in the different places, I think that's the way you have to do it. I've been urged, as an example, from time to time to do something about the pass policy. Well, I agree with the general idea that as we move along, there should be adjustments in the pass policy. But I am hesitant to specify what that is because I am not sure what I am turning loose or what I am authorizing. The guys that have got to do that for you are division commanders. You give them a philosophy and a direction and they're the ones that have to do it. And they have got to be equally careful about how they do it. Because they'll have colonels and lieutenant colonels in there who, one of them, for whatever reason, he'll take the view "God I've been waiting for this! I'll take every goddamned pass and stand in the door and if anyone wants one they're going to come to me!" Won't work.

Abrams also spoke about the diminishing value of past accomplishments that same year.

> You have to remember along with everything else, that it really is a tough and cruel world. The only thing that really is going to work for you is to settle on a program of sustained superior performance over a period of roughly 30 years, no matter what your assignment is. In the end—oh, you'll go talk to a rotary club or something, and the fellow will get up there and he'll tell about your great feats you've accomplished or the

things you've done and the places you've been, and so on, and it sounds good. If you're not careful you may even just get sitting there dreaming and forget it's time to get up and stop. [Laughter] Forget it! Forget it! The boss you've got at any point...he may be kind and refer to it sometimes, you know, when he doesn't have too much on his mind. He really doesn't give a damn about that. The things that are pressing in on him are the problems he's got, right now! And the way you fit in the solution of that, and the way you can get the things done, the way you can help, the way you can carry on your responsibilities, that's all that counts. All that went before is in a way meaningless. Oh, it has its meaning, because all of it [has] been experience, and it makes you more capable to face new and different kinds of things.

General Sullivan had some good advice in January 1993, when he covered leader comportment, saying "[Your soldiers] are going to be a reflection of you. If you walk around with the weight of the world on your shoulders, that's the way your troops will be." The next year he had advice for staff officers:

> I expect creativity but remember all good ideas aren't good ideas. Okay? So don't keep running into your boss with problems. Someone told me when I became Chief "Chief, I'm really worried you won't get bad news. I'm really worried, you know, you need to get bad news." [Chuckles] Every time I see this guy he gives me bad news, so...I'm getting like the dog, you know, I sort of cringe before I get hit here. Anyway don't just be a problem carrier. Try and solve the problem, try and do it right the first time. Remember though, the slide's going to get put backwards. Okay? The slides going to come up backwards, gang. Guarantee it. You know, the U.S. Army is a big muscle movement organization; it's not laser-brain surgery. And we're only human. Okay? We're only human, and you've got to be real. And if you expect 100 percent, you're going to be very disappointed. I can tell you that.

General Schoomaker offered far more sobering advice in 1999.

> [Shows slide: *Picture of destroyed helicopter with caption: Don't Confuse Enthusiasm With Capability*] I use this slide because I happened to be there at Desert One [Failed attempt to rescue U.S. Hostages in Iran]. I was one of the commanders on the ground. Never confuse enthusiasm with capability. I don't give a damn how many parades you've been in, how tight your chinstrap is, how wide the stripe is running down your trouser leg, or how loud you can yell "Hooah," or how many [physical training] formations you've run in, or how many Army Achievement medals you've gotten, it ain't going to get you a damn thing if you can't do what you say you can do. Another personal observation: It's very convenient to hide behind all the rhetoric and the hooah. Only you know whether that's what's occurring around you. What happens in your presence is your standard. And if you lead your soldiers, sailors, airman and Marines, just up to the edge of hooah so you can get the right checkmark and you can feel good about where you are and you really enjoy all this history—which is important, it's the foundation upon which all this is built—you're not doing your part. Because what you've got to do is take it beyond that. You've got to make sure that you're writing the history of your time just like those guys did of their time. And it's not about confusing these two things right there [referring to slide caption].

General Westmoreland put it more succinctly on June 4, 1970, when he told a gathering of junior officers "Nothing quite as sobering as responsibility." General Abrams added to this in 1974, saying "You've got to beware of the guy who is giving advice and doesn't have any responsibility. It's really easy." Similarly, in 1983, General Collins told the students that there was "Nothing like responsibility to develop ability."

At two different graduation ceremonies, General DePuy informed the students of the fact that they were changing roles. In both instances he notified them that they were now part of the problem, the first time being in June, 1974. "The ball is in your court. If the thing turns out badly, just look around to your right and your left and you'll see where the problem is. Don't look up, and don't look down, just look around." Three years later, he elaborated a bit.

> Now you are just about at the point in this business where, imperceptibly, you're changing roles. Pretty soon you won't be able, very comfortably, to talk about "them," because imperceptibly you're becoming part of the problem. And it's going to be harder and harder for you to pass off the difficulties on others. You can't point to the dumb old generals in good conscience, although there may be plenty of them. You can't complain about the colonel's wife, you won't get much solace from worrying about [the Officer Professional Management System]. But way back in the back of your mind, your conscience is going to tell you that, you know, all of a sudden you woke up one morning and you are the Army, instead of being a part of the army...So I really only have this piece of advice for you. And that is, just rise above your daily surroundings, rise above the irritations, rise above the distractions, rise above those superiors who are really inadequate, rise above the bureaucracy, and recognize the whole thing is in your hands. You know, to put it another way, if every major and every lieutenant colonel in the United States Army did his job right, the Army would be well-nigh perfect. And that kind of brings it right back to you, doesn't it?

In 1986, General Thurman tried to humanize the Army's legendary personalities, while simultaneously challenging the students to greatness.

> People ask me where are the Pattons and the Bradleys and the Eisenhowers? No one had ever heard of any of those cats before World War II. And the Bradleys and the Pattons and the Eisenhowers are present for duty in the United States Army, Navy, Air Force, Marines and Coast Guard today. They're driving Trident submarines under the surface for 30 days at a crack. They're on watch in aircraft all over the world. They're at the National Training Center. They're on the Berlin Wall. They're over on the DMZ [Demilitarized Zone in Korea]. They're in the Sinai Desert. They're in Honduras, they're in Bolivia even as we talk. That's where the leaders are of tomorrow. They're there, ready, and they're learning their job and their craft. And the young men and women who are presenting themselves for service in all of our services are looking for just one thing: and that's leadership. And you know what? This room is full of it. Good luck and Godspeed to you.

VALUES

Many speakers focused on the topic of values independent of leadership. To ears attuned to today's politically correct standards, a surprising number discussed faith, such as Secretary Pace in 1952.

> I have come to understand why it is that so many of our top Army leaders have become indispensable in public life, either while they are still in the Army or after they leave the Army. Because I have found how both a depth of integrity is created in the Army man by his training, by his life, by his responsibilities to troops. And I have found likewise how, with that sense of integrity, there is likewise incorporated the essential qualities of leadership that are imperative to any man who is to succeed in the Army. If I were to add one other quality that I think is imperative in the Army, and in our sister services, and in the free world, I would add the essential quality of faith. I think there is a great tendency today to think from time to time in terms of fate, rather than in faith. I think we in the free world will survive only as we believe, and believe strongly. And so I say to you that the ingredient that makes the great Army officer, the ingredient that makes the great Army, the ingredient that makes the great America and the great free world, are the ingredients of integrity, leadership, and faith. And I think that we who have had the privilege of serving with this great institution should always recognize and remember those three essential ingredients to the success of our way of life.

General Johnson repeatedly brought up faith in his many appearances, including this remark from January, 1963.

> When you get into a battle, there is always a very fine line between victory and defeat…And on the tough one, it's always the fellow who stands in there, who gives it that last little ounce, that finally wins. And you can cite examples, I'm sure, either from your own experience or from things you've read. This requires something that we can't teach, and I only wish that we could. But it requires something that you've got to develop in each one of you, for himself. Now for me, here's a case where I think that everyone here present recognizes that there is a supreme being, whether we call him God, or whether we call him something else doesn't really matter. Whether we approach him through Jesus Christ our savior, or we approach him through something else. In the last analysis it doesn't really matter. I believe that you do this through Jesus Christ. Some of you will not. But there's a requirement to have a supreme faith, an over-riding faith, in a superior being, something that will sustain you in the dark hours, when your every reaction says to fall back. And this is something that you've got to do for yourself. You can do it in a variety of ways. We have on the post fine religious programs. Both the Catholic and Protestant faiths have men's organizations. And I would urge if you do nothing else, plan to attend service on Sunday. There are many other activities you can get into. You're going to be busy, but take some time to pray. Take some time to open up a channel to this supreme being. Because only that way will you develop this inner strength you may not be conscious of most of the time. But [it is] this inner strength that will sustain you when the chips are down.

Johnson closed these remarks by leading the class in a prayer. In a 1970 appearance following his retirement, Johnson added more on faith and values.

At your age, 18, 19, 22, I had a lot of absolutes in my life. It was either right or it was wrong. Now I might not pursue the right, but I knew what was right. And every issue, same way, right or wrong. No grey areas. But as I've grown older I've learned that you're really living in the grey areas, somewhere. And as I've grown older, the absolutes in my life have dropped off, so now there are two. One: There is a God. I believe in God. Why? Because God has established rules by which we conduct our lives. God has established rules by which we conduct our relationships with other people. And after all this is a people world. So you've got to have rules for human relationships. Now ours is a Christian heritage. But all of the great religions of the world have some version of what Jesus gave to us as the Second Commandment. Love thy neighbor as thyself, and you know this as the Golden Rule. But it's important that you have some kind of a yard stick for your personal conduct and some kind of yardstick for your relationships with other people, and religion gives you this.

General Johnson often used faith to discuss one of his other favorite topics, integrity, as he did in November 1961.

In the book of Genesis, in the fourth chapter, in the ninth verse...well I've got to read it, I can't remember it. Well I can tell you the story anyway, before I read it. Cain and Abel had had their differences, and Cain had risen up and had slain Abel. And the Lord came looking for the slayer of Abel. And the Lord said unto Cain, "Where is Abel thy brother?" And he said "I know not. Am I my brother's keeper?" And this attitude has come right on down the line. Because the reason that we have these people in the years after the war is that you look around you and you say "But I'm not my brother's keeper. What he does is his business." Last year during one of the investigations of plagiarism that we had, during the course of the investigation one officer said "But other people are doing this!" And the investigating officer said "Who? Identify them." "Oh, I don't want to get somebody else involved, and I don't want to get involved in charges like this. I'd rather not say." Well, when I read that, that guy was cooked, for the simple reason that he wasn't measuring up to his responsibility. Am I my brother's keeper? Yes! Because of all of the things that we have in this Army, our most treasured possession is the integrity of the Army as a whole. And each one of these instances that we let somebody slip by is an erosion of this integrity. And you can't erode it very far before you don't have it. And when you don't have integrity in the Army, you don't have an Army.

Unfortunately, Johnson would have to put this principle into action during his tenure as Chief of Staff when his son was expelled from West Point for a violation of the honor code, that of not turning in a classmate he knew to be cheating. Johnson was obviously crushed, but ensured his son received no special considerations. Other speakers covered the West Point Honor Code as well, the first being General Bradley in 1967.

Character. This word has many meanings...I am applying it in the broad sense to describe a person who has high ideals, who stands by them, and who can be trusted absolutely. Such a person will be respected by all of those with whom he is associated. And such a person will readily be recognized by his associates for what he is. Unfortunately, one of our service academies recently lost some men because of alleged violation of the honor code. I would like to direct a few remarks to those that have criticized the honor system, particularly that part of the code which requires one to report on others who have violated the system. In my opinion, those who criticize this part of the code, and call it "squealing," overlook the element of dependence of each element of the officer corps on every other member. In combat particularly, success depends on every one doing his duty 100%. We don't want anyone of whose honesty, integrity, or character, there is any doubt. Therefore each member of the officer corps, or perspective member, must do whatever is necessary, to maintain the character of the whole group. This is not squealing in the ordinary sense. Voluntary tattle-taling to teacher on some insignificant matter is one thing. Overlooking or failing to report a breach of the honor code, which indicates a weakness of character, in the one who breaches it, and upon whom your own life, and the success of the battle may depend, is something else again. Instead of criticizing the system which makes for character, let's all of us do what we can to help develop this quality of character in each leader and in the service as a whole.

The honor code was again a topic of discussion during General Kerwin's speech to the 1976 graduating class due to an ongoing investigation regarding widespread cheating on a take-home engineering exam.

Standards of ethics. The battle lines of ethics and values have got to be guarded. And these battle lines, gentlemen, are constantly under attack, not only by the enemy without, but are sorely vulnerable from weakness and lack of will within. The officer corps, represented by you, is the sentinel of these ethical battle lines. You know that some elements of our contemporary society at times seem to be blasé about corruption and dishonesty. It's almost become unworldly to show indignation and anger when the weakness of man overcomes his obligation to the people he serves. In that case then, we blame "the system." High standards have always been difficult to keep. And there are many who weary of the constant burden of obligation to principle, and there are those who are always asking to have the load lightened, to make life easier, and their responsibilities, or integrity and honor a little less demanding. The unfortunate honor investigation at the military academy is not the first lapse, nor probably will it be the last. So long as man strives to maintain high standards, there is always going to be those who fail to meet them. But that does not mean that standards have got to be lowered. It means we should try harder…So it is not only the honor code at West Point that is on trial. There is far more at stake, far more. It's a universal code shared by all of us sitting here today, regardless of your source of commission. The standards and ethic of the Army have their essential foundations in the Code of the Cadet, which is carried over into you, and to me. And that's the underpinning of our professional values without which, neither you nor I have the right to lead.

General Johnson routinely covered the topic of integrity, as he did in January 1963, with a group of Associate Course students.

In my book, this is the most important single attribute: Integrity. What is integrity? Integrity is basically honesty. Now there are a whole lot of applications we can draw here, and I want to cite two. There are two things that are going to give you trouble: One of them is whiskey, and the other one is women… And [with women] you've got a great number of you that are pretty prime candidates. At this point I think there are 86 families with this associate class which isn't a very high percentage. You'll find that if you're willing, there will be other folks that are willing. I look at it this way. The marriage vow is the most sacred vow of all that we take. The fellow that will cheat on his wife is precisely the fellow that will cheat on me. When can I trust him? I don't think I can. Now I'm not looking for trouble, I hope we don't have any. But if you want it, I'm prepared to cope with you each time.

During those same remarks, he also covered the ever-present issue of plagiarism.

So everyone understands what I am saying, I want you to rise to your feet and sit down, right now. [Pauses while this happens] Subject: Plagiarism. Plagiarism is taking the idea or the writing of somebody else and passing it off as your own. [He repeats this definition] Now the reason that I emphasize this is because we prepare papers here. You'll be preparing a staff paper during the course of the year. Every class has had at least one person who has attempted to slide in a paper that is largely copied from some other paper that sits back up here in the archives. The reason given sometimes is because we thought you wanted it like that paper or you wouldn't have them out there. This is not the case. Everything that has preceded you up here belongs to somebody. It's his. As a matter of fact, some of them aren't, but from your point of view, they are! It's his. We don't object if everything in your paper is copied. You can copy everything. Put some quotations marks around it and tell us where you got it. Now the staff and faculty, despite any opinions that you may have as you go through here, are not stupid. You may think so from time to time. But they aren't. And some of the things that have been passed off as original, have been prepared by the people who are now on the staff and faculty, when they were at another service school fifteen years ago. These people review papers, Spring and Fall, Spring and Fall, Spring and Fall. They can recognize where some of these things come from. And when it looks too pat, they pull out a document or two and low and behold they'll find something. It isn't that we're looking for this, it's simply that when it occurs...most of the time, I'm sure we don't pick them all up, when it occurs, it just rises up and smacks you in the face. So watch it! Now I would be less than honest with you if I didn't say that if you copy everything and put it all in quotation marks, you're not going to be on the upper end of the curve. Because we do, we hope we do, give some credit for thinking. This is our purpose here, is to train people who can first identify a problem, and then go about the proposition of solving it. The same thing is true on what you write.

Three years later in 1966, as Chief of Staff, Johnson continued discussing integrity.

You have a second obligation, and this obligation is to your personal integrity. Now I don't know how many of you use an electric razor and don't have to use a mirror in the morning. I'm old fashioned, and I use brush and lather, so I have to look at myself every day. Sometimes it's not a pleasant sight, but I still have to look at myself. And you have to look at yourselves sometime during the course of the day, and you should like what you see. You shouldn't have to cast your eyes down, because you're ashamed of something you've done. You're leaders. And a leader cannot concern himself with concealing something with which he's not happy, about himself, especially. You've got to be proud of what you do, and you've got to be proud of the reasons that you're doing it. So that you've got this obligation to your personal integrity, because you've got to live with yourself. Not just for a few hours, but every minute, of every hour, of every day, of every week, of every month, of every year, you've got to live with yourself. And it's well to remember.

In 1994 General Reimer referred to his feelings regarding then-Army Secretary John O. Marsh's selection of 1986 as the Year of Army Values.

> The other thread of continuity that goes throughout the Army right now I think are values. And I think it's important to keep that in mind. I will tell you there was a time that I didn't understand why we had a year of values. I would tell you also having been the Vice Chief of Staff, after [the 1991 Navy scandal] Tailhook broke, I was darn glad we had the values. And I'm not saying that that's what prevented Tailhook for us, or that Tailhook was something that anybody needs to be ashamed of, but it happened out there, I think it was an abnormal situation, but I do understand a lot more about values because of my experience then. I think it's important to keep a focus on values. When we've lost the focus on values, we have paid the price very dearly. Some will say one of the problems of Vietnam was that we forgot about values. We forgot that we were a values-based organization. I think that there's a great deal of truth to it. The ironic thing it seems to me is that as society continues to march, the values-based families that we have out there don't exist anymore. I mean they're less and less important it seems like. Yet the values become even more important. And how do we in the Army continue to stress the importance of values to those people that come in and join the Army? And I think society holds the Army to a higher standard of values, which they probably should, than they do themselves. For example, with 17 soldiers killed in Somalia, a very tragic event. But yet when you look at the number of people that are killed on the streets of America, it does not get near the publicity.

Reimer continued this thought as Chief of Staff in 1996, echoing General Johnson's reference to the Golden Rule in 1970.

> ...I want to make sure we continue to focus on values. We had some extremist cases that bothered me a great deal. And basically when we got into that I think what we found is that we still hadn't eliminated prejudice in our Army. We have made great strides in that area. But I don't think I can stand up here and tell you that everybody has an equal opportunity regardless of their race or gender. I think there are some pockets in the Army that we—none of us should be proud of. And so I think we need to focus on the Army and continue to look at those things that we need to fix, and there's still some things here that we need to fix. I think the emphasis on values is designed to do just that. And basically what I try to do is to stress that to the chain of command. I'm one of those people that believes very strongly that you don't necessarily do this by gimmicks or...to me stand-down days never work. You do this by good chain of command, good leadership, and instilling and making sure that the right people are out there commanding our units. Now we don't do that 100% well, I understand that. But that's where this has got to all start. Get the right people in charge and make sure they understand the philosophy. And when you find somebody in violation of that philosophy, you come down hard on them. And you just have to hold them responsible. That's not zero-defects, that's being responsible for everybody's actions. And when I talk to commanders, I talk about three things. Basically command philosophy, and I tell them

after 34 years it's come down to the point that I've got it down to three things, and it's no more difficult than this and it's no more simple than this.

...You've got to empower people to do what's right every day legally and morally, and that includes yourself, when you look in the mirror. Second thing is you've got to create an environment where people can be all they can be. We've taken a lot of people in, recruited a lot of people with that catchy slogan, we've got to make that reality or else we've got a credibility problem we've got to address. And the third thing is just a spin-off of the old Golden Rule: Treat others as you would have them treat you. And I would tell you if those three things are your basic philosophy in life and your basic philosophy in the Army, you will do well in the Army. You really will. And where you get into trouble is when you start violating one of those three. You start losing sight of that, and so that's what we're trying to do in terms of—internal to the Army, is to ensure the people understand those three fundamental rules, and they're so simple and so fundamental I almost hesitate to tell you that and I certainly hesitate to tell the commanders that all the time, but I do anyway, because they need to hear it from me.

One of the best ways to convey information to a room full of students is by relating personal anecdotes, and many of the leaders that visited the college indirectly delivered leadership lessons by describing their own experiences during war.

3. The Army in Action

Most of the speakers addressed the Army in action, and in particular their experiences during Army operations, be they war, peacekeeping missions, or something in between. Many times these remarks offered an invaluable personal insight that certainly was not lost on the students.

WORLD WAR I & II

Field Marshall Bernard Law Montgomery, Deputy Supreme Commander, Europe, relayed a World War I memory during his visit to the college in 1953:

> I will tell you what happened to me when I first went to war. I was a young second leftenant in the First War. I don't suppose any of you gentlemen were born, it was a long time ago. First War. 1914. I went to war commanding a platoon of soldiers, a platoon of men. And eventually we had to attack the Germans. And my battalion, my company, and my platoon, we launched into the attack. Well in those days you went to war with a sword. And when you mobilized you sent your sword to the armorer's shop and it was sharpened. All made nice for killing Germans. I went to war with my sharp sword. Now when we had to attack, the first attack I ever took part in—no it wasn't—about the second—I drew my sword and I waved it around my head and said "Follow me." Which they did. And we rushed towards the Germans. And after a bit, when I'd been running some way towards the Germans, I saw in front of me a trench full of Germans, and a large German standing like this with a rifle shooting at me, or about to shoot at me. Now I was extremely frightened—it was the first German I'd ever seen. And I had a sword. Now I had spent the whole of my life up 'til then learning how to kill a German with a bayonet. Bayonet fighting. Stabbing the sacks. All that. But no one ever taught me how to kill a German with a sword. It was a new form of war to me, killing Germans with swords. I was quite close to him—I didn't know what to do. So I made a very quick decision—there's no doubt quick decisions are good things, I don't know if you learn that here. I made a quick decision and I rushed to this German, and I hurled my sword at him through the air and I kicked him as hard as I could in the stomach. The rather lower part of the stomach. The German—and you talk about the value of surprise in war—the German was extremely astonished, and he fell to the ground in great pain. And I took my first prisoner. But of course it was not good learning, see, it was bad. We went on in the trench for the rest of the day, and I got rather badly wounded, and was removed down the line to hospital. And I thought over this thing in hospital, and I came to the conclusion after a bit of thinking that the pen was mightier than the sword, and I joined the staff, and I got better!

Many of the speakers who appeared up through the 1970s relayed their World War II experiences. In his December, 1961 remarks, President Truman relayed how he had tried to play a different role in that war:

> …Had [Army Chief of Staff] General [George C.] Marshall agreed with me I might have got a little further than a colonel. [Laughter] When we passed the first draft act in 1941, I was a United States Senator and an active colonel in the Field Artillery Reserves. I went to see General Marshall, who was Chief of Staff at that time, told him that I had kept up with this situation and trained maybe 3 or 4 or 500 youngsters in how to handle a battery and I would like to be a colonel of a field artillery regiment or a group or whatever they had in those days. And he pulled his specs down on his nose like that and said "Mr.

Senator, how old are you?" I said "I'm 56." "Well," he said, "You're too damned old. You go on back and stay in the Senate." I said "General"—I was a Senator and I could talk back to him. I said "General, I'm four years younger than you are." He said "Yes, Senator, but I'm already in." [Big laugh] After I became the Commander in Chief, General Marshall continued to be Chief of Staff, and he was in to see me one morning, waiting a few minutes outside while I was talking to somebody else. My appointment secretary, Matt Connelly said "General, what would you say to the old man now if he'd come and ask you that same question?" Well, the general kind of grinned and he said "Matt, I tell you I'd have to say the same thing but I'd be a damn-sight more diplomatic about it." [Big laugh]

Major General (Retired) Ernest Harmon, who commanded the 2nd Armored Division in World War II, shared his thoughts on the true purpose of tanks with the students in 1952.

We had very heavy losses [breaching the Siegfried Line]. We lost about 60 tanks here in one day right off the bat. I remember General White complaining that he had lost 20. I said "How many have you lost?" and he said "20." I said "When you lose 100 let me know." After all what are tanks for but to lose? Spend your tanks and get your people over that's my attitude. You don't kill so many people in tanks.

Harmon also gave the students insight into his unique brand of leadership.

We were losing so many men to frostbite, you see. And of course it was varying degrees of frostbite...but we were sending them all to the evacuation hospital. So I asked my doctor "Isn't there a way we can save part of these people?" 'cause we were getting down to 40-45 men to an infantry company, and that's pretty hard. Well he said "If you'd establish a hospital of your own General...put the light cases in there we can save them." I said "Alright, you establish one of them, get the people out." I said "What are you going to give them?" "Well, I'll just put them on the floor there where it's warm, and have their feet exposed and rub their feet and give them a shot of whiskey every two or three hours and that will bring them around." So I said "Put the dentist in charge and get plenty of liquor down there and get them back up on the firing line." So I went down to see them and they're all having a fine time down there wiggling their toes. And we're getting about 150 back a day and everything's working well, and the Army heard about it, the Army medical got on it, said "Harmon was running a hospital. What's the idea of a combat soldier running a hospital?" Well they sent up word to stop it right away and close up the hospital. I got the order sort of mixed up in other papers and I didn't really get a chance to study it properly until the battle was over!

General Ridgway warned the students of the difficulty and perils of protesting orders in combat during his 1966 appearance, saying:

General Marshall...once said of decisions of this kind, "It is hard to get men to do this. For this is when you lay your career, perhaps your commission, on the line." Twice in my personal experience as Division Commander I felt compelled to protest against tactical decisions which were about to be assigned to my 82d Airborne Division...The second experience was the proposed attack by the 82d across the Volturno river [Italy], where the Germans had brought the allied advance to a halt. The sector chosen involved getting across an unfordable river, and then after an advance of roughly 1000 yards across open, flat terrain, the attack and seizure of a line of hills curving away from the river on one flank, then like a bow curving back almost to the stream again on the other flank of the zone of attack, so that the assaulting troops would be under concentrated fire from the front and both flanks. While the proposal to use the 82d was a high compliment, since it was the weakest numerically and much the most lightly armed of any of the divisions in the Fifth Army, I could only view the proposed operation as a suicide mission, which would result in the loss of most of the assaulting troops, and then with small chance of success. I could not accept such a mission without protest. But first I decided to talk to the commanding general U.S. Third Infantry Division, Major General Lucien Truscott, a field commander conspicuous for competence and gallantry, and an old friend. "Lucien," I asked, "What do you think of this plan?" "Matt," he replied, "I wouldn't touch it with a 40-foot pole, even with my heavier division." So I spoke my mind, first to the corps commander under whom the operation was to be mounted. And I recall I used the word "fantastic." Finally to the army commander. The plan was cancelled. In action and out, there is often a thin dividing line between recklessness, boldness, and caution. Even later studies of battle records may fail to erase that line, for it is next to impossible to reconstruct the exact picture as it was thrown on the screen of the commander's brain at any particular crisis of combat. Yet experience, your own and that of others which you have absorbed, together with common sense will be your best guides, and with good luck will see you through.

In 1967 General Bradley was asked about successful techniques to use when dealing with allied commanders and officers. He replied:

> War has gotten so complicated now that you must have allies. Somebody made the remark right after World War I, he was a senior American commander, "God forbid we have to fight another war with allies." Of course it's grown beyond that stage now, we must have allies. And you must have teamwork. I thought General Eisenhower did a wonderful job in keeping the troops under him, primarily the British and Americans, working together. You had to sometimes sort of question if he wasn't bending over backward, and giving more consideration to the British than he was to us, but after all he was an American and I suppose he had to. In North Africa for example he told us once that any American who made a critical remark about a British officer would be sent home. But it didn't apply to the British making critical remarks about us. [Laughter]

Along those same lines, in his discussion with faculty members in 1983, General Collins was asked about the delay in exploiting the Remagen bridgehead, and if Eisenhower had a reason for allowing Montgomery to go first.

> No, but Monty had a great deal of influence, and the British had a great deal of influence, no question about it. And the British Army, remember, had started the war and had fought in World War II for, what was it, three years, before we had fired a hostile shot. Along with that they took a tremendous number of casualties, and the ablest young men in the empire, practically. So it is natural that they were more conservative than we could be. We were a bunch of youngsters that didn't know any better, and we hadn't had the casualties that the British Army had had. And Monty was a fine defensive fighter up to a certain point. But Monty's basic trouble, and this was his state of mind in crossing the

Rhine, in contrast to Georgie Patton, for example, he had a set piece. Monty was a good set piece fighter. But he was always wanting to wait until he had everything in line, he wanted a great preponderance of artillery, and American artillery mostly, and tanks, American tanks also, and everything all set. Then he would pounce, you see. But he always tidied up the battlefield, to use his expression, which was a lousy excuse for not doing anything. Monty was a good general, I have always said, but never a great one. Too cautious, entirely. But maybe if we had had the same experience and casualties as the British had, maybe we would have been more cautious too.

Bradley shared yet another Patton story with the students in 1966, when discussing the risks a high-level commander must sometimes take.

You've got to go up once and a while and create the impression that you're not afraid to go up there, because they're up there, and not show it, at least, if you're afraid. Reminds me of a story about General Patton. He and I had our headquarters in the town of Luxembourg during the Battle of the Bulge, and usually I'd either go over and have dinner with him in his chateau, or he'd come over to my hotel and have dinner with me and we'd sit there and talk and every once in a while the bombs would start dropping and the German artillery would open up—we were actually in range. And we'd admit to ourselves that we're scared to death but we didn't have to hide it from each other. [Laughter] General Patton had a bulldog named Willie. And Willie didn't have any inhibitions about showing he was scared and when the bombing started he'd run under the desk or under the bed. One night the bombing had gotten particularly bad and I hadn't been with General Patton that time. George called up and he said "Brad, get [Ninth Air Force Commander General Hoyt] Vandenberg to send up a plane and stop this bombardment. They're dropping shells all around here, they hit my headquarters and killed one of the men, and one's just hit in my yard outside my door." He said "Brad, now don't get me wrong, I'm not scared, but Willie is." [Big laugh]

During his 1983 visit, a student asked General Collins how hard it was to change his mindset when he moved from command of the 25th Infantry Division in the Pacific to 7th Corps in Europe.

I just used my head I guess, that's about all you could do. Again, we had had experience both in open warfare and in jungle-type warfare in our Civil War and in the Spanish American War, we fought in the jungle down south. Not much fighting but we knew what a jungle was, we knew what its difficulties were...I was greatly relieved to get out of jungle, I can assure you, and greatly relieved to get into you might say a civil part of the world. The Japanese were very gallant men, they fought very, very hard, but they were not nearly as skillful as the Germans for example. But the Germans didn't have quite the tenacity of the Japanese either. But you were still handling men, and that's the basic thing. If you handle men properly, it doesn't make any difference whether they're white, black, red, or blue, if you know your business in handling men. And that, to me has always been the great appeal of the Army. Your basic tool is a man, not a damn machine gun or a tank or something else. You're handling men, that's the real thing.

Collins was also asked how the lessons learned in World War II were captured in post-war doctrine. He replied, "Well, if you let the, initially, anyway, let the men write the doctrine, the men who fought it. Make them do a lot of the writing. Pay attention to what they think, not what some staff officer thought. And I think that's the crux of it. And you can always use a General Marshall, too, if you've got any spare General Marshalls around."

At the end of President Truman's December 1961 appearance, then-commandant General Johnson felt he had to make a slight correction to something Truman said, causing Truman to reply in kind.

[Johnson] I want to give you my version of the [Civil War General John] Pope story. I wouldn't argue to the correctness of yours, because you're too much of an historian for me to argue with. But as I recall the Pope story, it was attributed to Lincoln, and Lincoln kept getting these dispatches 'Headquarters in the saddle,' and after one particularly bad dispatch Lincoln is reported to have said "Pope: He's got his headquarters where his hindquarters ought to be." [Laughter] [Truman] Since the General brought it up, I must tell you my Pope story too. [Laughter] Churchill sat around the table, Stalin and [unintelligible], and I was presenting because I was the only head of state there, this was at Potsdam [Germany], and we were talking about Poland. And Churchill was having an argument with Stalin about free elections in Poland. And Churchill made the statement "If that didn't happen, since Poland was a Catholic country, the Pope wouldn't like it." Well Stalin pulled his moustache and leaned on his elbow and said "Mr. Prime Minister, how many divisions has the Pope?" [Laughter and applause]

KOREAN WAR

Many of the guest speakers had Korean War experiences to share, and one of the most intriguing was General Dean, who was captured leading his division and held by North Korea as a prisoner of war (POW) for three years. In 1964, he discussed the beginning of the war and leading men in desperate times.

I thought surely they would attack at the end of the summer grain harvest of July 1949...and they didn't. Then I prophesized they would attack at end of the rice harvest in 1949. And they didn't. So I thought "I am a poor prophet," and I was really surprised when they did attack at the end of the summer grain harvest of '50. Our men had had battalion tests, but we hadn't had a chance to really have the live ammunition test that we had before we went to Europe. We hadn't prepared our outfit mentally for being shot at. And I found in those early days it had a very salutary effect to see someone up there with stars on his helmet, and stars on his jeep, out there getting shot at with them, because we had to sell space for time. We had to get time to get somebody over there to help us. Now the troops were good, but our equipment was false. Our communications equipment had been that which was used in the Southwest Pacific during World War II. Not only that, we didn't have adequate armor. As you've read, we had just inactivated the two corps that were in Japan that Spring before, the 9th and 10th Corps. We'd inactivated one active infantry battalion in each infantry regiment, so we only had two-battalion regiments. We had two firing battery field artillery battalions. But the thing that hurt us most was communications in those early days. And seeing the old man up there I think was worthwhile.

While You Were Sleeping

At the 1952 graduation ceremony, Secretary Pace shared a unique view of the Korean War.

> I think Korea ushered in a whole new theory, or philosophy for the military. For the first time in history, America has accepted the principle of buying insurance for peace. For the first time in our history, we are willing to spend big money to avoid a general war. We feel that adequate military forces in being, with an industrial military capability for immediate wartime expansion, spells something in men and equipment that the planners in the Kremlin can understand [referring to the government of the Soviet Union]. No one, we feel, will unleash global war if it means his own destruction. I can't tell you where today's military situation will take us. But I can say that the total implications of this period must be understood by military men and civilians alike, if this democracy is to fulfill its function as a world leader.

> The Army's mission stated simply, is this—to help prevent a global war if possible, or to help win it if it occurs. While the national effort is directed at avoiding World War III, the Army must be prepared for any fighting that may break out in the next few years. At the same time we are anticipating our requirements for the future, we must give our troops who are fighting and training now the tools to do their job. These requirements of today's partial mobilization will affect every one of you in your new assignment.

> I think it is fair to say, that at no time in our military history has our personnel problem been more complex or more exacting. To maintain efficiency will call for the highest degree of technical personnel management in an Army which is mobilizing, training, fighting, and demobilizing all at the same time.

Just a few days prior to this ceremony, Lieutenant General Anthony McAuliffe, who at that time was the Deputy Chief of Staff for Personnel, painted a far bleaker picture of the personnel problem and the requirements of partial mobilization. Although lengthy, the excerpt below is just a fraction of what he told the students about the personnel situation.

> Gentlemen, this personnel racket is a new racket to me, I've been in it about a year now. But from my limited observation I would say that everyone in the Army and everyone in Congress too, rates himself as an expert in personnel management. I don't think that's unusual, I remember before I got in the personnel business I always thought I could do it better than the way it was being done. And I often wondered at the screwy and inscrutable directives and so on that came out. I know that many of you have the same attitude and that some of the things we're doing are hard to understand, and I hope that by a discussion of some of the problems that exist at the present time that I can show you more clearly how difficult the personnel situation is under this present semi-peace, semi-war, half-mobilization under which we're operating.

> …In all the personnel planning up to the present and right now for the next fiscal year, '53, we've had an assumption that the combat in Korea would terminate. We've had such an assumption last December 31st. We have another one now, that the combat will be finished by June 30th of this year. Well, I'm sure that your estimate of how good that assumption is is about the same as mine. I don't think it's any good at all. But at the same time we don't have any personnel or appropriations for personnel to support continued combat in Korea, with the result that the replacements for casualties, the

combat rotation program, must come out of the General Reserve or some other place. The fact is that we cut these draft calls back under these imposed limitations to strength just at a time when we should be inducting many people. And why should we be inducting so many people? We need to because the great exodus starts in October and November this year and goes through February, March, and April. In other words, back in 1950 and '51, when we were having draft calls for the Korean situation as high as 80 and 85,000, those guys are leaving us two years later starting this October, and November and February and March and April. Now we're going to find ourselves in a situation, because of these limitations in strength, the reduced draft calls means that few replacements are going to be coming out of the training divisions four months after they go in, so that in October, November at the time when we most need a large number of trained replacements from the training installation we're going to have a low output from the training installation. And we're still going to have the requirements, if combat in Korea continues, to maintain the combat rotation, to have replacements in [European Command], to meet their termination of overseas tours and so on.

How can we make up the shortage? We can't get the replacements from the training center, there's only one way that we see of, no alternative, and that's levies on units in the Zone of the Interior [continental United States]. On the four National Guard divisions, on the training division, on the schools, on everyone. And it appears now probably, that starting about October, there will be a levy of about 25,000 a month, for a period of approximately six months, on units in the Zone of the Interior, to meet our requirements for overseas replacements. Now of course that's an alternative we don't care for, we don't like. You'll remember when we started levying the National Guard divisions last year there was a big storm in the newspapers and in Congress. They were warned, they were told, and the answer was "Well, alright, we either leave the guys in Korea in combat indefinitely, or we levy on these divisions and replace them." And everyone agreed that the only fair thing to do was to impose the levies, and carry on the combat rotation program.

So the pessimistic outlook is for '53 that as fluid and unstable as the personnel situation has been for '52 fiscal year, it's going to be even more so in fiscal '53. There are due for separation from the Army during fiscal year '53 alone approximately 800,000 men. All of those people who were inducted two years ago. In other words half of your Army is going to be turned over. Now we'll have a strong reenlistment program and we're very hopeful that we'll be able to persuade many of these inductees to stay with us. We have a big investment in these people as far as training and experience goes, and to lose these experienced men completely and have to bring in recruits and train them all over again is not easily done.

Now I'd like to go back to the assumption having to do with Korea. We have forwarded to the Secretary of Defense's office, with the [Army] Secretary's approval, and also the Joint Chiefs of Staff, a request for an increase in personnel to support continued combat operations in Korea. We made a similar request during the past fiscal year, and it was ignored, it was not approved. We are pressing for additional appropriations to take care of the pipeline, the combat rotation and the replacement of casualties in Korea. I don't know what possibility there is of obtaining this. I would say, judged on our experience in fiscal '52, that we're not liable to get it with the economy-minded Congress.

..The Van Zandt amendment to the last '52 appropriations act was one that provided that no officer who retired voluntarily could draw pay, unless a special certificate was made by the Secretary of Defense authorizing his voluntary retirement for either compassionate reasons, or second for the best interest of the service. That same Van Zandt amendment in the same wording...has been included in the new appropriation bill so that this same prohibition is apparently going to exist for 1953. We've made a request that they include a limitation of 30 years or maybe 35 years, exempt a man of 30 or 35 years of service and permit him to retire without such certificate. I don't know whether this will be included or not, but the fact remains that voluntary retirements are still going to be out unless they are certified by the Secretary of Defense as being compassionate or as being in the best interests of the service.

One of the policies that caused much consternation and debate during the Korean War (and the Vietnam War after that) was that of individual rotation (as opposed to unit rotation) into combat. Many speakers in addition to McAuliffe commented on rotation, beginning with Secretary Pace during the aforementioned 1952 graduation ceremony.

Another example in the personnel field which illustrates the point I make is rotation of troops from Korea. Rotation represents the best in the capacity of a democratic nation to readjust itself to a problem that it has never faced before, the problem of half-war and half-peace. We have now returned about 250,000 men from Korea. This has not been done easily. It has placed great stress on our personnel system at home, it has required ingenuity, intelligence, and tact on the part of our commanders in the fighting zone. But it has been done without an area of major complaint, and it has been done on a basis that I think is sound. The retention and expansion of this principle in the Army's future will continue to demand the highest technical competence.

In 1953, S.L.A. Marshall offered his opinion of the rotation policy.

Lest it be thought in saying these words that I am also approving of rotation. I want to make it perfectly clear that I think it is one of the most abominable policies that was ever visited on an army. And I think if we try to operate on any such basis in a real war it's going to destroy the Army of the United States. I think it's cheapening, it's selling the American character short. It's doing the one thing that we cannot afford to do, and that is destroy that vitalizing force that comes of a man in knowing that at last he belongs to something that's a little bigger than himself. I think the kids were given a bad break when we visited rotation on them, and the only defense of rotation was that it saved dollars, finally. But the idea that it was a relief to the youth was the way it was sold to the public. But you just had a short time over there, and this was hotsy totsy, but it took away from him all that strength which comes from a feeling for organization. I at last have found a thing to which I belong, to which I can fully subscribe my spirit. And in the end it killed men. It was a great killer.

He provided more context on the subject in 1962.

Five days before General Ridgway took over as Chief of Staff, I happened to be in Washington and he sent for me, and we went up to his small office, and he said "You've been around the Army as long as anyone I know and you've seen it under many conditions, and I want you to tell me what you think is wrong with the system, wherever you've run into things you disagree with." And I said "Well I'll go back to Detroit and write you a letter about that." He said "I don't want that 'cause then you'll be careful. I want you to just sound off." Well I'm not going to tell you all the things I talked about to him that day because it would be indiscreet. But the second point I made was rotation— never do it again. This is a certain way to destroy an army. I disagreed with the points system in World War II, I disagreed more violently with rotation as we used it in Korea, because it was destructive of unity and destructive of moral power. It did injustice to the individual.

And yet oddly enough I was in a sense responsible for it, because when I got back from Korea in the end of April, 1951, General Marshall, or Secretary [of Defense] Marshall as he was then, sent for me to discuss from my point of view the prime needs of the theater stated in order of importance. And I got down to rotation as the third point, and I said we have got to have some kind of rotation. We do not have a definition of the objective yet, and soldiers can't keep on going thinking that there's no terminal point. This is destructive of course, but I said beyond that argument Marines are rotating now, and the Army feels itself under handicap in Korea simply because there is no system. And he said "Well we've got a perfect system of rotation coming up within about two months." And I said what we don't need is a perfect system of rotation two months hence, we need an imperfect system right now. He said "Well what would you do?" I said "That's beside the point. You could say I was going to rotate all red-headed men out of the theater first, or determine it on the basis of wounds received, or on the basis of decorations." General Bradley was brought up and we discussed it. I think they tried an ad-hoc system based upon decorations received before the so-called perfect system was initiated. I did not know what we were planning to do. What we did, was in my judgment, 180 degrees wrong.

…as soon as I got back from Korea I went to General McAuliffe and said "Never, never again send men into line singly, or send them overseas singly. If we can't do anything else, let's send them in packets of four people who know one another, because you can put those men into a unit, and as long as you've got a friend right at hand they'll stay solid with one another and quickly they'll develop rapport with that unit. But if you send a man into combat by himself as a replacement, you have destroyed him." Do you realize, gentlemen, that something like 60 percent of the people that were combat fatigue cases in World War II were replacements that came up and were destroyed their first day in battle? They broke because they knew nobody. Suddenly they were put into a terror-filled situation and there was no one at hand that they could deal with as a friend. I think this is one of the most important statistics in our post-war history. That we have been careless about human nature in our handling of replacements. And I would say further, that if you are in a combat command, and you ever have the time come when you have lost people and you have a group of individuals come up as fillers to take over the gaps. If those men are not identified with one another, if they have not had time to feel their way around the new organization, it's better to leave them back, and wait 'til they get a chance than it is to put these rifles in your line thinking you are going to get strength out of this. You will get no additional strength out of this.

Indeed, in late-1953, S.L.A. Marshall had told the students about his group replacements theory when he was asked about his recommendations for a rotation policy, foreshadowing the Army's post-Vietnam unit rotation policy.

> I expressed some of my feeling about it in that document "Critique on Infantry Weapons and Tactics in Korea" which was done for the Operations Research office, in which the initial recommendation was made that, as far as Infantry was concerned, we rotate on the basis of a minimum of 4-man fire team groups. That we never go to individual replacement. But I think that *that* is a compromise, and that's simply argued as a replacement proposition to take care of battle attrition and not to take care of the Army in war, not thinking of policy as a whole. I believe that this country of 160 million people, despite all of our talk about manpower shortage, cannot afford less than the rotation on the basis of a unit, nothing less than a regiment. I believe that many times policies of this kind are arrived at because we're not willing to press hard enough for those things which we know are true.

Earlier that same year, James Van Fleet, who succeeded Ridgway as the commander of the 8th Army, was asked what he thought of group replacements.

> [Group replacements were] a tremendous improvement but only a drop in the right direction. Two companies of those arrived and they were sent to same division, and the idea was to keep at least four of those men together, as they arrived in platoons. And it was highly successful; it was a better morale there. However, that's *not* the solution. We believe that the only solution to replacements is *unit* rotation. All the U.N. units that go out there go by units. And they carry out there the tradition of those units…It's the only solution. We have recommended that for a long time, that 8th Army be replaced by units. Starting at Battalion, but getting rapidly up to the regimental combat team administrative and tactical units. That it would be cheaper and far more efficient in the long run. Now you will have to have individual rotation, of course, to take care of battle losses. But the bulk of the replacements, basically in this type of fighting, we believe should be by unit rotation. That has not been accepted yet by our country although 8th Army has long recommended it, and [United Nations Command commander] General [Mark] Clark, I'm happy to say, has approved it also.

In 1974, following the Vietnam War, Creighton Abrams had this to say about the rotation policy.

> We've always had an individual replacement system. Always believed in it. Always tore the Army up once a year or twice a year, depending on the circumstances. We've got to find a way. And the same thing applies to the artillery and the infantry. You can't build and sustain a high degree of professional skill and pride doing it the way we're doing it. If a fellow wants to sit down and dream about being in an Army that is really recognized by everyone as the finest in the whole world, then you've got to do things, something about things like that.

Regarding the Korean War, having just relinquished command of the 8th Army a few months prior, General Van Fleet had vital first-hand information that he relayed to the students in March 1953.

We are carrying out a one-armed fight by…our Air Force and Navy, and Marine air. Surely you should know that's not the way to conduct a war. A war should be a joint effort, and in the free world it should be a combined effort. And we have a piece of a joint effort there, and a piece of a combined effort. The American Army can keep up the momentum of attack, or of an operation of any type with whatever it takes. We put it into the plan ahead of time. That's one of the characteristics of 8th Army we can take advantage of any time. That is not true with the enemy we fight. He doesn't know anything about planning, or school, or indoctrination, or modern warfare, except what he's learning from us. And he's learning a great deal. Because I must repeat again what I said many times: That he is an apt student, and we are the best teachers. And we've been teaching him in Korea for nearly three years. And surely he's learning an awful lot about us and modern war for the first time. One of the great disadvantages of prolonging a war or any war we get into. We should clip it off short, finish it in minimum time, instead of staying there, and teaching him everything we know. Both in the air—especially in the air, training his air force—and on the ground, and on the sea. When it comes to tactics, there again, what we are doing is all wrong in Korea. We sit and wait, and the enemy then has the choice of time and place, this time to his advantage…The enemy has the initiative in the present type of warfare, in that he can choose first what's to be done, and we have to make the second move to counter. And that's the type of operation that has been going on—it started especially during this last summer.

Van Fleet was asked how costly it would be to affect a breakthrough. "All war is costly. And I think any price we pay to win a victory is a cheap price, and it would be much cheaper today than tomorrow, or this year than next year, or our generation and our children's generation, and it must be done. I don't think it is too big a price to pay, and it can of course be done." When asked if it could be done with the forces that were in Korea at that time, he replied "You're worse than a reporter. [Big laugh] Every commander would like to have more. If I was still there I would want more. Army, Navy, and Air, and ammunition too." [Another big laugh and much applause] Van Fleet was later asked how far north the U.N. Forces would go if a breakthrough occurred, which elicited scattered laughter from the assembled students.

Of course this war in Korea is just part of the whole global war, just as President Eisenhower has said, at present the most painful phase of it. As far as the far Pacific area, that is the whole Southeast Asia land mass, it's just one piece of it. We're fighting here now, the whole China mainland and Southeast Asia may not be doing much, but it's all the same war. This seesaw action, piecemeal action is not my particular recommendation. I'd say let's hit them on a broad front, and get the whole team of mules pulling at the same time instead of jerking individually. With such an effort would make this much easier of course. Where you go is not to be discussed, I would say. But that's up to higher headquarters to develop plans and tell us, at this level, what to do. So I'm not at liberty to discuss that. We can go where we want to and we can always win. I don't think this type of an army is a match for our forces. Very ill-equipped, ill-trained, poorly led, and they have none of our characteristics of superior know-how of command and staff planning, controls, communications, take care of fluid situations, do anything. Change in the middle of the night, do something else. Very elastic in our control. Flexible as can be. Our tremendous mobility and firepower. Those characteristics which you study here, which we practice out there, we can do anything we want to with that inferior North Korean & Chinese Army. Have no fear of that enemy, regardless of what G2 intelligence reports may indicate. [Big laugh]

He was also asked if he agreed that atomic weapons should be used against tactical targets in Korea. "You know, discussion on atomic weapons is left to Washington, not field commanders. I don't know how much you discuss that in your school courses. But I'll answer generally, by saying that if I have any advantage over the enemy, I'd like to use it. We'll find targets."

In 1964 General Dean was asked about his time as a POW, and what techniques he used to resist Chinese brainwashing.

"I was never a prisoner of the Chinese. I was the only American that was captured, that wasn't turned over to the Chinese after capture. In fact, I think the North Koreans, the Inmun Gun, [North Korean term for "People's Army"] used to take precautions that the Chinese troops in the vicinity didn't know they had a United States prisoner, because I was in small room, about 8' by 8'. You see I was never in a POW camp. And the Chinese outfit would be passing along and they would throw a blanket over my head so no one could see me in there, that is, the Chinese couldn't see me. That wasn't so comfortable some of those August days when it gets warm there. Took them a long time to march by. But, the first of your questions. Their method is an old method of first treating you with a great deal of sweetness and flattery, trying to flatter you. Try to sell you the idea that if you will communicate over the air to your troops, that you will be doing the world a great service. That we are fighting not a lost cause, but the wrong cause. They had a canned language. I was soon instructed and I soon became aware that I was a slave of Wall Street. That what we wanted was a wide brotherhood of man, the only way you could get it was under communism. And I don't feel that there is any preparation necessary for that, other than indoctrinating our services, officers and men, with the fact that we have here in the United States, not perfection, but the best government of the people that has thus far been achieved in the world. You don't ride on theory, you ride on actuality. There are injustices here in the United States, but there are greater injustices in the Soviet Union.

You know it's a wonderful theory, from each according to his abilities, to each according to his contributions. Now your inquisitors will say "That's not communism. That's socialism. That's what we have achieved in the Soviet Union today. But true communism is from each according to his abilities, to each according to his requirements." And then they will work on you and say "Now you are a very humble individual, you don't have many wants. But you can contribute a great deal to society. You can contribute a great deal to a communist world. But you have small demands, so you'll be very happy with a bicycle." Then they'll pound themselves on the chest, "I am a man of mediocre accomplishments. I can contribute very little to society. But I have great requirements. I have great requirements. So I'll give all I have, but I'll get a jeep." Now when he says he'll get a jeep, that's like you saying you'll have a Mercedes 220S plus a Lincoln Continental, plus the nicest Cadillac. That's what he was trying to put over. Difference between a bicycle and a jeep, because a jeep was a luxury in his eyes. Now that's what they tried to sell. It sounds beautiful, doesn't it?

But let's not go on theory, let's go on actuality. Look at those people in North Korea as I saw them, even those in the different echelons of responsibility. Always looking over their shoulder, fearful that their head might be cut off as an example. Always awaiting a weekly meeting where they had to go confess their faults to the crowd, to the assembled gathering. You're not a good communist if you don't have a good confessional, a periodic confessional before all the party members. Where you saw the whole populace regimented. You don't decide whether you are going to do this or you're going to do that. It's being decided for you. So if we can impress that upon our service personnel what we have, what the communists have, we'll be better prepared to resist if we're captured. But I feel very strongly in all our services we mustn't spend so much time in saying or teaching what you're gonna do when you're captured. Teach 'em how not to be captured, teach 'em how to fight and *do* some capturing. That's what we want to be doing. [Applause]

…Too much has been written of the few that failed. 22 [Americans] didn't come home. How many thousands of [North] Koreans chose to stay in South Korea although it meant leaving their families? How many Chinese stayed? I don't know the exact figures, but I know that there were 22 that stayed. And most of those 22 that stayed, stayed because they were fearful of coming back and facing up to their buddies that they had ratted on while they were prisoners.

In late-1953 S.L.A. Marshall used examples from World War I and Korea to discuss his "fatigue theory."

One of the things that I contributed to Army knowledge and military knowledge is the "fatigue theory." The determination of the fact that fear is a stress that is akin to work itself, instead of it being truly a mental process. It is a physically deteriorating thing that has the same impact on men as work. This came out of certain data that I ran into on the battlefield in World War II, and I developed it and presented it in written form and it was duly proven. And yet as I think back now, the thing that impresses me above all else is how long it took to see something that should have been realized in the first place. And I would have to go so far back to the roots of my youth and of my first experiences as a soldier to see how these ideas, impressions gradually added up to something important.

I remember back in 1918, walking with my regiment along the Seine going to the front, at the point where the Seine was scarcely wider than this walk here. And it was a hot day in July, up around 95, and we were carrying packs that weighed 65 pounds. I was right guide of the regiment, and I was in the best position as far as marching was concerned, of anybody in the formation, because I was out front. But even so, the weight of my ammunition belt blistered my waist in a complete circle, as did the weight of my straps on my pack, create blisters on my shoulders. And I saw this regiment go on that morning into the heat with only one canteen of water per man, and all the time this beautiful stream was trickling by us. And all the time that we marched with these heavy weights on us the regimental carts were running along parallel to the column, and they were absolutely empty. And at noontime I saw that regiment, as one body of men, stop, and without a word to anybody, take those packs off and put them on the carts and say to their officers "Alright, what are you going to do about it? Just try to make us take them on again." This was insubordinationism in a mass of men. And that was my first reflection on it. And it took me years to see that this was not so. This was a good regiment and these were worthy men. But they could not stand a condition of indiscipline in their command that required them to do something that, under the circumstances, obviously was not necessary. They were being unduly penalized; a hardship placed on them at the same time they were going into battle.

The next night we made our approach march and I saw that regiment go only eleven miles towards a starlit front, because in those days the thing that impressed you most about the western front was the vast amount of pyrotechnic display that you saw as you came up toward it. It was far more fearful and frightening than the amount of artillery you heard. Star shows and lights of all kinds, and I saw that regiment over eleven miles of roads to the point where we finally got into our positions that the men were completely worn out. They couldn't move. They sank down in exhaustion, some of them not even able to take their packs off. And it struck me as rather curious that this was so, because I had seen them march 20 miles, 25 miles under the same weights. And then six weeks later I saw them march again away from the front and they went 45 miles in a breeze carrying the same weight. And it didn't impress me at all, except I thought well, it is curious that it's so much easier to march away from the front than it is to march toward it. But I didn't see that it meant anything.

I regret very much that in Korea we did not go on to what I think is the study of the more important factor now and that is the nature of the recuperative process, and its application to military theory, because I am certain that many of our ideas would be altered, many of our tactical ideas. May I give you an example? What would be the natural reaction of the average young commander if he marched his men all day and then they worked on their entrenchments until the men were near exhaustion, and he knew that he was in the presence of the enemy? It would be to keep that force alert, wouldn't it? That's the way it actually worked out most of the times in Korea. That if they were dog-tired, he would still say "Alright, 100% alert." Or maybe 75% alert. Always the fear that if he let his men have rest he would be taking a supreme risk. And the thing that astonished me in Korea was this: That on those occasions where a company commander took the opposite risk and said alright, I'm going to get the men in the sacks and get them 50 or 20 minutes of sleep if possible, or two hours' sleep, or maybe a night's sleep if the enemy will be merciful, that even though the company had only twenty minutes' sleep, and it was hit, it would rebound and usually it was vigorous. That it was the shortness of the recuperative interval that was the astonishing thing. I remember one instance in the 27th Regiment, where a company that had been enveloped and fought to a standstill throughout the night so that when morning came was worn out—could not move, was given about thirty minutes sleep. They were thrown back into the attack about four hours later and came back with a terrific drive. It completely recuperated from the shock of the night before.

In dealing with the 1st Marine Division, especially in the operations room of the Chosin reservoir, I became convinced the period of recuperation, the time needed to get men back to the original level is almost exactly according to the length of the period in which they are under undue pressure. In other words, that if for three or four days they have had to take it on the chin, as did members of the 7th Division east of the lake, and under extraordinary rigor, then they may need something like 24, 48 hours of complete rest to rebound like soldiers. Whereas if it had been only three or four hours, they may need no more than 20 minutes. But as I say, here is an unexplored subject, and the reason I want to stress it is because I am convinced like the other sciences art, the military art itself has lain, waiting to be explored, running practically every direction. We think that we've learned so much, and yet as time goes on there is more and more that men have got to know. And it was never truer than it is today, that opportunities, challenges the imagination of men in your profession. The greatest discoveries of all are still around the corner.

COLD WAR

Between the wars in Korea and Vietnam, the Cold War was a pertinent topic for most speakers. Field Marshall Montgomery talked about the nation's readiness to fight in 1953.

I don't think you in the United States could produce a well-trained National Guard Division fit to leave this country and go and fight a good enemy under about five or six months. I don't believe you could do it. I put that question in Washington to various high-level people that I was discussing with and they agreed. To get mobilized, trained— you see it's training that counts when you go fighting, you must be trained—and then to go fight somebody it would take about five or six months. And that's no good. While you are training you lose the war. You don't lose it but you'll make it jolly difficult to win and you'll lose a lot of good men. Make it much harder to win. If that's the case over here you can imagine how difficult it is, how much more it is the case in a country like France, where the enemy is at your gates, and in two weeks or three weeks, if you haven't stopped him, you're very often replaced! When a nation goes fighting, you don't win the war with the forces in being in peacetime. They are only the shield. We all have our chunk, you have your forces and we have ours and everybody has their forces deployed in Europe. They are the shield. You have your forces deployed in Korea. That is the shield that takes the first shot and covers the mobilization of the nation. When the world conflagration starts, the nation springs to arms and mobilizes behind the shield. That's the best way I can describe it to you, and of course it's very applicable to a nation like France, or Belgium or Holland, which lives with the enemy at the gate. They are in contact with the enemy.

And if a nation cannot mobilize quickly behind the shield and spring to arms and get the national war machine into gear quickly it is no good in modern times. It is no good. And that's the chop. And that's one of the big things we've got to try and put right. And that is one of the main reasons that I came over here in this visit to the States to discuss with these people. Organization of manpower of a nation is the number two priority. The number one requirement in peacetime in the troubled world today is allied air power. Air power. You see the dominant factor in war today is air power. If you can wield your air power properly, and the Army will hold the bases and so on, then you are well-placed to win the war. And if you can't, it's very difficult to win the war. And when a war starts, the main offensive weapon with which you can hit the enemy at once is with air power. Therefore, air forces of a nation have got to be kept in peacetime at the strength you want, and at a very high degree of readiness. They must be, otherwise you can't strike at once. That's important. And in modern war, it is very important to strike at once. And people talk today about all this business "Would you use the atomic bomb, would you use this, would you use that?" I tell you what I would use. I would let him have the works: Atomic bombs, gas, bugs, everything. Everything! [Thunderous applause] I'd give him the whole damn lot. And if the war is due to begin on Monday morning, I'd give him the works on Sunday afternoon, because that's what he wants. But if you're going to do that, you must have these air forces properly geared in peacetime, and ready, and efficient, and deployed in the right places to do it.

In 1961, General Lemnitzer told the graduates of the importance of their efforts.

The effectiveness with which you perform your task will have the utmost importance to the great competition which confronts all of us. And that competition is of course the global struggle in which our nation is now engaged. The issue in this struggle is nothing less than victory or defeat, not alone for the United States but for the entire free world. We have no reason to fear this competition on the global scale any more than we have reason to fear competition on a personal scale. As individuals and as a people, we are a nation of competitors: In our professions, in our commerce, and in our entire way of life. In all of this it is in our nature to strive to win. Certainly in the struggle which involves our country and our survival, we must not be willing to settle for lesser goals. In brief there can be no substitute for victory. I think it is important to bear that fact in mind.

In December that same year, while introducing President Truman, General Johnson put the Cold War in starker terms for Associate Course graduates.

We are in a strange era right now, because while we have entered into conflict in the past, usually on the basis of a pretty grim incident that projected us in, we're now engaged in a conflict that gives us a good deal of time to consider. And when people consider, fears tend to accompany determination, and sometimes fears tend to temper determination. And so as you leave here this morning I think that you should remember that you're going to be confronted by moments of truth, just between you and your duty. That when this moment comes you've got to be prepared inside. We hope that we have done that for you.

VIETNAM WAR

The Vietnam War elicited many comments from the speakers, made all the more interesting by the benefit of hindsight. S.L.A. Marshall critiqued actions in Vietnam in December, 1962.

In war whatever it's form, either you seek and hold decisive ground, or you shouldn't start in the first place! In my judgment in Southeast Asia we are not doing that. The key to ultimate success in Vietnam is Southern Laos. Check the map again and follow the line of the Mekong river. It should become obvious that the key terrain for the general objects we seek is that which lies above this river trench where it flows from west to east to define the border between Laos and Thailand. If it becomes lost, there will be no stopping the Comms in Vietnam or containing communism anywhere in the peninsula. I quote you two propositions which should be inviolate in the determination of our strategy. First: Communist irregular forces will never be checked either by parading the force or political bargain when the military situation obviously affords them an inviting opportunity. Second: While it is perfectly correct that main policy must be regulated by political considerations, those policy decisions which proceed out of blindness to military values are but examples to deplorable ignorance. To say more than that would not be appropriate to this occasion.

In 1965, then-Vice Chief of Staff General Abrams discussed the personnel issues related to the war.

> In the Army, the war in Vietnam is being fought with what we have in terms of skilled personnel. And so what we have, over a year ago, is being stretched over a broader spectrum of structure, and new men by the thousands have to be trained, more than originally planned. [Officer Candidate School] is expanding tremendously, the aviator program, expanding. All the skills in the technical and administrative services are in intense demand.

Perhaps the most interesting comments regarding Vietnam are those of General Johnson, as well as his successor, General Westmoreland. In March of 1966, Johnson elaborated on the personnel issues.

> Then came a requirement to sustain deployments, in other words to maintain the momentum of deployments, and to sustain or maintain the forces that were in country. And of course here, I think we have at the current time, a great deal of misunderstanding and to a degree a certain amount of confusion about our ability to do these jobs. Now in the first place, trying to build up the Army under a peacetime condition is something like trying to fill up a bathtub with a bucket with the plug out. Now you can do it, but you've got to have a fair sized bucket, and you've got to keep moving with that bucket, because nothing stops the drain. Every day that goes by, every working day, we lose about 1,000 men from the Army. This means about 22 to 23 to 25 thousand men a month. So that the first job is to offset those losses, and then the second job is to provide for the buildup. Now we've got the bathtub analogy, which means we're right there with that bucket.

> And the other analogy is a little bit like it. We've been working pretty hard, really since about '56 or '57, on a very fine quality stew. We've had a lot of separation programs where we've eliminated troublemakers from the Army, we've had a great stress on educational programs in the Army for both our noncommissioned officers, our warrant officers, and our officers, these have paid off, because since about 1952, our enlisted educational level has increased from somewhere in the neighborhood of about 44% high school graduates to about 72 or 73% high school graduates. Our officers have gone up from somewhere in the neighborhood of 48-49 or 50% on up to about 78% with baccalaureate degrees. We have a pretty fair percentage of our officers, somewhere around 17 or 18% if my memory serves me, who have advanced degrees.

> And as a consequence, this stew, since 1952, and particularly since we have had some elimination programs in '56 and '57, has gotten very rich. Now on the 28th of July we got a decision that we are going to expand the Army by 235,000 people. 134,000 are going into structure and the other 101,000 were the people we've got to set aside to accommodate the individuals in our training centers and to provide trainers, both in our training centers and in our school systems. So what does this mean? It means that while

we've been building up this very rich stew over the course of the last nine years, we're all of a sudden going to throw a bucket of water in it because we've got company coming for dinner. Now to some people this is very distressing. But I think if you just think back to your own kitchen, now, on something that maybe a hunter's stew you've been working on, it gets to a point where the thickness and the richness of it gets to be just a little bit too rich for a fellas blood. It is not quite palatable anymore, so you want to thin it out sometimes. Now I'm not suggesting that our quality was that high, but on the other hand we can afford a little water in the stew.

Because we've got a fine quality officer corps, we've got a fine quality noncommissioned officer corps, it's just been enormously pleasing to watch the performance of our people. You never really train the people that you're ultimately going to take with you. You train most of them, but you've got some people that are going to come in in the last moment and you've got some people that are going to drop out at the last moment. And here, we figure that when a unit is alerted for movement, about 40 percent of them, since we're maintaining our peacetime rules, about 40 percent of them are in a nondeployable status. So that where you've got a unit that you've been training along, and say okay now we're going to move you. By the time you've reshuffled that unit, you don't have the same unit anymore. So take a pretty hard look.

In May of that same year, at an Associates Course graduation, Johnson commented on the war protests and family recognition.

We really are preserving and protecting the right of the people who are protesting. That, fundamentally, is what we're fighting for: the right to maintain this freedom of dissent. It's a curious paradox, but there it is. And I think if we just hold that attitude, we're alright. Last month in Vietnam I got the same kind of questions that I got in December when I was out there, "Why are these protesters making so much noise? Why doesn't somebody try to quiet them down?" Well my answer to the people out there was "Let's not be troubled by that, that's not really our concern."

Families. Your husband, or your dad, is as strong as you let him be. And he requires your support. And when I talk about the strains that we impose on family relationships, I know that they're very real ones. And it's hard to understand sometimes, "Why these requirements?" But I think that in each family, not in every one, but in most families, there is an understanding of why these separations are necessary, why it's necessary for father to go ahead, why it's necessary for sudden moves. But at the same time I think that you'd like a little recognition for this. Well I can say, in recent weeks, in some of the meetings with [President Lyndon Johnson], he's expressed this same feeling. A lot of times it doesn't get out in the papers like it does in the Washington area, and it's sometimes not picked up too much there. But when he has occasion to present awards at the White House, and so on, he makes these comments, just like last night he was out at Walter Reed, presenting some purple hearts to some individuals who have just come back from Vietnam. A couple of weeks ago he picked up a group of people who had been invited down by one of the hotels to spend some time in Washington for the weekend and be taken out on sight-seeing tours...the hotel does it each week. The president took them on a tour of the White House. He said "It always just renews my courage and renews my strength when I talk to these young men who had just come back from the battlefield, many of the who have a legitimate cause to complain, but who have no complaint. It's a strange thing."

General Johnson was back again in December for another Associates Course graduation, and provided another update of the situation.

> In the course of the last year and a half…a little bit less, we've deployed something more than 200,000 in the Army. We started out over there the first of May, of 1965, with about 14 to 15,000. We're over 225,000 out there now. And every man that's gone out there has had the wherewithal to do his job. And as he's used it, as he's fired his weapons, and as he's worn out his fatigues, and as he's put holes in his shoes, we've had replacement items for him. And never has an Army moved so far with as much of the United States of America in its knapsack. Ice machines, GE water coolers, air conditioners. [Scattered Laughter]. It's not a whole lot different as a lot of you know. Now it's a little different out there in the bush, but again, it's not a whole lot different than some of the ranges at Benning, or at Polk, or at Jackson, or at Gordon. Not a whole lot different when you get up in the highlands in some of the areas than it is at Carson, a lot of sameness out there. And we've put the troops in there and they're doing their job. Now what more do you want out of the Army, than to do its job? That's what you're doing, and that's what you will be doing. I think, what, 75 of you head out there shortly, don't you? I'll beat you out there and beat you back! [Laughter]

In March 1967, Johnson spoke to the students about the Vietnam planning assumptions that proved to be incorrect.

> All of a sudden, this plan [to use the Reserves to meet part of a commitment] fell out from under us. So Lesson #1 for today, and really the only lesson I want to leave with you today is, if you can avoid assumptions, leave them in your drawer. [Laughter and applause] I'm very serious when I say that, because there's a great tendency when sitting down to address a tough problem, to introduce an assumption that sort of walks you around a tough corner, gets it behind you, then you forget it, and then you tend to forget the assumption too. And it's very, very dangerous, because each of us, as we describe something or think about some activity, inevitably has in the back of his mind, some kind of a backdrop for the description that he presents, and it may not be the same backdrop that the fellow listening to you has in the back of his mind. And unless those two pictures are identical, you immediately have differences as to how you view this thing. So it's very important: Describe your conditions, be in agreement on the elements that are essential to the success of what you're doing.

> Well, we had word of this announcement [President Johnson's decision not to use Reserves in Vietnam] on the 28th of July [1965] of course, a few days before, and I tell you we started to scramble. Because virtually every plan that we had then was just sort of out the window, and we had to figure out how we were going to stretch a million men initially to about 1,250,000. How we were going to provide the increased leadership that we were going to have. Where the extra equipment was going to come from, because this was something on top of providing for the Active Army and Reserve establishment, this was a big addition to structure. Well we sort of—some people put it, perhaps a little bit unkindly, I don't know—bumbled along. And we've stayed at least a jump ahead of

the sheriff in most cases. Not in every case. [Laughter] But he hasn't kept us in hock for long, when he has caught us. But it's been just a tremendous lesson for not only the Army staff but I think for all of the Army. And it's been a lesson for this reason: Last May or June the general staff council, which consists of the Army deputies, some of the special staff, and headed up by the Vice Chief of Staff were sitting around the table reviewing the variations in guidance that the Army had gotten between the 1st of July 1965 and the 1st of July 1966, and there was unanimous agreement from the General Staff Council, that had they been looking at this guidance one year before they would all have said "We'll never get there." And of course at the time they were looking at this it was a year later and they were there!

....What does this mean for you? We've structured the force on the basis of 25 months between tours at a minimum. Our skill levels vary in terms of the number of people that are in them, some people have to go back earlier, some won't have to go back a second time at all. It depends on what particular skill. Basically, the planning factors that we've had with regard to casualties, the number of wounded, the number of killed, very happily, have been significantly less than the number that we started out to use. And so this means that there is some small increment less required to go over. I would visualize, however, that in the course of the next year and a half to two years the big battle, depending of course on what the North does, the big battle will be pretty well in hand.

During the same visit, Johnson delivered some general comments about Vietnam.

I've been a long-term man for couple of years. Two years ago I said ten years. This is two years and two months later, and I haven't changed it so it's now seven years and ten months. I did this deliberately because at the time there was a great tendency to have this thing over next week, or have it over at the end of the year. And this is not the kind of conflict that's going to be over that soon, because it's the toughest possible kind of conflict. Now we've had a lot of dispute about objectives, and I think that the dispute arises from the very simplicity of what we are trying to do. But it is simple. Restore law and order so government can function... the kind of government is not really something for our country to determine, because fundamental to our whole policy is the belief that the kind of government that a nation has is one for that nation to determine itself. Because we believe in the right of self-determination of peoples.

In December of 1967, Johnson gave an update of the personnel situation.

I think we're at about a break-even point and the only way we can go from here on is up. Now we've taken a lot of measures in this regard, in terms of shortening time in grade, in terms of waivers and exceptions on enlisted promotions, this sort of thing. We've tried to establish controls, and the basic reason that we've tried to maintain these controls is for the very simple one: That I am wrestling with problems that General Eisenhower left to me when he was Chief of Staff in 1946. And I don't want to leave a problem for one of you who could be Chief of Staff in 1987. Oh, I'm going to leave you some problems, I'm sure of that. But I am trying not to. Some things that we can't do: We can't keep captains. Now we're keeping some people who want to resign, these are regulars. The people who are in only for two years, effective the first of July last year, we have started to release. Now where are the captains? A lot of them are in majors' slots. Why don't we have the majors? Well, one of my predecessors, late fifties, early sixties, hard to figure out where, didn't keep enough captains for us that we could promote to majors. So, we're missing some majors. What do we do? We take some captains and put them into major's slots. And in some grades, we use up all the captains filling up the majors slots that we can't fill with majors.

This is why, then, when MACV comes in, and he wants to have 3,125 additional advisors next year, for 1968, [laughter] that's a little bit difficult to tell just who might have to do what here. What are these people going to do? These aren't all officers, a great many of them are noncommissioned officers. These people are going to be working with regional and popular forces, they're going to be working in the districts, they're going to be working in the provinces, but they're going to be working basically with the pacification effort. What are we doing now? From each of the divisions, there are mobile training teams now out with regional and popular forces. Two, three, four men. Now two years ago, when General Westmoreland and I were discussing this, this was back in 1964. We were discussing putting advisors at the district level. We debated about this a long time because of the security proposition, just what kind of a risk factor we were going to have? What were our losses going to be? And believe me, I watch losses, I read casualty lists every day, and some nights it gets to be pretty long in signing letters of condolence, which I still sign myself.

So we watch these, but we've had a very, I think, encouraging result from the district advisor. The loss rate has not been high there. He's been a significant influence, and it's been good. This is where the work has to be done. Just the night before last I wrote a letter to eleven lieutenant colonels saying that they had been selected on the basis of their record for an 18-month tour, not ordering, [but asking] "Will you take it?" This will be seconds and thirds [tours] in some instances for them. But they've demonstrated a very unique ability. Going back as the senior province advisor in this [Civil Operations and Revolutionary Development Support (CORDS)] set up. Before we get through there will be 24 or 25. Now there are going to be some emoluments with it. We're going to let them put their family where they want to, including quarters on post, we're going to let them join their family once during this period of time, at the expense of the CSA's contingency fund. We're going to let them pick their assignment, to the extent that we can meet it when they come out of there. Now these obviously are people with pretty hot records, because there is an extensive commitment there.

…I think I was quoted back in September…that in the course of next 12-18 months… I said we could think about withdrawing some force. Now I'm talking here about a stair-step process, and I'm talking about a stair-step with rather broad landings in between the flights of stairs.

In early 1969, Senator Jack Miller (R – Iowa), who happened to be a Brigadier General in the Air Force Reserves and was also on the CGSC faculty in the late 1940s, spoke extensively about the politics of the Vietnam War.

Now in ascertaining what is known as the 'legislative intent' it should be noted that during the debate on [the Gulf of Tonkin] resolution, the Congressional Record of August 6, 1964 shows the following: [Senator John Cooper]: "Then looking ahead, if the president decided that it was necessary to use such force as could lead into war we will give that authority by this resolution?" [Senator J. William Fulbright]: "That's the way I would interpret it." Now as Chairman of the Foreign Relations committee, Senator Fulbright was floor manager of the resolution. And his response to Senator Cooper's question during the debate would therefore have particular relevance. Precedence could be found for this resolution in the resolution on Formosa and the off-shore islands in 1955; the resolution on the Near-East in '57; and the resolution on Cuba in 1962. There were only two or three votes against the Tonkin Gulf resolution in the House of Representatives, and only two members of the Senate voted against it. It could be said that the resolution amounted to a de facto declaration of war. I might just say in passing that the two members of the Senate who voted against it are not back with us this year. [Laughter]

The change of [sanctuary] policy of course invoked some noisy criticism, with the critics receiving publicity out of all proportion to the numbers sharing their views. So that the leaders in Hanoi and Peiping [Beijing] would not retain any misimpression from this publicity that the criticism represented a substantial measure of public opinion in opposition to our security policy in Vietnam, the president submitted to the Congress a request for a $700 million dollar supplemental defense appropriation for support of our military activities in Southeast Asia. The presidential message which accompanied the request said: "This is not a routine appropriation, for each member of Congress who supports this request is also voting to persist in our effort to halt Communist aggression in South Vietnam. Each is saying that the Congress and the president should unite before that world in a joint declaration that the independence of South Vietnam shall be preserved and Communist attack will not succeed." The message also referred to the direct commitment of the United States to the defense of South Vietnam since 1954, when the United States signed the Southeast Asia Collective Defense Treaty, which was ratified by the Senate 82 to 1. And it also called attention to the Tonkin Gulf resolution, which I previously read. Most significantly, the presidential message said that failure by the Congress to pass the supplemental defense appropriation bill, or even to pass it by a less than overwhelming vote, would be notice to the world that soon the United States would pull out. Well only a handful of House members voted against it, and only three senators voted no.

If the Tonkin Gulf resolution, by itself, might not have been regarded as a de facto declaration of war, that resolution, together with the passage of the supplemental defense appropriation bill on March 22, 1966 surely constituted a de facto declaration. Now all of this is not to say that a majority of the members of Congress had been satisfied with the way the war has been conducted, much less with its prolongation and cost in human and materiel resources. However, dissatisfaction has not progressed to the point of refusing appropriations for the purpose of forcing a withdrawal. It has instead, this dissatisfaction, taken instead the form of speeches by members, hearings and reports by appropriate committees.

[Regarding restricting/suspending the North Vietnam bombing campaign] The subcommittee is firm in its belief that the desire for early end to the fighting, which we all share, must not cause us to be so naïve or foolish as to throw away one of our principle military advantages for shortening the war.

Developments since this report came out, a year ago last August 31st, truly demonstrate that the president, as Commander in Chief, and not the Congress, is the one who exercises the responsibility for the way a war is conducted once we are in one, whether it's by a formal or de facto declaration by the Congress. And this rests on the separation of powers provided by our federal Constitution. The line separating the powers of the Congress from those of the executive is not precise. Could Congress, in a de facto resolution such as the Gulf of Tonkin resolution, tie the president's hands by specifying the kind action that is or is not to be used? Ground forces only, sea forces only, air forces only, the place of the military action, for example, no air action over Vietnam? Or the reverse, no privileged sanctuaries in North Vietnam? Could Congress tie the president's hands by stating the purpose of military action as being defensive or offensive? Could Congress put a time limit on that resolution? So if it expired without being renewed the president would have to pull out? These questions may come up for debate in the new Congress.

Late in 1967 the Senate Foreign relations committee reported out favorably, a resolution expressing the sense of the Senate that no future commitment of U.S. Forces to hostilities abroad is to be made without affirmative action by the Congress. The committee report said that Congress could authorize the president to initiate hostilities either through a formal declaration of war or through a joint resolution similar to the Tonkin Gulf resolution, but if by resolution it recommended the inclusion of limitations along the lines I have just suggested. The committee's resolution was never acted on, and along with all the other bills not acted on, it died with the adjournment of the last session of Congress. However there are indications that it will be brought up again.

In answer to a question about the Vietnam-Paris peace talks and the feelings in Congress about ending the war, Miller had this to say:

Under proper leadership from the White House, I think a majority of the members of Congress will continue to support the objectives that we have stated [South Vietnamese self-determination and free from outside aggression, North Vietnamese troops back where they belong, Vietcong cease and desist trying to obtain their objectives]. Once those objectives are secured, we've won. If you don't attain those objectives, you've lost. They are minimal objectives. And I would say that under proper leadership from the White House, a majority of the members of Congress will stay with it. But there's a great amount of unhappiness...it's revealed in our correspondence. Some pretty hard liners of a year or two ago reached the point "let's get the hell out of there." It's a tough one. But you've got to have strong, positive leadership. This shifting back and forth is not going to get the job done. And I think that with strong, positive leadership that the Congress will respond. Quite apart, I'm not referring to partisan considerations at all. And I'm proud to tell you, that that unanimous report of the preparedness investigating subcommittee on the air campaign in Vietnam represented the combined views of 6 democrats, and 3 republicans ranging all the way from Margaret Chase Smith, the only lady member of the Senate, to Senator [Henry M.] Jackson, a past Democratic National Chairman. Not one iota of partisanship during the hearings, nor during the deliberations or in the report. So what I am giving you is a reaction at this early stage of the Congress. It's a little early to size up the Congress but I'm giving you my best judgment.

In April of that same year, General Westmoreland, Army Chief of Staff, appeared and spoke extensively about the Vietnam War.

Now what was our basic national strategy? In the simplest terms it was to hurt the enemy in South Vietnam, and through our bombing campaign to North Vietnam, to the point where he would agree to negotiate. And meanwhile our national policy was not to broaden the war, particularly the ground war which was confined to the territorial limits of South Vietnam. Now needless to say I had to develop a battlefield strategy that could not depend on negotiations. I had to assume a protracted conflict. On the other hand I knew that the American public would not allow us to keep troops of major magnitude in South Vietnam indefinitely. My strategy was therefore geared to the eventual turnover of more and more of the war burden to the South Vietnamese. Specifically my strategy involved grinding down the enemy using the total forces available, and never failing to capitalize on an opportunity to attrite the enemy—to attrite his ranks and his means of support. Now behind our military shield, which we establish by virtue of our presence, and that of our free-world allies, [we would] build up South Vietnamese forces, quantitatively and qualitatively, and this involved, introducing to their ranks progressively modern weapons. Associated with this strategy was the one-year tour.

Yes, the one-year tour was a major morale factor. But I also had a political thought in mind when I established the one-year tour and was subsequently supported by the administration. Without this one-year tour, I foresaw a situation that would perhaps destroy the morale of our forces in Vietnam, if there was a public hue and cry to bring the boys home, as we had observed during and following other wars. Now my answer in that regard was that the boys are coming home after one year, individually, unless they volunteer to stay longer, and in that connection over 100,000 have volunteered to extend their tours. Now my concept, which I discussed at length with Secretary [of Defense Robert] McNamara as early as 1966, was to build up a force in country of the size dictated by the enemy buildup, and by the requirements on the battlefield, only to such level that we could sustain indefinitely without benefit of national mobilization. It seemed to me that mobilization of manpower, the calling up of Reserves, large numbers of Reserves, was not in the cards, because of the political problems of the administration. And I therefore chose to develop a well-balanced force of such magnitude that we could theoretically sustain indefinitely, in consideration of our manpower and economy.

And my early estimates were to the effect that this was about 500,000, plus or minus 10%, which we could sustain by virtue of our manpower base and economy, for as long as was required. It always seemed to me that if we could get our message to Hanoi that we were going to approach the problem as I have outlined, of grinding down the enemy, maintaining a force level that we could sustain, and building up the Vietnamese and modernizing them, and they got the message that we were going to stay the course, that they would reassess their strategy, because they would realize that they could not win. But regretfully, every time we tried to transmit this message, it was usually fuzzed out by the dissenters. And this has confused, very much, the leadership in Hanoi, and perhaps as much as anything else has had an impact on some of their major policy decisions. Now I foresaw a time when we could scale down our level of commitment, although this would be token at first. I still feel that the day will arrive, regardless of what happens in Paris, when we can do just that. But I certainly am not going to forecast, particularly while negotiations are going on, when this will be done.

...As you well know, this has been a limited war, with limited objectives, fought with limited means. It has been a war that has been more political than military in the final analysis. The military has done what if was asked to do, and done it well. We've carried our burdens and attempted to pursue our task without complaint, under the rules that have been laid down by civilian authority. We have been successful within the context of our mission. As a professional soldier, and I hope that you will join in this view, we can be pleased with our performance, and we can be proud of our profession, operating under difficulties almost unique in the annals of history.

General Johnson returned in 1970 following his retirement, and spoke about Vietnam with the benefit of some distance and hindsight.

I expect that many of you know more about [Southeast Asia] at this stage than I do. But I would make this observation: You can't buy back time. That's something you can never buy back, obviously, or perhaps fortunately. So that with what has transpired there, and what is transpiring now, will result, I think, in two things. I have not changed my judgment, for example, that the Tet offensive of 1968 was a catastrophic military and political defeat for the enemy, despite the major propaganda victory that he gained from it. He is not going to be able to overcome the consequences of the military and political defeat that occurred at that time. Therefore his chance of achieving success in Vietnam is almost negligible. The prospect of the South Vietnamese controlling the destiny of South Vietnam I think is substantially better with the passage of each month. Now we hear a lot about Vietnamization now, and actually from 1954 to Feb of 1965 that's precisely what we were spending our time doing, for almost 11 years. Improving Vietnamization, so we don't really have anything that's new, the objective all along has been to permit Vietnam to control her own destiny and to manage her own affairs in South Vietnam.

He was asked about the impact of not calling up the Reserves for the Vietnam War.

...Now what's the impact [of not calling up Reserves or mobilizing the industrial base for Vietnam] to the Army of the future, I'll try to capsulize that just a little bit. This is hard to say. I think that perhaps we already have a part of the impact, and the extent to which it exists I don't know. Here's what troubled me. We reduced over a period of time, a relatively short period of time, the time necessary to progress from 2nd to 1st Lieutenant. We reduced the time pretty significantly from 1st Lieutenant to Captain. So what you had was a year as a 2nd Lieutenant, a year as a 1st Lieutenant, and then Captaincy, and I suppose most of you, or a great many of you benefitted from some of that curtailed time in the enlarged size of the officer corps. The question here is whether an individual, after 2 years—a year of which is usually spent thrashing around in orientation course, Ranger course, jump course, travelling, this type of thing, you have a year of good experience out of that first two years, maybe a little bit more—whether he's really qualified to go in here now and start leading a company? Because there you've got men's lives in your hands. On the other hand, you equate it against the fellow who is going to 48 drills a year and perhaps spending another day, two days a week, doing some facet of administration but he's not really troop leading he's administering in that extra time. As to whether or not

101

the Reservist is going to have a better capability or capacity to troop lead than the individual with this brief period of service, well it's just a debatable question. But, it means that the Majors of tomorrow, to take a pretty hard look at the range of experience that they've had getting to this stage, the variety of experience that they've had, and whether there will be the same depth of experience for a period of time as we had at the time that Vietnam broke out. Now this isn't necessarily bad. The reason is that all experience isn't good. I think impact in enlisted ranks will be different.

Not sure of impact of those who left? Did quality leave or stay? I don't know. High level of mediocrity or superb level of dedication? [It is] imperative that quality of the Army continues to improve. Now when we went in in one year and produced 19,700 second lieutenants from [Officer Candidate School] we didn't really improve the quality of the officer corps in that year because we abandoned an awful lot of our educational standards. Now I don't mean that a college degree is a guarantee of a good officer, but certainly the broadening effect of a good education contributes to the quality of an officer...My experience has been that a great many of the individual who's a superb platoon leader and company commander is a lousy staff officer because he can't write, he can't express himself when he gets in the staff positions. The smartest fellows in the world can have all the ideas in the world, but if he can't get them across, he might just as well be deaf, dumb and blind. Because you've got to get your ideas across.

On June 4, 1970 General Westmoreland returned and spoke about Vietnam (among other things) to an assembled group of Fort Leavenworth's junior officers.

During the last five years the Army has carried the major burden of our commitment in Vietnam. This has been a limited war, with limited objectives, fought with limited means. It has involved innumerable constraints that have been imposed upon the military. The military has made recommendations from time to time, but they are not the final decision authority. Appropriately, the strategy decisions on how the war would be fought, controls that would be exercised, are the province of elected political authority. But we've attempted to adapt ourselves to these constraints, these controls and this guidance. And we can hold our head high, because we have done, in my opinion, a truly remarkable job under the difficulties that have been imposed.

I think one of the biggest mistakes that has been made in the last decade was to exempt from military service young men from the campuses of this country. Undergraduates and graduates. Because the campuses in some degree, and degree depends on the campuses themselves, have become sanctuaries for individuals avoiding military service. By virtue of this policy, an unhappy attitude has been created on the campuses, and this has manifested itself in the disturbances and demonstrations under the name of dissent that has taken place. It seems to me these people who have taken refuge on the campus from military service, and are on the campuses in some cases, not necessarily to study and learn, but to avoid doing what we traditionally consider a duty to our country, to answer the call of our nation in a time of emergency. But they have somewhat of a guilt complex, and in rationalizing their actions, there has been in my opinion a tendency to blame everybody but themselves. And through this rationalization they conclude that their conduct, which involves escape from military service, as moral. But the Vietnam War is immoral, those of us who wear the uniform are involved in an immoral profession, and of course the establishment that's associated with the Vietnam War is immoral. And by virtue of this rationalization, born of a guilt complex, they lash out at the war, they lash out at the establishment and at the military services. And of course the military have been the victims of their emotional outlet.

One of the officers asked Westmoreland about moving troops into Cambodia or Laos.

...I don't foresee a day when we will be sending troops into Laos. The rainy season is on there now, and certainly this is not going to happen in the next several months. The place is a quagmire. Two years ago we could have gone into Laos and could have had a profound impact on the war. When we chose to fight a limited war with limited objectives with limited means, and to apply the political constraints that we did, we bought a long war. A war that's been longer than the body politic could sustain, it would seem. In other words our psychological staying power has not been equal to the task, it would seem. Now let me hasten to say that the so-called dissenters of the war are very much in the minority, but they are far more vocal than other factions of society. And I don't want to give the impression that the anti-war group necessarily are in a dominant position at this time, and comprise the majority of the people of the United States. I don't believe this is the case. But certainly the anti-war group comprises a significant fraction of our society, to the extent that their views, their activities have had, and no doubt will continue to have, a political impact. So in summary, militarily, you could make a good case for going into Laos. If this were permissible, or authorized, it could have a profound impact on the course of the war. (Not) now, but this could have been the case several years ago. But since we are reducing our forces in Vietnam progressively, our ability to run substantive and meaningful operations in Laos is progressively waning. Whether the Vietnamese could do it alone is very questionable. But our national policy of not broadening the war, the international implications if we violated the '62 agreement, despite the fact that the North Vietnamese have done it, could have a counter, could be counter-productive, at least, my feeling is that in the minds of the senior officials in the State Department, they will probably resist any such action, because of the international repercussions and the principles involved, since it would go counter to the '63 agreement.

Another student asked Westmoreland if he still felt there was a chance for a military solution in light of Vietnamizaton and the reduction of U.S. troops. In his answer he spoke extensively of the political nature of the war.

...we had planned, from the very beginning as a basic strategy, to build up the South Vietnamese to such a point where they could take over own security. And that we had projected a plan so that we could proceed to withdraw troops in the latter half of calendar year 1969, which of course was done. And we have been aggressively reducing our troop levels ever since. Of course national policy is arrived at by the military making their recommendations, the State Department making their recommendations, the Bureau of the Budget and the Treasury Department making their recommendations, and then the Commander in Chief, he has to reconcile all these points of view, some of which are competing for resources. He has to look at the political situation, and frequently takes into consideration the elections that are coming up, and they come up every two years, unfortunately, I would say. Fortunately, in a way, but policies are frequently influenced by these periodic elections, and this is part of our system. And this is why our system is so democratic. It's the way the people can influence policy. And of course the party that wants to stay in power or the party that wants to get into power thinks in terms of the next election. And these are all factors that have to be considered. So all of our military recommendations were not accepted and you expect them to [not all be accepted]. They were considered, and when they were rejected, they were rejected certainly for good reason by the Commander in Chief who had other things that he had to put into the equation in order to come up with his judgment, which was motivated by what he thought was to the best interest of the country. Certainly President Johnson tried desperately to end this war within certain constraints which were self inf—which were imposed by the economy, political factors, international considerations and so forth. President Nixon of course is doing likewise.

Now we are well on our way towards Vietnamization at the present time. This is not going to be a smooth road, this is going to be a rocky road. After this next 150,000 troops are withdrawn, the president announced last night that they will be by the 15th of October, they will be followed by another 100,000 that will be out by late spring. The South Vietnamese are going to be carrying most of the military burden. Now they should be able to more than hold their own with the North Vietnamese, because they are fighting from interior lines of communication where the North Vietnamese are fighting at the end of a long tenuous line of communication. The South Vietnamese have better weapons than the North Vietnamese. Better Supply. They have a very large force at this time, about a million, one hundred thousand men, and in addition to that they have a people's, members of the people's self-defense force, to provide security for the villages and the hamlets, or at least a great number of these, consisting of men too old to be in the active services, or too young. And of course a number of women have volunteered to assist the defense of the villages through the so-called people's self-defense force. So they've got a large force, and it's a well-equipped force, and well supplied. And they should be able to more than hold their own against the North Vietnamese, who are operating under greater difficulties.

The following day Westmoreland told the graduating class of 1970 that the Vietnam experience had improved their Army.

Although the tasks placed on the Army since 1965 have been demanding and unrelenting, a by-product of our Vietnam experience has been a quantitatively improved army. We have confirmed that our basic doctrine for ground combat is sound. And this is to the credit, not only to the United States Army as a whole, but particularly to the Command and General Staff College. And we have developed a new doctrine to match the tremendous mobility achieved by the helicopter. We have confirmed that our equipment and weapons are effective, rugged, and reliable. And we developed new equipment where our battlefield experience has indicated a need. From our experience with sensors, we may be on the threshold of a new battlefield concept, a revolution that could influence the future direction of the Army, an approach that may affect many of you in future years. But most importantly, we have reconfirmed that no amount of sophisticated weaponry, no amount of automation, no amount of supporting equipment will ever replace the individual soldier on the battlefield.

Later that year, in September, Westmoreland addressed the allied officers that were attending CGSC about his trip to Vietnam the previous June.

> Progress has been substantial in the last two years. The Pacification program…is succeeding. By virtue of military actions by Vietnamese forces and free-world allies, to include the United States forces, the strength of the enemy has been progressively reduced, and secure areas have been progressively expanded. And now about 85% of the hamlets, about 90% of the population are living in relatively secure areas. 95% of the villages now have elected councils. And voter participation has been greater than 75%. That's a far greater percent than my country can boast of, and perhaps even greater percentage than your respective countries can recognize. The enemy still shows the long-term effects of the disaster to the enemy during the 1968 Tet offensive. This reckless maneuver by the Hanoi-led enemy allowed us to inflict devastating casualties on him and he's never recovered. These casualties included a lot of his small unit leadership. He has been unable to wage a major offensive since that time. In fact, each of his attempted subsequent offensives have been progressively weaker. The Tet 1968 defensive also had a galvanizing effect on the South Vietnamese people. It shook the Vietnamese people to the core. War came to the cities for the first time. Now this brought about a unity of purpose and an attitude among the people that for the first time made mobilization of their manpower a reality, because for the first time it became acceptable to the people, and this fully was recognized by the leadership following the shock action of the enemy's Tet offensive.

> …At a lower community level, the People's Self-Defense force has been organized, and now numbers about two million trained citizens. These forces continue to grow and become stronger. They are an important part of the defenses for the South Vietnamese people. Now these People's Self-Defense forces also demonstrate loyalty to and confidence in the government, a desire to preserve the gains of the successful pacification program. All of these trained civilians are not armed with weapons. Only approximately 30-40 percent and this time, but more are scheduled to be armed in the future.

> …As I see the situation in South Vietnam, it is far less fragile than ever before. In fact I don't believe the situation is any longer fragile. I believe the South Vietnamese are strong enough to stand the stresses and strains of the near future.

> …[The Enemy] does not appear to have the capacity for sustained action at this time, especially in the heavily populated and productive areas of the southern part of the country. In summary, gentlemen, I was encouraged by the progress that I observed, and the discussions I had with the senior Vietnamese officials, officials that I worked with for four and a half years, as your colleagues well appreciate, and I must say, it's a great pleasure to see them…I think I know every one of your [Vietnamese] classmates, and have seen them in the field in Vietnam on a number of occasions. I'm optimistic about South Vietnam. I'm optimistic about the future despite the problems that I have noted, which are solvable.

During Secretary Melvin Laird's appearance in 1971, he was asked about the tremendous waste of resources during the Vietnam War.

As you know, there were great errors committed in 1966 and 1967 when great ships were loaded up with all kinds of supplies; just because they were available they were shipped. And the situation is not good. We've got enough horseshoe sets, and enough, well, many things over there—I won't even go into the details. It was not a good logistic build-up, but it was done in a hurry, and it had to be done in that fashion in order to get some of the needed things that were absolutely vital in Vietnam at the time. And it's easy to go back and look over and criticize for the manner in which that build-up went forward, but it was the greatest movement of supplies and equipment in the history of the world. These mistakes now are going to haunt us as this phase two of Vietnamization goes forward. But the reason that I think that we'll be in a better position than we were in Korea or at the end of World War II is that we do have the General Accounting Office working with us on a daily basis now, instead of second-guessing us after it's all over, and I think that this has been helpful.

POST-VIETNAM

The post-Vietnam period provides a fascinating glimpse into the minds of the men who led the way in rebuilding the military in the final decades of the twentieth century. Chief of Naval Operations, Admiral Elmo Zumwalt, spoke to the students in 1973 about the future construct of the Navy.

If today the United States eliminated its aircraft carriers, we would have zero capability of controlling and using the seas. We could be fairly confident that we could get the first third of the way to Europe [chuckles from audience], we just couldn't get the last two-thirds of the way. There is absolutely no way to provide air protection for the convoys necessary to reinforce our allies and to maintain our Army and Air Force overseas in bombs and bullets and food and fuel without those aircraft carriers. There is no way to make our fleet survivable without those aircraft carriers. The question is frequently asked, "What about the survivability of the aircraft carrier?" There you have to look at the thing in three frames of reference: First, a nuclear war. In a nuclear war, any target that's hit is gone, whether it's a city, an Army facility, an air force airfield. I would prefer to be on a moving target. Some carriers will survive, no important fixed facility will.

The next frame of reference is a conventional war. In the most recent one, Southeast Asia, the carriers slid into the gulf of Tonkin eight years ago and stayed there for the ensuing eight years. We covered the period when airfields were being built ashore, and we've covered the withdrawal, and made a major contribution throughout. Not a single aircraft was destroyed by enemy action on an aircraft carrier. 400 were destroyed by sappers and missile attacks on our bases in Southeast Asia and 4,000 damaged. In the Korean War, all the airfields in South Korea were overrun in the first few weeks. The aircraft carriers hung in off the Pusan Perimeter, saved the Pusan perimeter with tactical air support, with I must confess some assistance from the Air Force flying out of Japan, and covered the MacArthur invasion of Inchon which turned that war around. You've got to go all the way back to World War II to find a conventional war in which aircraft carriers were struck. There, the most modern class of that war is now the most ancient class we have, the three Essex Class carriers that remain. They were struck by as many as four of the most sophisticated cruise missile we ever had, the Kamikaze air craft, and never sunk. None of that class. Since then we have built much more armor, much more compartmentation, much more redundancy into our aircraft carriers. And in the most recent laboratory test, the tragic fire on the nuclear carrier Enterprise a few years ago, the equivalent of nine cruise missiles went off in U.S. bombs, and that carrier could have been back in action in a matter of hours. Finally, the third frame of reference is a cold war. We've never lost an aircraft carrier in cold war; we're losing airfields all around the world, in cold war. [Laughter and applause]

That same year General Max Taylor addressed the United States' ability to fight limited wars.

Another impression one has drawn from the Vietnam experience is one of uncertainty as to whether a democracy like the United States can indeed fight limited wars. We of the Army leadership of the past always felt that there would be the stalemate of nuclear deterrence. But that underneath that stalemate the nations would behave about as they had in the past. And I think the record will substantiate that roughly. But Vietnam has suggested that being the case, nonetheless can we, or a country like the United States, fight a limited war for prolonged periods of time and maintain national support? It raises the question of the dilemma which the next president will face when he is confronted by a situation where he feels in the national interest we should use limited military power, and then he must ask himself, "Shall I do so quickly, seeking a sort of Blitzkrieg effect so we won't have the prolongation of the Vietnam Experience, but in so doing risk overreaction and possibly World War III? Or shall we go the path again of Vietnam, incremental use of force and the likelihood or the possibility of another prolonged engagement?" Well now neither alternative is very attractive as I phrase it. But what's the next? To do nothing. Yet to do nothing may be even more critical and more dramatically wrong than picking either one of the former courses.

And then this same president would have to ask himself "If I do engage in limited military operations, can I count on the draft? Can I count on the Reserves?" Well as you know, the Nixon doctrine, President Nixon says very definitely that he is not going to count on the draft in a similar emergency in the future, he's going to call up the Reserves. I'm sure he means that, but on the other hand, his statement is worth nothing more than the duration of his own administration. And a very tough argument was within the Johnson administration which way to go. And there were some very strong arguments both ways, I'd be glad to discuss that in the question period if anyone is interested. But I'm just raising the point that no matter what the president today says, in the back of the mind of the war planner of the future, he's going to have to ask himself, how about the follow-on? Can I really count on the political endorsement required from Congress, to get the draft again, to use the draft, or to call up Reserve units?

During a later session with the college's Department of Strategy, Taylor was asked if it was conceivable that the American public would accept the plausible threats that Taylor laid out in his remarks regarding a rational national security, and if the rationality of the civilian leadership would even be relevant given what the public would or would not support.

I think you will agree that there is an interplay between leadership and people. One influences the other, and it works back and forth. The strong leader can indeed take a cause that doesn't strike the eye, so to speak, as being plausible. A Churchill, or FDR, these are the types, who can make it plausible. So that possibility always exists, except you can't fool the people all the time, bear that in mind too. So that you have to be justified in utilizing the limited war option that I talk about. The president better be sure he has a good cause—first that he's a Churchill, two that he has a good cause, and three he's got some damn good people around him that will never give up. Never give up explaining, re-explaining, over and over again, and controlling our media, which tries to work against all that, to drive a wedge between government and people.

He was then asked if it would have been better for President Lyndon Johnson to lay out the reasons for Vietnam up front.

Something like that, I say with the wisdom of retrospection, would have been justified. And he didn't do it, why? Because he was afraid of the right. He was constantly afraid of the reaction from the right. We've argued this case, I say we, his advisers, really, and they were always split on this. Should he get out there waving the flag, "C'mon boys," and he would have liked to have done that. But he became convinced and to the end he became more convinced as time went on that he must not overplay it because then things would get out of hand, and he couldn't control overreaction and so on. But having played it so hard the other way he paid the price.

When General Abrams visited in 1974, he gave an update on the status of the post-Vietnam War Army.

A few months ago I was talking with General Weyand, Vice Chief of Staff, and he and I have been getting out as much as we possibly can to see all of the pieces and parts of the Army. I'm sure you know, and we are certainly convinced, that you can't find out about it in the Pentagon. Where it's real and so on is out there where the people in the Army are. The Pentagon generally lags about nine months or a year on what is really happening. The fates of the military services sort of rise and fall like a sine curve, and the Pentagon maintains its distance over the years by nine to twelve months. Both in seeing it sink into the swamps of despair, and the same lag is true when it starts to rise to the peak. Anyway as we were talking about the Army, we thought that maybe...well we said "It looks like the patient has gotten out of bed and they've even opened a window, let a little fresh air into the room." Well, I think as much as we've been around we kind of underestimated the system, what had happened in the Army. So I think the patient's not only out of bed, but he is now out of the hospital and indulging in some exercise, and he's commencing like he's recovering. And I think when you go to your assignments that you'll—wherever you go—and most places I think you'll find that the Army has moved a little bit from the time that you first came here for your course at this school. I think it's a pretty dynamic thing and I think there's a lot of very favorable human chemistry going on out there. I don't mean to, I wouldn't minimize the problems that they all face, and so on. But they know them, and the attitude and aggressiveness with which they are being tackled and brought under control I think bodes very well for the future.

That same May, Army Secretary Howard Callaway was asked for help regarding how to explain the reduction of Lieutenant [William] Calley's sentence [for the atrocities committed at My Lai in March, 1968 during the Vietnam War] to young soldiers, civilian relatives, and foreign audiences, who might perceive ethnic discrimination. His answer, although long, is fascinating.

Let me give a fairly long answer to that because there were a lot of things that were involved. One part of it I'll ask you to keep off the record, and that won't help you in explaining it to others, but I think you will need to know a lot of what was on my mind. The part that I'll ask you to keep off the record is the part that I will say about the condition of Army at that time. I just don't think it's in the public interest for me to be making statements about the Army that are not complimentary of the Army. And that part, the uncomplimentary statements I make about the Army I'd prefer not to be used publicly because, you know, while we'll answer any question, I don't think it's my job to talk about bad things about the Army, I should talk about good things.

First of all, on your ethnic situation, I've received a lot of letters about that since the decision, and I was really frankly surprised—it never occurred to me, but I can certainly understand how people can feel that way. That's the old feeling that the Vietnamese aren't really people, they're "gooks" and all that sort of thing, and that did not occur to me but that is on people's minds and I'll a little bit address that as we go on. First of all let me say what I did about Calley and then what some of the considerations were. When it came to my desk there were two pieces of paper. One was the court martial and one was a very separate piece of paper asking for clemency. On the court martial itself, was much the easier decision. On that I did read the entire record. I read the entire [General William] Peers report. [General officer assigned the responsibility for investigating the My Lai incident] The file on that, on the Calley trial alone, is a four-drawer file cabinet full of material. That stayed in my office for about six or eight weeks, and I referred to—I didn't read all that—but I referred to it, tried to get myself very knowledgeable about it. I fairly quickly came to the conclusion in my own mind beyond a reasonable doubt, and of course that's the legal requirement, beyond a reasonable doubt that he was guilty of the crimes for which he was charged, that the sentence was appropriate, and I affirmed the court martial. That was relatively easy and clear, and my guess is that something above 90% of you would have done the same thing.

The next part on clemency was tough part. And on that as you know I reduced the sentence to 10 years…I think our system of justice has always looked differently at the question of innocence versus guilt, as it looks at the question of what's the proper punishment. For example, such things as character references, previous convictions, are not normally allowed in the question of innocence versus guilt, but they are considered as mitigating circumstances in the punishment. And I think that's why I looked at some of these mitigating circumstances. The two that I talked about and I felt were appropriate to talk about was one, that Calley was the only man convicted at court martial—we did court-martial his commanding officer, we court-martialed others, but none of the others were convicted. And the fact that he was the only one, while it didn't weigh too much, you know is sort of a mitigating circumstance. The other one which I thought was more of a mitigating circumstance was there was a good bit of evidence that Calley actually thought he was obeying orders. Now I had addressed that originally, and I had felt that if in fact he got those orders, he should have as a reasonable man—that's what the law says, as a reasonable man—he should have as a reasonable man have known that it was an illegal order and therefore I confirmed the conviction. But still it was there, the fact that he might well have thought he received the order, and that's a very different kind of murder from a pre-meditated murder where a man decides ahead of time to murder.

Very different from one where in the confusion of battle one might think he's obeying orders.

Now let me get to the real mitigating circumstances that I'd rather not talk about. Task Force Barker, as a part of the Americal Division, was not a unit that the Army could be at all proud of. It was a unit that was unbelievably poor. There was no concept in that unit of why we were in Vietnam. No concept that we were there to help the Vietnamese people. You know, we weren't going over there for any other reason and there was no concept. The only concept in that task force at that time was a body count concept of turning in bodies, and no thought about anything in the broader concept of what it was about. No checking by commanders on what's done. As a matter of fact, on that day at My Lai when they first turned in a body count of well over two hundred, not a single commander came to even check, and that would have had to have been one of the biggest actions of the month, of 200 VC [Viet Cong] killed. It was just a report to them, send upstairs, look good for the records, we don't care what you do, don't tell us about it, and Calley was not the only one doing those kinds of things. In the platoon next to him there were similar things done on the same day, and all throughout that unit there were all of these things being done. And that didn't just happen. Now you add to that that Calley himself was in the bottom of his class in high school, the bottom of his class at [Officer Candidate School]. You know, is a lower mental capacity. And to put on him the requirement of distinguishing between orders and all that sort of thing, might have been putting a pretty big burden on a man of that lower mental capacity.

Now you add to that this was his first real combat. Up until that what he had been doing was on some patrols and things, he'd had a number of casualties, but all to an unseen enemy, all to mines, and he'd had a lot of legs blown off and all that kind of thing. Building up the frustration, no way to attack back, all of that, and seeing his people hurt but no action. Then he gets his orders for going into My Lai. He is told that this is—and he believes, as a matter of fact Captain [Ernest] Medina [Calley's company commander] believed—that this was a really crack VC outfit. It was a battalion in strength, and that wasn't as strong as our battalions, but it was a VC battalion, really strong, hardened, seasoned VC. And this attack that's going to be made will be the biggest attack of the war that day in Vietnam, it will be a very major attack, and this is Lieutenant Calley's chance to go in and show that he's really going to do a great job. He was also told that there would be no friendly civilians in that village, that all the friendly civilians would have been out by 8:00 that morning. And there would be no friendly civilians there. He was also told to shoot anything that moves, all that kind of thing. Now you get into all that, and I think it's a mitigating circumstance. As a matter of fact as you read the trial, you're struck as a Shakespearean tragedy. And I think a New York Times writer put it better than anyone else I've seen when he said "You know that you yourself would have never come out where Calley did, you instinctively know that, but you can't find the point and time where you would have done different." It just sort of moved. Getting to the Americal Division, getting to that unit, getting with the kind of leadership he had, getting the kind of orders, and moving in the orders, and moving in to shoot anything that moves, and suddenly he's firing on defenseless women and children.

A bad situation about the Army, and the only thing I know we can do is get it behind us, go on to a kind of Army, and to keep from making the mistakes they made is what I'm talking about this leadership that the Army demands today. We have got to have the kind of leadership that knows what the Army's about and what it's to do. And it can't be numbers oriented and body-count oriented, it's got to be oriented on what the job is, and our job in Vietnam was to build up those people he was shooting, not to come in and count bodies and be the hero and all that. I don't know that I've given an answer that anybody is happy with. While I've said that I'm quite sure over 90% of you would agree with affirming the sentence, I would be very surprised if anything approaching 90% would agree with reducing it to ten years. Some of you might have reduced it more, many of you might have kept it at 20, some of you might have said fifteen years, you know, a thousand different solutions. And you just have to finally pick one. The one I picked I wasn't entirely happy with because there's a conflict there: A very serious crime and reducing in a sentence. But I tried to weigh only the justice of the situation, and not the publicity and not all that. The mail has been pretty much against me since I did it, but that wasn't why I did it.

In December 1974, Callaway told students about the reaction to his decision to release the report on the My Lai investigation.

I can't tell you how much heartburn there was in the Army about releasing that Peers report. There's no way for you to really understand how much heartburn there was. How many people just said "It's going to open old wounds. You just can't do it." If you read that report, and I've read every page of it, it's terrible. It shows the Army—you're not proud of the Army when you finish reading that book. There's nothing about it that I enjoy reading or would enjoy releasing. And I took the position from the very beginning we had to release it at the first possible moment we could when the problems were out of the way and we did. I don't know if you've seen the publicity from the Peers report, but every bit of it I've seen has been getting behind us the whole My Lai incident. And it's really come out to be really quite good publicity. And nobody is going back over everything because most of the stuff in it was already known. [Journalists] Seymour Hersh and Jack Taylor were writing all that stuff, they knew most of it, they just hadn't seen the report. And instead it came out, as General Peers said firmly, it came out to show that we, the Army, took on a very tough task and gave a good, solid investigation and that was a quality job done. Named names, pointed fingers, pointed at twenty people who did not perform their duty well, named what they didn't do well, and then tracked right through with what we've done with them. As I recall 14 or 16 were court-martialed, and it's true that only one served time, which was Calley of course. But we court-martialed Medina, we preferred charges on about 14 of them, administrated or punished a great many others, and a number of them, of course, were out of our jurisdiction by the time we found out about it. But here is something that almost unanimously the Army is saying: "You can't be open this time." We even had a court decision saying we didn't have to release it. And I promise you it's been good for the Army, enormously good for the Army, and it goes back to our credibility next time. And once the public understands that we'll tell it like it is in the Army, you've just got a different public. And why is it important that the public understand the Army? It's important for a lot of reasons. Number one, the mommies and daddies aren't going to let their little boys and girls join the Army if they don't think much of it. And it's important that they believe in it. But even more fundamentally at this moment in time, is if the public doesn't support us you can be sure that the Congress won't, because the Congress represents the public. And we've got to have the kind of credibility, believability, that when we go say it's important to have 16 divisions, somebody's got to believe us.

In late 1989, U.S. forces conducted Operation Just Cause in Panama in order to remove that country's military dictator, Manuel Noriega. Soon after the operation, in January 1990, Army Chief of Staff Carl Vuono gave the students a thorough overview of the event.

I'm here really on serious business, because we had something happen to the military and to the Army over the past few weeks that I think is really significant. And I think it's important that all of you out here, whether you're in one of the courses or whether you're on the faculty, to have a chance to hear early on a little bit about the operation, the planning, the execution, a little bit about some of the emerging lessons learned, and then some implications for the Army, because we're going through a watershed period in the military right now as all of you know, and I think what happened in operation Just Cause is not only a time to be very proud of the military, and I mean goddamn proud of the military, but also a time to reflect on what all that means as we reshape the forces that are really going to be the forces that are going to take us into the next century.

...These were the objectives that we were assigned: We were asked to protect U.S. citizens, ensure we operated the canal safely—by the way this was no small feat, support democratic institutions, and apprehend Mr. Noriega. And we were able to accomplish all of that...As we assessed the operation and developed the concept, it became clear to us that speed, surprise, and simultaneity was important. That we had to go in with sufficient forces to do the job. We had to go in as quickly as we could, with as much surprise as we could have. And that we had to hit multiple objectives in order to ensure that we met the objectives and that the commander's intent was carried out.

Now one of the areas that we worked on early on was to assist in the maturation of the [Guillermo] Endara government, and provide strong humanitarian programs. And I think it's important that you know that that was not an afterthought. There are folks who were saying "Well, it was slow getting started and so forth." Fact of the matter is it was in our initial intent that in the assault elements of the operation we had Civil Affairs and Psyops folks going in. So we knew exactly what we were going to have to do, and what had to be done. But the importance of the operation was to ensure that we neutralized major force units, captured Mr. Noriega, neutralized the [paramilitary] Dignity Battalion, and ensured sight security, and security from direct and indirect fires. So we had a plan to accomplish all of that.

I want to talk a little bit about deployment because I think it's important to put it in the right context. In order to carry out the commander's intent and put sufficient forces on the ground in simultaneous action, it was important that we reinforced forward deployed forces with contingency forces. And that's what we did with this operation. We knew we needed a mix of forces. We had to have light forces, heavy forces to do some things I'll talk about in a minute, and special operations forces. I'm not going to get into a lot of detail for security reasons on the role of special operations forces. Suffice to say that those forces demonstrated what we have been saying for a long time. They're truly unique and magnificent, and their performance in conjunction with heavy and light forces was unparalleled, in my view, to anything we've ever accomplished in the past. So we had that mix of forces, and we had to bring that mix to bear.

...On the Sunday before Christmas [December 24th], the decision was made to conduct the operation. The troops were not alerted on Sunday. Some of the key commanders were made aware Sunday night, but the bulk of the troop alerts came Monday and Tuesday. And we deployed Tuesday evening for an H-hour of 0100 Wednesday morning with a simultaneous parachute assault and mech link-up Wednesday morning. So what you had, was you had soldiers who went from Christmas shopping to combat in less than 53 hours. That's what you had here. And I talked to a number of those young kids, and not so young, and many of them had no idea on Sunday or Monday what they were going to be doing.

The 82nd went into an [Emergency Deployment Readiness Exercise (EDRE)] which was normal for the DRB, the division ready brigade. And it wasn't in a lot of cases, in terms of the trooper, until sometime late Tuesday, once they got locked in down at Green Ramp that they knew they were shooting up for combat operations. The in-place forces within [U.S. Southern Command (SOUTHCOM)] didn't know that it was the actual operation until Tuesday evening sometime. I use that to demonstrate our concern for the secrecy that we could get from a security standpoint, so we could protect not only our own forces, but protect loss of life among civilians in Panama, and indeed within the PDF [Panamanian Defense Force]. And that will come out I think as I talk. So I think from a security standpoint we did a much better job than any of us thought in terms of ensuring there were a lack of leaks, and as a matter of fact the plan was held close in Washington, and I think it paid off because you had very little leaks early on in the planning phase even in Washington, which is a major accomplishment.

...It's interesting to be part of planning something, and then seeing it on the ground, and then reading about it. [Laughter] And so the only point I would make here on that is you will see written and already written about an attempt to have everybody involved, so everybody got a piece of the pie and all that. I can tell you, I don't think that's ever happened in our military, but I can't say that [as I wasn't] directly involved. But I can tell you on this one, I was directly involved and there was none of that nonsense that went on. This was a plan that was developed based on the commander that was on the ground's intent, and what he needed in terms of combat power to accomplish his mission, and that's what he got. And this is the perfect case of that.

...Let me turn now and talk a little bit about ongoing missions. Combat operations as we know them have really virtually stopped several days ago. And we moved almost immediately from combat operations into stability operations. And what we tried to do in stability operations was to ensure that we assisted the Endara government in coming on board. But in addition to that, we returned the country as much as we could to a stable environment. And again I think you ought to be very proud of the troops for the way they switched gears from combat operations into stability operations. And you have infantry companies and platoons doing things in that stability phase that were not in their [Mission Essential Task List (METL)], and have done them very, very well. And I don't know if they're trying to make me feel good or not, but I asked about the METL, and everybody told me that they validated their METL at least to the 90% level. [Laughter]

So I left after that, I thought that was pretty good. But they said seriously that it was valuable having a METL and they validated it at the 90% level.

...I'm glad we went in. Because first of all I think the objectives the president laid out needed to be met, and we did so. But if you had a chance to see what I saw in terms of arms caches around that country, it said that this guy was up to something, and it wasn't good. When you have a force of 15,000, and we uncovered 76,000 weapons, he's doing more than arming his internal force.

In the question and answer session, an international officer asked Vuono if he would have been disappointed if the Panamanian forces had just laid down their weapons and refused to fight, considering they were trained by the United States. After some laughter from the audience, Vuono replied "Some did that, some fought very well. I think a lot of it depended on the leaders. I would say that Mr. Noriega was conspicuous by his absence in the fight. He turned tail and ran, and that's what you would expect, I guess, from him."

POST-COLD WAR and OPERATIONS OTHER THAN WAR

In 1992, future CJCS Lieutenant General John Shalikashvili spoke to the students about Operation Provide Comfort, an operation he led to, in his own words, "Help [our] Turkish friends to resolve an extraordinarily difficult situation that had developed on their border, and at the same time provide humanitarian assistance to those many, many Kurdish refugees that needed our help, and the help was beyond one country, namely Turkey, to provide." The border to which he referred was the Iraq-Turkey border, and as this was soon after the first Gulf War, the possibility of escalations with the Iraqi Army was an ever-present threat.

Early on we decided that there would be a period when we would go into Northern Iraq and the Iraqi Army would still be there, and the Iraqi Secret Police would still be there, and Special Police, and we would be pushing them out of the way, and every moment had with it the possibility of a confrontation. And so we decided that what we needed to establish was a Military Coordination Center, a facility where the Iraqis and we were in the same room with the right [communications], so when something happened somewhere in the [area], these guys could immediately get on it and try to resolve it. Now I will tell you, it all started on about the first or second day of the operation after we decided we were going to go into Northern Iraq, and you saw the units that were there. We had at that time about 3-400 Marines forward with us, and the rest of the stuff was flowing. But we really didn't want to waste any time, so we flew into Northern Iraq and landed in a place called Zakho, which was their largest town there in the area, and confronted the local commander. And I will tell you, you should have seen his eyes, because, you know, all of a sudden we showed up here with three or four helicopters and for effect we had a few gunships circling above. I don't know what the hell those gunships were going to do but it added to the drama of the moment. [Laughter]

My instructions from Washington were very clear, just kind of tell them to get out of the way. So I told them get out of the way, we're coming in. His response was the thing you sort of expect from him, "Say that again? You're going to do what?" ...We had a few tense moments, but low and behold, they began to move out of the area. And then for the rest of the operation, as we were taking over more and more territory, and eventually we went out some 120, 130 kilometers east and 60, 70, 80 kilometers south, and carved out a security zone. And pushed those military units you saw, pushed them ahead of us. And I am convinced that the reason we didn't have more problems was that the professionalism of the soldiers that we had on the ground. It wasn't anything they did or said, particularly, just the way they carried themselves. There was absolutely no doubt in anybody's mind, whether it was those Marines initially, Airborne units that we brought in later on, whether U.S., British Marines, Italians, French, Spanish, that those combat units that we brought in, through their bearing, their professionalism, just left no room for arguing. It was really tank company by tank company, artillery battery by artillery battery that had to be convinced and pushed out of the way. There was never a place where they had blown the whistle and everyone evacuated. It was said "We're taking over from here a circle of 30 kilometers." We picked, and said "Everyone out." And then we just had to push them out. And then we went east and drew another circle, and said "Okay out" and we pushed them all out. And never once did they seriously challenge us.

And I think partly because they had lost the stomach for a fight down south, secondly because I think as we took them on a small group at a time they felt really overwhelmed. They felt intimated by that professionalism. So you've got to be careful how daring you get, but you also have to remember that you can still get an awful lot done if you just set your mind to it, get out and do it.

When asked about the successes and shortcomings of the operation, Shalikashvili again brought up a point he made during his presentation, that this operation was a continuation of Operation Desert Storm.

Being the modest fellow that I am, there were no shortcomings. [Laughter] No, let me answer and kind of put a different twist to your question. Success and shortcomings of Provide Comfort in a larger picture of war termination, that I hope you have devoted some time to or will devote some time to. If you remember the setting, you can't disconnect Provide Comfort from Desert Storm. How successful we were not only on the humanitarian side of saving lives, but more importantly, or equally important, how successful we were in putting a cap on something that from the war termination point of view had been an extraordinarily messy issue, and could have had such a high political cost for all of us. And so if you view it from that perspective, I thought it was extraordinarily successful. I remember that we had probably daily the question raised about whether we're getting quagmired in Northern Iraq, meaning in the Iraq war really, the termination piece, just like we had been in Vietnam. And so I don't think—and at any given time we had about 400 journalists, newspapermen credited to our operation, and so I don't think a day went by when I was not asked in those early days, you know, are we getting a return of this? It was terribly important that we brought that to a close and put a cork in a bottle as far as that piece of war termination was concerned. And it was essential therefore that we did it very quickly, that we did it by erasing any implication that the United States was the cause of this. Or at least get it off the headlines that the causal effect was the United States somehow. And secondly that we do this with a minimum of suffering and a maximum of goodwill shown. And I think in that respect everyone who participated did that extraordinarily well.

He was also asked about the political interface during the operation, and if any guidance came directly from the White House or State Department.

> I took direction only from General [John] Galvin [Commander, U.S. European Command and Supreme Allied Commander, Europe]. Did anyone meddle, and did I ever feel like "Those damn guys in the White House and in the Pentagon" and so forth? I did not. I did not. I think that partly the reason was that things were going so quickly that we were ahead of power curve. So more often than not we were presenting the choices and options and the recommended solutions, and those guys would meet and give us the okay. As opposed to if you sit by and wait for them to tell you, you might get a direction and an answer that you don't like. But that's not how General Galvin operates. He always forces us to be about two steps ahead. So we were feeding to Washington what we thought was right to do, through Galvin.

Shalikashvili was also asked about the planning linkages between the military and civilian relief organizations that participated in the operation.

> No linkage among themselves. Not easy. Asked Civil Affairs to take all agencies who had voluntarily showed up, ranging from the largest ones to the smallest ones, and try to get to a cooperative effort that we would divide the tasks before us. It worked better than I thought, but it took some getting used to. Maybe I would illustrate one example. Early on when I flew into the mountains, I came upon a well-drilling operation out of Sweden. Somehow they had gotten this truck up there to the mountains where there are no roads, and there was this guy sitting, and he could drill a well. And he had all the apparatus with him, [and] he had about ten folks with him. There was no one else around. And I said "What are you doing here?" And he said "Well, I just arrived because I heard as I was leaving Europe that there is a company in Frankfurt, a humanitarian assistance kind of a group, that's sending pipelayers over here. We just thought we'd sit here until they come up and maybe we can find a place to drill a well and they can find a place to lay a pipe that will eventually get to the people who need the water." Well you and I just kind of go ballistic when you come across that. [Laughter] But that's how they operate. But it took a while to get through these suspicions that we're not trying to take over their operation or dictate to them what to do. And so it was a series of meetings of reaching a consensus. And lo and behold later on you found a well-driller drilling away and a pipe-layer was there and other guys were hooking up to it. You cannot approach it the way we would in the military. You have to find a cooperative mechanism. Ultimately, the Department of State was very helpful.

The fall of the Berlin Wall and the end of the Cold War brought a new security environment to the world, and a new and diverse set of missions for the U.S. Military. General Gordon Sullivan described these complex operations to the students in December 1993.

> [Referring to slide: *The Army's View of War*] The Cold War: Stop and go, stop and go [pointing to war and peace stoplight graphic on slide]. Now you have the same units [points to a graphic depicting war moving to peace as a red to green light spectrum] in the same battalion in the same country, you'll have people in shooting wars and doing a medical run. The same unit. That's a real challenge for us. We're handling it okay, but

our thinking is still back in here [points to cold war stoplight], green and red, stop and go. It is full go [pointing to spectrum] for us now.

Another of the post-Cold War peacekeeping missions was Operation Uphold Democracy which sought to restore Haiti's democratically elected president in 1994. General Wayne Downing, commander of United States Special Operations Command, spoke to the students in early 1995 about his organization's role in that operation.

I for one was very, very happy that when the Haiti invasion was called off that we did not send our Rangers in for peacekeeping duties. Because our Rangers were going to go in there to kill people, and we could not reprogram them in a 24-hour period to put them in there as peacekeepers. I think they would have done okay, except if we got into a high stress situation, and when you get into a high stress situation people react the way they're trained. And they were oriented to going in and doing a combat operation. I was very glad the 10th Mountain Division came in. The 10th Mountain Division on the other hand, knew they were going in after the first wave, they knew what their missions were, and they were prepared to pick up those peacekeeping tasks.

...As I talk a little bit about Haiti, as you know, we really had two plans. We had one plan for an opposed entry, and we [special operations forces (SOF)] were going to play very significantly in it. It was getting difficult. Part of the problem with operations other than war, it's not war, it's not peace. We were leveraging the military threat to try and get the FAd'h [Haitian armed Forces] leaders to quit and get out of the country. So we had to tell them what it was we were doing. And of course for us as military people that's anathema, right? It certainly is for us in special operations. We've got to rely on surprise as one of the key factors that let us execute many of our missions. And I'm telling you we almost had heart attacks several times with some of the stuff that was coming out in the press, because there's only so many ways to do a coup de main. There's so many ways to go after the seat of power. And the press was starting to get it right. I mean they were starting to nail it. So we were getting very concerned about the operational security of our forces. We had visions of coming into blacked out landing zones and having CNN and ABC and NBC there with the Klieg lights on taking pictures. We had visions of getting involved in a fight in situations like that. And, you know, broadcasting this into the American public's front room, and those things are not pretty things to see. And the press would have been right in the middle of it too. So how could we assure their safety? So we were very, very concerned about that. To a point that at the last minute— we waited and at the last minute we started making a lot of changes to our plan. So that we would hope to do things a little bit differently, but there's only so many ways you can change things. We were quite concerned about this. Of course, the good news is that it worked, you know? We did. We leveraged them off. The [President Jimmy] Carter team that went down there in conjunction with the threat, the 82d Airborne being airborne, was enough to let them throw it in, so when you look at the bottom line it was worth it. Had we had to have gone in and executed, I was worried about the security of our forces.

...The good news is we [SOF] were first ones in, did a great job. The bad news is I don't think we're [SOF] ever going to get out of [Haiti]. They like us, they like us a lot. The UN, they ain't coming in unless we stay. So we may have Special Forces in Haiti for a long, long time. I hope we're not there as long as the Marines were there. Nineteen years is a long time. But we'll see.

Another major operation of the nineties was the NATO Implementation Force (IFOR) in Bosnia, also known as Operation Joint Endeavor. This mission caused great consternation and stress in the military, particularly in the Army, as repeated rotations, high OPTEMPO, and shrinking resources made for a stressed force. Many speakers commented on the operation, led by General Sullivan in December 1993, when he gave a hint of things to come a full two years before an Army unit would enter Bosnia, saying "A lot of things going on. [CNN correspondent] Christiane Amanpour has gone from Mogadishu to Sarajevo. [Audience chuckles and applause] It's not a throw-away line gang. That's not a throw-away line. Pay attention. Pay attention to what happens next. I don't know what's going to happen next, but that is a factor. That is a variable in the equation."

Earlier that same year, Congressman Ike Skelton (D – Missouri) was asked if he advocated American intervention in Bosnia.

> No, I do not. [Applause] …I don't know what your mission would be. We have in that area a complete collapse politically, a complete collapse economically, and the old hatreds, centuries old, have come to surface. The United Nation's forces have done very little, if anything, in trying to keep a sort of peace. I don't know what the mission might be. I think there might be on the horizon, however, the possibility of trying to halt the Serbs' artillery devastation of some of the Muslim and Croatian areas. But for ground troops to go in there, that's a tar baby.

During a later visit in 1996, Skelton discussed the decision to send in American troops.

> As a result of the way I felt, very strongly, it was no surprise to the president, I co-sponsored a resolution in the House that disapproved of the deployment. And my language was in there calling for even-handedness, as opposed to arming and training. But it did support the troops very strongly, the language that we had. Whatever we did was non-binding because the president was acting as Commander in Chief. The Senate passed a very long resolution including arming and training the Muslims. Ours did not. Ours passed the House 287 folks in favor. Of course that did not affect the final result of the president ordering troops in. I am in the process of making a series of speeches on the House floor dealing with Bosnia. I will give a third one this week and maybe a fourth one next week. I hope we're successful, I hope things work out. Being there a year, however, I wonder if it will do little more than give the warring factions time to regroup, to rearm, to retrain. What's to keep some of the cousins of the Serbs from arming and training them? I don't know. But as you know, our policy is to be there about a year. Experts say that in order for us to make a real difference, we should be there, or NATO should be there some ten years. But that's not going to happen. Let's hope I'm wrong. Let's hope they take this opportunity to have peace and understanding, but you're swimming against the culture that Americans have a difficult time understanding.

Troops ended up staying well past the originally stated one year, and in September 1997, Secretary of Defense William Cohen was asked about lessons learned from the Bosnia operation, particularly regarding exit strategies.

Bosnia is a classic case of trying to respond to an international situation. I was not one who was eager to become involved in Bosnia as a member of the Senate. Because I asked the same question: It's easy to get in, how do you get out? What should be the standards? The president, the administration, and ultimately the Congress, decided that it was in our, not vital national interests, but it was an important issue, an important interest for us because had the conflict continued to spread and move south, and went to Macedonia, possibly got down to get involved with Greece and Turkey and other countries getting involved. Suddenly you would have a major vital national interest. And so at that point it was decided to go in for a year. I must tell you that sitting in the Senate at that time, I think it's not a wise thing to do to set time limits. Whenever you set a timeframe, then you are setting yourself up for a real problem in the future. But Congress was insisting. Without faulting the president, he felt compelled to try to do something, at the urging of our NATO allies, "You've got to help." We found out that when the United States doesn't lead nothing takes place. Europeans, it seems to me, and I know we have some representatives of European countries, but they don't seem capable of initiating action on their own without the United States' power and prestige. And so there was pressure being generated for the United States to take the lead to stop the bloodshed and we did…The military mission was complete.

The problem was that the so-called civilian side of the Dayton Accords wasn't being implemented for a variety of reasons. We didn't have an effective IPTF, the International Police Task Force, to get the money to start training a local police force, because we don't want our military to engage in essentially police functions but we don't have any policemen over there. We had refugees returning, and they're being either harassed or killed, houses burned when they cross over the lines. We don't want to be guarantors of refugee return. That should be a police function. The money wasn't coming in from international organizations that pledged the money, and so you weren't getting the capital infusion into that country to say peace is better than war. And so there was no civilian implementation of the Dayton Accords. And only recently because I and others have said "NATO has said 'Give us 18 more months. Give peace a little bit longer, a chance to have those seeds take root, and hopefully flourish.'" Now is it realistic? Time will tell, but what I have said is the [Stabilization Force (SFOR), which followed IFOR] mission should end, as I said it would end, in June of '98. The European allies, I must tell you, they don't like that idea. They feel that if the mission ends in June of '98, [the warring factions in Bosnia will] go back to warfare, the warfare will spread, there will be more killing, and all will have been for naught. My message to our European Allies has been stop talking about what takes place after June. What can be done between now and next June? Because that's what we are focusing upon: between now and June.

There has been an intensification of our effort in Bosnia. You've read about it, you're seeing it, you're seeing what it can produce, the danger that it might produce more conflict. For example, we are supporting Mrs. [Biljana] Plavsic, because she is supporting Dayton, although she originally didn't support Dayton. So we're supporting those who support Dayton. What you've got is Mr. [Radovan] Karadzic, and others, thugs, war criminals, who are in fact trying to poison the atmosphere by taking control of the media and putting out Hitlerian types of messages that are trying to prejudice the Serbian people against SFOR. So now the question is what are we going to do about the media? We may very well be forced to take action to interrupt that kind of transmission. That in itself can produce a reaction. And so what we are looking at very closely with our allies is to make sure that we are staying with the general guidelines of Dayton. To make sure that we don't move over into those missions that we said we wouldn't be involved with. And there's always that temptation, and there's always pressure saying "Well, we can't find the police, let's have the military do it." And that's the danger that we have to be worried about.

I don't know what will take place after June of '98. All I know right now is my message has been "That's what the mission is, that's what we're committed to, and let's do the best we can between now and then." And let's see how things unfold between now and then. Let's see what happens if you have elections, which are scheduled for the 11th and 12th [of September] at the municipal level. Let's see what happens with the elections in parliament on October 13th and 14th, or 12th to 14th, next month. And then let's see how this unfolds. But we're trying to keep the pressure on. June is the deadline. And let's focus our efforts between now and then. That's when the mission should end. That's what I'm going to tell the president, and frankly we have conversations on a periodic basis. He's following it very closely. He wants to make sure that we don't get more deeply involved than we currently are.

Yet we at the same time take into account what's happening with NATO. We've got a real problem coming up, because all of the NATO allies want us there. At the same time we've got a vote coming up in the Congress to expand NATO by three countries. If the United States, by way of example, would say "We're not going to be involved in Bosnia, period, under any circumstances, under any configuration," and then the NATO countries say "Fine. If you're out, we're out. We're not going to do anything to help the Bosnian people either." That vote comes about the same time you have the vote to expand NATO, so it's going to present an interesting problem and dilemma for all of us, the Congress, for the country in terms of how important NATO cohesion is going to remain. Because there are a number of people on Capitol Hill who don't favor expanding NATO, who feel we're going to weaken it. I don't agree with that, I think that by expanding NATO itself that we are expanding those who hold our values dear. That will, I think, minimize the chance of conflict in the future, minimize the kind of ethnic tensions that exist, and regional hatreds, and promote more stability.

In 1998, General Dennis Reimer was asked about the logic behind sending the 1st Cavalry Division, a unit designed for high intensity, conventional warfare, to Bosnia, a low intensity environment.

Well I don't know whether I can give you the logic of it, but since I made the decision I can tell you why I made it. [Laughter and applause] You'll have to judge whether it was logical or not. That is a very fair question, and one that's out there, and I know that it rumbles around from time to time. The decision that I thought we faced at that particular time was that we had been really riding Europe pretty hard with this Bosnia mission. We started out—we couldn't go anywhere else because initially—it was a one-year mission and it was June of '98, and finally June of '98 they said it was indefinite. So at that point in time we said okay, we've got to get Europe back to a stable state, let them focus on training and readiness, and those type of things, get back in a normal pattern. You just can't keep going back to that well that many times. We said okay, if you go to [the continental United States], where do you go? And the issue was, look: We need to make sure we do this thing right in Bosnia. Bosnia is still a dangerous place. Remember when we talked about going over there, and they talked about the millions of mines that were over there and how difficult that terrain was, and how nobody liked each other over there? You think any of that's changed? No, there are still mines there. There's still animosity amongst the Croats, Serbs and the Muslims. The difference is that the United States Army's over there and they look like a professional organization. It's like playing pick-up basketball and five guys looking like Michael Jordan all wearing Chicago Bulls shirts show up. The game just went up in terms of intensity, and I think that's made the difference. What I didn't want to have happen, since we were switching it over to another [major command (MACOM)], is for us to drop down a little bit. And so I said, Look, let's go, let's take the First Team [1st Cavalry Division motto] and send it on over there because this is an important mission. We've got to do that right.

Yes, I understood the risk associated with sending First Cav over there. And yes, it's going to take probably about 18 months or so to get them back into combat configuration where they will be ready to respond. And I guess my judgment will be tested in the next 18 months, if we have to pull them out and send them off to a major theater war somewhere then probably that was not a good decision. I don't know, but I can't see the future that far in advance in terms of whether we're going to have to fight or not. So we knew that we were going to have to do Bosnia right, we're switching it over to a whole new MACOM, coming out of the continental United States, look at where else you've got to go: Who else do you want to go to? Do you want to go to 3rd Infantry Division? We've got them going back and forth to Southwest Asia, just to make sure that Saddam Hussein doesn't get off the reservation. [Laughter] I'm not sure that (Bosnia) mission over there is a good light mission. The thing that helps an awful lot in deterrence is to have a few of those heavy vehicles and those Apaches [helicopters] over there, so that when people start to get a little bit unruly, you just say "C'mon there, we'll show you what this thing can do." And they have second thoughts then about all that, so we wanted to go with the First Team, we chose to do it with the First Team. Yes, there's a risk associated with it, but there's a risk associated with every decision I make. And I think there's going to be a risk associated with every decision you make. It's just different in terms of the degree of risk, I guess. But I think we have to be willing to deal with that risk. And I think the First Cav has done a great job over there, and I'm awful glad we sent them, because they have been tested already. And they don't take any monkey business off of those guys. One of the things I know from talking with guys like [U.S. Army Europe Commanders General William] Crouch and [his successor General Eric] Shinseki is that they're going to test whatever unit that we send over there.

Years into the Bosnia mission there was a lot of talk about how the focus on operations other than war had degraded the military's warfighting capabilities. On a return visit in 1999, Congressman Skelton was asked if he thought U.S. forces should be in Bosnia, and if that mission detracted from their ability to conduct a major theater war.

The answer to your first question is maybe and the answer to your second question is yes. [Laughter and applause] Our Military is not that large. I had serious reservations over the Bosnian effort. As a matter of fact I co-sponsored the resolution against our involvement in Bosnia. Nevertheless, regardless of the resolution, the Commander in

Chief sent troops in, and I along with others support the troops. Whether we like it or not, there are those instances when the military is the only organization or institution that can do the job, that can bring peace to an area. Especially the United States military, which is so highly regarded. It worries me that we are finding ourselves, I think as a result of CNN television, at least tempted to place our military in these positions, because if you look at it objectively no one else can do it unless we do it. It would be far worse, I suppose, had we not done something in Kosovo, which might very well erupt as it did in the first world war, into a wider conflict which we might very well have become involved as well as our allies. You are a great resource and I'm concerned about spreading you so thin, that if and when you are needed elsewhere, in a real conflict, your unit might be [readiness rating] C4, or unable to answer that call immediately. But this is the Commander in Chief's call. I do not disagree with what we did in Kosovo. We are there in the Balkans, I'm afraid, for a long time. But I think that we will have to make sure and backfill as best we can. I, for one think that the Army is too small. I, for one think that we should increase the size of it so that we can have all our divisions at C1, C2. You are the national resource that we must carefully guard. But there are places that you will be sent. By whoever the Commander in Chief is. And Congress, the only thing Congress can do is cut off the funds. Which of course, we're not about to cut off the funds of troops in the field.

The Kosovo campaign (NATO's Operation Allied Force, U.S. Operation Joint Guardian) dovetailed out of the Bosnia mission, and when Chairman of the Joint Chiefs General Hugh Shelton appeared in 1999, he was asked if that campaign's larger allied contingent covering the ground portion supported by a smaller U.S. force in the air was a NATO model for the future.

The answer is very simply that all of us face parliaments, or congresses or whatever we have as political things, and we had placed a tremendous amount of resources—well resources is the right answer I guess, you know planes and bombs and everything else— into the Kosovo operation. And therefore it was felt that when it came to going in to do the peace enforcement piece after it was over, that we should not do the heavy lifting, so to speak, but that our European allies should pick up more of that. And the agreement was that we would do about 14 or 15 percent, and that the European community would pick up about 85. And that has consistently been what it's been in Kosovo. Today we have about 6,200 [personnel] in there, the percentage is right at 15 percent today. I'm getting a little concerned because as we speak today the Italians have more troops than we have—as we look at the new [Statement of Requirement (SOR)] that just went into effect—the Italians have more than we do and that's it. With 6,200 in there we are the second largest ground contributor, and I think that the next thing we are going to see is a Congress saying "What are we doing, why aren't we bringing that force down some?" We went into an area that was originally set up to be a U.S. only area. Of course we now share that with the Russians, who have come into the area with a couple of battalions. Yet we've kept our three there. So we did not reduce, some of our other allies, in fact, when other nations decided they would contribute, partners, or NATO members said that "we'll give more," they in fact reduced their contributions, which is why we ended up with as high as we have compared to some of the other allies.

I don't see us ever splitting out and saying we'll do the air piece, you do the ground piece. We're in this together, that's one of the beauties of the alliance, the fact that it was a consensus of nineteen nations that hung tough during this thing, and each one contributed within their capabilities. And we did not complain because we had to provide 53% of the strike sorties and 79% of the support sorties because we have the force to do that. We thought one way, however, since our allies had the other types of forces to contribute to the ground operation, that would be one way to reduce the criticism of our Congress, who keeps saying "Why are we giving so much in an area that is more strategic and of more vital national interest to our European allies than it is to us, yet we're contributing?" So we're trying to balance this thing between being a great partner and also not getting beat up too badly back in Washington.

A student then asked him about the NATO strategy, and, alluding to a hammer and nail analogy Shelton frequently made, asked if the United States was hammering a nail or a screw.

I think we were screwing them down pretty tight, to tell you the truth, and we were doing it with the hammer called the airpower that we had. You know, there's been a lot of discussion about ground now. I've got 840 of the world's pre-eminent ground element sitting there [referring to the 82d Airborne Division]. I'm a member of it. I was raised in it. I believe in it. And I think in the final analysis if you want to achieve your political objective there is only one way that you can assure doing that. And that is you're going to occupy the territory. That is precisely what I told the president. We looked at what the objectives were from a political standpoint, we looked at what we could do militarily, and we set our objectives within something that was achievable militarily. And we pointed out that there's a gap. And I also pointed out that you might achieve this political objective but I can't guarantee that short of a ground plan that will go to Belgrade. So we knew that going in. But I also understood that as you looked at the campaign plan that we had laid out, that in the end, this guy [President of the Federal Republic of Yugoslavia Slobodan Milosevic] was going to be left with one of two choices: He was going to be left with seeing his country completely destroyed, and he might have liked to do that, and that was always an option for him. Or he might live to see the UCK [Kosovo Liberation Army] start to rise up and start attacking him in a way that he was having trouble managing his civil populace, keeping his people alive as the bodies started being brought home etc. And somewhere in there there might be a combination of the two. And so somewhere it might be hard for him to hold on, particularly as the winter months would start to approach. I didn't know how long it would take but I knew going in it would not be a 3-day war or 12-day war. I didn't think it would be, at any rate. There were those who believed it would and I won't call any names but you've read enough about that. I wasn't even sure we'd do it in the long run, but I felt confident. And the longer we went, the more intel that started coming in, the more confident I got. About a week before it stopped I was in the oval office one night and I was asked "If you were king for a day what would you do right now?" And my answer was "Stay the course but turn the thumb-screws. Let's raise the ante a little bit. We've got to get a little bit higher and harder." A week later we had the thing, and I must admit I was— "Whew—thank goodness." You know, it worked. But I think a lot of us were, because we did have that gap and we knew it.

Exit Strategy. I'll be very frank and candid with you in here. The exit strategy is the same exit strategy that we've seen in Bosnia. I can't give you a date. And it's why you heard me in testimony say, a couple of times I think if you've heard or read that, that the civil implementation piece of it—this interagency piece that I've talked about today, except applied at an international level—is what it's going to take to get us out of Bosnia or get us out of Kosovo. If a peaceful and stable environment is the requirement, and the only way that you can keep it is to keep an armed force in there, a NATO force in out doing the work that would normally be done by police, by highway patrol, by DEA, by FBI, you know, putting in American terminology, by the elements of law and order, the rule of law, the courts system, then how are you going to get out? You're not going to get out unless you have a civilian government that has a rule of law, has a court system, has a police system. It is why right now to really guarantee the level we want you need the International Police Task Force, but you also need the [Organization for Security Cooperation in Europe (OSCE)] in there working their butt off training indigenous personnel that will become the law enforcement people of the future. And that's the way we'll get out in total. Now the longer we stay there, like in Bosnia, the further we can reduce the troops and get them down. You know the new SOR, I think we'll probably end up going down to about 4,600 from the current ceiling that we've got. So that's another fairly significant reduction. But the next one's going to get tougher, because you're now getting down to a point that all you're doing is occupying space. You're not posing much of a threat, you're not out there with an intimidating force that's moving through the area, and unless you've got police in there it's apt to start flaring up again. So the exit strategy is tied to the civilian implementation plan, and that is the toughest piece, because we aren't in charge. And that's why I say we're a hammer, that's not necessarily a nail. I don't know if I'd call it a screw, maybe it's a gimlet or something, I'm not sure.

Later in 1999, General Wesley Clark, the NATO Supreme Allied Commander during the Kosovo operation, referred to his 1975 Master's thesis *Military Contingency Operations: The Lessons of Political Military Coordination*, telling the students "When I was a student here 25 years ago, I wrote a [Masters of Military Art and Science (MMAS)] thesis I had to live in the Air Campaign over Kosovo." He then proceeded to discuss the operation in great detail.

[*Slide showing the mission of the air campaign*] This was the mission of the Air Campaign. I used to keep this in my desk drawer and slide it out, and look at it, and shudder, and put it back in the desk drawer. [Reading slide] "Halt or disrupt a systemic campaign of violent repression and expulsion in Kosovo." We wrote those words in July of '98, nine months before we executed the campaign. It was one of a series of [Operation Plans (OPLANS)] we wrote. We thought "Well, we're pretty sure we can disrupt it, we're not sure we can halt it. It depends a lot on the circumstances." And so we hedged our bets, and that was the mission of the air campaign. We operated on two axes. A strategic axis going against the integrated air defense command and control, the force throughout Serbia, sustaining infrastructure and supply routes, and we attacked in Kosovo against the deployed forces.

[*Slide: Allied Force— Measure of Merit: Avoid Losses, Impact Serb Forces in Kosovo, Minimize Collateral Damage, Maintain Alliance Cohesion*] The way I managed the campaign was through measures of merit. These measures of merit are all logical, but they are inconsistent, one with another. If you try to optimize any one measure of merit, you'll fail in the other. And so the strategic art in this case was keep them all moving. Avoiding losses. No politician ever called and said "Don't take losses." I want to make that very clear. This was not a political imperative. President Clinton didn't say he wouldn't take losses. In fact, the President, the Secretary of Defense and all other allied political leaders said they expected to take losses. But what we knew, we the military was, if you're running an air campaign and you start to have aircraft shot down, then the clock starts to tick against you. The first day you lose two aircraft, people say "Okay, you had 360 aircraft when you started, you lost two, that means two into 360, that's 180 days," the clock's ticking on the air campaign. The next day you'd lose six aircraft and they'd say "Now you've lost 8 in two days, that's four a day, how many days can this go on?" So it was a military imperative to protect the aircraft. We wanted to impact the Serb forces in Kosovo. I knew we could take out hard targets; we're very good at striking hard targets and fixed facilities on the ground. But can you hit forces that are dispersed and mobile and camouflaged?

That was the key problem, and that's why I put my priority here [pointing to "Impact Serb Forces in Kosovo"]. It was an extremely difficult problem for the Air Force. They weren't doctrinally ready for this, and they weren't fully equipped for it, to do this in the absence of a ground component. And so we put a lot of effort into that during the war. We knew we had to minimize collateral damage. An air campaign has a certain half-life, in part based on collateral damage. Because if you start hitting innocent people and blowing up bridges, then people start to question what are you doing, and why, and is it worth this? And so when you start an air campaign, you're going to hit targets that are purely military and that won't have collateral damage. But as the campaign goes on, the low-hanging fruit has been picked and you have to look harder for the targets, and the enemy gets smarter in positioning what you're trying to strike in areas that cause collateral damages. So we knew we had to work to minimize that. And finally there were no targets that were more important than maintaining the cohesion of the alliance. Ultimately it was a political-military operation, it wasn't just a military operation, and so we had to have allied unity.

[*Fallacies slide*] There was a lot of discussion about this. Frankly, I don't know how I could possibly have succeeded in this operation if I hadn't gotten the advice every night on television from my retired colleagues. [Laughter and applause] But let me tell you there was always a strategic plan, the strategic plan was very simple: It was to escalate and make the campaign unendurable for Milosevic, and to escalate as rapidly as it was politically feasible to do so. Some people think that if we'd just bombed Belgrade the first night that would have been the end of it. Well, we bombed Baghdad the first night and Saddam Hussein didn't pull everything out of Kuwait. I'm sure it would have shocked Milosevic if we had bombed Belgrade the first night, but it would have also shocked about 18 NATO allies. And there was no single target worth tearing apart allied cohesion. NATO allies believed that use of force should be more incremental. And they were going back to NATO's Cold War doctrine of flexible response. We've learned a different lesson, we view it a little bit differently than they do, but I think everybody's learned as a result of this and I'll talk about that in a minute.

But don't believe there was a simplistic, easy, one-night solution there. Some people say we didn't do effects-based targeting. I don't know if there are any airmen here that participated in this, but I sure thought it was effects-based targeting. I was asking the questions every day in a VTC "What's the effect of striking this target?" and "How come we struck only one petroleum refinery instead of all of them?" and "Why did we just strike two storage tanks and not all of them?" So there's a lot of methodological confusion when you're running an operation like this and you have to more or less run audible plays to keep it rolling, you never get everybody on the same sheet of music. This is not something that we operated off a prepared, detailed war plan. A lot of people complained about political micromanagement. But when you are in a campaign like this you'll always have political micromanagement. It's inevitable. If you want to bomb the bridges going over the Danube River in Belgrade, that has some military significance, it has a huge political significance. And I for one don't want to do it unless alliance political leaders are prepared to back me up. I don't want them at the press conference the next day to say "How come this was bombed? Gee, we had no idea. This looks like the military is out of control." The military was never out of control, we always operated with political guidance, and within NATO political guidance. And that's essential in a campaign like this. Some people thought that when the Russians came down to Pristina airport they'd be pussycats because they didn't have any logistics. That's certainly one way to look at it. They said to me "Don't worry about the Russians. When they come down, they'll have to eat our food." Well, three, four months later when I look at it, I look at it from the Russian point of view. They said "Hey let's get down there. Don't worry about the logistics, NATO will feed us." Some people think ground forces didn't have anything to do with this. But the actual truth is ground forces had everything to do with this. The [Kosovo Liberation Army] ground forces pushed the Serbs out into the open at the end. And the NATO force buildup, including Task Force Hawk, is what made the ground threat credible, and I believe it was ultimately not only the air campaign but the threat of the ground forces coming in that persuaded Milosevic to try a new tactic and give up Kosovo.

Clark was asked about the centers of gravity of the operation, and elaborated on the political aspects of the mission.

…We knew that when we targeted Milosevic and the people around him it was going to be a tough target. It was a political center of gravity. What you have to understand about the centers of gravity issue is if you're going after the strategic center, this is not like attacking Ploesti [Romania] oil or German ball bearings in World War II—by the way, neither one of those attacks was particularly successful—it's not a physical resource, the strategic center of gravity. And therefore it's not something that even good command and staff graduates can plot out and promise "Sir, if you'll just strike these five targets, you'll destroy Milosevic's will to continue." And therefore it's not possible to link a certain set of bombing targets with a certain political outcome. You don't know precisely how to get at what Milosevic's level of pain is that he'll tolerate or how to get at the people around him. It's not like doing weapons effects calculations. Now in the operational center of gravity down in Kosovo, you could do that. But you couldn't at the strategic level. Why this is important is because it says that you will always have a certain amount of political interference in your targeting process when you go after a strategic center of gravity like this. This is not something where an Air Command and Staff or U.S. Army Command and Staff graduate can stand up and in front of the president and say "Mr. President, you're wrong in interfering with us on attacking these bridges because I can promise you if we attack these bridges Milosevic will cave in." I mean what an absurd position. Nobody could make such a claim.

I went to see the NATO Secretary General [Javier Solana] about a week into the war. It was time to attack Belgrade, and I said "Secretary General, we've got to attack Belgrade." He said "Oh! My God! What are we going to attack in Belgrade?" I pulled out the picture, I said "Here, I want to attack these two headquarters buildings." He said "But can you hit these two buildings?" I said "Yes, we will hit these two buildings." "But what if you hit something else? What is around these buildings?" I said "Well, within 400 meters there's a hospital, a school, here's a church," [Audience chuckles] and this is not what any political leader wants to hear. And so he said "Can you be sure you won't hit these buildings?" So I went to the probability of hit charts and said "Yes, I'm 97% confident that we're going to strike exactly what we're striking, and nothing else." Then he said "Yes, but there's a 3% chance..." Then he said, and here's the key question, he said "Can you promise me, if you strike these buildings, that will be the end of the air campaign?" I said "No, I can't promise you that. But I can promise you if you won't let me strike buildings like this, that this air campaign is going to go on a long, long time."

And when you ask about the strategic center of gravity, what I'd like to explain to you is that you will always have a certain amount of political guidance that comes down from the top. Because the people at the top, they know Milosevic, they understand the history—or any other leader. And they understand the political dynamics, maybe better even than a Command and General Staff College graduate does. And so what this does, this sets up a very difficult dynamic of military leadership that will impact on you. It will take away from you your sense of responsibility. It will take away from you your sense of achievement. It will make you feel interfered with. And you'll be complaining about "Those people up there." You know how when you're a company commander the battalion staff is really screwed up? But when you're a battalion commander wait until you see how dumb the brigade staff is. And if you're the brigade commander you really have to work the division staff. It's even worse if you're on a corps-sized post, because I guarantee you the corps staff doesn't understand the first thing about training or about your unit. And just imagine what this is like in an Allied operation when you are actually using force, and people are telling you not only do they understand the post and the system, but they're not even giving you a mission you can have. They're telling you to do a, b, and c, but "Wait a minute, come back and talk to me on that." It's very confusing, it's very difficult, it's very demanding. But I think that's the command climate that you're going to be going out and working in. And so you have to understand about the centers of gravity and the strategic piece, that all of this is interconnected.

Politics and civil-military relations have always been part of the Army experience, and both were a frequent topic with guest speakers, both military and civilian. One of the more fascinating (and famous) to address these topics was President Harry S. Truman.

4. The Buck Stops at Fort Leavenworth: Harry S. Truman Addresses the Command and General Staff College

Benefiting from the proximity of his Presidential Library and home, the Command and General Staff College (CGSC) at Fort Leavenworth, Kansas, hosted Harry S. Truman at least three times in the early 1960s. On January 13, 1961, he addressed the Regular Course as part of their guest speaker program, followed that afternoon by remarks to the Fort Leavenworth Women's Club. On December 15th of that same year, Truman returned to deliver the address for the Associate's Course graduation. He appeared for the last time on the Bell Hall auditorium stage on February 15, 1964, presiding over another graduation ceremony, this time for Reserve Officers. Each time the folksy, sharp-witted former president never failed to please, especially when he departed from his prepared remarks.

GRADUATION ADDRESSES

At all three of his appearances, President Truman delivered a variation of the same address. Although the content of his speech was interesting, it was his off the cuff deviations that captivated the audience. He began by calling the presidency the most misunderstood constitutional office in the United States. He lamented that there were official records and publications covering the Congress and Supreme Court, but "there is no single publication that preserves the utterances and the acts of the presidency. And many of them can only be found *inadequately* in newspaper files. And in a lot of instances that inadequacy is purposely done. I know from experience."

Truman discussed the importance of preserving the personal papers of the president, and how those of past presidents had tragically been lost, destroyed, or scattered. "You know every paper a president touches, even if it's cussing out to a music critic, is an official document [interrupted by big laugh] and ought to be preserved." He went on to explain his library's founding in relation to his presidential papers. "I built a building down there in Independence, Missouri, and turned over between four and five million documents…and they all belong to you. They're public property… If you want to know something about me that's not printable, you come down and take a look. You'll find plenty!"

Truman then stated that being president is the most difficult job in the history of the world, and that it is more like holding six jobs at once. "You must bear one thing in mind: as a former President of the United States, my sympathies are with the man who has to hold down these jobs." First, Truman said, the president must ensure laws are faithfully executed. Second, he is the Commander in Chief. It was at this point when Truman normally took a not-so-thinly-veiled shot at General Douglas MacArthur, who Truman relieved during the Korean conflict:

> I don't know if you remember or not, if you read your history, President Lincoln had to fire four generals before he got one that worked. I only had to fire one, but that was one too many. It shouldn't have happened. I didn't get any pleasure out of it at all. I didn't appreciate that situation and never have and never will appreciate it, because there wasn't any necessity for it to happen. It was just a big-headed fool who thought he was better than the president and found out he wasn't.

The next three presidential responsibilities, according to Truman, are the foreign policy maker of the country, providing information on the State of the Union and approving laws, and acting as head of his political party which, Truman noted, is not outlined in the Constitution. Regarding this last duty, he offered a caution:

> [The president] must never forget that he is responsible to all the people in the nation, regardless of party, and he must always think of the welfare of the nation as a whole. The president and the vice president are the only officers elected from the United States at large, and as I've said time and again, the president is the only lobbyist in Washington who looks after the interests of 150 or 160 million people.

This led to a discussion about lobbying ("a perfectly legitimate function") and the president's relationship with Congress:

> Separate powers was [sic] NOT devised to promote efficiency in government. It was devised to prevent absolutism and dictatorship. So a certain degree of struggle between the president and Congress is a natural and a good thing. [It is] the duty of the president to see that the constitutional powers of the presidency are not infringed. Some elements in the Congress are always trying to legislate him out of office, and make themselves an English Legislative Government, which is not what the Constitution provides at all.

According to Truman, the final duty of the president is the social head of the nation. It is quite apparent that Truman didn't enjoy this job very much:

> A great many of the stuffed-shirt-social-life people in Washington like this very much. They think it's the finest thing in the world, to be able to meet Dukes and Princes and Kings and Queens and other dignitaries of foreign countries... The president gives five or six state dinners each year, and holds several large receptions. And if you think it's a lot of fun, to stand in line for two hours and a half and shake hands with 2,700 people whose names you can't even understand and whose names you don't give a damn about just try it sometime and see how you like it.

Truman continued his remarks with a discussion of the past presidents, in order, adding commentary to some:

> [John] Tyler's brother was the father of my great-grandmother. We never thought much of Tyler and didn't brag on him much, but uh, still we have to admit the connection...The greatest thing that [Theodore Roosevelt] did was when he split the Republican Party and caused the election of Woodrow Wilson...one of the greatest of our great presidents.

Truman stopped with himself, not mentioning President Eisenhower at all. Given the animosity he felt for Ike, he probably thought that any negative comments would not be well received by his Army audience. Following the presidential history lesson, Truman encouraged the audience to become curious about United States and world history, in order to "keep this republic the greatest in the world."

Truman fielded questions during all three of his CGSC appearances, even though this was not normally done during graduation ceremonies. The question and answer sessions during his visits were fascinating and humorous, as Truman was more enjoyable when he was off script. When asked to comment on the Peace Corps, Truman responded that the more nations know about each other the easier it will be to get along. He then added:

> This little snot down in Cuba is trying to make it appear that we're...[interrupted by laughter]. Trying to make it appear that we want to be aggressors. We could have kept Cuba as part of the United States, just as Puerto Rico is now if we wanted to do it. We wanted Cuba to free, and we still want Cuba to be free. That fellow's no good. I've always said if that fellow had a shave and a haircut and a new set of clothes he'd have a different outlook on life.

This was followed by a question concerning the advice he would give to President-elect Kennedy regarding the U.S. relationship with Cuba. Truman responded that Kennedy wouldn't want his advice, adding that "fellas on the sideline got no business trying to tell him what he ought to do." Ironically, the Bay of Pigs incident occurred three months after these remarks.

Inevitably, questions regarding the use of the atomic bomb came up. One student stated that some historians felt World War II was over before the bomb was dropped, and asked Truman why he decided to use the bomb. Clearly he had fielded this question before:

> There are a lot of Monday morning quarterbacks that know exactly what ought to have been done after the fact but don't know a damn thing about it before hand. The atomic bomb, at that time, was a weapon of war. That first bomb cost 2 billion, 600 million dollars to make. And the objective was to win the war. And that bomb was dropped in Japan when they absolutely refused to consider surrender. A few days after that bomb was dropped they surrendered...250,000 youngsters were saved on our side, 250,000 on the Jap side, and about a million were kept from being maimed for life. That bomb was a weapon of war, and if I had to do it again on the same circumstances I'd do it just like I did then.

This answer was followed by thunderous applause. When asked about his most difficult decision, Truman's answer probably surprised a few people in the audience: "Korea was the most difficult decision, because that involved the whole of the United Nations, and not only the United States. They're all bad enough, but that's the most difficult one that had to be made."

THE BACK STORY

Perhaps as interesting as Truman's appearances are the stories surrounding them. Following his presidency, Truman was inundated with invitations to attend functions and speak at "special" events. Those emanating from Fort Leavenworth included the dedication ceremony of Munson Army Hospital, the Officers' Wives club, the Protestant Men of the Chapel, and the National Sojourners to name a few. As he was a busy man, he almost always had to send his regrets to these numerous organizations.

Fortunately for CGSC, Truman was able to accept some of the invitations. It is almost certain that compensation was not a requirement for his appearances, as Truman was violently opposed to profiting from his association with the Presidency of the United States. He apparently wasn't above accepting unsolicited honoraria, however. Following his January 1961 visit, MG Harold K. Johnson, then the Commandant of the college, sent a letter and a $100 check, stating "Perhaps, as you said, 'Great presidents are followed by mediocre ones.' But fortunately, our country was spared that misfortune in 1945." He also received thank you letters from both the President and the Program Chairman of the Women's Club for his remarks that day, along with a "check as a small token of our esteem and respect for you."

Truman was invited to speak to the December 1963 Associate Course graduation, and accepted on September 30th stating, "If nothing unforeseen takes place, I will be with you." Sadly, he was forced to send another letter on November 27th cancelling his appearance due to the assassination of President Kennedy. This may have made him more eager to appear at the February 15, 1964 event since he hated not to keep his commitments.

The February event involved delivering an address to the graduates of a two-week long Reserve Officer Associate Course, which concluded five years of part-time study. According to the letter inviting him to speak, this was the "first time in the history of the staff college that a group of Reserve officers has been selected to conduct a course of instruction during the academic school year." Ordinarily it would be somewhat unusual for someone of Truman's stature to address graduates of a two-week long course. Truman appearance, however, is explained by the fact that he had risen to the rank of Colonel of Artillery in the Reserves, as he reminded the students during his January 1961 appearance:

> I was a Field Artillery Colonel in the Reserve when I became president, and when I was sworn in again in 1949, General [Omar] Bradley was Chief of Staff. And I suggested to him that I'd like to keep that Colonel's commission until I finished the job in the White House and he said "alright, that'll happen." [laughter from audience] So along in the spring in 1952, here came a nice engraved certificate: Colonel Harry S. Truman, Field Artillery, Reserve, is hereby transferred to the Inactive Reserve, by command of the President. I'd never seen it until it came to my desk. So I called General Bradley and read it to him. He spoke in good soldier lingo and said "For Chrissakes send that damn thing back down here. I don't know how it got there." I said "General, there's only one, and this is it. And if you get it back you're going to have to come take it away from me."

Regarding the February appearance, Major General Harry J. Lemley had invited the Trumans to come to Fort Leavenworth the night before to hear a concert on post by the Kansas City Philharmonic Orchestra. The president declined, and according to the itinerary Lemley picked Truman up at his library at 8:45 a.m. for the 10 o'clock ceremony. Following the ceremony, Truman was the honored guest at an Association of the United States Army luncheon held at the Officer's Club, at which he spoke briefly.

THE KOREA DECISION

The most interesting and little known part of Truman's visits to CGSC took place after his December 1961 graduation address. He had been working on a collection of television programs that would eventually become the series *Decision: The Conflicts of Harry S. Truman.* The producers of the series felt that Truman's actions during the Korean conflict would have to be included in the program. It was decided that Truman would meet with veterans of the Korean conflict and answer their questions, and all of it would be filmed for use in the series. Nineteen officers—fifteen Regular Course students and four faculty members—met with Truman following the

Associate Course graduation ceremony for introductions and as an ice breaker of sorts. Following lunch, the two hour filmed session began.

According to a proposed script for the event, the session would begin with Truman providing some opening remarks. The notes themselves are an interesting read, as the "script" was clearly offered as a suggestion: "The president may wish to say that as far as he knows never before in the history of the United States has a former Commander in Chief of the United States spoken to veterans in a war in which they both took part." The script suggested the president cover his service in the Army and his time as Commander in Chief during the end of World War II. The script went on to suggest that he highlight how World War II was an "old fashioned war" that began with an attack and ended with a surrender, likely the last time this would take place. Additionally it was felt he should cover some Korean history, his reaction to the first news of the invasion by North Korea, and related United Nations Security Council actions, among other recommendations.

It is unclear from the remaining recordings of this event whether any opening remarks actually took place. Based on some of the questions it seems clear that Truman didn't follow these recommendations. What is left, however, is a fascinating and fairly candid question and answer period that has been well-hidden from history. According to tapes compiled and edited by Merle Miller, a Truman biographer and someone involved in the television project at the very beginning, there were over fifty questions asked. This prompted Truman at one point to remark "You're full of questions, but go ahead. I want to give everybody a chance." With so many questions, numerous aspects of the conflict were covered, including the decision to commit troops in Korea, possible utilization of Chinese National troops, captured weapons analysis, and the role of the press. Some themes did emerge, however, although not necessarily in an organized fashion.

Public support and understanding of the Korean conflict was a recurring topic, beginning when an officer highlighted the appearance of doubt on the part of the American people, and asked the president if he felt they understood that it was absolutely necessary to go into Korea. Truman began his answer before the question was finished, stating

> They understood it at the time, and there was nobody against it. The again' didn't happen until the campaign came along a year or two afterwards. Nobody was against it, everybody was for it. I never heard of anybody being against it at all. Even Dewey was for it.

Later, Major Lewis L. Millet, who was awarded the Medal of Honor for actions in Korea, said that while en route to receive his medal, he had spoken to many civilians. They seemed "very disinterested and didn't care anything about what was happening over there," and Truman was asked if he felt that the public was psychologically prepared to support the Korean War. He responded "Well, of course it was. I never had any trouble with it at all. All that trouble came on account of that campaign that came after that, and nothing whatever to do with the reasons or the why it was necessary to save the Korean republic."

Along these same lines, Truman was later asked if he felt calling the Korean conflict a "police action" downgraded it in the minds of the American public. Again, he interrupted the question with an emphatic "No, I don't think so. I think those that would want to downgrade it would have downgraded it no matter what you called it." When asked to explain the difference between

133

a police force and an Army, he responded "Well if we are at war, a declared war, with any nation then the military are in control. And that's an Army of the United States. When we are in conjunction with the United Nations to prevent aggression, that is a police action to prevent the whole world from being involved in an atomic war." Truman was then asked if he thought police actions were an example of what would be faced in the future, he said "That was the intention, exactly."

Understandably, the students were keenly interested in Truman's thoughts regarding the readiness of the ground forces and the restrictions placed on the commanders in Korea. This theme began with a question regarding the extreme austerity of the U.S Forces in Japan. Truman's response was remarkable: "Because it was the opinion of all concerned that the war was over and we were going to have a peace and get things straightened out and mama and papa and all the kids were crying [in a mocking tone]'I want to go home'..we had to bring them back home, that's all there was to it. They still do that." A similar question addressed the age and dearth of equipment available to forces in Korea. Truman replied (sounding much like Secretary of Defense Donald Rumsfeld in 2004) "We had to use what we had. That's all we had." When asked about funding limitation for Korea, Truman continued: "A great many of the appropriations I asked for were turned down, or they came too late to be of any use."

The most dramatic line of questioning involved the support given to the effort and the restrictions placed on the command in the Korean theater. Sometimes these questions seemed to irk the president. It began when he was asked if he had given any guidance to General Matthew Ridgway before he took over 8th Army. Truman replied "Well of course. I told him he was Commander in Chief, go ahead and win the war the best way he could, just like I did to every other field commander. He had completely [sic] freedom of action." "Complete freedom?" Truman was asked. "Except that he was not to cross the Yalu river if he ever got there. That's all there was to it."

At this point an officer relayed that his division had been ordered to stop at the 38th Parallel around October 1, 1950, "while the United Nations made certain deliberations as to whether or not the UN would be authorized to go in to North Korea." This delay allowed North Korea to fortify its position in front of the U.S. division, causing heavy casualties once it was authorized to continue. The officer asked why the necessary authority to cross the 38th Parallel hadn't been foreseen to prevent something like this. This seemed to put the president on the defensive:

> Well now you'll have to ask the commanding general in the field, I wasn't there. I gave them freedom of action and the man in the field is the man who does the commanding. Makes up his mind what tactics and strategy should be. The president can't make tactics and strategy in the White House because he's not there. If I'd have been on the ground I could have told you exactly what to do if I'd been there, but I wasn't. Wasn't because I didn't want to be…I was not the commanding general in the field and that's his business. He had all the support he could get from the president.

Another officer followed up: "In other words there was no restriction at all?" Interrupting and raising his voice a little, Truman stated: "I said he had all the support he could get from the President of the United States, and that was up to him, if he had some good reason for it, I'm sure. The best way to find out is to ask him, if he's still alive."

A bit later, an officer asked "Back to your previous comment about the commander in the field. Am I to understand Sir, that you gave the commander in the field the authority to marshall all available resources to defeat the enemy?" Truman's answers on this subject were getting shorter. "Yeah, of course. He always has that, and if he doesn't he's handicapped. But, he had one restriction. And that was he was not to go far enough north to bring on a third world war. That's what we were trying to avoid. We didn't want an atomic war. Nobody wants it."

The drilling continued: "Well in that same vein, Mr. President, when the Chinese planes would take off from beyond the Yalu, and bomb the American forces and our planes in pursuit had to stop at the Yalu river, this was a restriction imposed by the president, is that right?" Truman answered "Yes. That's correct. That's absolutely correct." Then, feeling perhaps he had been a bit rough, followed up with an encouragement for more questions: "Come 'on boys, don't be backwards."

Nearly all of this question and answer period ended up on the cutting room floor. Fragments of seven of the president's responses ended up in the *Police Action* segments of the *Decision* program, and most of those were altered and re-recorded. The reason for this is summed up in a draft page of the Preface of Miller's *Plain Speaking: An Oral Biography of Harry S. Truman.*

> ...one dark winter morning in 1961 [Truman] drove alone from Independence to the Army Staff and General Command School [sic] in Fort Leavenworth, Kansas, where he discussed [the Korean] decision with a group of young Army officers, all of whom were veterans of the Korean fighting. Several of the questions annoyed him, and he said so, sometimes unkindly; we had to photograph the seminar several times. It was not a happy morning.

The program's producer, Robert Aurthur, was less subtle in his assessment, writing that Truman's performance was "terrible." The president was extremely impatient with the delays of lighting and camera preparation, and "wandered from the room two or three times, disappearing into the office of an eager major general." More than likely he was referring to Lemley. According to Aurthur, at one point one of Truman's advisors said "We'd better get going. They've cracked open a bottle of bourbon in there." Once the filming began, Aurthur wrote, "[Truman's] answers to the questions reflected his irritation and wrath; he was abrupt, even rude, and worst of all, some of his facts were obviously wrong."

Perhaps it is understandable that after this experience, Truman didn't return to the college for two years. Three months after the final February 1964 visit, he turned eighty. Later that year he tripped going into a bathroom in his residence, cracked his head on the sink and fractured two ribs. There is no record of any further CGSC speaking invitations, although the Officers' Wives continued to invite him to their luncheons, and in 1968 he received an informal open invitation from MG Michael Davison to visit the post any time. Truman died December 26, 1972.

On three occasions in the 1960s, students at the Army's Command and General Staff College were treated to something truly special: a living legend who was also a fantastic public speaker. Fortunately these appearances by President Truman were recorded and will forever remain available to future generations of students at CGSC, and to students of history as well. The fact that the college played a small role in the legend that was Truman's life makes these appearances a unique piece of Fort Leavenworth history.

5. Photos

There are not many photos of guest speaker visits to CGSC. Below is a small sample of photos and cartoons related to these visits. Most, including those from the CGSC Yearbook (The Bell) appear courtesy of the Combined Armed Research Library archives at Fort Leavenworth. If a photo isn't from this source, its origin is indicated.

This undated photo of Anthony McAuliffe is presumably from his 1952 visit to CGSC
(Leavenworth Public Library Collection, Leavenworth, KS)

Bell Hall was the home of CGSC, and the Eisenhower Auditorium ("The Blue Bedroom"), from 1959 to 2007

Students assemble in Bell Hall's Eisenhower Auditorium in 1983

President Harry Truman greets an international officer during his January 1961 visit

Joseph M. Heiser, Jr (1969)

Harold K. Johnson (1969)

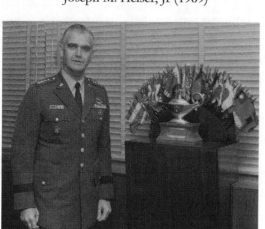

William Westmoreland (1971)

Creighton Abrams (1973)

Secretary of the Army Howard Callaway arrives at Sherman Army Airfield during one of his visits (Leavenworth Public Library Collection, Leavenworth, KS)

William DePuy speaks at the 1974 CGSC Graduation (Leavenworth Public Library Collection, Leavenworth, KS)

Gordon Sullivan (1992)

Dennis Reimer (1997)

Students were not above poking fun at the guest speaker program in the yearbook:

(1968)

(1972)

(1972)

(1986)

6. Civil-Military Relations

A common thread running through the speakers' presentations was that of civil-military relations. A majority of the speakers took time to remind students about the concept of civilian control, the president as Commander in Chief, and the meaning of their oaths. Additionally, the thorny topics of candor and dissent were addressed, made all the more interesting considering the careers of the speakers who discussed this topic. Coverage of civil-military relations was rounded out with discussions regarding Congress, the military's credibility, especially in the post-Vietnam era, and its relationship with both American society and the press.

CIVILIAN CONTROL

Harold K. Johnson frequently spoke of civilian control of the military, and always as an absolute. Knowing what he went through during his tenure as Chief of Staff, it makes for remarkable reading. In May 1966, he made sure the students understood their chain of command.

> We work for the Commander in Chief. The Commander in Chief has said [Vietnam] is where we belong. Here we are, here we stay until the Commander in Chief says "Come home." Very simple. Very simple. Now we have a voice as citizens in what goes on in this country, but on the other hand our voice is somewhat restrained simply because of the obligation that we have when we put on the uniform and because of a liability of sorts that is unlimited when you put on the uniform. And this liability is to go where you're told, and you do what you're told, and you place your life on the line. Sobering. Sobering. But that's why the profession of arms is an honorable profession.

That December he had a similar message for the graduates of the Associates Course.

> …Your first obligation is to your oath: To uphold and defend the Constitution of the United States of America against all enemies, foreign and domestic. And you take this obligation freely, without purpose of evasion. No fingers crossed, you're going to select what you do and select what you don't do. You do what you are told to do. I might add that when people ask what we're doing in Vietnam, I don't worry about that, because I work for the President of the United States. And he says "You get some folks in Vietnam" and I said "Yes, Sir." Very simple for us, you see, when we look at it that way. [Scattered laughter] It's well to understand the broader purpose, but don't ever forget that when somebody yells "Froggy!" we have to start to jump. This is just inherent in what we do. And that's where your oath comes in. To do, fundamentally, what you're required to do.

In 1967, Omar Bradley was asked about problems with civilian control under the present-day organization of the Joint Chiefs and the Department of Defense.

> I'm glad I'm not there. [Laughter and applause] I don't know what the final result will be, but I know that a lot of senior leaders, both on active duty and retired, are concerned. I don't know if you saw the article in the recent Army, Navy journal where the number of high ranking civilians—or civilians I should say—in the defense department increased from, if I remember the figures correct, it's something like 1,500 to 57,000 in the last six years. That is bound to infringe somewhat on the military leadership. I don't know how it would work out in a serious war. 'Cause after all, experience does count, even if it does come from bad judgment. But it is something we can help on. It's our life, it's been our

lifetime study, and I just hope that the situation never comes to the point where our experience, our developed leadership, our integrity, our love of country, is forgotten. [Applause]

General Westmoreland also frequently reminded the officers of the concept of civilian control of the military as he did on June 4, 1970, when speaking to Fort Leavenworth's junior officers.

> The Army has undergone during the last five years a very difficult time in its history, primarily because of our commitment in the Vietnam War. You know well that the Army does not make policy. We do not decide when and where military forces will be committed. This is made by political authority, because in accordance with our Constitution the Army and the military services are firmly under the control of civilian authority, and no professional military man would want it any other way. Our job is to try to carry out national policy which has been formulated by our civilian leadership, a leadership elected by the people. And when an officer raises his hand to take the oath, he swears allegiance to support the Constitution of the United States. He also swears to support and carry out the orders of the Commander in Chief and those appointed in authority above him or her. This is the way an officer must look at his role. He has a role to play, the role is very carefully proscribed by the Constitution, and this is of course implemented by the oath of office that he takes.

Westmoreland spoke about this oath at the CGSC graduation ceremony the following day.

> This oath is unique. Its charge is not for the defense of any man, nor the support of any partisan cause. Our solemn oath is the affirmation for the defense of the cornerstone of our government, the Constitution of the United States. Implicit in the oath is loyal response to our Commander in Chief, the President of the United States. As a group our armed forces have never swerved from honoring this oath. Loyal dedication to civilian leadership as set forth in our Constitution has been and continues to be our obligation. Nowhere has the Army better demonstrated adherence to this loyalty embodied in our oath than in Vietnam. There, halfway around the world, the Army with the other services, have supported selflessly and diligently our national commitment to guarantee the South Vietnamese the right to choose their own way of life free from communist intimidation.

In 1973 Max Taylor was asked about the principle of civilian control, and whether the current organization of the Department of Defense was beneficial to the defense of the nation.

> I haven't been in the Pentagon [recently], you see, and you really have to be on the spot. You can't just sit on the outside of the wall and know how the relation works. What you have said against it now had been said against it when I was active in the Pentagon. I never felt oppressed by the civilian leadership. I always had a very good relationship with the people at the top, I'm talking about when I was Chairman of the Joint Chiefs or the [Army] Chief of Staff. And there the relationship must be good; if it's not good it should be broken up at once. A Chief that kept that kind of reaction and feeling of [not] being on the same team as the Secretary of Defense, he'd better leave. Or the Secretary of Defense ought to ask him to leave. In my time generally speaking that's been a pretty good relationship. It's when you get in the bowels of the Pentagon and these endless

civilians who come and go, many with the best of intents, just not knowing what the game is all about.

One of the most frightening things as you get old is to stand back and see a new administration come to Washington. Very able men full of beans coming in there and taking over the most powerful machine in the world—the United States Government, and not knowing where to put in the gas, where to turn the throttle, how to make it whistle even. And that goes on for about a year. A terrible time. And meanwhile these young men are doing things we military people think is practically treason because they don't worry about security. We were going to the White House for the first time in the Kennedy administration, and a civilian I knew slides his head out and wants to talk about Southeast Asia. And I talk to him and as I started to leave he said "Would you like some papers on this?" and he had about two or three Top Secret documents and passed them to me "Take them along." It never occurred to him that that was not the way to pass on information. And that's pitiful, that's really too bad, because these fellows ought to be trained.

General Edward "Shy" Meyer revealed a different side of civilian control to the students in 1979.

Now let me…address the need for a draft. I believe that the role and responsibility of the military is to state clearly what the requirements are. To indicate what the needs are of our country to have an Army, Navy, Air Force and Marine Corps that's capable of going to war. We have to articulate that, based on what we are told to do by the President through the Secretary of Defense. We're essentially told that we have to be ready to be able to go to war in Central Europe as first priority; we have to have a capability also at the same time, simultaneously, to be able to go to war, Middle East, Persian Gulf, Northeast Asia, or somewhere else. Those are the kinds of priorities that we're given based on whatever the needs are…So those are the kinds of things that we're called upon to do, and we need to define what the manpower requirements are to do that. We also have a responsibility toward the administration and toward Congress to articulate how closely we are able to meet those requirements, alright? In the case of the National Guard, the combined National Guard and [U.S. Army Reserve (USAR)] we're about 130,000 short. We're short in the National Guard, we're short in the Reserves today. We're short in the Individual Ready Reserves, which are the replacements. We're going to have the trained end strength shortfall that I told you about in the Active component. Alright? Those are the parameters of where we are now.

I object personally to those in Congress or to those in other high places who are trying to use the military as the belled goat or sheep, whichever one of your historical reference that you want to use, is being used to lead the country toward a draft. The decision on the draft is a national issue. It's an issue that has to have a national support and national consensus, and there are two ways that you can have an adequate National Guard. One is to go through some sort of a draft, and the other is to provide sufficient incentives and opportunities so that people will, in fact, join the National Guard, if the nation wants to do that. I'd just tell you, I personally object to being used by folks who want the Army, or the Navy, or the Air Force to be the ones that say the only solution to the problem is a draft. I object to that, because the draft, in my opinion, is a national decision that has to be taken. What I am ready to do at the drop of a hat is to say what we can do with the programs that are proposed, to indicate whether they fall short of what's needed, to indicate that without draft, without registration, what we are and are not able to do as far as being able to go to war. And I think that's the proper mode and the proper role for the military in what is a national debate. I think it's improper for us to be forced into the role of being out in front leading a decision in one way in what I believe is truly a national issue. I'm entitled to have personal views on that, but I have to say that I don't believe in the role as Chief of Staff that I should be the one that's forced to be speaking out for what is truly a national issue, as a sole solution. Because I can show you all kinds of ways, if our country wants to pay for it, that there are ways we can fill up even the Minnesota National Guard. [Laughter] So that's possible. If you gave free fishing rights I think you might be able to do that.

General Vuono had a different issue with the National Guard in 1986, as he explained to students the ramifications of a decision made by state governors that forbid their [National] Guard units from performing their annual training outside of their state without approval.

…That governors' proclamation was very, very disturbing to us. And it should be not only to us in uniform but it should be to the nation as a whole. I think it was a step in the wrong direction. There were several governors who you all know were opposed to putting any forces at all into [U.S. Southern Command] on those exercises. A couple of governors went down and were persuaded by virtue of what they saw there, it was great training for those Guard elements. There were some, very knowledgeable and very well-meaning, who felt that there was a fundamental mistake to allow us to do that. Not that they themselves had any hang up, but because it was a fundamental mistake from the standpoint of their state and so forth, and that's why they went for it. I personally believe that it was not right for that to have been signed.

CANDOR, DISSENT, AND LOYALTY

Along the theme of civilian control of the military, many speakers broached the topics of candor, dissent, and loyalty. Again, the most fascinating remarks are delivered by Harold K. Johnson, beginning in November, 1961, when he was the CGSC Commandant.

About three weeks ago we had an article come in for the Military Review. This was written by a civilian. He'd had two years of service—I think in [the Army Security Agency (ASA)]...I'll recognize ASA as existing...[Laugh] And he was talking about officers in politics. And he was making the point that if the trend of officers discussing political conditions is permitted to continue, that there comes a time when a particular zealot is convinced that he must be supercritical, go overboard, and be undermining or undercutting the people whose responsibility it is to determine or chart the course of our national policy. Therefore it's better for the officer corps as a whole to stay out of politics and keep their mouths shut. Well, this was a very good article and we were about to buy it for the military review, and I read it over one afternoon and I thought 'Nothing wrong with this.' But I'm a procrastinator, to a greater extent than most of us, probably, so I flipped it over on the left side of my desk, and I picked it up in the morning and I had some time and I spent about an hour reading it. And then the more I read it the madder I got. So I sat down and wrote a nice long letter to this fella, because, I said, loyalty is a two-way street. We can be loyal to the policies, but when we're upholding the policies the loyalty also has to come back. And I raised the question: Why did one Chief of Staff of the Army [get] put out to grass or pasture, not with full honors, and suddenly he is recalled, and is a foremost military advisor? This is General [Maxwell] Taylor. No reason for not naming names. Why and who is undercutting General [George] Decker? What are the reasons for the repeated attacks on him? What's the basis for it? Who's defending them?

During this same appearance, Johnson was asked "The feeling is prevalent that the way to succeed is a middle of the road approach, not rocking the boat. Many of our higher-ranking officers have attained high positions through this approach. Would you care to comment on this?"

As you grow a little bit older you begin to see that to get from point A to point B there are usually an infinite number of ways to get from point A to point B. Sometimes there is a tendency to be critical of our superiors because they choose route one instead of route ten, and we neglect to look at the fact that in the end, they get to point B, which is after all the important consideration. It doesn't really make any difference how you get there. To answer your question directly, you build up resistance in a great many cases by lashing back before you take a look at "Is your objective attained?" I think you come back to thing we try to teach here, "Remember the mission…what are you trying to do?" I would say that middle-of-the-roading is not characteristic of our people. I think that the times have changed so that the people—General [Matthew] Ridgway is the first example, General Taylor is the second, of Chiefs Of Staff who were ostensibly fighting the system who were put to pasture.

If the same environment or climate of opinion existed in 1961 that existed in 1953, General Decker might be in the same position because he is pursuing substantially the same line that General Ridgway did, and that General Taylor did, and that General [Lyman] Lemnitzer did. The environment has shifted; the line hasn't shifted too much. So that you can come up with a conclusion like you had if you don't stand away from the problem, but you've got to stand pretty well away from the problem. And I would say this: You must stand for your convictions. You must stand for them. I have a philosophy that has worked well for me, but you're not yet in a position where you can afford it. I say this to myself: I've gotten further that I ever expected to be, and I'm further than I ever deserve to be, and anytime they want to fire me, they can. I'm here to get a job done. I go lashing back, but lots of times I'm overruled on something. I don't fight it, I see what they want, and this is what I do. Sometimes I wonder whether I'm right or whether I'm wrong.

It was obvious Johnson spent some time mulling this answer over, because the following April when he once again stood before this class he elaborated on his earlier remarks.

A [Student from his November 1961 Lecture] was raising the question "Did I think that our senior officers sometimes took the course of expediency as opposed to a right course when it appeared there might be an exceptional criticism raised?" And my answer to that question, I think, was not what I had intended to put across, because I believe that I answered the question somewhat along the line that there are many different ways of getting a job done. And I left an impression in reviewing my answer on the tape of supporting expediency to a degree. This is the furthest from my own concept of the responsibilities of senior commanders. A problem never goes away by ignoring it. You've got to stand up to them, you've got to face up to them. And if your first attack doesn't succeed, then you've got to fall back, regroup, and plan another method of attack. Now frequently during this regrouping phase you may double the basic load of ammunition, if you can discover some more ammunition somewhere. And that is what we have started to do with the study [Visualization of the Nuclear Battlefield] I am going to present.

In January 1963, Johnson had a slightly different take on candor.

Caution: We are here in soldier suits. We are here to do the bidding of the government. Our job is to do the bidding of the duly elected governments, whether they're our own, or you represent another government. Our job is not—and I repeat—not to quarrel with what our government tells us to do. There's this old dodge "Ours not to reason why, ours but to do or die." And this is very true, as far as people in uniform are concerned.

When Johnson was Chief of Staff, one of his mentors was Omar Bradley, who discussed candor and resignation in 1966 in answer to some controversial testimony he had given regarding income taxes and the defense budget while in uniform. Bradley's comments below are interesting because General Johnson sought Bradley's counsel regarding resignation during Johnson's difficulties with President Johnson and his administration.

Of course, I shouldn't have said that. I don't know what led me on to say it. Of course at that time, I think that was probably when Secretary [Louis] Johnson was Secretary of Defense. He was trying to be very economical, he'd cut our budget down a lot. And I've had people ask me why I didn't resign in protest. Well, I don't believe in resignations in protest because you lose your value. I figured I could get more out of Secretary Johnson by staying on there than having a new man come in. As a matter of fact, he had agreed to increase the budget the next year, much of it due to my keeping after him, I think, until of course he was relieved. But I should not have gotten into that subject because we [found out] now income tax can go pretty darn high. [Laughter] Normally I think that an officer should be free to express his opinion and be objective in his remarks. The minute we lose that image of being frank and being free to be frank, we have injured our usefulness. One time I was approached about running for the Senate. I said unh-uh...I don't want to get mixed up in any politics. But the big point is I just don't believe military people ought to get mixed up in politics. There are always exceptions—that's what trues the rule of course. And there are special reasons for it. I never criticized General [Dwight] Eisenhower for getting into politics, but in general we should not get mixed up in politics. Because the minute that becomes general in our actions we will lose a lot of our effectiveness in going before committees. When we go up there they should look upon us as being absolutely objective, saying what we think.

I know there [are] certain restrictions sometimes, but I think we must do that. I got pretty harsh one time in a hearing when the Navy kicked over the traces about the B-36 [bomber]. The hearing went on and on, and I finally made up my statement—a pretty tough one—and went up and gave it and that ended the hearings. About three months later I was over in Tokyo and rode in from the airport with General MacArthur, and he said "Bradley, I want to compliment you on your action before that B-36 problem." He said "I followed it very closely from here, and it got down to the point where either you or the Secretary had to really take the Navy to task and end it, and I was glad you did it." And I said "General MacArthur, here you are 7,000 miles away, and you are the only one that I've heard analyze the problem as I had at that time. I prepared my statement, I told the Secretary that I would not show him the statement, but that if after I made it I had outlived my usefulness I needed a vacation anyway." (Laughter) And here's MacArthur 7,000 miles away, the only one that ever realized why I had to make that kind of a statement. There are times when you have to be pretty dog-gone frank if you are going to uphold the prestige of the services, and if you're relieved afterwards, why, you probably need a vacation.

Johnson, now Chief of Staff, covered the subject of congressional testimony in December 1967.

You have a sort of pendulum swinging all the time with regard to the argument concerning civilian control of the military, as an example. There really is not now, and never has been any question of civilian control of the military. Oh, you might find isolated cases in our history, 150 years ago, one or two, a very tiny body of men who were pushing against the restraint. The curious thing is that the argument is not between the civilian and the military, the argument is really between or among civilians as to whether or not the executive or the legislative will control the military. All of the things that you've seen written here in the past several months, particularly as they relate to [Secretary of Defense Robert] McNamara's departure, as an example, talking about the resistance or the moves by the military to upset the military control, none of this has come from the military, curiously, when you look at the source. I get asked every once in a while by the people that I talk to as to whether or not there is any question among military people as to the necessity of the continuation of this subordination to civilian control. My response to it is "Where do the charges come from? Where do the so-called indications come from?" They come basically from the release of testimony of military people before congressional committees, and the testimony is shaped somewhat, that part of it that is released, to make a particular point.

Now how is this testimony developed or derived? In response to questions. "Are you suggesting," I ask the question, "that you want the military person to lie, or to shade the truth in response to question?" "Oh, no." Well obviously not. Obviously you can't do that, and the military man, in this relationship, has a very thin line to walk, and it's one that each of you must remember, because many of you will be preparing back up sheets next year for congressional appearances, or you'll be providing inputs from somewhere for this sort of activity. Or fact sheets directly to congressional committees in response to questions that are raised by the staffs over there. And the military man must recognize that he really is the ham in the sandwich. Slice on one side, the executive. He is a part of the executive and is responsible to the executive. Slice on the other side the legislative. Under the Constitution, [Section] 8, the legislative has the responsibility for raising and supporting armies, and they are entitled to forthright answers from the military witnesses that appear before them. So you just have to take a little bit of pressure and hope that not too much cheese gets mixed up with the ham, I guess. [Laughter] But I have dwelled at that length on that topic because a) it tends to be at the forefront these days, and b) it is illustrative of what I am talking about when I say the purpose of armed force is to operate within the law. Not a part of the law, all the law. And it's important that we remember there is no case where we find ourselves above and beyond the law.

In 1971, Defense Secretary Melvin Laird requested the students' candor, saying:

> We have had difficult times before, as we've faced challenges in the field of national security. And I believe that with your help, and with the understanding and cooperation of all Americans by carrying on a better program as far as communications by being frank and honest in our discussions of the threat we face, we will be successful, and we will be able to adequately protect our people and ensure a generation of peace. That's what our job is all about. To work towards peace. To ensure peace. We truly are the Department of Peace as far as our nation is concerned.

During his visit in 1973, a faculty member asked Max Taylor if he had reconsidered some of the Joint Chiefs of Staff reforms he had outlined in his book *A Time for Trumpets*.

> Times have changed. In all seriousness, when I was—to my great surprise and everyone else's—called back from retirement and became Chairman of the Joint Chiefs believe me the Senators hadn't forgotten that: "When are you going to get that horse of yours out and start firing all your colleagues on the Joint Chiefs of Staff?" Well I promised at the time that I was not a crusader committed to past concepts. I was willing to look the situation over as it was in 1962, which was quite different than in 1959. And I did find it quite different, and the difference being two. First there had been some changes in the civilian high command. We had a new Secretary of [Defense], Robert McNamara. Whatever these others want to think about Secretary McNamara he was one of the greatest administrators I've ever met—a man of great character. He made a lot of mistakes, but his home runs were a lot more frequent than his fumbles. Furthermore, within the Chiefs themselves, they had worked out a committee system, the evils of it could be circumvented to some extent, the Chairman really was allowed to issue orders, and even the Secretary, by simply informing of issues when they were simply carrying out decisions in which all had participated, and getting away from the idea that a committee really moved a battleship or decided on what deployment to make for the Army overseas. So a good bit of the committee handicap in view of operational matters had been done away with and it's even better now. So I would say that just by evolution the chairman has taken on a good part of the functions which I would have given to this guy as I perceived of this in 1959. But bear in mind I didn't want to abolish the Joint Chiefs of Staff as an advisory body. They stayed as a board, the equivalent of the Joint Chiefs, to give advice in the field of strategy and so on, which should be and usually is a major part of the responsibility of the Joint Chiefs.

Taylor had more to say about McNamara in a post-lecture discussion with selected students.

> The president has endless advisors on many, many subjects. And military advice, he may get it from his barber if he wants to. Maybe he does, I don't know. The Joint Chiefs used to get mad when I was Chairman, at McNamara. Quite a fellow. I was very fond of Bob McNamara although he had many qualities which disturbed the Chiefs. They would say "Look, these whiz kids down the hall with their computers, look at this paper they turned in to the Secretary of Defense." And surely, right in the middle of the issue was

purely one of military strategy and they had an answer and so on. And I said "Well, what about it, is it a good answer?" And they said "No, it's not worth anything." "Well, do you think Bob McNamara is a fella who's going to take a recommendation that isn't worth anything?" Well, no, they would concede that he wouldn't be. "Well then, what are you mad about?" Then I would give this speech: "Look, the Secretary of Defense has not only the right but the duty to get advice on important matters from any source that may contribute to solving his problem." And I would say "He might get it from his barber, his bartender for that matter. He can get it from his whiz kids, he gets it from us, he has to because by law he has to get our advice. Now if our advice doesn't appeal to the logical mind of the Secretary of Defense as well as that of his bartender, his bartender ought to win in the argument. Now let's—boys we've got to get on our horses and be sure our logic is better than the competitor. If it's not we ought to lose."

During this same exchange, Taylor was asked what the students could do to strengthen national character.

As long as we are in uniform our freedom of action is restricted, that's one of the prices you pay to be an active officer. When you get retired then you can indulge in these other things but I would tell you right now the compensations from the freedom of retirement aren't nearly the pleasure you get out of wearing the straight-jacket of the uniform of the Army. The easy answer and maybe the only answer is we can influence the situation by our example. If indeed we are this excellent force I have been talking about. If our officers are obviously men who are leaders and men of character, if we don't have any more of these scandals, [U.S. Army Provost Marshall Major General Carl Turner] and Lieutenant [William] Calley and people of that such, that's an area in which we can act effectively, even though not consciously, and brilliantly in a short period of time. So really that's about as good an answer as I can give you. Meanwhile, don't hesitate to speak up when you have a chance to speak your mind, especially with civilians. Don't avoid speaking in public, going out and accepting invitations, especially when it is consistent with your duties. We've been rather shy and rather inclined to run away from the press. Don't run away from them, you have to get to know the press. You have to get to know their good things and their bad things. The average Army officer I grew up with was always afraid to speak up to the press, and to speak frankly. Yet I've found—I believe in the equal distribution theory, namely in a thousand men of any profession of any race you get the same percentage of sons-of-bitches. And that applies to the press. So if you take that point of view you can put aside any inhibitions to talk about those things you really know about. Don't talk about things you don't know about. Sometimes we're guilty of that too.

Another Chairman of the Joint Chiefs, General Hugh Shelton, talked about his relationship with the Service Chiefs and the President in 1999.

As you know in [the Goldwater-Nichols Act], which passed in 1986, the role of the Chairman was changed into that of principal advisor to the Secretary of Defense and to the President. Now that doesn't mean that I'm the only advisor. The other members of the Joint Chiefs are advisors also, but it's normally me that goes over and makes a recommendation, and I do not have to have their concurrence to give my recommendation as we did prior to Goldwater Nichols. But I would tell you that I value their comments and their judgments, and we normally discuss these items that are of utmost importance to our nation, to our armed forces, in the "tank," the conference room that we call the "tank," before I go over and make a recommendation to the president or make a recommendation to the Secretary. Most of the time it's a unanimous decision, and if it's not unanimous, I will tell the president, you know, "Five out of the six members strongly support this, one individual has reservations about such and such." But that's the way that I give the advice. I think that it is best when it is done in private. Once I go over and make my recommendation to the president, he makes a decision, I don't comment one way or the other in public or in front of the Congress or anything else. My recommendations to him are private. Now you can argue, say whether or not you think that's appropriate or not, I happen to think that in a town where it's too often that people are looking for publicity, it's too often that people are trying to get publicity for themselves, a lot of egos get involved, that you can gain more trust, more confidence, and carry more weight when they know that what you're going to present is not going to be spread all over the Washington Post the next morning, and so that's the way that I operate.

That same year General Wesley Clark gave the students some advice about candor and loyalty.

You say "This is what we need," and you put it in writing, and you live with the consequences. Because that's what being a professional military officer is all about. You're not in this for yourself. You're in it, put in the position, you have to serve in that position to the best of your abilities, you have to discharge the duties that are assigned to you in accordance with your own best judgment. And if you're given orders that are illegal or immoral you don't obey them. If you're given orders you don't like, well you can either execute them or get out of the chain of command. But when you're giving the orders, when you're giving the political advice, then it's not nearly so clear-cut and so simple. But ultimately you have to do what's right. And then you take the consequences. And that's what it is. Now it's a lot better to take the consequences when you're a four-star than when you are a major. So be careful what battles you want to fight. Because when you get into battles like this, you may not win every battle.

In 2001, Senator Pat Roberts implored the students to use candor.

I'm going to ask you something right off the bat. And this is the one thing that, whenever I have the privilege of addressing people like yourself in Washington, at the War College, or wherever, I ask them for their candor. That raises a few eyebrows. And I know that we all take a look at the chain of command dictates that our military must live by—I know that, nobody quarrels with that, nobody wants to change that. But to demonstrate what I mean let me give you two examples. It was about three years ago. All of us who serve on the [Armed Services Committee] who take time to go to bases all over America and talk with people like yourself: Enlisted, NCOs, field grade, and company grade, and the [commanding generals]. And everywhere we went, I don't care what base it was, within [the Continental United States (CONUS)] or in regards to overseas, it seemed to us that we were getting the stories about the stress and the strain and the hollowness, wearing out the troops, wearing out all of our materiel. And yet when we had the Joint Chiefs before the Senate Armed Services Committee they were testifying "steady as she goes" in regards to the military budget, the Defense Appropriation Bill and the Authorization Bill.

I can remember that this Senator [gesturing to himself] asked all of the members of the Joint Chiefs, "With the current budget the way that it is and how you see things out in the field, more especially on behalf of the warfighter, are we making ends meet? Can you perform your mission?" And almost to a person with the exception of one, why they indicated "Yes we think we can do this." This was in [February, 1998]. This is right during the appropriations process—right about now. With the exception of one. And that was our Commandant of the Marine Corps at the time, Charles Krulak. Now I asked the Commandant, I said "General, can the Marine Corps perform its mission with the same amount of funding that's in the budget?" And that's a pretty tough question. And it's a pretty tough question for any member of the Joint Chiefs to answer. And General Krulak said "No, Sir, we can do it better. You ask the Marine Corps to perform its mission we will put cold steel on the enemy anytime, anyplace, anywhere and we will be victorious. But we do not have enough money in the budget to perform the mission as I interpret it to be." I think the White House had Chuck Krulak's number on speed dial, but he didn't much care—well, he cared, but I mean the one thing he cared about were his Marines. Then along about [September, 1998] we had another meeting and all of a sudden all members of the Joint Chiefs and the Chairman of the Joint Chiefs, with all due respect, came in and said "We can't do this."

…And my question was if we were so damn smart in the Spring, why were we a lot smarter in the Fall? And so the Senate Armed Services Committee, with the help of the bipartisan members and the House, set about trying to appropriate more money in regards to what we think your obligations amount to. And we went through the pay raise and we went through the health care, retirement fix and all of that. But we still have a lot to do. it just seemed to me that if we had a little candor right off the top, if in fact the Joint Chiefs—I'm not trying to pick on anybody, or the political circumstances that were coming down on top of the Department of Defense or the White House or the budgeteers or whatever—if, in fact, that that opinion or those decisions had reflected what we were learning in the field we would be in one hell of a lot better shape.

My whole suggestion to you is, and I know that, where especially after the election in Florida and more especially after what happened to us in the military that you may have a little feeling about expressing your personal views to a member of Congress, or a Senator, or State Legislator or whatever. Get to know them. Sit down with them. We have fewer and fewer members of the Congress who ever served in the military. I'm the only member of the Kansas delegation ever serving in the Military and having the privilege to serve in the Congress. That doesn't mean the rest of the delegation's not interested. They are, big time. Have your interests at heart. But we need your candid advice and we need your honest assessment. No, don't go out of the chain of command, I understand that. But damn it! If we're going to make changes, and we could have made changes a lot quicker, part of that depended on the candor that we got from the troops in the field.

RELATIONSHIP WITH CONGRESS

The military's relationship with Congress that Senator Roberts referred to has been an uneven one throughout the years, and was a frequent subject with the guest speakers. In 1952, Lieutenant General Anthony McAuliffe described a part of the relationship in answer to a student's question regarding legislation that had a negative impact on the military: "This so-called "spite" legislation, do you consider it a violation of contract under which many of us came in the service? And second, as a particular result of this legislation, have you noticed an appreciable increase in resignations in any one of the ranks?"

> Well you're putting me right on the spot. One of the Articles of War says you don't criticize the Congress, and I haven't so far. [Audience chuckles] I use "spite" legislation in terms of I was quoting the Army, Navy, Air Force Journal. [Big laugh and applause] I don't see any evidences of resignations. The Army, Navy [Air Force] journal, however, did carry an article on the 17th of May which was picked up by Mr. Mark Watson of the Baltimore Sun and Mr. Hanson Ball of the New York Times, in which they enumerated about a dozen things that made a Regular Army career to a young man less attractive now than it [was] four or five years ago. And that was where I picked up this comment about "spite" legislation, which includes such things as the Davis Amendment and the Van Zandt amendment and the baggage reduction in the household baggage allowance. And they talked about the restrictions imposed on the post exchanges and commissaries and so on. So while we see no reflection in the way of resignation of Regular Army officers, definitely in conversations with Regular Army officers who have sons who might seek an army career, I don't know whether it's all talk but I've heard a number of them say that they wouldn't urge their sons to take on this thing. We have had a couple of resignations of men who served about 18 years as Regular Army officers and submitted letters along the line of this Army, Navy, Air Force Journal. So there has been—it's probably an exaggerated perspective by reason of this Army Navy Journal article and by reason of these two letters which also were publicized to some extent.

During his 1975 visit, General DePuy was asked whether Congress agreed with his assessment of the future battlefield.

> I would say that the Congress doesn't agree or disagree with it, but they're oblivious to it. [Laughter and applause] We make efforts. In fact I personally have been asked to make a substantial effort along the same lines we've discussed today. It's not easy. You go to a committee meeting of some kind with 16 or 17 senators on the committee, you're fortunate to have one or two there. And they wander in and out during the time. That's right. You young fellas haven't had that experience. You someday will. So, answering that question with the Congress is almost an impossible thing. Up to now it's been answered within the Armed Services Committees and within subcommittees of the Armed Services Committees and that's the way Congress has worked.
>
> Now, given all the other problems, the general membership of the House, for example, has become active in the defense arena with amendments and so on, which are offered on the floor. And I would say that a very large amount of misinformation, disinformation, lack of information permeates the Congress of the United States right now. As a matter of fact I think I'd have to say in all candor that the chances are that

their visualization of the thing would be something like this: That the Army has too many generals, too many colonels, too many headquarters, loves tanks and other expensive things, and that given the economic situation in the United States they can afford to be cut a bit. There's a large number of people in the Congress, particularly some of the new members, who feel that very strongly. They feel as strongly along those lines as you feel probably along opposite lines. And that's precisely the problem that General Abrams was trying to attack when he went for a 16 division Army: To prove that we were not all tail and indeed we were more, and increasingly so, more teeth. Cutting headquarters, cutting generals and so on and so forth. And all of that has in fact had a considerable impact among the older members of the Congress.

And in the Armed Services Committee the Army today is in very good odor, except among the very new people who have come in with a focus on the economic and social problems of the United States, are not informed and don't care, and you can understand that. Simply it's another world with which they're not familiar. And with them there is a deep lack of understanding. You've got to go after that problem with a great deal of discretion. The country doesn't want, the British system doesn't allow, by the way, but our country doesn't want a lot of generals running around, you know, like the Salvation Army, trying to get contributions from Congress. That's just not the way that policy is supposed to be made. I believe, because pendulums do swing back and forth and we always move on some kind of a sine wave of enthusiasm and lack of enthusiasm, that events, not arguments, will again prevail. In my some 34 years in this business, it has always impressed me that it's never the clever study, it's never the eloquent argument that carries the day. It's events. The murder of [Saudi Arabian] King Faisal for example, may turn out to scare the pants off a lot of people. It may have more effect than all the arguments that all of us could make together over ten years. The fall of eleven provinces in Vietnam, and it looks like that's not—it's only the beginning of the problem.

So, I believe that our business as soldiers is to be professionals, to learn how to use what we've got. To get the best we can out of it, out of our troops, out of our weapons. To think hard, to be smarter than the enemy, to be bolder. At the same time to be realistic. And I would say that's what you fellas are faced with...The problem you face is not the Congress, because the Congress is going to go its way based on larger sweeps of the tide than anything you can effect by going up there and arguing with them. The Congress is going to move based on what happens out there in the world and in our economy and so on and so forth. The problem you face is to take your little bit of the Army and realize its full potential. Your little bit, when you go out of here you may be brigade S3s, battalion S3s, soon you'll be battalion commanders. Don't worry about the generals. A lot of people say "Ah, the Army's all loused up because of those generals. They're too old and they're living in World War II" and all that sort of stuff. Well it's always been that way. I didn't think much of generals either, I was awful smart when I was your age. I went out here, or in Gruber Hall, I thought the generals were all outdated and obsolete. But that isn't going to help you do your job. Don't worry about the colonel's wife either. Don't blame anything on her either. You just take your little bit of the Army, your little battalion, and perfect it. And then if the guy sitting next to you takes his little battalion and perfects that, and the guy next to him takes his—we've got all the battalions in the Army represented right here—nobody could beat us. Don't look at me. Just look to your right and left fellas. That's where the problems are. [Laughter and applause]

When he was the commander of Forces Command in 1976, General Bernard Rogers gave his views of congressional relations to a more senior audience at the Combat Division Refresher Course.

But what the hell? We shake our heads and go "What the hell?" We get our day in court in front of those committees. I've been the Chief of Legislative Liaison for the Army. And it's our job to educate those people. And it really is shocking to find the decisions that are being made and the bills that are being constructed over there, and written by these legislative and administrative assistants, bright, dedicated individuals, who don't know what the hell they're doing. And it's our responsibility to poop them up, you see, and if we don't then we aren't doing our job. And here's one of those kinds of times you don't—you know you're not supposed to lobby. Because we're not a registered lobby over there, legislative liaison, you're supposed to—sort of like the readiness group— you're supposed to respond to requests for assistance. But sometimes in that business you have to find ways which requests for assistance are generated so you can get in there and talk to them. I'll give you a case in point.

Young fellow from the—the most junior and the youngest man in the House of Representatives from up in New York, Tom Downey. You know everybody has Tom Downey cast as a man who's anti-military. And when I went up to talk…to the Reserve Officers Association in their headquarters, they'd asked some congressmen and some staffers over, to talk about what we're trying to do in Forces Command with respect to the readiness of the components and all. He couldn't stay for the question period, so I arranged to go see him, for an hour, when I was back in Washington the next time. And it was a very interesting hour. He is on the House Armed Services Committee. And he says "Everybody comes up to me expecting me to be an expert in military affairs." He says "Hell, I never served." He said "A four-star general commands a division, doesn't he?" I said "No." He said "I just don't know but I want to learn." Well, boy! There's the chance, you see. And it was very interesting, some of the positions that Tom Downey had taken, and some legislation that he had introduced with respect to changing certain legal matters with respect to the Guard, when we had a chance to talk to him, why, he understood and I think he would have done differently had he known.

That's why I say it's up to us to find way to educate these people as best we can, who are drafting this kind of legislation. And secondly to get their constituents to make their representatives know how the hell they want them to vote, and I tell you I've seen some of them change almost overnight, when I was in the [Legislative Liaison] business. From a position that they had, with which we were quite comfortable and could depend on, until the next day they got up on the floor of the House and the Senate and made a speech which was completely different. I said "What the hell happened to you?" He said "The voice of my constituents has come through." So we've all got work to do in helping educate them. But [Senator Sam Nunn's Legislative Assistant] Jeffrey Record, if we can—and Senator Nunn—they'll give us our day in court. And if we can present a case that's cogent and makes sense, and oftentimes that's kind of tough, you know, it makes so much sense to us, it may not to them. But if we can, why we'll get what we need.

In 1988, General Carl Vuono was asked if he was concerned about the lack of military experience in Congress.

One of the real joys of my job is being able to deal with Congress. [Laughter] I say that seriously, I enjoy dealing with Congress. And I'll tell you why. Because, just as he suggested, there is a lack of experience over there in terms of the military, in terms of serving in the military, and in a volunteer force you have that. But I enjoy working with Congress because they don't understand the military, [so] they listen. They are willing to listen. Now they don't always agree with you but they are willing to listen. And our job is to make sure that we clearly articulate what it is we're trying to do in the military. You've got to have a very sharp focus on what the military is trying to do. What it is we're trying to do, what we need, why we need it, and what it costs. And you've got to lay it out for them four square like that. You've got to be direct and up front with them. You can't just knuckle in when they don't agree with you, you've got to come back at them with common sense and judgment.

And then you've got to make sure that the entire service is on the same azimuth. You can't have one guy in the service talk about one program this way, another guy talk about it over here. It's not just members of Congress, it's staffers up there too who have no experience. When they see two diverse views within one service they say "What the hell? I don't know who to believe so I'll go this direction." And so we work it. I personally work it very hard and the leaders inside the Army work it very hard. But I find that by explaining the programs, talking to them, establishing with them that you know what you're doing and what direction you want the Army to go; getting them out to visit the Army. We have yet to send a congressman or staffer to visit any organization in the Army that he didn't come back singing the praises of the Army. Because our soldiers and our young leaders make a difference as they tell them in very clear terms what it is we need and why we need it. There's also a very, very strong sentiment building up on the importance of conventional forces, and the need for conventional forces. And we have reaped some benefits of that in terms of additional resources. We got 103% of what we went over there for in the '89 budget. Now the top line wasn't as high as I'd like to have it, but we got 103%, which is not bad. And I think that's because of the recognition of conventional forces and there's an understanding that we are willing to discuss with them and explain to Congress our programs.

Now it's not going to get any better in years ahead. Those [in Congress] who served in World War II are starting to retire and leave, and frankly, a lot of those are out of date with today's army anyway. And there's not many of those that are in now who served in Korea and Vietnam, although we are getting a few more Vietnam veterans, particularly in the House of Representatives, that we're working. And there's also a very good feeling about the military over there, a very good feeling that the military is not only important, it's necessary. On the other hand, when we have difficulties such as the fraud investigation on acquisition, that doesn't do our case any good. I mean it does not. Even though the uniformed military has not been as greatly involved in it, it's still the military, and when folks are saying, like the question over there, "Where can I put more military money?" They say "Well you guys waste what we give you, so we can take it away." So there's our own internal act that we've got to make sure is cleaned up, and then we've got to deal with them direct and to the point.

Senator Roberts gave a different view of congressional relations during his appearance in 2001. A student referred to *Dereliction of Duty* by H.R. McMaster and asked if the executive branch could similarly involve the county in a protracted conflict without the support of Congress.

> Well, there was a Senator from Kansas [referring to himself] and a Senator from Georgia by the name of Max Cleland, I think we all know who Max is, he's a legitimate hero of the Vietnam War. And he and I sit on opposite sides of the Armed Services Committee and when we were getting involved in Bosnia and Kosovo, or for that matter post-Somalia, and we would ask the experts to come in, and then in again in my service in the Intelligence Committee when I was trying to figure out intelligence-wise what would happen if we started a gradual war of escalation in regards to our bombing campaign, what did intelligence tell us? And then after getting that, asking "Where the hell did it go?" you know, to the decision makers, Max's eyebrow would go up. And I guess mine did as well…So he raised an eyebrow and I raised an eyebrow and we started a foreign policy dialogue series…And we advocated something called realistic restraint. Okay? What is [General Hugh] Shelton's comment about the hammer and the nail? And I think a lot of other statements that indicated, again, it's one thing to have a cause to fight for but another thing to have a cause to fight and die for.

> And what were we doing? When we went in to Kosovo I had an amendment during the Defense Appropriation Bill and I said "Before we would commit any troops in the Balkans that the military would have to come back and inform the Congress of the following things." We had about three or four. What is the mission? What is the definition of victory? I think we added one about esprit de corps and several other things. We said you had to do that before you would commit any troops. The Pentagon didn't like that worth a damn, really. And I got a lot of calls. [Secretary of Defense] Bill Cohen, who I know and love and appreciate, former senator, called me up and read me out. And I said "Damn, if you can't answer those questions, what the hell are we doing?" And so we got about ten senators to support that amendment, went in, and I talked to the Admiral who was put in charge of answering that. And he came in to visit with me about two years later and I thought "Oh boy, am I in trouble." And he said "No I want to thank you. I want to thank you on behalf of all the staff that worked on this, because we had a hell of a time explaining it." Well, I think that's fairly obvious.

> Senator Cleland went a little farther than that. He got into the War Powers Act. And boy is that nettlesome. And there aren't many times when we have utilized the War Powers Act, we always go around it. And presidents want the flexibility to respond without having to invoke the War Powers Act and get a vote in regards to the Congress of the United States. Now you saw last session [Senators] Bob Bird and John Warner had an amendment on defense appropriations that…put a time limit out here with regards to our involvement in NATO in the Balkans depending on Congress voting affirmatively to continue that involvement. And also contingent on the fact that the other folks who are part of the force, I think it's about 31 nations now involved, not only NATO, in sharing the proper burden. And I think we had some language in there which made a little sense. I voted for it. Everybody went nuts on the other side saying "Oh my God, you are not supporting the troops abroad." We didn't think that was appropriate. So we're still out there and we're trying to deal with this. Cleland on the War Powers act,

Roberts with an amendment now, "Whoa, wait a minute you can't commit until you explain to us what the hell's going on." All of that. I think a lot of that has to do with, quite frankly, a change in administration where I think [President George W. Bush] wants to become less involved, or if we are involved we ought to have a very specific game plan. And I'm not trying to perjure the past president's intentions by any means.

CREDIBILITY

Emerging from the Vietnam War, the Department of Defense and military services' credibility with both Congress and the public was in shambles. Many of the speakers addressed this topic as the services worked hard to regain the trust of the American people. Secretary of the Army Howard Callaway spoke at length on the topic in 1973.

> In talking about the entire relations with Congress I haven't talked about the fundamental point. And the fundamental point is that we in the Army have got to regain our credibility with Congress—and remember when I say Congress I mean with the American people. The Army's credibility with the Congress and the American people today is probably at an all-time low. Not just because of Vietnam but that certainly contributed to it. People just don't believe what we say. And an Army that, those of us who've been a part of it, think that integrity is our cornerstone, and yet the people of America think that the Army's always trying to pull something. They think we're promising things that we can't produce. They think that we're procuring new weapons and saying that we can do it in a couple of years and it really takes us five or six. Or that we say we'll build a helicopter for a million dollars and it costs two million dollars, all these kinds of things that you've been reading in the paper. And we've got to build back that credibility. And there's only one way to build back that credibility: And that's to be entirely open with everybody in what you do. Now we've got an Army manned by humans, and humans are going to make mistakes. And we're going to have a lot of things we'd just as soon nobody know about. We'll have scandals. We'll have officers who did not do as well as they should have. We'll have noncommissioned officers who did not do as well as they should have. We'll have people spying on folks they shouldn't have been spying on, and we will have all these things going on and we will tend to say "Oh, let's just hide that and maybe it will go away."

> Well General [Creighton] Abrams, who is probably the greatest Chief of Staff we've ever had, he's just one of the great soldiers I've ever known and he has a feel for the Army. We were talking about this the other day and he says "You know, I've never found bad news to improve with age."[Laughter] And you know, it doesn't! And you know it doesn't, and I know it doesn't, and yet every one is tempted the first time this comes up to hide it, and put it under the table, and give a quick answer, an answer that doesn't tell all about it, when that's not the way to do it, because they're going to find it out. If we try to say something is better than it is, or don't tell the full story, in today's world they're going to find it out. Congress will find it out. The American public will find it out. You'll have the problem you always had and you'll have the additional problem that they'll say "You're hiding that, what else are you hiding?" And they won't believe anything you say. And this is probably the key problem that we have with the Congress and the American people. And to the extent that those of you are involved, and you will be involved, both now and in the future, with talking with media, talking with people in the

community, talking about the Army...I don't mean you have to go out and try to let all your dirty linen hang out, you don't have to try and find something wrong with the Army and talk about it. But if you have something that you're not proud of, and if somebody questions you about it, let 'em know the full story.

The next year, in May, Callaway returned and elaborated on this point.

We just don't have credibility with the Congress today. We're having a problem right now with the Senate Appropriations Committee; I mention that because they're in mark-up today. But if there were just some way that I could say to that committee "We really need the forces that we've asked for and we need them for the following reasons," and if I could have them take that at face value we'd have no problem. But they're going to say to me "We've heard all that before." Now we've got to get that behind us. We've got to get where—I'm not talking about the integrity of the Army, the Army has integrity, I'm talking about the credibility of the Army. It's just not there. And how do we go about building it up? We go about by surprising [Congress], by being so open with them they just can't believe it. And this doesn't pay off the first time, this doesn't pay off the second time. But when you finally get a history of that, you finally get where those staff members and the congressmen and even the press start believing you. And I just think that's going to take us about a year, but I'm already seeing a lot of good results. I would really commend it to you, the same kind of thing. There's a tendency in the Army, a tendency for all of us to close in, come in tight, don't tell anybody. You know protect yourself, CYA [cover your ass], all that sort of thing. I understand that tendency, and I'm not objecting to it, but I just think that's not the way the Army should go today.

...We've got a policy in my own office called the "Glad You Asked" policy. And there's nothing we can do in the Army that doesn't—it's got to fit the "Glad You Asked" policy. And the "Glad You Asked" policy means that whatever that action was, if [syndicated columnist] Jack Anderson picks up the phone and says "How about that?" you've got to say "Jack, I'm glad you asked about that." [Laughter and applause] And you know what this will do for you? It will change your whole attitude. I've had a lot of things that I didn't think through too well and people on my staff would come in and say "Sir, I'm not sure that's a 'glad you asked.'" And you have to think, is it? [Laughter] It'll keep you straight on all of that. As a matter of fact it's amazing what it'll do. We had one little thing that on the surface didn't look so good, and it was one that was very sensitive politically, one that could have gotten on the front page in a moment. And I didn't get the phone call, but one of my staff did, from a reporter, and—this actually happened, he told me about it later, it was not Jack Anderson but it was a reporter. And he said "I'm glad you asked about that." He said "I thought you weren't interested. Let me tell you about it. What would you like to know? Here's what we did, here's how we handled it, here's the facts, here's all about it." And said "We really thought you weren't interested, we're delighted you're interested, what else can we get for you?" And the story never appeared. [Big laugh]

And you know to the extent that you get a congressional [inquiry] on something. You know, first of all, you want to be on a "Glad You Asked" with congressionals. Whatever you do, just assume, I'd say for you instead of Jack Anderson calling on the phone, just assume you're going to get a congressional on that. And to be in the position where every night as you go to sleep you can say "I hope I'll get a congressional on that in the morning." [Big laugh] And when it comes you'll write back "Dear Senator, I'm glad you asked about that." And tell it all and tell it open, if it's bad news and something—you know, one piece of bad news came in, and it had to do with a very sensitive area. I remember it well, it happened about eight months ago and General Abrams found out about it at six o'clock in the evening. And at 6:01 his [Secretary of the General Staff] was there, wires were going out, the back-channels were humming throughout the Army, and by about nine o'clock that night several actions had been taken, by the next morning further actions were taken. And while it's something we really didn't want to talk about, if Jack Anderson would have called, we would have been in a position to say "Jack I'm glad you asked" while swallowing a little bit. And sayng "Jack, here's when we found out about it, here's what we did about it. What suggestions have you got for doing about it?" And while it would have been an unpleasant story because it was a very unpleasant happening, certainly the Army would have, at least, minimized that by trying to grab hold of it and doing the right thing. And fortunately Jack didn't call, but we would have been ready to answer.

That same month Secretary of Defense James R. Schlesinger spoke about earning the confidence of the American people.

Let me make two observations, and they're observations I've made before. First, democracy gets the kind of Army that it deserves, the type of military establishment that it deserves. If it does not treat the people in the military establishment with respect, the consequences for the health of the body politic will be quite unfavorable. The other observation is that the confidence of the public must be won, and some would say won anew every day. The services have been blamed in the last five years or longer for things which were not their responsibilities. Some of the sillier aspects of the Vietnam War, or most of the sillier aspects, can be attributed to political decision makers. And political decision makers, part of the way you get elected, I suppose, are specialists in ducking down in the weeds. [Laughter and applause] I think that this is not unique in recent history. If you recall during the period after the firing of General [Douglas] MacArthur, which was a political decision, and a wise one, that the administration at that time was so weakened, that it chose the tactic of sending General [Omar] Bradley to the hill, who was the only five-star general who would outrank MacArthur, in order to defend the political decisions of the administration. And that is unfortunately true, that administrations, when weakened, will exploit the prestige of the military—to detriment of the prestige of the military, by the way. I think it is notable for example that in 1972, in December, there was a political decision to bomb Hanoi, and to mine Haiphong Harbor [in Vietnam]. And at that time [Defense] Secretary Laird was leaving office, Secretary [of State William P.] Rogers was not to be found, one person who went to the hill to defend all those activites was the Chairman of the Joint Chiefs of Staff, Admiral [Thomas H.] Moorer. He bore the principal political responsibility.

The Service record in Vietnam is probably not without blemish, and serious blemish. There must be, I think, a higher degree of candor than we have reflected in dealing with the public and the public's views. During the great period of the Cold War, one could, in the military establishment, get by with any kind of "bunkum" simply by citing authority. That will not work any longer. And to the extent that it is attempted, it will tend to bring out a flock of greater critics. Leveling with the public, candor, is the way to restore confidence. I believe that we have made progress restoring confidence in the military establishment. And, to a large extent I think, to the degree that confidence of the military establishment in itself was somewhat shaken by the events of recent years, that there is underway the restoration of confidence in itself, which is a prerequisite, in effect, to the restoration of public confidence. The military, under all circumstances, must be proud. They must also be scrupulous in weaning out, winnowing out deficiencies that exist in their own institutions. They know them. If the military fails to root out the deficiencies in their own institutions, somebody else is going to do it, and it's going to be in a clumsy way that does greater damage to the institution.

Secretary Callaway returned in December 1974, and covered the credibility issue with a new group of students.

I have a lot of paperwork to do. A lot of things...Have any of you have ever been stationed in the Pentagon? Have you? There's a lot of paperwork that goes on in there. And a lot of it, for some reason, somebody thinks I should see. So, I'm used to an inbox and an outbox. Well, when I got this job I got about 6 inboxes. One won't hold it, you know, they've just got them all in there, the people who shuffle them back and forth, and I choose, have a big time. [Laughter] Well one night, it was late, it was tiring, and I was a little bit tired, I was reading all this stuff in my inbox. And what they do, my staff, it's a very good staff, they occasionally put things in one of those in boxes to see when I'm reading whether I'm awake or asleep when I read it. And they'll put something in there that's just crazy, you know, and I say "Hey I was awake this time." Or if I just send it back and sign and they'll say "He was asleep" and they'll go back and look at some of those.

Well, it was late at night and I was tired, and in came one of those that I, you know, I wrote down at the bottom "Caught ya, I was awake." They came back "No, serious!" They were serious. [Big laugh] Here's what they said. You know, I'll tell you the truth. Here's what they said. They said "You know that UTTAS?" I said "Yes, I know that UTTAS." [Program to replace the UH-1 Iroquois helicopter] "The one we already spent a couple hundred million dollars on?" I said "That one, yeah I know that one." "And do you remember what we do with it?" I said "Yeah, we fly it" and all that sort of stuff. They said "Well, you know about loading it on airplanes?" I said "Sure, we're going to fit it in a C-130, a C-141, and of course a C-5 [cargo aircraft], all that sort of stuff. As a matter of fact, I'm sort of pleased with that, because it's the only thing that I've ever understood about these technical research and development. I cannot understand all the performances and design of the rotor blade and how they wiggle and all that," I said. "That's above me. But I can understand that, it's great. Because what you do is you get a box, and you fit the plane in the box, and you know, I understand that. And that's good. I'm serious, I'm an infantryman, and I can understand about that." So that was good. They said in this little memo you know, that UTTAS, we just found out this afternoon that the UTTAS won't fit in the box! [Laughter]

We had one officer, he may be here in this class, whose sole—I'm serious—whose sole job was air transportability of the UTTAS. Now, it didn't fit in the plane, you know. I said "Does the Air Force mind if we take a crowbar and stretch the plane a little bit?"

And they said "Well, we don't know." My point I'm making, I'm making it sound funny because it did sort of get my attention. That night about 7:00 the Assistant Secretary of the Army for Research and Development, the Under Secretary of the Army, we got together and said, you know, what do we do now? And I said "Well, we're really going to put to the test this idea of openness...Tomorrow morning at 9:00 when Congress opens we're going to be there. We're going to go to all four major committees, we're going to tell them what's happened." And we did. We told them we really don't know the full story, all we know we've got a major air transportability problem. We may have something where the UTTAS really won't fit in the aircraft for which it was designed. And that's all we know right now, we're looking into it, we'll keep you informed. What do you suppose the unanimous congressional reaction was? "How can I help?" Right. "Thank you for keeping us informed, what can we do to help?"

Now let me change the situation. Suppose we had taken the reaction that we were tempted to take because it was that bad. And suppose we had taken the reaction that we'd better really fix this before we go to Congress? You know, some way we'll find a solution, as a matter of fact we did, those of you who are worried it now fits, it's fine. I don't know what we took off of it but it fits. [Laughter] What do you suppose would have been the reaction? If, in doing this in perfectly good faith, trying to get it fixed before we went to Congress, we're trying to do all that, if about the time we were working on this, about a week later, a story had appeared in Jack Anderson's column and it had said "Guess what the Army has done? The Army has spent a couple of hundred million dollars and the plane won't fit in the box. And isn't that just like the Army?" And *then* we went to Congress, and went to those members of Congress and said "Hi, we've got an air transportability problem." What do you think their reaction would have been then? Somewhat different. Yeah, you bet. They would have all been on the floor. They would have been doing everything they could to say "Again, you can't trust the Army." You get credibility by being open and honest and you get help by being open and honest, and I promise you that applies to you in your job, and it applies to me in my job and every single time we try it, it works. It's just amazing how it works.

Years later in 1987, Georgia Representative Newt Gingrich paid a highly entertaining, no-holds-barred visit, and he was asked about the credibility of Army Leadership during congressional testimony.

Well in the first place most of Congress doesn't pay any attention, because Congress is a highly fragmented body, and [the Army leadership] go to testify in front of an Armed Services Committee, and out of, what, I guess 54 members or something, you've got nine present, and three of those are busy signing mail. So you've got to start with that presumption, and I'm overdoing it but—and it's something all of you can appreciate in your own business—getting people's attention is very expensive. So when you get their attention you have to say something. Read the testimony sometimes, and I don't mean just for the Army. But sit down sometimes and read an armed services hearing. I mean they'll just put you to sleep. Because it's like the minuet, it's very structured, it's very stylized. And notice I didn't say earlier 'testify,' I said educate. You may educate by getting them to go visit bases, you may educate by getting them to go visit Reserve units in their own district, you may educate by getting them out to the National Training Center. You may educate by having drinks with them. There are hundreds of ways to educate human beings. Those of you who have taken over and shaped up a unit, know that there are many things you do that are informal that may be more powerful things you do that are formal.

…And then candidly I say the reason that you have to educate is simple: Where's an average civilian supposed to turn and look for advice that we need to survive against the Soviets? I would think that you'd want us to look to the uniformed military. When we look, what do we discover? We're told that if we buy 612 M2s [Bradley Fighting Vehicles] and 694 M1s [Abrams Tanks] it'll all work, and by the way here's the rest of the shopping list. Well that's not the way the world works. How am I supposed to think? I have very, very limited time. I have 500,000 constituents, 12 counties, I serve in the Aviation Subcommittee as the ranking Republican, we're writing a bill this spring which is the basic airport bill for the country, I've got to go vote on 900 things a year, and by the way I've got two hours—what would you like me to know? And what you discover is, frankly, there are no places where people have really thought that through very carefully. And you can learn it over time, but again, let me make it very clear, because I don't want to sound, you know... 4-star officers in all four services tend to be very impressive. It's a reality. They are better educated than most congressmen, certainly better trained and spend more time learning professionally, they tend to be very aggressive, dominant figures or they didn't get to that level. So it's not that they're dumb. Remember professions are not a function of genius and IQ. Professions are a function of skills and doctrine mastered, to which you subordinate your ego, so you can act professionally.

And all I'm suggesting to you is that if your profession is defending America, not just winning on the battlefield, that part of that profession has to be explained to me, because after all, I've got 18 staff people, total, to do everything I do. You have more full colonels studying some minor aspect of the battlefield than my entire staff. And so I turn to you and I say "Show me the profession of civilians defending America." I do this to all the services, not just you all. I do it to the State Department. What is it I should think? How is it I should know? And then try to break it down so that someday we can have a six-week course—you know, you train captains more at Leavenworth than we train congressmen in their lifetime? Have you ever thought about that? And then we wonder why congressmen end up being as the gentlemen described them? [Earlier in the question period a student had some disparaging remarks about congressman] There are no systems of training. And I'm not saying that you have to do it. But I'm saying the largest pool of professionals who care passionately about defense happen to wear uniforms. So as a person who reads books and who cares about this stuff, I come to you to say it seems to me you're the best place to start thinking this through. And then I think you'll see us start to get educated, but it will not happen in formal briefings, or in formal hearings. They're the end of it, they're the cherry on top of the cake. They're not the cake.

SOCIETY AND THE PRESS

Two other aspects of civil-military relations involve the press, with which the military has had a love-hate relationship during most of its existence, and the American society at large, from which the members of the military come. General Ralph Haines reminded the faculty of the

Leadership Department of this during his visit in 1973, sounding a warning that would prove prescient some 35 years later.

> The Army, more than any of the services, must be identified with the people of the country. We can never allow the Army to be separated from the people it's designed to serve. We operate in an environment that's heavily contaminated with people—the ground. We do not normally operate in the more antiseptic environments of the sea and the air as our sister services do, so we do have to have a very close relationship with the civilians we are designed to serve.

Admiral Elmo Zumwalt Jr. provided an example of why the military was averse to dealing with the press in 1973, when asked about an NBC news program on defense spending.

> The program is one in which we faced the choice to appear or not appear. The public relations advice was that the least worst alternative was to appear and make our case. And it proved to be just that—the least worst alternative. [Laughter] The way in which the thing was prepared was typical of the objective that had been set for that particular producer, namely to do in the [CVN-70 aircraft carrier and F-14] program. As witness, the fact that the most magnificent advocate of defense programs in the Senate, Senator [John] Stennis, was quoted once, extremely briefly, using two or three sentences that didn't permit him to make any point particularly at all, whereas Senator [William] Proxmire, for whom I wouldn't use similar adjectives, [Laughter & Applause] appeared some 15 or 20 times, and would give the nation the impression that he was a great defense expert. The same technique was used throughout. Fortunately, I am informed, as a result of some fine detective programs and others going on at the same time, only 300,000 people watched the program. I don't believe that's going to have any appreciable impact on the outcome.

During his 1979 appearance, General Meyer also commented on some of the military's responsibilities to society outside of national defense.

> ...We [have] a responsibility in our development of the individuals that we bring in to attempt to create a whole man. A man who while he is with us, if he chooses to go back, is a man who has had the opportunity to develop mentally, he has had the opportunity to develop physically, who has had the opportunity to develop sort of an ethical approach so that he can contribute more to our nation, and an individual who has an opportunity to have a social awareness of the other needs of the nation. The great history of our military in the past has been the ability to have brought people in and then to have sent them out so that they have a great respect out in society for the military itself. And that's why, when I get back to the question I bridled at over here about saying that the people that come in aren't capable, I bridled at that because I think we have a responsibility to do that. And if we do not do that, and if we assume they are not capable, they are going to assume no one cares, they are going to assume that they can't do anything, and ultimately we're going to end up with a whole host of people out there who, assuming no one cares, and who assume they can't do it who really can't do it. So that's why I believe by using those programs to develop the individuals we have, whether they stay with us or whether they go on, that we have the opportunity to influence the future of our country, because we have the opportunity to work on that total individual and return back to society, either

at the end of twenty years, if you change the current programs, at the end of ten years, or the end of two or three years, an individual who goes out and can contribute and improve our total society. So that's, in my judgment, the side benefit that we get. But I will say that, and you can use [Marshall of the Royal Air Force] Sir John Slessor's comment, and that is that the greatest social service that we do a nation, our nation, is to provide them the security under which all the other social services can be conducted. And I think that's a great service which the military provides to our nation.

General John Vessey gave the students an update on how the military was viewed by the press during graduation ceremonies in 1981.

How is that Army out there today? I just returned from my annual inspection of the troops in Europe, and I can tell you that the Army is good. I saw some of the best training that I have seen in all my years of service. The officers and noncommissioned officers know their business. The soldiers were skilled and well-disciplined. But in the same breath I must tell you that they're not inhibited by a lack of room for improvement. There is much out there for you to do. I'm sure you also realize that you're leaving CGSC at a time in our country when you, we, the warriors, the guardians, are getting mixed reviews from our fellow citizens, particularly those citizens in the business of informing other citizens, the news media. You've been reading and will continue to read some very sharp criticisms of the armed services, of the Army in particular, the institution you serve. Some of that criticism is justified, and deserves to be heeded. Most of it is not. I view our job as being that of exerting great effort to give the nation the best and the most economical and effective defense that we can give it, and demonstrating that capability, so that our citizens are confident in our ability. We'll just have to let the unjustified criticism roll off our ponchos.

In 1999, General Shelton gave his view on the relationship between the military and the press and Congress.

Now myself, and [Lieutenant General William] Mike Steele [CGSC Commandant] and many of us here are veterans of Vietnam. Some would say when it comes to the press, victims of Vietnam. And so our slant on the press sometimes may be a little bit skewed. One of the things that I've learned, and I learned a lot when we were doing the Haiti operation, is that the press can be very responsible, and regardless of whether they are or not, we've got to work with the press if in fact we're going to keep the American people informed about what its armed forces are doing, and if in fact we can present the facts as they are, rather than let them paint it as they believe them to be. And so you really do need to learn and start thinking in terms of treating the press as a part of our operations that have to be contended with. The CNN effect is real. They're going to be there no matter where you are, and they're going to be reporting live in most cases. In many cases as you know from Iraq, we weren't there but they were reporting. Same way in Belgrade [Yugoslavia/Serbia]. And that can be very helpful as well, in terms of battle damage assessment, etcetera. But certainly we have to deal with them. And I have found in my dealings with them that most of the time, you treat them with respect, they'll respond accordingly. Doesn't mean you always like what they write, I certainly didn't say that, but they'll report it factually.

And then the other one is the Congress. As you know, less and less representation, veterans in the Congress means they know less and less about what we do. And so it really is good when we can take the time, senior level, at your level, you can get them out to the field visiting your units, to take the time, introduce them to the great men and women that serve with us, let them see what a quality force we have today, and take the time to explain to them what it is we're doing and why it's important we do that. The fact that we have such a contest going on over Vieques Island [Naval bombing range in Puerto Rico] as an example, is a lack of real understanding of what the PhD level of warfighting is all about, and how trying to pull together close air support, naval gunfire, shipboard fire, and Marines coming in the shore, why that's important to our joint Navy-Marine team. If you don't understand it then it's very easy to listen to the governors say "You know we can't tolerate this" even though you've got a ten mile buffer zone, and as regretful as it is, in all of its history only one individual has ever been killed at Vieques Island. That was the one guy, you know, the one individual that caused the most recent uproar. While we have lost two pilots in the process, and that's all a part of what we consider to be training, as regretful as it is. You know, we know that the business we're in is hazardous, but we'll lose less in combat if we do it right in training. And so you take the time to explain all this to congressmen and show them what it is and why what you're doing is important, and it will pay dividends for our armed forces, for each of our services.

As seen above, many politicians visited the college, and provided a unique insight and perspective that would serve the students well in their future relationship with Congress.

7. Politicians

Many politicians visited the college over the years, and provided the students a glimpse into their world in the hopes of bettering understanding between the military and those who would direct their activities. One of those was Republican Representative of Missouri (and World War I veteran) Dewey Short, who was the Chairman of the House Armed Services Committee when he spoke to the students in 1953. He wanted them to know that Congress was their ally: "I want you to realize, gentlemen, that you've got a friend in court. And that's because practically every man in the House Armed Services Committee is an ex-serviceman who served in WWII or in the Korean conflict. We've lived with your problems. We're careful who we put on our committee." He also suggested a post-military career for them.

> You think it is pretty tough on you at times? I suggest sometime, if you ever want to leave the military service, you run for Congress and find out how easy it is to get there, and then how delightful and pleasant it is after you arrive. [Laughter] Politicians? Just a bunch of crooks. Just no good. S.O.Bs. Every man has his price. No love of country or patriotism. Indifferent to the people he represents. Brothers, unless you have a hide tough as a rhinoceros, and [are] capable of smiling when you want to fight, don't you ever run for any public office. Now do we have these congressional relations built up, General Hodes? We've got a better understanding today between the Pentagon and the Congress? There is a disposition on the part of civilians and many uniforms to cooperate and work together more than ever before in our history. And I've never seen much difficulty, I certainly didn't see it a year ago when I [was out] in Korea with [Commanding General, Eighth U.S. Army General James] Van Fleet, and [Commander, U.S. IX Corps, Lieutenant General Reuben] Jenkins and [Commander, 7th Infantry Division, Major General] Wayne Smith. I saw no great difficulty, after talking to [Commander of the U.S. Pacific Fleet and subsequently Chairman of the Joint Chiefs] Admiral [Arthur] Radford…and the rest of the boys out there concerning unification. Unification worked fine in the field. About the only place you got all that hell-raising was in that Pentagon. And that doesn't disturb me too much. A healthy rivalry is a wholesome thing. Its only when it degenerates into petty bickering and jealousy, and I think we've gotten over that. We should have learned our lesson by this time through World War II and the Korean conflict. No, you've got communications, good teamwork, out in the field. You had it in Europe and Italy, in North Africa; you had it all throughout the Pacific, regardless of whether it was an admiral or a general in command. They worked together as a team. And their learning…of course even some soldiers in uniform learn hard…but they're learning in Washington to get along together because we've got a few hard-boiled businessmen that are knocking some heads together. Sometimes you have to do that, even to high-ranking officers. It keeps you motivated, though.

In December 1961, President Truman also gave students post-military congressional career advice, while at the same time admitting he had not wished to be the vice president.

> And another of the greatest of our great presidents came along and saved the Republic again, and his name was Franklin Roosevelt. I'm a little prejudiced because I was elected vice president with him. Didn't want to be because I was afraid I'd get what I did afterwards. I didn't want to be the vice president, I'd rather stay in the Senate, it's the best place in the world to serve. If any of you youngsters ever have a chance to go to the Senate or to the House—of course you have to run all the time with the House. With the Senate you have four years where you don't have to.

Truman was always good for a story or two, and delivered these during his appearance in 1964.

> I was with President [Herbert] Hoover up in Iowa and we went to [Kennedy's] funeral in Washington and I came back with him, went up there, and he has established a place up in a little town in Iowa [pronounces it Eye-oh-way] where he was born, that will take care and maintain his papers, and his papers not only as Secretary of Commerce but as President of the United States. He has a library out at the University of California, eh, Northern California [Stanford University], where he has more things that have to do with revolutions that have taken place in South America and the rest of the Western Hemisphere than they have in their own archives. I was talking to a fella the other day who was close to him and told me that they [South Americans?] had come up to his place in the hotel in New York where he lives and asked him if they could go into his library in California to look up some things about Venezuela, and Panama, and two or three of those other ungrateful kids that we've set up into business you know. Nothing in God's world is as mean as a youngster who goes back on the people who have made him. And that's what Cuba, and Panama, and two or three others of these things have done. I had the sassiest letter you ever saw from the President of Panama the other day who wanted to know what I was thinking about. I told him he would find out what I was thinking about if he'd learn that the kid ought to respect his daddy.

> ... I always told them [Truman's Secret Service detail] if anybody tried to shoot me I'd take the gun away from them and stick it down his throat (only I didn't say throat) and pull the trigger. They said "Listen here, Mr. President. You can't do that, for the simple reason you can't get to them." And when they did try to shoot me I found out I couldn't. Two of these Puerto Rican people that didn't like what had happened in Puerto Rico in the election came up to the White House for the purpose of shooting me. And I was taking a nap upstairs right over the front of the house—this was in the Blair House [the White House was being renovated]. And pretty soon the madam came in a said "They're shooting our guards down here." I said "Oh no, it's just a backfire." She says "you get up and look!" I got up and stuck my head out the window and there's a fella lying out in the street who'd been shot all to pieces and there was a dead man over behind the bush and dead man down at the foot of the steps and another fella who had been shot and I said "What's going on down there?" And they come hollering "Get back there Mr. President, get back there." I went downstairs and met Jim Riley who was head of the Secret Service who said "Mr. President have you ever been in an air raid?" I said "Yes, lots of them." He says "Is it customary to go out and look up when they sound the siren?" I said "You've balled me out well enough, I won't do it anymore!"

Senator Miller spoke to the students in 1969 about the duties and obligations of Congress with respect to the conduct of foreign policy and war, particularly as far as Vietnam was concerned.

> Although I share the concern of a lot of my colleagues over our treaty commitments, and over what some of my colleagues have called an imbalance of powers in favor of the president in matters of foreign relations, it seems to me that Congress has only itself to blame, if there is to be blame, for treaties it ratifies, resolutions it passes, the statutory powers it gives the president, and the appropriations it makes. Congress has passed all of

these. And if perchance, Congress should feel that is has been deceived or misled by the executive, then the power of the purse would surely enable it to take remedial action.

The president in another administration submitted the [Southeast Asia Treaty Organization] Treaty to the Senate for ratification. Without the approval by the Senate there would have been no basis for House and Senate action on the Southeast Asia resolution. Without the Southeast Asia resolution, the president would have had questionable justification for asking the Congress for money to conduct a war. I say questionable because there is argument on both sides. And of course without the money we would long ago have been forced to pull out of South Vietnam. Fortunately both the executive and legislative branches of our federal government were in agreement on this phase of our national security policy. But the life or death power over that policy clearly rested with the Congress.

...It's expected these days by members of the committees that questions might be asked of the military witnesses which may well reveal that their requests to DoD, in the preparation of the DoD program budget, were eliminated or curtailed. And it is here that the Congress may decide that the Secretary of Defense was wrong in overruling the Service Chiefs.

... Broad discretionary powers are usually given the president, however if Congress feels deeply about how this power is used, Congress will move. A good example occurred when Former Secretary of Defense McNamara proposed to merge the Army Reserve with the Army National Guard. Some 270,000 reservists were to be merged into the Guard so that the Guard would be composed of 650,000 instead of only 380,000. Reserve-minded members of Congress threated to appropriate only enough money for a Guard of 380,000. And the secretary could see if that happened of course the merger was gone, so he backed off and said he would leave the matter to Congress...The point to be made is that unfortunate as this controversy was, that Congress has power to prevent certain action through limitations written into appropriation bills. On the other hand, the Congress does not have the power to force positive action. It may appropriate money for a new program or for a new weapon system, but the chief executive cannot be forced to spend the money. Of course if the new weapon system or the new program was deemed vital to our national security, and the president refused to pursue it, Congress has the power of impeachment. This is pretty much textbook theory. In actual practice there has usually been most commendable cooperation between the two branches of government in matters of national defense, and I'm pleased to say regardless of party affiliation.

...But the ultimate answer about what makes Congress tick is public opinion. Opinion translated into votes at election time, an opinion expressed in the millions in telegrams, letters, phone calls, and personal contacts that descend on Capitol Hill 365 days a year. Public opinion expressed through meetings of citizens, and the occasional visits with members of Congress on main street or at a county fair or at a homecoming, and any one of a thousand different places. Public opinion can of course be affected and sometimes molded by speeches made on the floor of Houses of Congress, by speeches made by members at conventions and public gatherings. Public opinion can also be affected and sometimes molded by the way these speeches are reported and even more by the failure of some of them. I am reminded, for example of the time when one of my colleagues made a speech in the Senate during which he criticized the myth, he called it, of the danger to our security posed by Cuba. The speech was promptly and fully answered within a few minutes by other senators. The next morning the "myth" speech was headlined and reported at great length on the front page of the New York Times, but nowhere in that paper, nowhere, was there one word reported about the answering speeches.

Thomas Jefferson once wrote: "That for the great American experiment in self-government to succeed, the will of the majority is a necessary condition, but is not a sufficient condition. The will of the enlightened majority," he said, "is the necessary and sufficient condition." And so it is today. If our citizenry is informed and public opinion is enlightened, the law of the Congress, which mirrors public opinion, in National Security Policy will be well carried forward. But if the moral fiber of our people is weak, and if they are uninformed, public opinion will be inadequate to meet the challenge of our national purpose, and a great amount of blood, sweat, and tears will have been to no avail.

Miller was asked an odd question regarding government influence of public opinion:

Q: There seems to be a lack of understanding of American people of our national policies and an awareness of the communist threat, an example of this is the opposition we've had with the war in Vietnam. In view of this, do you feel that we should have more positive means of influencing public opinion in the United States toward our national policies and if so, who should be responsible for doing this?

A: Well first of all, I don't think we can legislate more means. I think it's a matter, as I said in the wind up of my statement, that the majority had better get busy and get aggressive and espouse its views. Too many people who react to this situation and say "Well, they're just a bunch of troublemakers...I know what the situation is, I understand the danger." And they somehow assume that all the rest of the general public understands that. You'd better be careful if you follow that idea. It's about like a court case; you may have a client and you may say "Look, if I ever saw a lead-pipe cinch, this is it." But you'd better make an argument before that jury or you're going to lose that case. So I think the majority has got to vigorously espouse its views. Of course another thing that helps is leadership. If you have good strong leaders they have the potential to get the press media more so than the rank and file citizen. But we need a combination of strong, outspoken dynamic, right leadership, and a tremendous amount of backup of other leaders in the communities. And there hasn't been enough of it.

Now with some members of Congress, they'll do what they can, but what happens if the New York Times doesn't pick up the rebuttal to a myth speech? This is going to require a tremendous amount of effort. I'd say if we could just give about 90% of the effort that the minority gives to their public relations we wouldn't have a problem. We'd better get on with it. And I look down the road and to me this is one of the most serious problems. It was even alluded to yesterday when the astronauts appeared before the joint session, and one of them said that "We can't do anything except what the public backs up." They understand what public opinion means. And it's an odd thing that after a good education and a reasonable amount of experience I had to go to Congress before I appreciate it, fully appreciate it. That public opinion makes or breaks our country. It's vital. Now public opinion doesn't make or break the Soviet Union because public opinion doesn't exist there, at least in a closed society, it doesn't count. But public opinion in a democracy will make or break the future of the democracy. I don't care how much military power we have, it isn't worth anything if public opinion doesn't support its proper usage.

When Newt Gingrich spoke to the students in 1987, he gave a very candid presentation that included some very specific ideas he wanted to share with the students.

I want to talk about some central issues that you ought to think about as a professional. The first one is, I don't think you can master Air-Land Battle and learn how to fight an irregular war. I think we're asking the officer corps to do two things that are impossible. You can do either one, you can't do both. And that's a very profound challenge. And it's compounded—I think you could have fought the active defense and irregular war. You would have done both of them pretty badly but you could have done them. But in fact if you look at Air-Land Battle and take it seriously the level of elegance and synergism and synchronization and all that stuff that you have to have in order to move inside your opponents decision cycle while knowing who your opponent is, that takes so much focus that for the life of me I don't see how in one professional career you can master it well enough to be brigade commander or above and master the almost exactly opposite skills of irregular warfare. Because Air-Land Battle is high-tech, high-speed, synchronized. Irregular warfare is low-tech, low-speed, decentralized. And they're antithetical.

And I would suggest to you that one of the reasons we're doing relatively badly in irregular warfare is that we're not fighting irregular warfare. There's a famous story out of World War II of American soldiers capturing a Japanese soldier and asking him "Who is the greatest jungle fighter in the world?" And the Japanese said the Australians. And the American was very offended, and said "Well, who's second best?" And the Japanese said "We are." And the American said "This is ridiculous. We just captured you, you said the Aussies are better than we are, you now say you're better than we are, how come we captured you?" And the guy said "You cheat." [Laughter] He said "Americans never fight in the jungle. You bomb the jungle, you bring in the bulldozer, you knock it down, and then you win out in the open." [Laughter] He said "If you quit doing that and come into the jungle we'll show you how much better we are." Well let me suggest to all of you that that's our problem in El Salvador, and in Nicaragua and Angola…The rhythm of mastering another culture, so that we can compete successfully in that culture is antithetical to the rotation system of the U.S. Military.

So I would leave for you to think about the explicit challenge I don't think you can do both jobs. We're going to have to, in the long run, are going to have to have two officer corps. We're going to have to have a very tiny officer corps that has very few general officers and are made up of people who are slightly wacky and they go off and they win irregular wars. [Murmurs and chuckles] And historically that's the nature of the people who win irregular wars. I mean you can't find me very many good staff officers who fight irregular wars. Because they're nutso. [T.S.] Lawrence, [Robert] Clive, I mean go back and study people who win irregular conflicts. And they're charismatic personalities who rise above the bureaucracy and are universally detested by normal people, [Laughter] because they're an enormous threat. And if you will look at [Edmund] Allenby's campaign against the Turks and look at Lawrence, and there's your model. Allenby was a main force general leading a main force effort in Palestine, Lawrence was an irregular. And Lawrence could not have fought Allenby's campaign, and Allenby could not have fought Lawrence's.

Second problem. You desperately need to develop a core doctrine for civilians to understand. Let me explain. You have this thing that talks about areas of interest and areas of influence and all that stuff, and then the area of intense emotional concern which used to be the FEBA [Forward Edge of the Battle Area] or the FLOT [Forward Line of Own Troops] or something. [Laughter] It took me years to figure out that when I'm dealing with [the Office of Congressional Legislative Liaison (OCLL)], they are the tactical arm of the Army or the Navy or the Air Force or the Marines. And OCLL walks in panting heavily for $9 million for X, because that morning at breakfast with the general in charge of OCLL they were told "Get this." And so it's sort of the charge, the machine gun mentality. They're ready. And they run over and find out whoever is going to get this for them, because at the end of the day they have a simple scorecard. And again it's much like being a battalion commander at Fulda [primary avenue of advance for the Soviet Union into Germany]. You know, are you still there or aren't you? [Laughter] So it's that sort of thing, and you can't ask them to educate Congress because that's not their job. Their job is to win the immediate skirmish on behalf of whatever they were told to win that day. And they will say and do pretty well what it takes to win the skirmish. Now that means, however, that if you're a congressman, you spend twenty or thirty years in Congress dealing tactically with the Army when it's passionate and being ignored when it doesn't matter. And so your learning curve is zero.

And I would suggest to all of you to think about the notion that if you elect a congressman who's an insurance agent and he or she doesn't know anything the first year, that might be a comment on the civilians who elected them. If they've been there twenty years and they still don't know anything, that may be a comment on the system of defense's failure to have thought through the central problem of defense. Now I say that because I became a congressman because my dad took me as a freshman to the battlefield of Verdun [in France, World War I], and we stayed with a friend of his who had been in the Bataan death march, and at the end of three days at Verdun it occurred to me—this was in 1958—it occurred to me that my father would fight where the Congress sent him with the weapons the Congress gave him under the rules of engagement established by the Congress. It's important to remember that. The president is Commander in Chief; he is only allowed to be Commander in Chief of the war we declare using the weapons and the army we create. The Constitution is very clear. And yet, you spend more time thinking through how to defeat the BMP [Soviet fighting vehicle] than you do thinking through how to educate the Congress which is going to cripple you enough you can't defeat the BMP. Then you blame me because I'm ignorant.

And the second thing I learned is not only do you not think about it, but the truth is, at the level of defending the nation, there is no professional doctrine in this country. When I turn to senior officers and I say "Tell me the ten things you wish I knew," they're not sure what they are. Fighter pilots know what I should know about fighter pilots, and

Marines know what I should know about Marines, tell me the ten things I should know to think about defending America. And all of a sudden it turns out they don't know. They've never thought about it at that level. They know it's not done well and it must be somebody's fault. They know we would have won in Vietnam if somebody had known the right ten. What ten things should Lyndon Johnson have known to ask? Now that's a tough question. It can't be more than ten because they won't remember more than ten. Nobody does. So what are they? Just something for you to think about. And you can't say "Well, they should trust their military advisors." Would you like to read the history of the Civil War and Lincoln and his generals? Would you like to look at [British Prime Minister David] Lloyd George and his senior officer corps in World War I? Give me a break. [Laughter] You may think we're dumb. We don't think we're professionals. We're just politicians. And officer corps over time, particularly in peacetime, become bureaucracies, and bureaucracies set up cultures which define the internal reality as more powerful than the external reality. And you can read [C.S.] Forrester's brilliant novel *The General*, and when you think about what the British paid for avoiding knowing about reality at the Somme [France], and the fact that no senior British general went to the front. So you can't just turn to me and say "Trust the ones in the uniform." Plus, think of what some of you think of your friends. [Laughter]

…It's very, very important from an Army standpoint because the Army is fundamentally the easiest of the services to criticize, because you're on land. I was explaining this to a group earlier today, but you have to understand the world as seen by congressmen. All of you know that body language matters, right? And you're taught that I guess as second lieutenants. If you look right and you feel right and you have a command presence, everybody but the noncoms [noncommissioned officers] will think you are competent. [Laughs] And if you tell the noncoms you'll let them run the platoon they'll think you're competent too. And they'll run the platoon for you. Well, I'm a congressman. I call over to the big building and I say I need a briefing. There are basically four very different service styles. The Navy sends somebody over. An admiral, erect of bearing, command presence. And essentially in nonverbal language and cultural body language the admiral communicates that in his entire career from the time back when he was a young ensign first given command of a ship late at night, he has learned how to command at sea no matter what nature does. And he has been prepared instantaneously to defeat the Soviet Navy at sea. And he has had thousands of men under his command and he has been calmly willing to put them in harm's way to save the nation. And he knows that I have not had that opportunity, and that I'll never fully understand it. But he is willing to talk to me anyway. [Laughter]

The Air Force essentially sends two people. And they differ in styles, you know, the target acquisition problem. [Laughter] The first one walks in, is a fighter pilot. You always run into fighter pilots in the Air Force. And the fighter pilot basically says, "You know, I could whip your ass. [Huge laugh] I could take your wife, and both your daughters will regret that they were too young to have known me. [More laughter] So why don't we just cut out all the baloney. Sign the check. And in later years you'll have been proud of this moment." [Laugh] Just as you get ready, just as you understand that style, they switch on you. A guy walks in who is not as physically fit, not as dynamic and overpowering, but he's a missile expert. And he starts off usually with something friendly like "When I was getting my doctorate at Cal Tech, and we got involved in these equations, using the Cray, I said to my Nobel-prize-winning tutor, do you think I'll be able to explain this to a congressman someday? And he said no. [Laugh] And I found that he was right. But if you'll sign the check, you won't look ignorant, and I won't be frustrated." [Laughter and applause]

The Marines send in a guy. Who basically says "You may not be able to give me the money. Nobody really cares about us. And we have a fight in four minutes. [Laugh] And we may die without adequate equipment, enough training. But that's what the Marines are for. So if you'd rather sign a check that's here on the John Wayne embossed seal, I'll take it, gratefully, and do what little humble bit I can. We now have three minutes 'til the fight." Now, faced with this array of frustration, because none of those are answerable, right? I mean if you're a civilian, you can't answer them. What happens with the Army?

And this is [General George] Marshall's great legacy and also his curse. And if you study Marshall, and this is true: Marshall spent more time with civilians and guardsman and reservists as a young officer than probably any young officer in the Army. I mean as early as being a first lieutenant he was considered, I think, the greatest trainer in the U.S. Army. It's a small Army back then. The equivalent of being a Major now in terms of relative importance. But look at him, his reputation was awesome. And he understood the central problem of an American army. Which is in a real war, a big war, I don't mean, and with all due respect, Vietnam was not a real war by nation-state standard. In a big war what happens to you is you surge. I mean if we are fighting a serious war that lasted more than 40 days, we would move to a 6 to 7 to 9 million-man Army within three years. So what is the first thing an Army has to do? In a free society it has to be reasonable towards all those civilians who it's presently going to send into battle.

So Army officers walk in and they go "Hi. You know, we know you're not going to give us all that high-tech stuff. And frankly we probably don't need it because we can make do. And we don't want to be involved in all those skirmishes like that Marine. And we're just here to keep protecting the world from war like we have in Europe and we have in Korea. And we're just here to be very reasonable. What questions would you like to ask?" Now here's this congressmen who just went through three services, none of which let him say anything, and you ask what questions we'd like to ask. And then you point out to us "Why don't you come ride in an M-1 tank, it's easy." And it is, apparently, I've never actually ridden in one. I've seen them, they're very big. [Laugh] But what does that say to me? It says "A ha! I know how to drive on land. I may not be able to be a fighter pilot, I may not know about ships, and I may not be in the middle of combat like that Marine, but I know how to drive because I've done it all my life." So now I get to ask questions. And I then promptly reduce the questions to the level I feel secure at.

Like, when the M-1 first came in, we had such breathtaking armored warfare questions as "Why does the track keep coming off?" Now why did the congressman and staffers focus on why did the track keep coming off? Because it's secure. I don't want to know about the battle of Kursk. I don't want to understand the battles around the Suez. Those are complicated. I don't want theories of operational maneuver groups. But by God I can tell you what a track that falls off looks like. But personally, as an Army brat who's studied this stuff for a long time, I never worried about the track question. I mean my dad was infantry, but he had friends who were Armor. [Laugh] And I knew that every guy I'd met as a kid was embarrassed when his tank just sat there. That armored guys had placed a high value in finding a way to make sure the track stays on. So as far as I was concerned the armored guys just out of self-respect would solve the track problem. I'm a lot more worried about whether they'll solve the armored warfare problem. But you have a problem in that sense because until you can figure out how to move congressmen from hardware to doctrine, you're at an enormous disadvantage because all of your hardware tends to be understandable. And therefore we can ask questions about it, and if you pretend that our questions make sense then we'll think we're doing what's right. It's a very, very complicated and sophisticated issue.

We are currently failing at implementing the Reagan doctrine. The Reagan doctrine is a great doctrine, it says we ought to help people who want to be free figure out how to get there. We're failing, we've been playing with it now for six years, the Afghans aren't free, the Angolans aren't free, the Mozambicans aren't free, the Nicaraguans aren't free. I would suggest this is a problem in visions and strategies and projects. And it's something you need to think about. It's not useful to fail for this number of years at a doctrine named after a president particularly while he's still in the White House. And what's even more frightening is that most of them don't even understand they're failing. And it's something very important for you to think about. There is no Western doctrine for winning that makes sense in terms of the Reagan doctrine. If you take the Reagan doctrine seriously, and you should, because that's the primary violence we're involved in in the 21st century. We'll resemble the Reagan doctrine more than we'll resemble Air-Land Battle. Do not think that Nicaragua is more important than Germany. We start with nuclear war, we have to be good enough at that, we go to central front war in Europe, we have to be good at that. We then go to saving the oil fields, we have to be good at that, then we get down to the question of irregular warfare—because if you lose the first three it doesn't matter if you've just won in Nicaragua. You lost the planet. So if you have to choose relatively, it is important to keep them in that sequence. But it would be useful, we have a large enough military, we have enough smart people reading books, it would be useful to be good at all four. And we're currently pathetic at irregular warfare.

…The second problem you have is how do you educate a democracy? Because no irregular warfare doctrine for America that is confined to the battlefield makes any sense. You have to win at least the permission of the American people, and I would suggest we're approaching that almost exactly wrong. Rather than saying "Will you give me positive approval to be in Nicaragua or to be in Angola?" what we should be saying is as long as we keep it below a certain threshold, will you ignore it? Because you can get permission from the American people not to pay attention very easily. And we've just been asking the wrong question. It is impossible, short of Pearl Harbor, to get positive approval for violence. We just won't do it, it's not who we are. It's not the way a democracy works. It is possible for a national government to get permission from people who believe that the government knows more than they do about obscure areas they would like not to think about. That's doable. And a very different issue.

Last big point I'm going to make. And I'm hoping to be able to convince General Vuono to undertake this study during his tour as [Army Chief of Staff]. The U.S. Army is much too small to be a serious player on the Eurasian continent. Period. That is objectively, professionally true. Period. You can't possibly argue with that. Most of you wouldn't. We are also not going to become, in terms of the all-volunteer Army, any bigger. Period. Now, the German and French and Russian armies solved that problem before World War I. They built enormous reserve armies. And the German Imperial Army's reserve divisions were so good, that in coming into contact in 1914, the French army could not tell which were the reserves and which were the regular divisions. Now how do you do that? You have very big reserve units. You practice regularly. The development—we were talking earlier about microprocessors in the classrooms. Simulators. You use all sorts of technology. You make it fun to be a soldier, because you let the guys at the soldiering levels practice being soldiers. They like doing that. No other system in America could give you the fun you'd have in a weekend if you were a salesman during the week, and you actually got to play in an M-1 simulator during the weekend. Now I don't mean to degrade it or make it sound simple, I understand it's a lot more complicated. But at the level of getting those tank platoons that helps. And it is a part of why people sign up. It means that you probably have to pay more for reserve forces.

[Talks about supporting a 4,350,000-man Reserve] And I'll give you the money for it. Why? Because in every congressional district I'll have 10,000 reservists who are sitting there every month studying the military and going "If he doesn't buy more M-2s, I'm going to get my ass shot off." Now that's an incentive program. And you design the program that shows what a 4,350,000-man Reserve would look like, and let me show it to the current reservists who are captains and majors. And let them start to say to themselves "If we went to 4,350,000 men in the Reserve what would my rank be?" [Laugh] Now you have a large enough critical mass of informed civilian citizens. They will show up at the town meeting. And they'll say "Let me tell you what I learned in this month's video tape from the Chief about what happened in Chad. Let me tell you what I learned in this month's video tape about the new Soviet equipment, or about last month's operation by the Soviet army in the Ukraine." And now you've changed the whole dynamic of informed intelligence on the part of civilian leadership in the United States of America. It is impossible, short of that size of Reserve, to do two things—and they're interlocking. It is impossible to sustain the United States in the Eurasian continent in a real war. And any of you seriously think that the Russians and the Europeans are going to let you pull enough troops out of Bavaria to go into Iran? If you do look at 1973 when we could not use German fields to pick up equipment for Israel. We are not big enough even to defend the oil fields. We are certainly not big enough to defend the oil fields and Europe. Second, once you design the right-sized system, you now have to right-size the civilian base to support the system. You don't have the right-sized system if you don't have enough civilians. It's an interlocking tautology. I've been preaching it out here since '79 and I have hopes that sometime in the late nineties the system will gradually figure out that that's unavoidable. There is no other technical solution to the problem. But it really does go head-on to a lot of assumptions in the Pentagon.

Along these lines, Gingrich was later asked whether he supported some form of national service. He said he "personally would prefer universal military training. [Applause] Pershing wanted it, Marshall wanted it. It would lead logically into a four-and-a-half million-man force, and it would give you a base of minimum understanding on a nation-wide basis. And it may well be demographically you don't have much choice by the late nineties."

Obviously candid and pointed remarks such as these generated an intense question and answer period.

Q: You indicated that there is virtually no difference between your position and ours, except for the fact that Congress has the ability to give themselves massive raises, retire after five years with pretty decent pensions and so forth, and also give themselves, as they did in 1981, a tremendous tax break that for some senators was up to about $47,000. Do you ever foresee the Congress extending the same generosity to the military personnel that they do to themselves? [Huge applause and laughter]

A: Now, [Laughter] should I make a comment further or was that...? Let me comment on that at a couple of levels. We lived at Riley in the mid-fifties when my dad was earning captain's pay and had three kids. I have to tell you from that historic bias you are not underpaid. I understand from your own bias you are. I have friends—I'm a college teacher, I'm probably overpaid. I have friends who are lawyers. Their law school classmates are earning four times their income, playing golf five weeks a year, and have much bigger tax breaks. I am, in fact, under the current tax bill—congressmen have less of a tax break than businessmen. The change in 1981 was a temporary change, it didn't survive political pressure, that gave us the same tax advantage that any other citizen has. We have a $3,000 limit on expenses we can take for living in Washington. So I have a second home by necessity for my occupation for which the ceiling on my tax deduction is $3,000. And what we did in 1981 was we temporarily gave ourselves the same pattern as businessmen, which frankly since I'm not rich I thought was crazy because you're right, it meant that some wealthy—I mean J. Rockefeller could now take off half the income of probably two battalions as taxes. But he owns this huge mansion and he can take the whole tax break. So that's what happened, okay? We got a pay raise last year. I happen to not believe you should get pay raises in the term to which you're elected. I'm giving the entire pay raise for two years to students in high schools in my district as a scholarship to go to college. [Applause] My wife is not overjoyed by that, but she accepts it as reality. I will also tell you if I get reelected next year I will then take the pay, because I am running next year for the following two years and people know what the salary is.

Finally I want to go back to your point about masters. In the end in a free society we get the government we deserve. All of you have the right to vote. At some point when you retire you have the right to run. Or you have to right to become precinct leaders or whatever. I happen to think the current Congress is corrupt. I happen to think that it needs to be overhauled dramatically. I think that it is wrong for one party to have been in power in the House since I was eleven. I think over time that Lord [John] Acton's injunction that power tends to corrupt and absolute power tends to corrupt absolutely is true. I think the current Congress is in some ways ignorant. That we had one congressman recently who said he couldn't be for the Contras because they were communist, and he didn't like the 'Uno' guy who was in charge. UNO is the name of the faction not the guy [National Opposition Union]. But let me remind all of you, one, you can change it if you take your career as a lifetime career, not just as a job. You have plenty of time, that retirement pay, and lots of extra energy, and most of you are going to live long enough. You can spend more years in politics after you retire than Lincoln spent in his entire career. So I'm not totally sympathetic in that sense, it's your country, not just mine. And you get to ultimately fire me. Two, it ain't never been much better.

You think George Washington's Continental Congress was smart? Read his letters to them. You think Lincoln's Congress was smart? Would you really like me to go out here and randomly pick 435 battalion commanders and drop them into Congress? I want you to think about that for a while. The Army would be a lot better off for a brief period, and they wouldn't know anything about all the other things we worry about every morning. My only point is that it is the nature of a free society to be very clunky. And it takes constant, unremitting effort by each generation to reform this society despite itself. It's just the nature of free societies.

Gingrich was then asked about his comment regarding fighting wars out of the public eye, and how that was possible given the state of technology and the appetite of the media.

First of all you educate the media to some extent. Second, most people don't pay attention to most news. We live in an information rich environment, and it's a little bit like walking into a grocery store with the mental attitude of somebody who came out of a primitive society, where somebody lives in the Kalahari Desert, where if you didn't eat all the food you found, as soon as you found it, it would spoil. If you go to your local Krogers and try going through with that attitude you'd die somewhere around the asparagus. [Laugh] The same thing is happening to us with information. The average citizen has the remarkable capacity to avoid information. And the trick is what triggers them to look at the information? If you say to them "Oh, Nicaragua's incredibly important and you've got to pay attention to it." You may get them up to a point of saying "No, I don't want to do that." But the average citizen's barely going to get up to that level of enthusiasm. If on the other hand you say to them "Hey, we've got an all-professional force, a handful of volunteers that want to go down and do some work, no big deal." They go "Good, pass the beer, I've got to go to the ballgame." [Laughs] Now, that frankly is the way it should be.

Why should an average citizen in a country of 250 million people, with all the things we've got to do to compete with Japan and Germany, all the things we've got to do to dominate the ocean, all the concerns we have to stop AIDS and to clean up drug addiction, with everything we're doing to build SDI, why should we care about little-bitty wars? I mean, how many Americans do you think were glued to their set for CNNs vital report on the Chadian defeat of the Lybians? How many Americans could spell Chad? [Laughter] And I'm not sure I would argue they should be able to. There are now more countries than it is reasonable to memorize. They should know where Africa is, they should have a general sense that there are things over there that are important. But I've got to tell you, people who grew up—remember? Many of you were part of this generation. My wife was at Kent State during the shootings. And that generation worked hard. I was a graduate student during that period. I was at Tulane. We learned about Vietnam. And Laos. We learned about Cambodia. Cambodia has disappeared, it's now been replaced by Kampuchea. Just about the time we finally learned all those we pulled out, wasting that intellectual investment. People who were able to spell Montengard have not been able to use it since 1974. [Laughter] Then they decided we had to learn about the Middle East, and we learned about the Sunnis and the Shiites and we learned about the Christians in the Amal militia, and we had just gotten up to speed in Beirut and where the airport was and where the Marines were and they pulled out. And the average citizen says "I've only got a certain number of things I can learn in a lifetime."

The most heated exchange was the following:

Q: Sir, until you came here I never knew why they have a non-attribution policy.

Gingrich: Okay, before you go on I should say something to you. This is being taped. I never speak for non-attribution. I say it the way I see it, and if they want to fire me that's their right.

Q: Well I won't fire you, Sir, I'm from New Mexico. I noticed how easily you passed off the responsibility for raising an Army on to the Army. Congress has the responsibility to raise and maintain an Army. I guess your point was as we all make [the rank of] general it's incumbent upon us to educate Congress because congressmen will not go out and get their own education. I don't understand why you guys don't get off the dime and figure out that you're responsible for the strategic levels of war, and it's your responsibility if you think we need more Reserves, to raise them.

A: Okay, now let me give you my modest answer. And just for fun, and I hope you won't take this personally, but I'll reduce it to the same level of directness that you just did. [Big laugh] And I would be glad for any of the more experienced officers in the room to correct me if what I am about to say is wrong. In the first place I, modestly, "got off the dime." I went to Georgia in 1960 as a junior in high school student after my father had taken me to Verdun [France] when we were stationed in Orléans. I ran for office from 1974 to 1978, I lost twice and won the third time, arriving in Congress $50,000 in debt because I'm not a wealthy person. I fought a protracted conflict that began in August of '73 organizing local cadres and built civic action teams in 12 counties. I arrived in the Congress with a PhD in history. I began my first year by going over to see [Army Chief of Staff General Edward] "Shy" Meyer and saying I'm an Army brat who has now gotten to the point I think the Army wants me at, and in the fall of 1979 [TRADOC Commander General] Don Starry sent General [Don] Morelli to see me to give me my first briefing on Air-Land Battle doctrine, which was at that time in its first design stage. I helped write parts of Air-Land Battle doctrine. I have sat in rooms in this building and helped redesign it. I think I have a very good idea, in fact, what vision, strategy, project and tactics are about, I understand the operational art, and I was part of the first group that argued that the original Army doctrine which some of you grew up under, which had only strategy and tactics was an inadequate doctrine, and that you should adopt the Russian doctrine, which is operational art, which is based on the German doctrine. In fact the operational art is a translation into Russian from the German and now from the Russian into the English. So I think I have a reasonably good idea.

I also understand that you are a 780,000-man professional force with an officer corps paid full-time to think about defending the country. And that you have hundreds of thousands of civilians who are out there already, and if I get up there on the floor of the Congress and I have a professionally done study which shows me how one could professionally build a 4,350,000-man Reserve, and how it would fit into continuous operations and why we would therefore be a safer country, I will not look like a jackass. On the other hand, if I get up in my current situation and said that, and I've been saying it in this room since 1979, I will be attacked by senior Army officers because they will have never seen the study, they will not understand why it's valid, they will see it as a threat to their immediate procurement, and they will promptly rush over and testify in great seriousness about how impossible it would be to put through basic infantry training that many people. And I can show the quotations because it's happened before. So my job is to educate the Army and Navy and Air Force and Marines adequately enough that at senior levels—and you'll notice we're only having this conversation once you reach this point in your career, I don't talk like this out in the field—that you in the rest of your professional career and after you retire in your citizen career, that you will write the documents and create the doctrine which allows those of us who care passionately about survival to have an informed base within the bureaucracy so when we say something the bureaucracy is not threatened, understands what we're doing, and can reinforce it. And we can do it professionally well. Now that's sort of what I've been trying to do.

Gingrich closed with some comments regarding democracy.

In a democracy, we are occasionally going to be stupid. It's a guarantee. Dictators are always smarter than democracies in the short run, and always dumber in the long run. It's a problem of information flow. Now if that's true, and I would argue I can prove that it is, then there are bound to be moments in your life when your country's dumb. It's just the nature of a democracy. The incredibly important job you play is to be the line that defends us long enough to get smart. You saw it on Bataan, Corregidor, North Africa. We saw it with Task Force Smith in Korea. It's the nature of a democracy. It's not fun, it's not pretty, it's not wise. It is simply as Winston Churchill once said: The least bad of all those forms of government. And there's one other thing: If we don't die as a country, freedom is, within a century or a century and a half, going to exist on the whole planet. I think that's unavoidable if we don't die as a country. All of you know that your civilian masters don't know very much. Therefore you have to be a professional. Nobody wants me to be a professional.

During his many visits, Representative Skelton frequently addressed congressional topics of the day. In 1993, he began with domestic issues, and then spoke extensively about how the free world should assist Russia.

If I have any complaint with the military collectively, it's that so many people who wear the uniform either don't understand or forget, number one, the Constitution of the United States, the role that Congress plays in what you do and the uniforms you wear and providing and maintaining you, or the communication that should exist at a better level than it does.

…Here at home we face serious challenges. The recessions and slow growth the past two years took their toll on our collective confidence. Domestic problems can be summarized by concerns about unemployment, our national debt, budget deficits, trade deficits, and what can be described as a social deficit. The social deficit encompasses concerns about the rising cost of health care, less than adequate education at primary and secondary levels, a crumbling infrastructure of roads and bridges, and the decay and violence that plagues not just inner cities of our nation but the rural areas as well. The recent election, the promise of a new administration, the improving economy, and the vigor of a young president may help to restore some of the national confidence we lost over the past few years.

...The right kind of Western aid from Europe, Japan, and the United States to the right people can make the crucial difference between success and failure of the democratic capitalist experiment in Russia. Such a program should include a social fund to cushion the shock of those who lose their jobs, to supplement the income of pensioners, to provide medical supplies, and to house returning officers from Eastern Europe and the Baltics. Another aid would go to bolster industries such as energy that can help the Russian economy and have lasting impact. Repairing Russia's energy infrastructure with modern American drilling practices could provide jobs for Americans and a source of hard currency for Russians. Another way to help the process of reform along the way is to provide skills and know-how to local councils, banks, businesses, farms, hospitals from the bottom up. The goal of such aid is stabilization. To help Russia and the other successor states stop their descent into economic chaos. It's a goal that can be achieved. Success by [Russian President Boris] Yeltsin would be a most resounding victory for democracy.

The restoration of the economies of the Eastern Block may well require another Marshall Plan [which rebuilt Germany after World War II], but this time it cannot be done alone. We must work closely with our allies. There will be a long, drawn out campaign taking years to show progress, and yet a lasting victory there would pay great dividends in the long run. American generosity after World War II helped restore the shattered economies of Europe and Japan, permitting the most rapid expansion of world economy in history. A similar development could take place within a few years in Eastern Europe, in Ukraine and in Russia.

Twice before in this century, the United States was confronted with revolutionary changes after an epic struggle. After World War I, we retreated from the world stage and lapsed into isolationism. Weimar Germany in 1923, like Russia today, was experiencing hyper-inflation, collapse of government, capital flight and economic chaos. Hitler did not come to power for another 10 years. The ultimate result was another world conflict in 1939. On the second occasion we remained engaged. The Marshall Plan, aid to Greece and Turkey, the Formation of NATO, Douglas MacArthur's enlightened occupation of Japan. All these helped stabilize difficult situations in both Western Europe and Japan. The result has been prosperity in Europe, Japan, and the United States, and the avoidance, ladies and gentlemen, of World War III.

...If there is to be collective action, it will happen only if the United States leads. The response to the Iraqi aggression in the Gulf succeeded because of American leadership. A more recent example in Somalia. Yugoslavia is an example of what happens when the United States refrains from taking the lead. We should have learned from history that wars, even major ones, can come about when least expected. The peace and tranquility of the European summer of 1914 was shattered by that assassin's bullet. The world was ill-prepared for the tragic events that followed.

We must maintain a ready, modern, and sufficiently powerful military that can meet any unexpected contingency. We need to remind ourselves that despite all the problems we have, America is the richest, most productive nation in the world today. No other nation comes close in terms of economic output, and none seems likely to overtake us for at least a generation, if then.

We have both the ability and resources to continue leading the free world. All we need is the will. Those who would pose a false choice between meeting our responsibilities abroad, and meeting the needs of our people at home do our nation a disservice. For the truth is that we either meet both responsibilities, or we shall meet neither. In the multi-polar world of the future leadership will not be easy. But the United States will have a leading role to play far into the 21st century. Now is the time to realize that taking the initiative is preferable to inaction. That leadership is preferable to self-doubt. That securing the gains that democracy has made in the past decade is within our reach. We can do all this, if we look upon the design of the future, not as a threat, but as a challenge.

Skelton was asked a question about the conditions under which aid to Russia would be provided.

Q: Regarding U.S. or Western aid to Russia, you used two historical examples of Germany and Japan and that of the Marshall Plan following World War II. Given that both of those nations unconditionally surrendered to allied forces and stood down their militaries, not necessarily as a condition for the aid, but definitely prior to the aid being given, don't you feel that, given the fact that Russia still maintains forces under arms [and] still has strategic nuclear forces, that we need to look at some sort of a guarantee other than the statements of the current leadership in terms of their future intentions prior to we [sic] rush in and rebuilding their infrastructure?

A: If you have any ideas I'd love to have them. [Laugh] I don't know what they would be, Major. There is a definite distinction, and I felt this, and I agree with you there is a definite distinction between the Marshall Plan of 1947 and what is occurring today. I do know this: That number one, we cannot do it alone—economically, we cannot do it alone. We can provide the leadership, but there are other economies that can be of help. And number two, if something isn't done, it may not work. It may turn the worms. But if we don't give it a try you may be the ones to pay the price. You, and the young men and women who serve under you. I don't know of a better answer. If you do, tell me.

During his April 1994 appearance, Skelton was asked by a British officer if he felt the European elements of NATO were not doing enough for their own security, and were instead relying too much on the United States.

No. I think, quite honestly, I think this has been reflected by those who have chaired the helm of the NATO forces through the years, that it works well. Has worked well. It appears from what I see, and I have had innumerable briefings through the years with the NATO forces, including officers from other countries, that the joint venture is working quite well. I think in this country in some areas, including some members of Congress, you will find some criticism that America is doing too much. I do not share that, I think that the bargain that we have works well, it's important for us to be there. NATO is a success story. If you look back through the history of Europe, I doubt if you will find a comparable term of peace throughout the centuries as a result of what NATO has been able to do. I hope that it will continue. The same proportion? I'd hate to see us frankly go below the 100,000 soldiers that are there. It's important that everybody row their oar together. It's a great success story, let's not tinker with it.

In December of that same year, Skelton once again lamented the lack of understanding between Congress and the military.

…What I do and what my fellow members of Congress do is raise and maintain you, and yet I find on both sides, those of you in uniform and those of us in the political arena, we pass each other in the night. Not really taking the time to understand or appreciate one another. It's too bad. You know in the Armed Services Committee I've had that privilege, and it is not work, it is an absolute joy—frustrating at times—but an absolute joy, to work with people in uniform. Agree, disagree. Top flight people in our country. But I think that in your school, earlier than now, and those of us in Congress should do a better job of understanding one another.

Skelton also discussed the future of the military, as well as its past.

Where do we go from here with our military? And I suppose we could term this as lessons from our recent Persian Gulf crisis. Most Americans don't realize that we came within a gnat's eyelash of armed conflict three times this year: Korea, Haiti, and Saddam Hussein once again. And the lessons that we should learn from this last soirée to the Persian Gulf many people have forgotten. But let's think out loud for a moment. Saddam Hussein shocked us all once again when he deployed some 70,000 troops and 800 tanks within twelve miles of Kuwait, led by the infamous Republican Guard, to again threaten the oil fields in that part of the world. And his maneuver was quick, it was orderly, indicating that it had been well-planned and had had careful rehearsal. President Clinton responded positively and decisively, and within a week American forces had multiplied in that region. The Iraqi army saw M1 tanks in front of them, and the shadow of American airpower overhead. Well, that crisis moved from the battlefield to the negotiating table, and America demanded that the Iraqi army, at least the Republican Guard element, be barred from maneuvering below the 32d parallel, which is about 100 miles north of Kuwait. And that's where we ran into trouble. Some of our previous coalition partners, democratic governments, undermined the coalition solidarity, and failed to support us in that effort. Saddam Hussein, you will recall, made his move just 12 days after we had our attention toward occupying Haiti, and our attention was riveted there as a nation, as a military, and where we executed the largest peacekeeping operation we have ever done.

But he'd been watching America for some time. Through the previous six months we had concerned ourselves, you'll recall, with North Korea. Nuclear weapons were the issue. In June the president put our forces on alert, sent Patriot missiles to Korea, and moved battle groups there, and I am convinced that Saddam Hussein began planning his strike when he saw America moving toward a possible conflict on the Korean peninsula. And while the U.S. and South Korea would defeat North Korea, Saddam Hussein knew the cost would be high. Though the second Korean War was averted with diplomacy, and looking at the events at the time, I'm convinced that Saddam Hussein began planning his move back then. The present Gulf crisis ended without combat, as you know. But the dictators and their armies remain intact, both in North Korea and Iraq. They remain poised to threaten the vital interests of our country once again. There are various lessons we should learn, and that's what you're all about is learning lessons from the past...So let's learn these lessons and see if they can't help us in the future.

Lesson number one: Our strategy to fight and win two major regional conflicts nearly simultaneously is an appropriate one. As you know, it was established by the former Secretary of Defense Les Aspin who was a former chairman of our committee, and a document known as the Bottom Up Review that set forth the force structure was written to take care of the two regional conflicts. Well we need to be prepared to defend our vital interests when those two unforeseen things come to pass. I think that's a good premise. The second lesson is that American diplomacy must be backed by strong, credible military power. If it's not, we speak without much avail. We need credible military backing to have a potent American diplomacy. We should never, never forget that.

[Lesson number three] The Persian Gulf crisis teaches us to dampen our expectations about coalition partnerships. Our present Secretary of Defense [William J. Perry] wrote an article back in 1992 about the future, and much of it being around coalitions with other countries. And of course, Desert Shield and Desert Storm was a very successful chapter in coalition military workings. But it isn't always going to be that way. When we wanted to establish the line at the 32d parallel, south of which no Saddam Hussein Iraqi forces could come, some of our allies did not agree. That was unfortunate. That's why we here in this country should work hard with our allies, do our best, but not put all the eggs in that particular basket, because we may be forced to go it alone.

...As sure as God made little green apples, we're going to need you somewhere down the road, and if the caliber of officer erodes, if you vote with your feet. If the caliber of the young Soldier, sailor, Marine, airman erodes, they vote with their feet. When they're needed, we may come out second best, with casualties that were unnecessary. So if I have a message for you, it would be a Navy phrase, "Steady as she goes." I hope that each you will continue to do well, and have a strong and prosperous career.

In answer to a question about military education, Skelton stressed its importance.

Concerns: I chaired a panel in '87. We came out with recommendations involving jointness, strategic thought, and rigor. Military education is so very important. In between the [world] wars the only right thing that America did was to educate its military leaders for the future. Everything else went to pot. Everything went to pot. But somebody, somewhere, insisted that they have this fine course, two-year course at Fort Leavenworth, that the Army War College do a good job, that the Navy War College do a good job. They had time—Bull Halsey had enough time in his young career, in between the wars, to go to both the Army War College and the Navy War College. And the real heavy hitters, they asked them to come on and be instructors. And these instructors by and large ended up division commanders or above in the Second World War. That was the golden era of military education. That's what I hope our panel has revived and I have good reason to think that we did. And it costs money to do this, not a lot of money to do this, but it costs money to bring in top-notch civilian instructors and pay them and we had to pass an amendment on that. To require the right kind of mix, so you have enough sailors teaching you as well as soldiers. And airman teaching you as well as soldiers.

And I was shocked when the Senate Appropriations Committee cut $14 million out of professional military education for this year. Well we got it turned around. But one thing we did not get turned around was the devastating language that looks toward next year. Hopefully we can get that voided this year in conference. The importance of military education should be the top of everything. It's learning about those times when people stepped in holes. People who didn't survive the mistakes they made, or how they learned from the mistakes of others, or how they did something right in battle. If you don't intellectualize it, you're going to fail on the battlefield. That's why we did well in World War II, by those majors and captains and lieutenant colonels that were going through what you're going through now. Thank goodness for that. I'm going to do my best to keep the whole military education funding up…That's why you ought to study as hard as you can while you're here because sooner or later—sooner or later—you're going to be called upon to use those examples, those lessons that you learned from the lectures and text here.

An international officer asked Skelton whether "Congress [had] largely forfeited its constitutional role in declaring war…giving one individual the power to initiate military operations, largely without public debate,…in areas sometimes…where our vital interests are not threatened?"

A: You have posed the question as so many of us have. It is clear in the Constitution that Congress is the sole repository of the declaration of war. On the other hand you have the provision that states that the President of the United States is the Commander in Chief. And where the vital interests of America come, and where they fuzz into a necessity for a declaration of war is a line that has never been drawn, either by the courts or much further than the War Powers act, which really doesn't answer that question. I felt it necessary that Congress speak [during] the Persian Gulf crisis back in 1991. I handled the first two hours of that debate in favor of a declaration authorizing our troops to use force. Looking back I think everyone, constitutional lawyers included, would agree that that was the thing to do. That same issue has come up since, in particular with the issue of Haiti. As that was resolved at literally the last moment through diplomacy, that became moot. I don't think you will ever really have an excellent answer to that, but hopefully in the clear-cut cases where the voice of the American people should be heard and debated, regardless of the outcome, we would do it. Emergencies being laid aside, I think that should be the case.

In 1996, Skelton discussed the relationship between the three branches of government and provided some history on the Goldwater-Nichols Act of 1986, which caused a major reorganization of the Defense Department.

In gluing all of this together, the framers intended for the two houses to be at war with each other. They intended for the White House, what later turned out to be the White House, the presidency to be at war with the Congress and the Supreme Court's role at that time was not clear, but *Marbury versus Madison*, [Chief Justice] John Marshall established it as the arbiter of the Constitution and could strike down laws made by the

Congress and the acts made by the president. And it's worked pretty well through the years. Actually it's worked very well the years.

The Goldwater Nichols bill. Interesting history there. Dick White, a congressman from Texas, had a series of hearings. [Chairman] David Jones, [Army Chief Edward] Shy Meyer, of the Joint Chiefs of Staff both testified that something was wrong with the way the Joint Chiefs of Staff was working. That they were yielding to the lowest common denominator to reach a consensus. Well, Dick White had some excellent hearings, he put a bill together, he retired, I picked up the ball thereafter in 1983, and introduced the first bill, and the Joint Chiefs of Staff really didn't like it. I abolished it. They had no sense of humor. [Audience chuckles] I got a letter from P.X. Kelley, the Commandant of the Marine Corps. We had to have a special lead folder because it was still so hot. But we had a series of hearings. [Alabama Representative (D)] Bill Nichols, the chairman of the particular subcommittee that dealt with this, didn't become interested in it right away until he went over [to Beirut, Lebanon], shortly after I was over there. I was in Beirut when they were still, sadly, bringing Marine bodies out of the tragic bombing. Bill Nichols went over a few weeks thereafter. Had a series of hearings aboard ships about the chain of command from the president to the Marine colonel. There were 22 links in that chain of command. Twenty-two. And he became interested. Something has to be done in this reorganization of the United States Military.

Over the next three years we developed bills. Passed them individually, they died in the Senate. One year we made it part of the DoD Defense Authorization Bill, most of it died. Senator John Tower, the Chairman of the Senate Armed Services Committee, was not enthralled with it. The Navy being the greatest, but not the only, opponent to reorganization, and he [Tower] being a Chief in the Navy Reserve, it didn't have much chance, although we did get a few paragraphs. Then in 1986 the Chairman of the Armed Services Committee in the Senate was Barry Goldwater. We again passed our bill as a free-standing bill and Barry Goldwater, Sam Nunn as his ranking minority at the time, picked it up and ran with it.

And we came out with what is now known as the Goldwater-Nichols bill, which was a sweeping reorganization of the entire military in the United States. It was bitterly opposed, bitterly opposed by the Joint Chiefs of Staff, especially the service chiefs. We had some very unpleasant sessions, individually and collectively, with them, but for probably a good reason. If you and I were in their position we probably would have opposed it as well. What we ended up doing was increasing the power of the Chairman of the Joint Chiefs of Staff, lowering the power of the other four members of the Joint Chiefs of Staff, who ran their respective military branches. Inserted a Vice Chairman of the Joint Chiefs of Staff, and we later gave him additional powers. And then we increased the power of the [Regional Commanders in Chief (CinC)]. Testimony was that Admiral Bill Crowe when he was [Commander in Chief, Pacific Command] he asked his Army 3-star commander, he told the commander to move an ammunition dump from one place to another he said "I'm not going to do it, you can't make me do it, I'm not." If he did that today under Goldwater Nichols he'd be gone in two hours. Because we gave that CinC, in times of peace as well as in times of war, complete mastery of his domain.

In late 1999, Skelton returned, expressing his concern for the military's future well-being.

> I have a concern that I'd like to share with you. I think that you and your leadership here are addressing it. But it's as a result of success that your predecessors have had. We won the Cold War. As a result of that and the Berlin Wall coming down and Europe having a new face on it, the American military, as well as other militaries in NATO have been cut drastically. 40% in the United States Military. Yet insofar as the Army is concerned, your operations tempo has increased some 300%. There is a clash of events there. But with the downsizing of the military, of course conscription ended in 1973, fewer & fewer young men and young women are joining. Fewer and fewer families have someone— father, son, aunt, uncle—in the military. And consequently the understanding of things military across our nation is waning. This is a challenge for all of us, including myself. Because if we are to have a substantial military to do what is necessary to maintain a peaceful world, and we are the only superpower on this planet, we have to back our diplomacy with strength. And that is you. The young men and women that you command, and will command.

> ..This is "The Year of the Troops." But each year is on its own and I am concerned about the following years, particularly in the areas of research and development, and the area of modernization. That if we don't do something about it in the future, you will find airplanes, helicopters, trucks without spare parts. You will find serious problems with readiness that can only be fixed with infusion of dollars.

> ... The front page of the Washington Post reflected, what, three or four days ago, that two of the Army divisions, the First Infantry which has its flag in Germany, and the 10th Mountain Division, which is up in New York, both are at C4 readiness [the lowest level]. And of course this is alarming for me to read. However it's also interesting to note that parts of these divisions are doing 'other things' or recovering from doing 'other things.' And it's not a great surprise. I was pretty upset when I read it and I wanted to know where my copy of the report was. General [William M.] Steele got the Army I guess a little exercised when I asked for my copy and they had no copy. It was as a result of a briefing that allegedly was blown out of proportion somewhat to some Senate staffers. However it is true that when you have ongoing duties and a small—you only have ten divisions. They can't go to war because they are being drained off doing other things. It's understandable. But it is also something we must do our best to keep them as close to C1 or C2 as possible. When they're drained off like that there's just not an awful lot that you can do.

Skelton was asked a question about a disconnect between the civilian leadership and general public regarding military casualty rate expectations and acceptance of casualty rates in operations.

> I think it goes to the gap that exists between the American military and the American civilians. It also touches on the success that America has had in recent engagements. In Desert Storm, the low casualty rate there, when, I think General Schwarzkoph, didn't he suggest we might have some 10,000 casualties? My recollection. And of course there were far, far, far fewer than that thank goodness. But we were victims of our own success in that area. We've been very fortunate as you know in Bosnia and so far in Kosovo. I think the root of this is a lack of basic understanding and appreciation of the

role of the military, that there are casualties in serious engagements. But when the American public does not understand, as I think so many don't, you're victims of your own success, and consequently expect no or few casualties with a great success in whatever the mission may be.

Senator Roberts touched on a host of issues during his April 2001 appearance, including resolving a serious issue with China, United States foreign policy, and budgeting.

We have many challenges—there's no question about that—within our military today. And the truth of it is we're making some long overdue progress. Finally. But I want to let you know, in my personal opinion, and in the opinion of some who have the privilege of serving on the Armed Services Committee, in too many instances our military is still stressed, constrained, and in too many cases, hollow. And speaking to you as a former Marine, as a Senator who fought and won the privilege to serve on the Armed Services Committee and Intelligence Committee, like yourself, I don't like that one damn bit.

Let me turn to China. President Clinton described our relationship with China as a strategic partnership. President [George W.] Bush has described it as a strategic competitor. Some now in the Congress, my colleagues, are instant national security advisors and secretaries of state, have described China as a strategic adversary. My view, they're probably all three. And that's what we face today, more especially in regards to the week that is coming upon us and the tough negotiations that are going to take place. Last week was quite a week. My staff and I were visiting 23 counties out west [in Kansas] and we were at Colby and we were headed toward Goodland. Special occasion because at five o'clock in the morning the Intelligence Committee that morning gave me a call and said "Senator, we think there's going to be a breakthrough." And I said "Can you give me any details?" And he said "Yes Sir, just turn on CNN." [Laughter] So I did. There was the Chinese Foreign Minister going through his diatribe but also indicating that our people were going to be released. And in Goodland, Kansas, America, there is a family, the Vignery family, and I think you saw on television young Jeff, who was one of the pilots. And his dad is Ron and his mom is Judy. Ron is an attorney out there.

Wind is blowing about 60-70 miles per hour. We're having a hell of a time getting down Highway 70. They had it blocked off and I pulled rank and I said "Hey, I've got to get to Goodland. [Lieutenant] Jeff Vignery is about to be released, and I want to be at that bank where they're having the celebration and all the yellow ribbons you see, you've got to let me through." "Alright Senator, be careful." I saw a bunch of TV trucks on their way out there to film that, and they were underneath the underpass. Sort of made my heart glad that—well, never mind, I won't go there. So we went out there to the bank and there were about 150, 200 people braving the wind and the rain and the snow out there for Ron and Judy. And I got to hold the telephone to my ear and say "Ladies and Gentlemen it's wheels up and Jeff is coming home." Boy, tears and smiles and hugs, what a deal. I think as a result of that we are now in a very—I hope it's a longer period, but from time to time we do this in our country in regards to the national awareness of the role and mission of people like yourself who wear the uniform of the United States. Maybe a little education as to why we fly reconnaissance aircraft, in terms of what reconnaissance missions are necessary for our country. Real spark of renewed patriotism in our country. Made your heart beat a little faster.

...I believe, in regards to [the role of vital U.S. national interests in our foreign policy], that a case can be made that following the Cold War, the United States seemed to lose focus and direction in its foreign policy. It seems we drifted away from certain basic fundamentals and understanding of our national interest. We seem to treat all events around the world equally, but more importantly the decision to even participate or pass appeared to be based more on public concern, fostered by CNN and others, rather than an evaluation based on what our vital national interests were. Based on this senator's observation, if we as a nation become involved militarily in an event in the world that is *not* a vital national interest, or even one that has significant national interest, then it appears that we do not fully commit to winning. Or even define what winning is.

Two examples of our military involvement with and without significant national interest: The Gulf War and something called Kosovo. We were fully committed to winning the Gulf because our vital national interests were at stake. Now I know Saddam is still there. We get 8% of our energy supply now from [Iraq ruler] Saddam Hussein. And then use the fuel in our aircraft to go bomb him. If that is a sustainable energy policy I'll be damned if I can figure that out. But we are reassessing on a regional basis just what it is that is our policy in regards to Saddam, but I think you understand that we made a full commitment at the time. But I think Kosovo, even though there was a compelling—let me underscore that—a compelling humanitarian situation—And talking with many students of this school several years ago down at the best steakhouse in Kansas and maybe America, Mama Mias, with a little Wild Turkey served aside, I said "What the hell is it that we are accomplishing in Kosovo to the people there?" They said "Senator we're making a difference. We're making a big difference." And I think from a humanitarian standpoint certainly that is correct. But it is not a vital national interest, and as a result, with all due respect to [General] Wesley Clark and the 19 other generals involved, we did not construct a smart, robust military campaign. In Kosovo we did not have clear objectives, we had a poorly defined end-state, still do. And we were unwilling to commit to using the full military capability of NATO to win. To win the victory, which is very hard to define. And the situation in the Balkans is still unresolved. As I indicated I was just there about a month ago. We had 11 Serbs killed, some on the border and some in Mitrovica [Kosovo]. And they got the U.S. Senators out of there very pronto, I can assure you of that. But from Bosnia to Kosovo to Montenegro to Macedonia to Albania—we're now talking about a greater Albania—and that continues to fester.

Well what are our national interests? Two commissions, one in 1996 and one in the year 2000 looked closely at a system or a way to assess and try to really prioritize. I was fortunate to serve on both commissions. Basically let me just indicate to you what this was all about. [Reading] "Challenges for the Decade Ahead: Developments around the world pose threats to U.S. interests and present opportunities for advancing Americans' well-being. Because the United States is so predominant in the economic and the technical and the military realms many politicians and pundits fall victim to a rhetoric of allusion. They imagine that as the sole superpower the United States can simply instruct other nations to 'do this' or 'stop that' and expect them to do it. Students of history will recognize a story line in which a powerful state emerges, even if accidentally, engenders resentment, even when it acts benevolently, and then succumbs to the arrogance of power, and thus provokes new threats, from individual acts of terrorism to hostile coalitions and states." Sound familiar? [Continues reading] "Because America's resources are limited, U.S. foreign policy must be selective in choosing which issues to address seriously. The proper basis for making such judgments is a lean, hierarchal conception of what America's national interests are, and what they are not. Media attention to foreign affairs reflect access to vivid and compelling images on a screen, without much consideration of the importance of the U.S. interests. Graphic international problems like Bosnia or Kosovo make highly consuming claims on American foreign policy to the neglect of issues of greater importance like the rise of Chinese power"—this was written in 2000—[continues reading] "the unprecedented risk of nuclear proliferation, the opportunity to increase the openness of international trading and financial systems, or the future of the Southern Hemisphere of Mexico."

A student asked Roberts about the disconnect between long-range military planning and an annual budget cycle, and asked how Congress could reconcile these two diverging processes.

Very carefully. Like two porcupines during that amorous period. [Slowly building laughter] A little slow here today, I don't know. Jesus, you think it's difficult for you to understand, what do you think about me? I'm an authorizer! That means we sit on the Armed Services Committee and in the infinite wisdom of our founding fathers, the Congress—well, first the president will propose, which he has done in his budget. Now I understand it was $8 Billion, now it's $10.5, it will go up to $15 by the time that we're through, to pay for the increased fuel costs and all of the things that were talked about in the campaign, by the way. So we're going to have to have an urgent supplemental as long as we continue to rob these funds to pay the readiness funds for all the missions that we talked about. So that's up now to about $10.5 billion. So the president will propose and then your Armed Services Committees of the House and the Senate will authorize this. And we go through a very careful process. I've got everything under the sun under the emerging threats subcommittee. I've got terrorism, I've got weapons of mass destruction, I've got crime, I've got four or five other topics that take an awful lot of money. All the Nunn-Luger programs. And so we carefully go down that, we try to shape it within the budget that we have. If you're going to err, you'd better err on the side of readiness...So we're very careful as we go down that. Then we turn it over to the appropriators.

I love appropriators. In the House, when I was the Chairman of the Agricultural Committee, and we were trying to get adequate funding for agriculture, I thought seriously about shooting appropriators. In the dead of night I still might go over and shoot some appropriators in the House. But in the Senate I decided "This is ridiculous" so I smother them with the milk of human kindness. I press their ties, I shine their shoes, I clean their windows, I do KP [slang for military mess hall duty], I do everything for appropriators. And I say "Please, Ted [Stephens]" There's the Chairman of the Appropriations Committee. "Bob Bird, we'll pave West Virginia if we have to. [Big laugh] All I want is a little money to fix up the housing in Leavenworth. Please! For majors. A few light colonels." And so you beg, borrow, and say "Please, these are the priorities." Then you work that out as best as we can under very difficult circumstances. I think that you're going to see—Oh, we asked the Joint Chiefs to come back after three years after that remarkable display of 'Hear no evil, See no evil,' and then they changed their mind after six months, no reflection on these great Americans, they were under a lot of pressure to do what they thought was right. But now if you ask the Navy and the Air Force and the Army and the Marines what they truly need to get the job done, my God! We're into 40, 50, 60, 70, 80 billion dollars more than we are now.

And that's why Secretary Rumsfeld has said "Whoop! Time out. We're going to do an assessment." Do the assessment first, and then we'll do what's necessary down the road, and we're going to come up with about $10.5 billion. A lot of talk about a two-year budget cycle. You appropriate the money and you go back in and do oversight and you try to figure out what's working and what isn't. I'm not too sure but what you wouldn't spend more money on in emergencies than you would on an annual cycle. But what we're going to try to do is look out over the next 10 years, and that's what we're doing in the Emerging Threats Committee, to say, alright, what are those threats out there, what should we be investing in? Admiral [Art] Cebrowski and the Streetfighter Warship, sort of like a giant catamaran [A littoral combat ship]. That doesn't make regular Navy troops who want more destroyers very happy. But you've got to take a look at that. So we're doing that. And it will be driven a lot by this study that Rumsfeld has.

These politicians generally covered heady, serious subjects, as did many of the guest speakers. Most tried to significantly lighten the mood and grab the audience's attention using levity. Some succeeded, and some did not. The following chapter provides some of the highlights.

8. Jokes and Oddities

In order to grab the audience from the start, lighten the mood, or keep students awake, most guest speakers made some attempt at levity during their remarks. A few samples of the jokes that worked are below. Additionally, some speakers, as well as some students, said some things that must have caused their audience some discomfort.

DID YOU HEAR THE ONE ABOUT...

In 1953 S.L.A. Marshall took the stage and copped to feeling less than 100 percent.

> I am speaking under some difficulty this morning, because my voice is pretty well shot. That's due only in part to the lingering on of a cold. The other part of it is that I was out with some friends last night and they treated me as an old newspaper man is supposed to be treated, meaning just as often as possible. [Laughter] And the truth of the matter is that even the kind words that were said about me by [Deputy Commandant] Colonel [Charles] Beauchamp a few minutes ago couldn't possibly make me feel good. [Laughter] But, as the porcupine said as he walked away from the toothbrush, "Well anybody could make a mistake, and I made mine last night." [Laughter]

General Lemnitzer treated the 1961 graduating class to an anecdote from his time at the school. "On the final general terrain exercise across the river we had the usual minstrel show, and one of our Chinese officers was asked what he thought of the school and the course. And his answer was this: 'Most peculiar school. Many questions, no answers.'" The next year, General Johnson prefaced a lecture he was about to give about the nuclear battlefield with an apology: "Now regrettably I'm going to join your long roster of illustrious guest readers. [Laugh and applause] But I have read this enough times, and I have gone over it with my pencil enough times, and I can assure you that I have a reasonable degree of familiarity with it." [Another laugh]

During his February, 1964 appearance, President Truman kept the audience laughing with stories such as the time he visited the University of Wisconsin.

> They had about 3,200 students in a hall that would hold 1,100...when I got through talking to them, some little old gal said to me "Mr. President, what are we going to do about birth control?" I said "Young Lady I'll be damned if I know...That's in your department, I don't have anything to do with that." Then a little later on a boy over here on this side said "Mr. President, what'll happen if we have an all-out atomic war?" "Well," I said. "I don't know young man, but the young lady won't have to worry about birth control." [Laughter]

An audience member asked Truman for his thoughts on a potential female president of the United States. "They've got everything else in the country I don't see how you're going to keep them out of there."

General Bruce Clarke, former Commander, U.S. Army, Europe, spoke about one of the freedoms of retirement in 1964.

> After you are retired, you're not inhibited by responsibility and you can become an expert in a hurry. Now that I have been retired for two years, I am far greater an expert than I

was two years ago. Because I have no inhibitions and I am willing to approach any question and express an opinion on it, which I will do with great abandon later.

Omar Bradley didn't feel quite as free in his retirement, saying in 1966 "I should have said to start with: Excuse me for reading this, but still being on active duty I have to get my speeches cleared."

Admiral Zumwalt had some dry zingers buried in his remarks that were not lost on the students in 1973: "The amphibious ships [are] capable of projecting that very fine missile—the Marine," and "I tell one of my favorite flag officers that I think we have at least one mental group IV flag officer." [Referring to the lowest mental category] General Bruce Palmer lamented how his U.S. Readiness Command was an underutilized resource in 1974, saying "The problem is I feel sometimes like General Halftrack in [the comic strip] Beetle Bailey: Waiting for the Pentagon to call."

General Abrams was another speaker with a dry sense of humor, as he demonstrated in 1974: "I've looked forward to this meeting here this morning with a great deal of pleasure and anticipation. I'm delighted to see such a fine turnout. [Laughter] At least permissiveness has not infiltrated this fine institution." Later, in response to a question about how the Unified Command Plan reworking would turn out, he said "If I made a prediction on the outcome of that I would be telling you something that I really don't know. I would be indicating some insight into the machinations of [the Pentagon] which I don't have." [Big laugh]

That same year Army Secretary Callaway realized his power did not reach to the Bell Hall stage, after pointing at a paddle handler to receive a question, only to have the moderator call on a different number. "I find a lot of things I don't have authority for, excuse me Colonel Brown." [Big laugh]

General Vessey repeatedly brought the house down during his visit as the Deputy Chief of Staff for Operations in 1975.

> I've got an outline of a talk and it has a bunch of slides because I remember that we used to sit alphabetically, it wasn't in this place, it was in the theater. And it used to be fairly dark underneath the balcony. But if the guy didn't have slides and you were back in the 'V' rows as I was, it was difficult to sleep when some guy just kept the lights up through the whole talk. [Laughter] Well I've got some slides and when you feel like you want to grab a snooze back there kind of give it this [gestures] and we'll turn them down and I'll show a slide.

> …The best talk I ever heard at a service school was Curtis Lemay, the old Chief of Staff of the Air Force. He came down to Norfolk [Virginia] when I was a student there [at the Armed Forces Staff College]. And at Norfolk, I don't know how you work this question business here but at Norfolk the students got appointed to be monitors and you had a microphone. And you had to peddle that microphone to somebody that was going to ask a question, or you had to ask one yourself if you couldn't sell it. [Laughter] And I was number one in the microphone roll that particular day, and they told us to expect anything when LeMay comes. And he said about the way I feel about my outline here, he said "I've got a talk. It's a pretty good talk, I read it on the way down here." And he said "I'm going to give it to the commandant and he can put it in the library and you can read

it too." [Laughter and applause] Then he said "What are your questions?" [Big laugh] Well, there I was stuck with that microphone. But fortunately we had a spring-butt [big laugh] that was there in my section, and he took the microphone and immediately launched off into some great theoretical speech on roles and missions, and after about 10 minutes he came to the question mark in his speech. And LeMay said "That's a helluva dumb question. Next question." [Big laugh]

...You can say things as a division commander, and there are guys who will hear you say things, and you say one thing, and it's the old semantic triangle, they hear something else. And you have to be very concerned about that. As General Abrams used to say, the higher up the flagpole you go the more your backside shows. And you want to be concerned about that, because you'll go around and you find some soldier doing something very nutty and you say "Why are you doing that?" And the kid says "Because you ordered it done, Sir." And that happens all too often. As a battalion commander I was concerned about—it was in another day of constrained resources, and I went down to the paint sheds one day and looked in here and geez, we had all these gallons and five gallons of paint, open with a wet layer of scum on the top of each one, none of it very useful anymore. And being sort of a scotch jerk I got the battery commanders together and said "I'm going to give you a little lesson in saving paint. And I have here a gallon of paint, unopened, OD paint. I have here a putty knife. I have here some wax paper. I have here my pen knife, and I have here a paint brush and a board. And I will paint that board. Now, before you open that can of paint you ought to put this can of paint down on the wax paper and take your pen knife and cut out a piece of wax paper the size of the paint can, and then just set that aside." I said "The smart thing to do is not paint out of the paint can, but soldiers are going to paint out of the paint can, so recognize it." So I had two other things, a hammer and a ten-penny nail. I said "Now, take that putty knife and pry the lid off that paint can carefully so you don't bend the lid. Now you take that hammer and that ten-penny nail and you put about 6 holes in the rim, down inside the rim here so when the soldier paints out of the can, the paint will flow back down through those holes into the can. And when you hammer the cover back on, it won't splash all over and get his fatigues all full of paint and you'll get a good seal." Then I painted the board, to show them it was real paint"—I learned that [Method of Instruction] in Leavenworth—[laughter] "then you take that piece of wax paper and you put it on top of the paint and you push the bubbles out and just have it sit on top of the paint, put your cover back on the can, hammer it closed, and you can save that paint forever as long as it doesn't freeze out there in the paint shed. All you have to do, next time before you open it, cut another piece of wax paper, take the old piece of wax paper out, no scum, stir it up, and paint."

I went home, I thought maybe I'll get a green-weenie [Army Commendation Medal] for that, that was so smart. I'd never gotten one and I was looking for some way to do it. If this worked out well I might even tell my leader how smart I was. Well about two weeks later I was down around the backside of the motor pool, I got down in old bungle battery's motor pool and I said "Hey Sarge, who's got the key to the paint shed? Let's open it up and see what it looks like." So we opened it up and God, was it a mess. It was an artillery battalion and of course they had a little red paint around there, and the whole inside of this thing was just gooey with red paint. And I looked in there, and here is a can, it was obviously red paint, and somebody had punched about six holes around the outside of the can about two inches down from the rim. [Laughter] And being sort of a maintenance-minded commander I always had a screwdriver in my pocket, so I pried off the lid, and there's a big crumpled up chunk of wax paper pushed down inside the paint. [More laughter] Couldn't you just hear these soldiers while they were doing this, saying "You know, if the dumb son-of-a-bitch wants it this way, we'll give it to him." [Applause]

…I've talked so long I'm probably in trouble already, and I just have to tell you the story about trouble. You guys have had so many guest lecturers that you've probably heard this thing, and if you have don't stop me because it's my best story and it's so funny I want to hear it again myself. This is a story of a Russian. A very compassionate man who was out in a very cold day and he was walking back in town, and he found a bird about two-quarters frozen to death lying on the ground. He picked up the bird and held it in his hands to try and warm it. He blew on the bird to try to bring it back to life. He could perceive the signs of life but he could see that the bird was pretty far gone. So he finally put it down inside his jacket and walked on into town. And when he walked into town he had to go into some kind of business establishment and he didn't want to have to take his coat off and have a half-dead bird drop on the floor, so he looked around on the ground. He found a fresh pile of steaming manure on this cold day in the middle of the street. So he parted the manure very carefully and put the bird down inside the manure and packed the manure up around the bird's neck. Well the warmth and the other theraputic effects of the manure brought the bird around. And the bird began to sing. Well, it was a small village and there was a fox going by the village out on the edge, and the fox heard the bird singing. So the fox came over to check it and he found the bird in the pile of manure and he pulled the bird out of the pile of manure and he ate the bird. Well there are three morals to this story and they're so obvious that I feel guilty repeating them but I will. And the first is that the guy who sticks you in it isn't necessarily your enemy. And the second is that the guy that pulls you out isn't necessarily your friend. And the third one is when you're into it up to your neck, don't sing. [Laughter and applause]

Less than a week later General Weyand tried his hand at humor.

I was going to say it's a pleasure to be here, but I'll have to hold judgment on that until all this is over…Bear Bryant had a story that he told at a Touchdown Club thing I went to about a year or so ago. And he was describing the trials and tribulations, travails of a coach. They didn't end when that game ended. He had the interests and problems of the team and the team members to worry about. It was a 24-hour-a-day job. And he said "It's like making love to a gorilla: you don't quit when you get tired." He went on to say "You quit when the gorilla gets tired." And it's obvious that the Pentagon never seems to get tired.

General Meyer poked a little fun at himself in 1979.

When I came to the Command and General Staff College I came on an athletic scholarship, [laughter] they didn't have the same sort of strict criteria they have today for selection.

196

...One of the things they tell you when you become a general officer, when they send you through charm school, is they tell you the first thing you have to do is go hire yourself a good speechwriter. And that way you'll always sound brilliant and you'll be able to make the right kinds of sounds, and you won't screw it up out there. So I did that when I started out, and I asked the guy to write me a 20 minute speech. So he gave me a 20 minute speech, and I got up, and it kept going and going and going and going and going when I was reading it, and it ended up it took me about 45 minutes to finish it. Afterwards I took Frank off to one side and really chewed him out and said "I thought I told you to write a 20 minute speech?" And he said "I did write a 20 minute speech but I didn't tell you to read it through twice." So that's one of the reasons I decided I wasn't going to use speechwriters and speeches anymore.

...I also then was kind of entranced early by 3 x 5 [index] cards, because when I was first assigned to a division I was assigned to a National Guard division, the 40th National Guard Division. And of course that was right about the time of the Korean War, and when you went into a National Guard division you went into a division which had great longevity, as you can imagine, a great cohesiveness kind of experience that exists over time, where everyone knows one another quite well, everyone has known the families and everything else. But when I got there I went to the first hail and farewell and I found that we had a regimental commander who had a very short memory. So he used 3x5 cards in order to ensure that he didn't forget anything, and I'll never forget that first hail and farewell, he was saying goodbye to his adjutant and it went something like this: "Tonight we're gathered together to say goodbye to— [looks down at card] Major and Mrs. Jones, and Major Jones has been my— [looks down at card] adjutant [big laugh] for the last— [looks down at card] four years. During that period of time he's done a— [looks down at card] excellent job. [laugh] He's going off to the— [looks down at card] 12th Cav at Fort Lewis. He goes off with our best wishes and those of our Lord—[looks down at the card] Jesus Christ." [Big laugh and applause]

General Vuono also used self-deprecating humor when he visited as the TRADOC Commander in 1986.

I want all of you to turn around and look in the balcony. Now you see up there that's all the faculty of the Command and General Staff College. And I'm sure you're wondering why they're here, because they normally don't come. You probably think they're here because they want to hear what the guy who's speaking is going to say about some substantive matter. Well you're wrong, that's not why they're here. They're here to see if I do this time what I did when I talked to this audience in 1984. And it was November of '84, and I had [General] Jerry Bartlett's job [Deputy Commanding General, TRADOC]. And the fellow who had [Deputy CGSC Commandant, General] Fred Frank's job was a guy by the name of [General] Dave Palmer, who's now the superintendent of the Military Academy. And I was the [CGSC] Commandant, as is Jerry, and occasionally they would invite me down. Only when they didn't have anybody else, or they needed a filler, so they'd ask me to come down. And so they did this day. And I came down and had the audience, just like this, had them in the palm of my hand. They were all just sitting on the edge of their chair, just couldn't relax because what I was telling them was so great. And at the end of it, I got a standing ovation. I mean I got people cheering in the aisles. I felt pretty good about it, until Dave Palmer was standing there waving his arms at me. And then it dawned upon me. You see, you all get a Thanksgiving weekend. And Thanksgiving weekend, as you know, starts on Wednesday night. And then it goes Thursday, you get Thursday off for Thanksgiving, and then you digest Turkey on Friday and Saturday, do a little hunting Sunday and come back Monday. And so I told the class after my presentation how great they were, how much we all liked them here, and that they were going on a long weekend, and that we wanted them to enjoy themselves, be safe, no accidents, and come back bright-eyed and bushy-tailed on Monday morning. And I said "Have a good holiday." That's when I got the cheer and that's when I got Palmer waving his arms. It was Tuesday. [Big laugh]

In 1988, Vuono repeated this story, and added a little extra, describing a utopian version of CGSC that "existed" when he was the Commandant.

This was a few years ago, back when the course was a good course. [Laughter] Did you get that Binnie? [Referring to Deputy Commandant General J.H. Binford Peay III] That was back when class was nine 'til twelve. And then of course we had a policy here, no outside work. [Laughter] So you were free. And there were no writing requirements or speaking requirements. We certainly didn't have a block of tactics instruction, who would ever want to teach tactics to Leavenworth? And we worked a three-and-a-half day week, because we believed in being fair. So three-and-a-half on, three-and-a-half off was the policy back in those days.

General Max Thurman demonstrated his dry sense of humor in 1986, starting his presentation with "I've got one ear stopped up from landing there, so I can't hear myself, which is probably fortunate—I've heard this before." He also ribbed the student moderator when he said "Sir, traditionally I'll ask the first question." Thurman replied "But will it be a good one? [Big laugh] Has it been rehearsed by the faculty?"

In 1992, General Shalikashvili told the students about the reception the much-maligned Meals, Ready-to-Eat (MRE) were given by the local Kurdish population during Operation Provide Comfort.

You do not sustain babies who are beginning to go into shock because of malnutrition through MREs. You do not sustain old, sick people through MREs. I'm not sure you sustain you and I with MREs. [Laughter and applause] I'll tell you two stories about MREs and then I'll stop because otherwise the [Deputy Chief of Staff for Logistics] will get on me. Both of them are true stories. At the beginning of the operation when the special forces guys got in there, and they were helping recover these bundles and divide the MREs, they came upon an old man who had, with his frozen fingers had somehow gotten this damn bag open, doing better than I do most of the time, but he had gotten it open, and do you know that dehydrated fruit in there? I swear to you it's true. He was looking at it, turning it around, and not knowing what to do with it, he started cleaning his shoes with it. [Big laugh] Now, I for one think that's the only edible thing in that bag! We knew, however, that we had a big problem of teaching them how to eat MREs. And so one of the first tasks our [psychological operations] guys had was to in fact develop leaflets and other programs to teach those folks how to get the most out of MREs we were giving.

The other MRE story and then I'll quit. When we got to the point of building the camps, we wanted to make sure that we would bring people from the mountains, Kurds from the mountains into Northern Iraq, and have them help construct the tent cities. And at lunch time, we offered each one of them an MRE. And of course by this time they had been on MREs for 30 days. Out of some 40 guys in that crew that I watched, not one accepted an MRE. Not one. They chose to go hungry all day rather than eat it.

In 1992, General Sullivan reacted to a common problem in the days of overhead slide projectors when his briefing slide came up backwards. "Slide is flipped. Look gang, let me tell you something. This is not a zero defects outfit okay? [Laughter and applause] For those of you who think it is…this is a big muscle movement organization, alright? You're going to get lots of hand-wringing about zero-defects while you're here. Stuff happens." [More laughter] In December 1993, Sullivan joined many guest speakers in commenting on the CGSC catch-phrase "The Best Year of Your Life," when remarking on a slide titled *The Leavenworth Experience*: "The worst year of your life. Next slide." [Laughter and applause]

In 1994, General Barry McCaffrey, Commander, U.S. Southern Command, had his issues with slides, when twice he couldn't get the slide he wanted shown on the screen. "I think these are actually the second slides so what I'll do is I'll just talk to whatever they want to stick up there." [Big laugh] He covered another obscure topic of speaker logistics as well: "I might also tell you, those that haven't been up here, there's a net down there [in front of the stage]. Must be for the airborne troops…or those that are dismayed by the audience reaction and want to jump."

General Downing relayed the joys of dealing with other government agencies in 1995.

The most difficult thing that I've had to do in my 33 years in uniform is go to Washington and participate in the interagency process. Sit down with our counterparts from State, CIA, from the FBI, from Justice, from DEA, United States Information Agency, Agency for International Development, Department of Transportation, Department of Commerce. I mean, you name it. FAA. Sit down and try to put together policies and actions which are going to promote U.S. goals in the world. Very, very difficult. Very difficult. And I always like to tell people I'll take any rucksack of any size, any jungle you want me to go in for any duration—just don't make me go to another interagency meeting. [Laughter]

General Reimer won the class over with his introductory remarks in 1996 when he said, "I'm not going to tell you this is the best year of your life. [Big cheer] And it wasn't the best year of my life. But as I reflect back on that and I realize as I get older I can remember things very vividly that never even occurred."

In 1997, Secretary Cohen had fun with a student who asked a lengthy question—so lengthy, in fact, that it earned an entry in the Guest Speaker section of the 1998 CGSC yearbook. When the student was finished, Cohen asked "Would you repeat the question?" which caused the audience to go wild. "No, I'm just teasing," he continued. "I can see you have the sympathy and the empathy of all your colleagues." Two years later General Shelton ribbed the students as well. "I'm told that you've got quite a few individuals here that always have questions [laughter] and I'll look forward to them. Particularly after the four hours of grilling that myself and the other members of the Joint Chiefs took from the Senate Armed Services Committee just the day before yesterday."

THEY SAID WHAT?

Reviewing these tapes in the social, cultural, and military environment of the 21st century occasionally causes some of the remarks to come as a bit of a shock to the system, such as those made in 1953 by Representative Short.

> We've got to do away with corruption in government. No more five or four percenters or mink coats or influence peddlers, and bribers. And I'm glad there's sort of a new moral climate in Washington today. I'm glad that 117 homosexuals and persons considered unfit and unsafe for the security of our nation have voluntarily left their posts. I'm glad that the [Ethel and Julius] Rosenbergs and the [Morton] Sobels and [David and Ruth] Greenglasses are all being brought to the bar of judgment [for espionage]. There's still a lot of work to be done. I don't fear Russia or any foreign power half as much at as I fear at times the weaknesses within our own country.

In January 1963, when General Johnson was the Commandant, he led the Associate Course class in a prayer at the end of his opening remarks.

> I think I've talked long enough. I wonder if you would join with me now, while we offer a prayer for this class. Our Father in Heaven, we ask thy blessing on this class as it opens today, on this institution and its staff and faculty as it prepares for another part year. We ask that all that we do here be done in thy name and in thy sight. We ask that you keep our hearts open, that you remind us each hour of each day that you stand beside us, that you are guiding us each step of the way, that you will show us the right if we will keep our eyes on you, that you will help us if we turn to you in prayer. That you are our strength, and that you are the salvation of the world as we know it. All of this we ask in the name of the master of men. Amen.

Four years later in March 1967, Army Chief of Staff Johnson would lead the class in singing 'Happy Birthday' to General Michael Davison, the CGSC Commandant. In 1969, General Westmoreland recognized the fact that CGSC was co-ed, and then appeared to promptly forget that fact.

> Leavenworth is an institution of tremendous importance...and has stayed abreast of our requirements. It has looked ahead. I'm impressed that you've even kept abreast of the trend in the academic world now to go co-ed. I never thought I'd address the students as "ladies and gentlemen" but you do have seven ladies in your class. And I understand incidentally that they're very good students. The credentials of you gentlemen as members of the student body are very impressive...

In 1973, Max Taylor pointed out a strange fact that elicited an even stranger reaction.

> We were somewhat a backwards generation; it took us two years to get through the place. And furthermore we had 130-some marked problems, which if we didn't pass, quite frequently, if not always, was going to involve and affect our subsequent careers to an

important degree. As a result it was quite normal, in fact it was somewhat expected, that we have at least one suicide in a class. [Scattered laughter] My class didn't make that, and on graduation day one of the members of the faculty commented to me that he'd always been a bit disappointed in the class of 1935. [Big laugh]

Defense Secretary Schlesinger in 1974 left no doubt as to the types of questions he did not want to field.

I have talked for thirty minutes. We will shortly have a question period. I am informed that there is an indication of what the state of morale is in the Army by the questions that are addressed to the speaker under such circumstances. If they concentrate on pay and housing, the sense of dedication to the Army's mission in such a period tends to be lacking. So let's concentrate the questions on the Army's mission.

Clearly Army Secretary Callaway should have laid down the same ground rules during his appearance in May 1974. If he had, he wouldn't have received what is probably the longest (almost four minutes), strangest, and most inappropriate question ever asked at the college, when a Vietnamese international officer complained to him about the poor treatment he was receiving (it is unfortunate there is no video of this event to capture the expression on Callaway's face).

Mr. Secretary, Sir. Lieutenant Colonel Tuan from Vietnam. [Quoc or Pham Van—the 1974 yearbook shows two Tuans in this class] First, I apologize [to] you for asking the question. I should not ask the question, but if so, maybe I do not have any opportunity to ask you. Here is the problem. We allied officers having per diem when attending school within the United States. We feel very miserable. Miserable for many reasons. We feel the training here. We recognize three good opportunities to have, maybe we will have the opportunity to see the beauty of the United States of America, one in Christmas time, second in New York and Washington tour, third, we have leave whenever we have the graduation day, after the graduation day. But during the Christmas time, the weather was too cold to us to travel [murmurs and chuckles] so we forget about it. Second, the tour in New York and Washington last week was very miserable. We feel very insulted, not because of the trip, but the way we have been treated. Within the New York and Washington area, $15 or $16 a day for three meals, and not much, but we are expected to take the receipt, to turn in the receipt in order to be refunded after eating. So we never feel free at any time.

Every morning it was done when you were in CGSC, because almost every morning we have to get up at six o'clock in order to catch the breakfast. Then, after that, an overloaded trip for the whole day [murmuring grows] and we were not released until 18:30. We have one evening at New York, one evening and one day in Washington we call free. But we did not feel free, because any time we travel we have to worry about the receipt, we have to take and turn in to Major Pate or Colonel Dodson in order to be refund. [Murmuring increasing] So the second trip was no more good. The third trip we are going to plan is our leave after the graduation day. But two days ago in the evening day before last, we have been informed that you authorized us leave without living allowance, so what is the reason, Sir? [Much murmuring]

A clearly dumbfounded Callaway answered in the most polite manner possible: "On that question I'm sorry I'll just really have to plead ignorance. I don't know. I'll give you that answer you hear so much around Washington and I try not to give but I've got to in this case, I'll just have to check into it and let you know. I really don't know." It was clear the Vietnamese officer didn't speak for everyone, as officers from Yugoslavia and Germany made immediately clear.

> Your excellency, I am Lieutenant Colonel [Slavko M.] Jović from Yugoslavia. I want to thank Colonel Dodson for excellent trip we had recently. [Thunderous applause] I want to tell you also that I am very happy to be among the first section, a really big section. I am very happy here.

> ...Sir, Lieutenant Colonel [Manfred S.] Eisele from Germany. I do not want to ask a question, I just want to state that I think the majority of allied students here are very delighted by the kindness, helpfulness, and generosity of the American people, and of the American Army that gave us the opportunity to visit your beautiful capital and New York City. Thank you. [Much applause]

In 1976, General DePuy, in answer to a question about artillery, seemed to discount the abilities of noncommissioned officers.

> Let me say one other thing about artillery: The artillery has always been the best trained element in the United States Army, and the best performing element. The question is why? The answer is the artillery is run by officers. The forward observer is an officer. The [Fire Direction Center] is run by an officer. The battery exec runs the battery. Yeah, once in a while they don't level the bubbles. The infantry fighting element at the squad level is led by sergeants, tanks are commanded by sergeants. And so wherever you have a high level of intelligence, training, dedication and reliability, you have a relatively effective battlefield system. You have pilots who are officers in your F-15s, you get that same payoff. So anyway I don't worry too much about the artillery. As long as it's going to still be run by officers. We may have to add some officers for the supervision of the platoons in order to be sure they do, in fact, work right.

Once past the obligatory comedy in their opening remarks, most speakers that appeared on the CGSC stage spent a lot of time discussing and being asked questions about current events, providing a fascinating time capsule that revealed the world in which the United States Army operated.

9. Events of the Day

When guest speakers come to CGSC they spend most of their time talking about the events of the day, and it is perhaps in this area where the tapes in the CARL archive yield some of their richest material. It is fascinating to hear the leaders of the day discussing events of their time without the benefit of hindsight or in possession of all the information. Topics of discussion included: The Cold War, social changes such as integration and gays in the military, the all-volunteer force, readiness, increasing world complexity and the rate of change, operations tempo, DoD reorganization, President Clinton's impeachment proceedings, and terrorism.

THE COLD WAR; NATO

The topic of the Cold War occupied many minutes in the Eisenhower Auditorium, as the Soviet Union was the prime focal point of the military for decades following World War II. In 1951, Major General Hugh Milton, who would become Under Secretary of the Army, spoke of the uncertainty of the future.

> We all hope that wars will cease, and that peace may reign. But no man, no man in this nation today, knows what tomorrow is going to bring forth. When our leaders had been called before the Congress of the United States, and when I say our leaders, I mean Generals Bradley, Marshall, and Eisenhower, they constantly emphasized that we're living in a very dramatic period in the world's history and you know it as well as I... These [Soviet] forces may move against us with the speed of lightning, or they may resort to a delaying action, which may extend over ten, twenty, or as General Eisenhower has said, possibly thirty years.

In 1953, Field Marshall Montgomery also spoke about the difficulty in predicting the future actions of the Soviet Union.

> And nobody knows today whether the East would resort to World War to achieve its aims more quickly. Nobody knows that. I certainly don't—I wish I did. Nobody knows. And the further disadvantage that we suffer from in the West is that we have no clear-cut political aims. Our political leaders don't really, in my view, know where they are going to. I've told them all, but they don't know where they are going to. And that makes it very difficult for us fighting men. And of course you must know where you are going to...otherwise you don't go anywhere.

> ...It is my view that you cannot continue indefinitely with a divided Europe. There used to be one Europe; today there are two Europes—East Europe, West Europe. And the dividing line goes straight through the middle of Germany. Now I don't believe you can continue in that way indefinitely. And you've got to remember that everything being done today is based on the fact that there will always be two Europes. The Marshall Plan, The European Defense Community, the European Army Plan, the Schuman Plan for steel and coal. All that, you see, is based on the fact that Europe will be permanently divided into two. It is my view that this is entirely wrong. You can't go on like that. There has got to come a time when there will be again one Europe. And if you were to say to me "What do you mean by one Europe?" I would say, "Well, I mean what we call today Western Europe, plus a united Germany, plus Poland, plus Czechoslovakia, plus Yugoslavia. I would stop with those.

…We soldiers have got to understand that the defense effort made by a nation must be balanced with the economic possibilities. It's no good saying you want a hundred divisions or whatever you want, if to produce that the nation is going to go bankrupt. No. And that is a very difficult thing, to get the thing right, to get the balance between shield in front and reserves behind. The shield in front is expensive, the reserves behind are cheap. And governments are dependent for their lives on votes, the votes of their people. But I think we soldiers are to blame very often because we say we must have this we must have that. It's got to be balanced with economic possibilities, and if you don't it's no good.

General Gavin talked to the graduating class of 1956 about the feelings of the people caught between the two world superpowers.

This is the world in which you now go forth to serve in the armed forces of many countries. You have an ancient, decadent, latter-day feudal state, from whence comes forth a very aggressive pattern. And then we have our own Western World, symbolized by the focus of industry, concept of a way of life here. Between these two power centers are millions, millions of people, who look very uneasily to ourselves; concerned about what we might do in the event of war to them and their institutions. Likewise they look very anxiously to the Russians. And yet, it is these people in between who are the balance in the scales of the future. Let us never forget this. I say that out of deep conviction having served two years with the Philippine Scouts years ago in the Asian area. I've been six years in Europe out of the last eleven years of my service. I know how uneasily they feel, how anxiously they look about.

To the graduates of 1961, General Lemnitzer warned against compromise.

I feel that today there are too many advocates of compromise, too many people who forget that in the international field, and especially in war, there is no prize for the second best. I have little patience for the talk of the so-called glorious defeat. A nation which is defeated, no matter how gloriously it may be, never determines the shape of the future. Only the victor does that.

A retired Harold K. Johnson spoke in 1970 about what he saw as the demise of NATO.

NATO has done one thing for us—we've had no conflict in Western Europe. We have lost no territory in Western Europe. I'm sure, before the end of the year, I would expect General Lemnitzer perhaps to be out here because he, in retirement, is endeavoring to continue to make the NATO case. And desirable as it might be, desirable as it is to assure the security of Western Europe, I think the fact is that NATO tends to be deader and deader and deader. If not dead, moribund.

In his 1973 visit, Max Taylor also questioned the future of NATO.

We Americans have always been far more fearful for Western Europe then the Western Europeans have been. They have never extended themselves to defend themselves with any of the earnestness that we have put, at least in the early years, in our contribution to NATO. That fact is apparent in Europe, it's apparent here in the United States. And you can have only to listen to the debates in the Senate to have the feeling that the size of our NATO commitment and probably deployments elsewhere is very much under scrutiny and sooner or later congressional action will reduce those deployments if we don't do it as a matter of military judgment.

...Credibility of course, is everything. Does anyone feel that the French are going to sacrifice Paris in France for Hamburg? The Germans don't think so, that's why they're so anxious we stay there. Incidentally, don't everyone walk out of the room and say "Taylor is recommending we butt out of Western Europe." I'm not. I'm just saying we'd better be looking where we're going because we're going out someday, under some set of circumstances. I would hope that it would be after getting all we can in the negotiation field from our presence there, and then going out with agreement of our allies, because they can't really talk back when we look them in the eye because they haven't believed in this war for ten years! Ten years, but they still want to keep us there. And I think we should stay there for some purposes, to see how Germany's turning out. But Germany is solving that for us. Their 'Aus Politik' is really their answer: This is the way we're going, and we're acquiescing in that, we don't find that terrifying. Hence the fear of the German reaction tends to decline. So I'm just telling you the arguments that show up whether you like it or not. I'm not particularly happy about it; it's just a fact of life.

Taylor was asked that since France had an independent nuclear arsenal, should West Germany get control of the nuclear weapons within their country to send a clearer message of deterrence to the Soviet Union and strengthen the Western Alliance.

First I would not be at all sure what the effect on the Soviet Union is, the fact is the French have a very limited nuclear force. Whether that really impresses them I wouldn't be sure. If I were a Hamburger I would be very doubtful that the French would use that nuclear force to [unintelligible]. I'd be doubtful about the Americans for that matter. Now in the case of the Germans however, it's a good question. How about a limited force for the same purpose in the case of Germany? I know there are some Germans in the audience and I would be very much interested to hear one or more of them comment. I'm quite sure that many a thought from Germany is asking that question, it has in the past and still is. I'm not revealing any secrets to say however, that it's a different thing for Germany to have these weapons than for France. If Germans had it it would scare the bejeezus out of a lot of people around the world. [Big laugh]

Secretary of Defense Schlesinger spoke of the perceived lack of European commitment to its own defense in 1974.

We might become sufficiently impatient with the European contribution that we decide that "'Tis true, what you say, that it is in the United States' interest to defend Western Europe but we think it is even more in your interest to defend yourself. It might be a disaster from the American standpoint for Western Europe to be overrun or fall under the shadow of Soviet hegemony, but for you it would be an unmitigated disaster and you'd better think seriously about it."

...There has been a tendency to rely on the American presence, the American crutch, meaning the nuclear crutch, not to deal seriously with military problems. There has been this tendency to go—to talk about weapons acquisition—the hawking of weapon systems in NATO is shameful. I don't know what you're taught about that here when you study security assistance. But the principal objective of the United States Government should not be to sell equipment to its allies, particularly if it will result in a decline in the combat effectiveness of said ally. [Laughter and applause] Within NATO though the history has been sort of like selling picture cards—filthy pictures on the corners of Paris in the old days. Everyone is sort of going around showing his weapon system. [Big laugh] That was accidental. [Referring to joke he just made. Another big laugh] But I presume I should apologize now to the ladies who are present. I am told that that is expected of all visiting lecturers to apologize to the ladies who are present, even though they have been apologized to on countless prior occasions. [Big laugh]

...NATO has a problem that they tend to play the weapon systems game. They also have the problem of a sense of psychological inferiority vis-a-vis the Warsaw pact which has gone on ever since they failed to meet the Lisbon goals of 1952, there's a great deal of mutual distrust among the alliance. All of the Europeans are watching the Americans because it is recognized that the Americans are untrustworthy, and as a result you have the somewhat paranoid discussions that occasionally go on at the highest levels, in which you say "By God we ought to make this alliance stronger." And the question that immediately comes back is "Now what does he mean by that? Does that mean that they've cut a private deal with the Russians under the condominium to deliver us into their hands? Or does that mean that they are unilaterally planning to bug out?" It's very hard to carry on a good substantive conversation under those circumstances. [Laughter]

...Some of these [doubts about the moral stamina of Western democracies], as you know, are attributable to Vietnam. But many of them go far beyond that. There was a decay, a disarray, that began to crop up in the societies of the West even before the discontents associated with Vietnam started. And this is reflected in a fair amount of carping and self-flagellation that afflicts our societies. We wonder, we should wonder, about the moral stamina of these societies. And the moral stamina of the societies, to the extent that they can carry on a coherent foreign policy based upon the creation of military forces which serve those foreign policies, ultimately rests on the moral stamina of the public. One can go on piling up weapon systems, developing force structures, but unless there is the public support, and the public stamina, all of these things will be unavailing.

...To a large extent the NATO alliance has rested on the U.S. Nuclear crutch. And while that may have been satisfactory from the alliance standpoint in the past, as the balance in the nuclear area has shifted, it has meant that less and less, or fewer and fewer are the contingencies on which we can have reliance on nuclear response. And that means building up the conventional capabilities. NATO can easily suck up 10 or 11 Army Divisions.

Schlesinger was asked about what the current force reduction talks meant for the future of NATO.

I think we can make the case [to prevent congressional pressure for unilateral U.S. withdrawals from Europe]. And I think for the reasons I mentioned earlier, the 'discovery' that the Soviet Union was a totalitarian society, and the impact of the Middle

Eastern War, plus the fact that American involvement in hostilities ended, has brought about a substantial change in opinion with regard to NATO. Until a few months ago, the fashionable attitude with regard to deployed forces was wherever you see deployed forces they should be withdrawn. Sort of on the [Mount] Everest principle, redeploy them because they're there. [Laughter] The 190,000 men that we have in Germany play a critical role in the development of a conventional deterrent, and I think the arguments for that are being better appreciated.

But as the passions involved in Vietnam fade, there will be those who are recalled to their rightful minds [laughter] and will recognize, I believe, that simply because they were infuriated by the presence of 600,000 servicemen in Southeast Asia that the appropriate response to that is not to flail away at the 190,000 men in Germany. So I do not believe that we will be forced in the near term to withdraw our forces outside of the context of [a Mutual and Balanced Force Reductions (MBFR)] agreement. Provided one thing—and that's a big proviso—that the Europeans demonstrate a willingness to do more on their behalf. And by more I mean absolutely not as a substitute for the American effort. The German forces are improving and we continue to advertise all that the Germans do, because there isn't all that much else to brag about in Western Europe. We are proposing a percentage reduction of U.S. forces and Soviet forces. Since the Soviets have about 460,000 men there and we have 190,000 men there, they are sufficiently good at arithmetic to figure out that that is not necessarily advantageous from their standpoint. And it's not clear that we will be able to get them to withdraw the 68,000 men, which is 15 percent, in exchange for 29,000 which we are offering to withdraw. The Soviet objectives at MBFR are long run. And the bait that they hold out falls under the heading that the Americans are under sufficient pressure or sufficiently disillusioned with the Europeans, that they will snap at the bait of the reduction of 20,000 men of their forces and for that we [the Soviet Union] want to get commitment on two things: First that there will be no common European defense effort, and second there will be national ceilings applied to European forces. Most notably [the Soviet Union] would like a cut in the Bundeswehr [German Defense Forces]. Apparently they notice the same things that we do. And this will be tempting in the short run for the United States, to risk the long run security of Europe in order to succumb to the local pressures. I hope we can resist those pressures, but if the Russians play the trap right, I'm not sure how well we would do. I do not think, however, that we will be forced unilaterally to withdraw forces. We might be.

In December 1974, Secretary of the Army Callaway gave his justification for a 16 division Army.

Why do we need to build back up to where we were? At that time [between Korean and Vietnam wars], several presidents, different parties, secretaries of defense, said we needed 16 divisions. My question is is the threat greater now, or less now? Clearly greater, without any question. At that time the Soviet Union had a half a million more men in arms more than we have. Today they have two million more men in arms than we have. At that time NATO was sticking together and the Western European countries were financially very stable. Now they're certainly financially in much less shape. The southern flank of NATO was strong then, and of course we've got Greece and Turkey of a little bit different bent at the moment, while the southern flank of NATO is much weaker. The Mideast of course much more volatile now than it was then. The Soviet Union since that time has outspent us in what they're doing with their ground forces, the number of tanks that they've got is improving in numbers and the quality of their force has come up enormously. So the threat is certainly greater now than it was at that time.

In 1975, Army Chief of Staff Fred Weyand spoke of the scope of the Soviet threat.

This threat that we face is no longer a narrow military threat. It's a challenge that challenges not just our military capability and strength and credibility, it challenges our political cohesiveness and national sense of purpose, challenges our economic system, it challenges our psychology as a nation or our ideological base. It challenges our technological superiority, and it just presses in on us from all sides, much more so than it seemingly ever has in past history. And it's a global thing that seems to extend far beyond what it used to be. I was looking at pictures and intelligence for example that have to do with Somalia day before yesterday. And it's startling to see, like on a global radar screen, these blips popping up all over, as a force whose ideology, whose values for the most part, are absolutely incompatible with ours seems to be gradually gaining ground and gradually encircling us. And another trend is the increasing raw military power of that force. In this case I'm talking about of course the Soviet Union. And then of course we have the loss of our once overwhelming nuclear superiority. And this is something that we haven't thought through entirely, just what does this nuclear stand-off mean?

We do know one thing it means and that is that it greatly heightens the importance of conventional power, conventional military power. But we don't know much beyond that. Would we have handled or would the outcome of the Cuban crisis have been different had we not had overwhelming nuclear superiority as Kennedy in a sense faced down Kruschev? Is there now a greater temptation on the part of the power that normally, ideologically is aggressive and tending towards adventurism and aggression to make a quick grab of something in a conventional way and then simply hold it, waiting to see what the response will be? Testing credibility, testing capability, knowing full well that in the era of nuclear standoff the mutual incineration of the two antagonists is not something that would be a likely option. And then we have a problem such as ours of a nation tending to turn inward. An introspection, a preoccupation with our own problems.

And this is disturbing because most of us that are in the military have come in contact with problems outside our country and we know instinctively that we cannot live in isolation from others. And yet our people tend to be preoccupied with that, and why not? Say in Kansas, for example. The farmer is selling his surplus wheat to the Soviet Union. Wheat that he could not sell at a worthwhile price, but now all of a sudden he can sell it and make a profit, and he benefits greatly from that. And then someone like Weyand comes along and says "My friend, we need more money from you so we can defend you against that fellow you're selling wheat to." Very complex. And I don't think I've made any great strides as a salesman as a matter of fact, in that regard.

General Vuono spoke of the dangers of isolationism in 1988.

And although burden-sharing is something we want to continue to talk about and dialogue about whether it's in Europe or whether it's in the Pacific, the idea of saying

"Well, because the allies' contribution is not what it ought to be, the way we'll handle that is, we'll just back off, and back out with our forces" is absolute nonsense. Absolute nonsense, because the security of the United States is tied very, very closely with the security of Europe and with NATO. And we can ill-afford to make some dumb move based on burden-sharing that will have long-term implications to this country, and to our people in this country. And if you think that unilateral withdrawal from anywhere because of burden-sharing makes sense, if you're a member of the Soviet Union you'd be on the sideline cheering, because that gets your force levels down without going through the tough negotiations that are going to take place on arms control.

In November 1994, General Sullivan discussed the shift from NATO to United Nations (UN) missions.

Forces of change. I think that this one here [points to the UN flag on the slide], at least in the United States, certainly we need to pay more attention to this. [The UN] is becoming more and more important, for us. NATO was dominant, now the United Nations is beginning to emerge on the scene in a much more expanded role for us in the United States, and we are paying more attention to it. And you'll see in Haiti, for instance, the UN mission in Haiti, will be another example of that.

Secretary West described the complexity of the post-Cold War environment in December 1994.

The end of the Cold War, and certainly with that end we have had some great change. But one thing, perhaps more than any other, is our whole national security environment has been turned upside-down. The big challenge we thought we could plan for here, that you would come and discuss, one block against another, the East against the West, those blocks, the easy divisions, the easy ways in which we plan has been swept away. We undoubtedly rest more easy, but do we plan more easily? Or have we found a more complex challenge, a more complex environment?

West spoke about this planning the next year.

In our national security planning we now plan against the possibility of three kinds of conflicts: Global conflict, regional conflict, communal conflict. We can pretty much agree that the prospect of a global conflict seems to be disappearing more and more, or if not disappearing, at least, for the moment, seems much less likely than it was just a few years before. However we don't, and never will, be so foolish as to eliminate all planning against such a contingency, or preparation against such a contingency, it no longer dominates our national security thinking and planning as it once did. As I said, there has not been a conflict that consumed every nation state in the world since World War II fifty years ago. The second kind, regional conflicts, based on the notion that there continue to be heavily armed nations in regions around the world, because of their national aspirations or their transnational aspirations, constitute a threat to their neighbors. For that reason if those neighbors are our allies, to our interests, or for other reasons having to do with economic positioning, global location, a threat to our interests. But they could cause the kind of regional conflict that could quickly spread and ensnare us and our allies…The third kind of conflict are communal conflicts, those that can grow out of ethnic passions, ethnic antagonisms, long-nurtured and long-held.

And by long I don't just mean years or decades, I mean for centuries. And certainly what we face in Bosnia, what we are trying to ameliorate with negotiations at Wright-Patterson Air Force base in Dayton, is as good an example, both of the kind of conflict that springs from these communal concerns, and of the dangers of such a conflict can pose to world interests and to United States interests.

In 1996, General Reimer discussed some of the impacts of the end of the Cold War.

It's important for all of us to remember the last six years. I always start off by saying that the 21st century for the U.S. Army began in 1989. We're not talking about building a bridge to the 21st century. We're already doing that, and we have been doing that for the past seven years. When the [Berlin Wall] came down in 1989, I don't know where you were, but I know where I was. And I know I totally underestimated the impact of that wall coming down. It has changed business, it has changed the way we do business, and it changed the U.S. Army in a very substantial way. Think about those last seven years, and think about what's happened to the Army. We have taken over 500,000 people out of the Army, Active component, Army [National] Guard, and the United States Army Reserve, and [Department of the Army] civilians.

Secretary Cohen gave some interesting insight into the post-Cold War decision making process in 1997.

We have to ask these questions about ourselves in terms of who we are and what we hope to be and where we want to be in order to decide this question of where are we going with the U.S. military now that the Soviet Union no longer exists...And so we spent a good deal of the first few months, and we only had a few months to develop this entire [Quadrennial Defense Review (QDR)] process, because Congress had mandated that it would be filed and sent to the Hill by May 15th...What should be the strategy of the United States in this new post-Cold War world? And of course at that time you may recall there were a lot of academicians who were writing at that time. Francis Fukuyama, you may recall that name. A very brilliant academician who wrote a piece called [*The End of History*, where] he basically said that now with the fall of the Berlin Wall that we were going to see the 'end of history.' That democratic liberalism is going to sweep across the globe. And this prompted a South African academician named Peter Veil to say "Rejoice my friends, or weep with sorrow. What California is today, the world will be tomorrow." Of course, Fukuyama's thesis was a bit overstated, because he didn't take into account the fact that you have a Muslim society, many Muslim countries, who aren't going to embrace our democratic capitalism form of government and ideals. That you had China, you had Japan, other countries who wouldn't necessarily just follow our example. The clash of Asian values versus those of the West for example. But the thesis about spread of capitalism I think generally was right.

...I was criticized somewhat again, by [people] saying "There goes Secretary Cohen talking about two [Major Regional Contingencies (MRC)]." My answer is "Well, which one do you want to give up? Do you want to give up Korea? Do you want to give up Southwest Asia? Which one would you like for us to give up?" And I don't hear many answers, I hear the sound of silence, when that question is posed. Now it may be in the future that the Korea peninsula might become united. It may resolve itself in a peaceful way. It may be that we only have to contend with one MRC in the future. No one can predict that far in the future, so in the short term, we have to be concerned about how do we maintain the level of commitment that we have, unless we're willing to give up the commitment? Now we can solve some of our problems by simply cutting back on our commitments, but then we have people here who represent some other countries who might take a dim view of that.

INTEGRATION; GAYS IN THE MILITARY

In 1952, three years after President Truman signed the Executive Order integrating the military, General McAuliffe gave the students an update.

The next subject I have is a delicate and sensitive one, and one of great concern to the department and particularly to [the Army Personnel Office], and this is the subject of integration of Negro manpower in the Army. This has been a subject of study and controversy for many years, as you know. In fact, when [CGSC Commandant] General [Henry] Hodes and I were at the War College it was one of the big studies at that time which a committee of students worked very hard to come up with a solution. We've had about four different boards of general officers discuss this subject and study it and make recommendations in the last decade. From the point of view of the Department of the Army, our interest is solely from the viewpoint of efficient utilization of manpower. The actual fact has been that we have carried a Negro overstrength in all-Negro units in the zone of the interior which has really been a waste of manpower, and which rose to a number as high as 16,000 at one time last year. Aside from that, it was clear that all-Negro units were not as efficient, particularly in combat as they might be. And based on these considerations, last July an integration of White and Negro troops was initiated in Far East Command, specifically in the combat units in the 8th Army, 25th Division.

Prior to that, as you know, we had complete integration in the reception centers, in the training and in the schools here in the Zone of the Interior. And it had all gone forward in fine shape, even in such a place as Fort Jackson, South Carolina, where many of you have served. The training has been carried on very effectively on integrated bases. The integration moved forward in Far East Command. After adoption in the combat units it was extended to service units, and now is fairly well on a complete integrated basis. The reaction of commanders has been favorable. So favorable, in fact, that this program is being extended now. It started in European command about the 1st of April, for some of the combat units. And, to a limited extent, there has been integration in the zone of the interior. Most of this is left to the discretion of the commander, the objective being to do it quietly, and routinely, with as little fanfare and publicity and public attention as possible, and to move slowly and gradually so that we don't have any untoward incidents involved in this thing. Actually there's a lot of emotional stuff that's stirred up by every move that's made in this very sensitive area. Certain people from the South of course are bitterly opposed to any type of integration, on the other hand there are other groups farther north in other organizations that are always urging the Army to go much more rapidly than it has gone in the integration with Negroes and Whites in units. Suffice it to say that we're satisfied that the program is necessary from an efficiency point of view. We think that it's gone well and we think that it's going to continue to go well and we're hopeful that it will do so.

In 1973, Secretary Callaway was asked about race relations within units stationed in Europe.

> ...I think the company level is about the last place where a commander really knows all of his men intimately and can really influence the action of all his men. Now if we can at the company level, with good battalion commanders and others helping out there, if we can get people to return to the principles of leadership that the Army's always been proud of, and the basic principles of leadership are looking out for your men, and treating everybody alike. If everybody's treated as a soldier, and if everybody knows he's treated as a soldier, and if everybody knows his commanders are interested in him as a person, and that he can take his problems if he perceives he is discriminated against, and can have them explained and discussed and worked out. Once we can get everybody in the Army to believe that they are all soldiers and treated alike, and that if you are Black you have an equal opportunity for promotion, and if you're White you're not discriminated against by reverse discrimination, and if you go out and get in trouble you'll get the same penalty whether you're Black or White, once everybody understands that and it is clearly communicated and it is in fact true...once all of that happens I think we'll have solved most of our racial problems, and that's the area I think we should work hardest in. [Applause]

General Abrams addressed the problems of race relations in 1974.

> Now for a long time there has been first a quiet social revolution, then a little more active, and then violent, going on in our country. And every facet of that not only is reflected in American military forces, but it should be. The military forces have got to be a child of its people or it's really meaningless. You don't have anything. And so we've got race problems, that's for sure. And it's working both ways. You have Whites in the Army who—it just seems like it's impossible for them to see other men, Black, or Mexican American or Puerto Rican American or Japanese American or Indian, see them like themselves: As humans with hopes, with aspirations, with prejudices. And we've got some that are not that way. But until we arrive at that day when as human beings we can see all humans as we believe the Lord saw them, then we'll be able to say we no longer have a race problem, or a minority problem, in the Army. So yes we have it, and we've got to keep working, and we've got to work intelligently, and we have to be able to speak frankly about it with each other. So I'm glad that you're going at it in earnest here, and I think it's the proper thing to do, and it's important to the Army.

In May of that year, Secretary Callaway was asked about the possibility of allowing homosexuals to serve in the armed forces. Even the way the question was posed provides a glimpse into the attitude of the times.

> Q: Sir, in recent times there has been an increasing trend in public life to accept homosexuals even to the extent of electing them to public office. I noticed in an article this morning by Tom Wicker that he believes that equal protection under the law would allow homosexuals to be accepted into government service and even into the armed forces. I've heard this echoed in several other articles recently. My question is, Sir, does it look like we're going to have to put up with homosexuals in the Army? [Long disturbance, talking and laughing]

A: You know, all the time you were talking I was trying to think how I was going to start off my answer with 'I'm glad you asked that question!' [Big laugh and applause] But I'm glad you asked about that. I don't think the Army, certainly as far as my input into this, I don't the Army is in any way prepared to accept homosexuals at this time, and I don't see any kind of input that does that. Seriously as you know the courts may take a very different view. We will abide by whatever the courts say…I know there are a lot of people who, politically, feel that we are going to have to accept that. Well, I think it's just like my attitude on women at West Point. Somebody asked me the other day "What would it take to get you to admit women at West Point?" And I said very simply, "A direct order." And I feel—[interrupted by laughter and applause]—I feel the same way about homosexuals. I'm not for it. [More laughter]

General Sullivan addressed social issues in 1992.

Sexual Harassment. I want you to pay attention to that while your here. It's going on in your Army, I don't like it. I presume you don't like it. You need to think about that, you need to talk about it, 'cause it's going on, and I don't like it. If you want to know how I feel about it, think about the golden rule while you're here running around this place. Homosexuals in the military. I've stated my position. My position is I don't think they have a place in the organization. I'm well aware of the fact that we have some. I think it is against good law, order and discipline. And my position is clearly stated and I'm going to hold to that position.

He addressed both of these topics in January 1993 with members of the Pre-Command Course, eleven months before "Don't ask, don't tell" became law.

[Pointing to "Homosexuals in the Service" on the slide] I don't know what is going to happen here gang. I truly do not. At the moment I don't. I've met with the president now—I met with the president Monday. I met with him—the other Chiefs were there, we were all there, the president, vice president, and other members of the president's staff were there. There was a dialogue back and forth, we stated our position on it—I think you all know what my position is on the subject. There was a subsequent meeting in the tank with the Secretary of Defense. We've had a couple more meetings, one yesterday afternoon, I was down at Fort Chaffee [Arkansas], [so] the Vice [Chief of Staff] went to that. Then there was a meeting last night at the White House and Senator [Sam] Nunn made some comments when he came out of the building. We saw those in the paper…I'm a little unclear as to where we are at the moment on the subject. It looks though, as if there'll be a six month period to take a look at it in detail, and I think the question now is if we don't ask at the MEPS, how do we handle the self-declares? That's the issue. What do you do with the person who pops up and says "I am"? The regulation says if he or she says "I am" then you process for—as long as there's no crime committed—then you process for release. And that's about where we are.

[Points to Sexual Harassment] I want you to pay attention to it, because it's going on. It's going on; don't think because you are in the 9th Cavalry, 7th Cavalry, 3rd Cavalry or whatever in some line unit, infantry unit or tank unit, that you don't have to pay attention to it, 'cause you do. Because women are in the Army and they're all over the battlefield.

ALL-VOLUNTEER FORCE

The move to an all-volunteer military in the early 1970s was a frequent topic of discussion, even years after it was officially implemented in 1973. In 1970, a now-retired General Johnson shared his views of the all-volunteer force (AVF)—views that would prove somewhat prophetic.

> ...I do not agree with a volunteer Army. I don't agree with it for three reasons. One is I don't think that we can get the number of volunteers that are required for the size force to meet the obligations and commitments that I think we'll have over the course of the next 10 to 15 years. If we do we're going to get it by lowering standards. If we lower standards we're then going to have to have elimination programs, because you can't keep a whole Army full of bums. And when you have your elimination programs you're going to then have to maintain the same size or even a larger training establishment as we have now, so all of the savings that ostensibly occur as a result of the volunteer Army are going to just kind of go flying off. Reason number two is over time, and I don't look for this in five or ten or even 15 years, I think it will be out in 25, and 30, and 35 years, and it will be a very gradual process, a gulf [will] grow between the military establishment and the society that it's designed to serve...But there's even a more basic reason than that. And it's this: I don't think this country can ever afford to let the idea get abroad that every citizen of this country [doesn't share] a responsibility for the security of the country. It's important that we all remember that we grew up in this land of the free and the home of the brave by sharing the responsibility for our own safety and security. And the moment that you can turn and say "I am paying somebody to do that," at that moment we're on a downhill slide, and the slide is greased, and we're gone as a nation, and we certainly are not going to be the land of the brave and we won't be the home of the free for very long. [Applause]

Secretary Laird's discussion of personnel cost issues in 1971 sound very similar to those that accompanied the post-Iraq war drawdown in 2013.

> With manpower costs going up to the extent that they are, 52-53% this year, 60% of our budget overall in the Department of Defense in 1974, there is no question that we're going to have to rely upon the Reserve and National Guard to a greater extent than at any time in the past. It's just facing up to the realities of the 70s, the manpower reality and the fiscal reality. And if we don't do it, we're in pretty bad shape. And we're letting down the security interest of our country. As far as making a volunteer force a reality, it's going to entail pay, allowances, educational opportunities, but more than anything else, it's going to be the acceptability of military service in the eyes of the people of this country, a recognition of the need and respect which we should hold our military men and women in, and their absolute essentiality to the future peace of the free world. Now I believe that with all the incentives and if we do the job that's needed and necessary to build up a greater degree of acceptability, we will be able to induce enough to join the National Guard and Reserves.

Admiral Elmo Zumwalt gave the Navy's perspective of the AVF in 1973, as well as resistance to change by some of his senior personnel.

In order to deal with [the all-volunteer force] problem, it was clear that we had a major need to revise our approach to personnel administration. The reenlistment rates for the Navy had been running downhill at a dramatic rate. The first crew reenlistments were down to 10 percent, an all-time low, and those for career personnel were down in the low 80s. We [implemented] a series of changes: The highly publicized ones were a change in hair standards, the authorization for beer in the enlisted barracks, hard-rock music in the clubs, and women going to sea in the one ship in which it's legal to send them to sea. I like to point out that in regards to the changes in hair standards during my 20 months in Vietnam, I estimate that I talked to some 15,000 of the 37,000 young officers and sailors out there, and I don't ever recall being challenged about why they were out there, or why did I have to be the guy that was wounded, or lost a leg, but very frequently they would ask the question "Why is it that we are willing to volunteer to join the Navy, and we're willing to fight an unpopular war, and are not permitted to look like our generation?" And then I came back and took this job and saw the pictures on the bulkhead: the first Chiefs of the Navy had long beards and mustaches and sideburns and realized that they had been permitted to look like their generation. And it proved to me that a small change to return to the conservative styles of their great-grandfathers. [Laughter and applause] The beer in the barracks...our married petty officers have always been able to go home and reach in the refrigerator and have a beer, I contend we've eliminated discrimination against the bachelors. With regard to the hard rock music, I can't stand the stuff myself. I've got four children who are squares and listen to it all the time, it hasn't hurt them and it doesn't seem to hurt our sailors. Finally with regard to women, I believe that they have a very important role to fill in the Navy, and if we're going to head for an all-volunteer era it's absolutely mandatory that the services be able to double the manpower pool, or the man and woman power pool, available to us by taking advantage of this very large area of talent.

...Let me speak for a moment about the phenomena that transpires when one seeks to make major change in any organization, as we've had to do to change ourselves from one served by the draft pressure of those who didn't want to go into the Army to one which had to be able to compete in peacetime with the other military services, which, if you really analyze it, have a better deal to offer than does the Navy. Because with the exception of that unfortunately too infrequent nut who enjoy going to sea for six to nine months at a time, in peacetime it's only the Navy that has very, very long family separations to offer. And furthermore, only the Navy that can't offer most of its people frequent liberties in the case of the unmarried personnel. So that we've got a tougher problem. And in making that dramatic change in an organization which is as tradition bound as was the Navy or any military service there is bound to be a set of polarization. There is one category of personnel which immediately seeks to go further than the changes permit, and this sets up a set of internal and external reverberations. There is another group of personnel which resists change partly through resentment, partly through comfort for the old, and partly because of fear of the new, and they dig in their heels and have to be dragged kicking and screaming into the twentieth century. [Laughter] And it is from this group that you have heard most of the expressions of discontent that have appeared in the newspaper. And then there is, in any organization going through a major transformation, an overwhelming majority who recognize the need for change, who support it, who get with it, who insist that the new changes be enforced to the letter. And that majority has increased from about 85 percent at the outset to about 97 or 8 percent at the present time, and it will be pretty close to 100 percent by the time I get through. [Laughter and applause]

In September 1973, Secretary Callaway spoke of the Army's own resistance to embracing the AVF.

The other thing that of course I spend my time with now and the thing that all of us spend the most of our time with is manning the army—manning a volunteer army, if you will, because we have a volunteer Army. You know, whether we have a volunteer army or whether we have a draft is a political question, that's not the Army's question. That's dictated to us by Congress. And we get into some very wrong kind of arguments when we talk about the volunteer Army. Members of Congress, particularly those who support the military, are frequently saying "Do you think we should have a volunteer Army? Do you think it would be better to have universal military training where every young man and woman serves his country in one form or another as a part of his life? Do you think it would be better to have a draft so that all Americans have some obligation to their country and understand it?" And you know, those are fine questions to talk about, and they may be a lot of fun, but they don't have a thing to do with anything that's happening now, because we don't have a draft, and we're not going to have a draft. Not this year, not next year, and not the year after next, and not in the context of what we can see in today's kind of timeframe, absent some major change in the world situation. We just don't have a draft. So instead of asking the question of what would we like, and I think all of us would like some systems slightly different than what we've got now, the proper question for every congressman to ask us is "How can we help you make the volunteer Army work?"

My point is there is no acceptable alternative. The only alternative in today's context of the political situation as it affects the Congress today, the only alternative, is not a draft. That's not available. The only alternative is failure for the Army. And the Army has never failed this country in 198 years and I don't propose to start it now. So our alternative is only one: To make the volunteer Army work and work well. And our dedication of all of us has got to be to make it work. The alternative that some people think of, "Well, let's show them it doesn't work and then go back and get a draft" is not there. The only way for that to work is for us to fail so miserably that the Army would be irreparably damaged before we could get back to the draft. There's no chance that this Congress or the next one is going to give us a draft just because we're not quite meeting quotas. They're not thinking that way at all. Their answer would be a severely reduced Army rather than a draft. I'm saying this because while I find 90% of the people in the Army supporting all-out the volunteer Army, I still find, particularly on the fringes of the Army, certain of our supporters in veteran's groups, Army-related organizations, are taking a strong stand against the volunteer Army. And I think we can show conclusively that that's very counterproductive to the Army, and very against the best service to the Army. So my plea to you is to get fully on board with making the volunteer Army work as a far better solution than any of the alternatives that might be available to us.

In May of the following year, Secretary Callaway spoke of the difference between soldiers in a draft army and those in a volunteer one.

Reenlistment of Field Grades [officers] is not my major problem. My major problem in making the volunteer Army work is with the first term soldier who's got to be satisfied. Who's got to go back to his sweetheart and his buddy and his parents and say being in the Army is important to him…It's your job as a leader in this Army to see that that individual soldier has his legitimate expectations met. And if he joined the Army to be a mechanic, and he comes to your unit, you can't make him a cook. And I'm not talking about [Military Occupational Specialty (MOS)] mismatch; I'm talking about MOS satisfaction. And our job is to suddenly realize that in a volunteer force we've got to treat soldiers as people and not as numbers. And I still find throughout this Army a mechanical approach of numbers to so many of the things we're doing. And we can't look at numbers; we've got to look at people. We have the same job with our young soldiers that General Motors or any other company has. And you know [they've got a] problem on an assembly line where a guy does nothing but screw on the same nut every day, and after three years if he's tired of it, and he comes to his foreman and says "I'm tired of screwing on that nut every day," you know that foreman doesn't go up to his supervisor and say "What we've got to do is ask Congress to draft this fella to screw the nut on." You know, and that's the attitude that a lot of people in the Army still take. "Well if a soldier doesn't like it, we'll have a draft."

We've got to do it just like General Motors. If he's tired of screwing that nut on every day, General Motors has got to find out a way to get him interested in that job. And if we've got a soldier that's bored to death, I don't care whether it's in a support command, or whether it's in an infantry rifle company, or whatever it is, we've got to have leadership good enough to make him excited and challenged. And I really think that's the basic key to this Army: Will our leadership be good enough so that that young man who's come out of basic training highly motivated, he's probably come out of AIT highly motivated— depending on which AIT he goes to—he comes out of there excited and wanting to do a good job. And when he gets to his unit, do we turn him off or do we mold that young man into an excited, challenged fine soldier? And it's up to the leadership of the Army. And if we can do that, everything else will work. It really will. 'Cause I can look a young man in the eye who's planning to go to Princeton or Harvard or whatever school he wants to, and I promise you I can give him a good argument on why he ought to spend two to three years in the Army first. And it will make sense. But it will only make sense if when he gets to that unit, he's doing something important to him, and that he's challenged. And that he understands why he's doing it, and he's part of a mission that he understands. Now I'm sure no one misunderstands me, but just so I'll touch on this point. You don't challenge him by making it easy for him. You don't get his loyalty by giving him lollipops and babying. You make what he's got to do tough, you make it clear to him why he's doing it, and you let him understand that he's part of something important, and then expect him to do it, expect him to carry it out, expect him to carry it out well. I would even go so far as to say the discipline in the volunteer Army must be far superior to the discipline in the draft Army. Because if you haven't got discipline, if you've got a rag tag outfit, there's no way a man can feel a sense of pride and purpose. And without that sense of pride and purpose, there's no way to get him to communicate to his buddies to make the volunteer Army work.

In December 1974, Callaway was asked how the AVF could continue to be as representative of the society it served as the draft was.

It's one of the toughest jobs that we've got, and one of the toughest jobs getting the Army on board for. Back last year when I was talking about this, you know everybody nods, but nothing was happening. And I think we're starting to get people on board. There are just so many good things about a representative army. I'm not talking about just Senator [Ted] Kennedy's concern, and he's concerned it will be all black, all poor, that the blacks will take more than their share of casualties, and you know that's a concern. I'm not just talking about that. I'm talking about the advantage of having an Army where, in every neighborhood, there's some kids from the block that people know that are in the Army, that feel like it's theirs. If we start to get in a war and have casualties they feel it. You know we don't want an Army that's a foreign legion over there, we want a part of everybody. I think that's enormously important. Well we're beginning to get not only quality, we're beginning to get representation. And the kind of thing, and the reason this is so sensitive is anytime you do anything and say representation somebody thinks you're trying to give some minority group an un—take away some opportunity and all of that. You talk about something emotional, it's really there. What, so far, we're able to do, and so far I have at least the grudging support of the members of the Black Caucus that I've talked to, and people of that kind, is to say that where we have an over-representation, and by over-representation I mean more than 100%, of the [Qualified Military Available (QMA)] that we're supposed to have, where a recruiting district or area or command has more than 100%—see what we've been doing is take good recruiting places like the South, Jackson, Mississippi, Jacksonville, Florida, or even a downtown ghetto in New York, all of that, very high percent of people who have low employment opportunities. What happens? We not only recruit hard there, because it's easy to get people, all the 'unit of choice' canvases converge there from all the divisions, everybody's recruiting there. Instead of getting the normal amount you'd expect of QMA you get 400% in some cases. Well, we are saying that we're going to take those marketing assets—we're not going to let the 'unit of choice' still congregate there. We've got to spend some of the time in, let's say, the upper peninsula of Michigan, where we never get many people, and that kind of thing.

...What do I see is the Army's job while the economy is bad? I see the Army's job is to get so good, and that includes the presentation, which is enormously important, get so good and so fine that the country understands it, and then we can travel on our own. If we got caught right after Vietnam, with the enormous problems we had at that time, and the enormous lack of public support, and got caught with a really going economy where everybody could get a job, we might have had a real problem. But by the time this economy gets good, which, you know I hope it's tomorrow it gets good, but however much time we've got, we want to use this time to make this Army just the best Army it can be. I sincerely believe we can do it...It's extremely important, to have an Army that's felt by the American people to be a part of America and not them versus us. It's the guts of the whole problem we've got. And when we get that it'll feed on itself. And when we've got that, you know, I don't care how good prosperity is, I can take, you can take, we can take, the Army can take a high school graduate who is number one in his class, an Eagle Scout, has every kind of job opportunity, can go to any college he wants to in

America, and I promise you, we can sell him to join the Army and it will be the best thing he ever did. And I'm talking about as an enlisted man—obviously ROTC and all of that—but as an enlisted man. Spend three years in the Army, get a challenge, get an excitement, learn something about himself, learn some discipline, some self-discipline, learn a trade if he wants to. Get an education, come back with the GI Bill, which is worth $12,000 to him, come back to college on Uncle Sam and the G.I. Bill. Get a maturity he gets nowhere else. They don't know at 17, 18 what they want to do with their lives. Get him out of the Army after three years, they know where they want to go, they're charged up, they make a better student and make a better employee. You know we can sell the top quality, but we've got to get an attitude that is different from the kind of attitude that we had a couple years ago. And as long as everybody says "Oh, that old Army's over there, that's not a part of us," we'll have a hard time getting that attitude.

...The leadership needed in a volunteer force is very different from the leadership needed in a draft force. In a draft Army we could afford to—probably wasn't smart—but we could afford to treat the first-term soldier as one who was in the Army because he owed it to his country, an obligated service, and we could afford to treat him as someone just sacrificing because he owed it to his country and we didn't have to look after him too much. Should have, but didn't really have to. I'm not talking about getting a hot meal to troops in the field, we've always been good about that, but I'm talking about genuinely treating that person as a human and understanding that his life is important. And if he likes to tinker with automobiles and that's something he's good at, he wants to be a mechanic you don't make him a cook. And likewise if he wants to be a cook you don't make him a mechanic. You are genuinely concerned about the legitimate needs of our best soldiers, in ways that have to do with their satisfaction in their job, their importance in their job, to challenge him. You don't run a rifleman up a hill again every day when he's done it before. Once he's trained in that you must find ways to keep him challenged. You've still got to keep him trained, you've got to keep him disciplined, but you've got to keep him challenged. And this was not as necessary in a draft Army. And the leadership that we must have, particularly in our NCOs and our company and battery-grade officers has got to be outstanding to bring that man where he's doing what he wants to do. And once you've got that you've got an Army that won't wait. When you've got an Army where everybody in it wants to be in it, believe in their leadership, they're doing what they're excited by. I've seen units that you just cannot believe how good they are, and you have to—our job is to get the Army that good right now.

General Meyer elaborated on the challenges of the volunteer soldier in 1979.

We can't blame the society for the kind of young soldier we are getting. He is the soldier we are getting. He has the same kinds of needs. He needs to have the opportunity to develop mentally. We can provide him with that. He needs the opportunity to be able to develop physically. Many of them come from a society or come from a climate or come from an environment in which they have not had the opportunity to develop totally. That they have scabs and scars on their minds and on their psycho [sic] which prevent them from being able to take part. We have to attempt to establish some moral or spiritual standard for them which explains to them, for the first time in many of their lives, some sort of basic tenants in which they can believe, so that they can believe in their fellow man, they can believe in the soldier next to them so that a bond of trust and confidence can develop because that's the only way that soldiers can fight when they go to war, is if they believe and trust in the guy next to you [sic]. The absolutes in war are one, I don't want to get killed. There might be one or two guys out here who didn't really care if they got killed. Most folks start out with one very basic thing, I don't want to die. And then you start looking around for the kind of folks near you who you have trust in, that you can work with and have confidence in, who are going to ensure that that unit you're in is operating well so that you're not going to die. So that's the kind of trust and confidence that we have to inspire in any young soldier. And finally we have to ensure that we have a social milieu in which that individual has an opportunity to understand other people and be able to operate effectively.

Meyer added the following on selective service registration.

The United States of America has to be able to go to war. And one of the elements of being able to go to war, in addition to the forces in being, is the ability to mobilize. So registration is linked directly to our ability to mobilize. I am convinced that an element of deterrence, one of the things that would deter my counterpart in the Kremlin from recommending to [Soviet Premier Leonid] Brezhnev that he ought to begin conflict is his historical remembrance of the great capabilities of the United States to be able to mobilize its industrial and manpower base. So registration relates to mobilization…So I think registration needs to be linked very carefully in your mind with mobilization. And that's why, as a member of the JCS, I have supported registration, because I think it's essential to mobilization. I said as a member of the JCS, my friends, that's where I end up supporting it, because of the military need for it to be able to do that.

One of the issues which sort of clouds registration is Vietnam. If you talk to people about registration one of their concerns is their view that it was, in fact, an unpopular war. Their view that they do not want their children, they do not want themselves to go off to a war in which they don't agree. Very clearly in the case of registration, essentially, that is not possible. Because we now have a War Powers Act, which was enacted by Congress, which prevents people from being sent off until Congress itself, representing the will of the American people, has agreed for people to be sent off for any period longer than ninety days. So nobody who has registered, mobilized, comes in [and] is trained could possibly be sent off before the will of the people is in support of it. So the arguments against registration that relate to Vietnam in my view are specious, based on the baffles that have been currently placed into how we go about deploying forces by Congress and the War Powers Act.

General Max Thurman, who commanded the U.S. Army's Recruiting Command at the launch of the "Be All You Can Be" era, spoke to the class in 1986 about personnel issues.

What about the people side of this, which makes it hum? Our organization is inherently built around people, so how are we doing about that? First of all, the standards which we require people to operate on: We'd like for two thirds of them to be in the upper half, no more than 10% Cat IVs [lowest mental category], and we'd like 90% or better to be high-school graduates. Then you've got to pass the moral, mental, and physical standards. And you say "Well, why do you need to specify smart people?" And the answer is…that smart people are smarter than less smart people. [Big laugh] Here's the upper half [points to chart] operating on Stingers [shoulder-fired air defense missiles]. Two-thirds of the people can fire the Stinger well if they're [Category] I-IIIAs. Mental Category IVs a little bit less. Air Force take note. [Big laugh]

…This is a reminder about the fragility of personnel business. And every time I do a pitch, you will see me give you this chart, by emphasis of repetition. Here is the track record for the Reserve, the Guard, and the Active, and remind yourself the nadir of the personnel situation in the Guard and Reserve was 1978, with those kind of numbers, and the nadir for the army was '79 when the endstrength was missed by 17,000. You go back and look at some of the factors embroiled in that, pay comparability, unemployment, education benefits, and recruiting resources. Start [at the onset] of the volunteer force [in 1973]: plenty of resources, plenty of pay comparability, G.I. Bill. End of 1976, answer: "You're doing so well, we'll slam-dunk that and see how you do." Well they stopped the pay comparability, the employment situation began to turn around, and they gave us a thing called the Veteran's Education Assistance Program, which is on the lips of every single person in America, can explain it to you in gory detail. [Laugh] [They] said take a 40% cut in recruiting resources, and said "Now how ya doing?" The answer is we flunked. Now no Air Force, Navy, or Marine should get complacent. Because in 1979 the Army, Navy, Air Force, and Marines, everybody, failed to make their mission…in the recruitment market.

And [Senators] Sam Nunn and [John] Warner came along with a pay comparability restoration here, begin to give us a little incentive and began to turn the market around, notice all the curves begin to go in the right direction. But now we're in a declining pay comparability zone again, a decreasing unemployment rate, although we've broken the direct linkage between unemployment rates and enlistments of high quality people. We do have a new G.I. Bill, and we're getting adequate resources, but it requires minding the store. And you'll notice now I don't call it a volunteer army anymore, it's the five recruited armies, because if you went down to your local recruiting station—which I'm sure that you have been to, and all those who have not served in the Recruiting Command will be given orders from this class to go directly there. [Laugh] The point is they're not lined up outside trying to get in, you've got to go hustle the market.

…We're going to let the Guard and Reserve rise as high as they can get commensurate with the quality of accession meeting the standards that we set for the Guard and Reserve. Would it be a bad deal for America for the Guard to have a million-man force, or a million person force? Would it be bad for America to have a million people in the Reserves? Answer is of course not. Because if you and I perceive that we have a values set that is useful to transmit to the population of America at large, why would we want to turn people away from the Guard and Reserve? And so we're going to let the Guard and Reserve rise as high as it's going to rise, commensurate with the people who volunteer for entry there can meet the standards for admittance that we set for ourselves. Happily, these two numbers will exceed the Active component next year. And so the Guard and Reserve in aggregate, and that doesn't include the Individual Ready Reserve, will exceed the Active component in 1987, and that's good news. If you had asked me in 1980, and I've been in the manpower business for about six straight years, "Could you raise another 250,000 people in the Guard and Reserve in six years?" I would have said not a chance. And yet there are 250,000 more on the active list than 1980. So we've come a dynamite long way in that process, and many of you work with Guard and Reserve, [I] know we have some Guard and Reserve members in the audience, but the work that you do in the summers and in training, round-out work and the like, is absolutely essential to our total force concept, and the Reserve and Guard are integral to our processes.

General Vuono spoke about recruiting challenges in October, 1988 that would be repeated many times over the next couple of decades.

We're going to continue to put the money and put the effort in quality soldiers. And I'll tell you there are some dark clouds on horizon out there. So I don't want any of you in the Army to sit back and be complacent and say "All we've got to do is throw a few bucks into it, we're going to be okay." It's going to be tough over the next few years to continue to get the kind of quality for a number of reasons. First of all the pool of personnel that are eligible to be recruited has been dropping. Secondly, there is a market out there for jobs. There's no lack of jobs out there today. The unemployment rate is lower than it's ever been. And thirdly, industry is competing for the same kind of quality kids that you and I want in the Army.

In December 1993, General Sullivan pointed out an interesting aspect of the AVF, stating "…Over 70%, by the way, of the Army is married. The numbers keep going up, because interestingly enough, the married couples stay, the single soldiers get out. That may tell you something…There is a message there, and I'm not sure I fully understand what it is." A year later Secretary West discussed the possible impact of the first Gulf War on the minds of America's youth.

A year ago to a different class I reported that we were having a marvelous amount of success in recruiting quality soldiers for our Army, quality members for all our Armed Forces. I did warn that there were some disturbing signs on the horizon. One of the lessons of Desert Storm, I said, was not just that the armed forces of the United States can respond and perform quickly and effectively and efficiently in a way that brings credit to them and to the republic that they represent, but also that part of being in uniform is going to war, and that in war people are injured and die. Our American youth have learned that. That is one of the things they learned from Desert Storm. And although I would not suggest, and don't ask you to take the message, that they are somehow any less reluctant to take on the burdens of citizenship that have generations before them. Nonetheless, we have seen a bit of a decline in what I would call the predisposition of youngsters to enlist in any of the Armed Forces. It is not a source of worry, but it is a source of concern, and we continue to watch it.

In 1997, Secretary Cohen addressed the gap between military personnel and the society they served that General Johnson warned about in 1970.

You've been reading some of the same things I have about some writers who are worried about: Is the military becoming an elitist institution? Is there a widening gap between the military and civilian society to the point where there are different standards, in which the military starts to look down in condescension and with contempt upon the people they are protecting? And if that's the case, that presents a problem, because you have of course civilian control of our military. Or does the military march to a different

222

drummer? So that's not an idle question—it's a long one, but not an idle one. And you point to something that's almost fundamental that you all have to deal with, we have to deal with. Senator Patrick Moynihan wrote a piece [in 1993], and the title of the piece was called "Defining Deviancy Down." And it was a very catchy title to this article, and what he was trying to point out is that our social norms have been really reduced over the years. If you think back, how many people, for example, were killed during the St. Valentine's Day massacre? How many in here know? It was less than five. Five people killed during the St. Valentine's Day *massacre*? And it's still a note in every world book of records. And yet today we lose five in a weekend in Washington D.C., and very few people think much about it, so that we have defined deviant behavior down. And it's a problem that we have to face as a society, and you're seeing some change taking place. We've seen kind of the excesses of the sixties and seventies reach a point where there's a swing back now. People are starting to look at what happened to those core values that are so important to us as a society, about truth and honor and courage and commitment. And when you say, you're suggesting that somehow people coming into the military today are getting it pretty easy, not tough enough, is interesting. I went to Paris Island last week, and I went through their training program. And they have something that's been introduced by [Commandant of the Marine Corps] General [Charles] Krulak called Crucible Week. Really putting them through a test that final week before they graduate. A 54-hour ordeal in which they go through sleep deprivation, food deprivation, put through all kinds of mental tests as well as physical ones. I just came from the Naval Training Center. And they have instituted something called Battle Stations.

But what I've found is that all of these training centers that we have are drawing upon a society which is less physically prepared, softer, more complacent. Many of them come from broken homes, single family homes, maybe without parents at all. I read the piece written by [Rear] Admiral [Kevin] Green, came out in the Early Bird back in July 18, on my way out to visit the training center. And what he pointed out is a significant portion of the people, when they mail their civilian clothes back home, they would find that checking the records, too many percentage of them would mail it to a post-office box, to some kind of an institutional setting, and too often the clothes came back addressee unknown. We are drawing people from a different kind of society than you came from, where the standards are much lower, perhaps, much more violent in many cases for those who have to live in the inner cities. And so it's a greater challenge to those of you who have to train them. But I must tell you, even though the pool of people coming in may not have had the same kind of stress that you went through, may not have had the same kind of challenge that perhaps you were presented with, by the time they leave, they are sailors, and Marines, and airman. They are fully capable of joining you as the finest fighting force in the world. And so I have gone to each of the training centers, from the Air Force to the Marines to the Army, and now the Navy. And what I continue to be impressed with is no matter what they are coming in with—and most people would tell you they're brighter, they're smarter. They may not be as physically fit. They may not have the same respect for authority as you all did. But when they get through that basic training, they are professional. And they have a sense of esteem, and a sense of confidence, and they have a team spirit.

And that is reflected, for the most part. We have our exceptions; you will read about it tomorrow. You'll hear about the Aberdeen [sexual assault case] story, you'll hear about

223

what's taking place in the Army as far as a deficiency in leadership and so forth. But essentially I think what's taking place is that our country is swinging back from the excesses of the sixties and the seventies, and I believe that we should not lower the standards in the military. The reason that we are the best in the world is because we don't tolerate the least. And what we want to do is to make sure you hold those standards as high as you possibly can, and not be forced to degrade them. You don't have to be politically correct to the point where you are softening your training so that the people who are coming in are unprepared to carry out the duties and responsibilities. I think you're seeing a swing back and I think that over a period of time you will see that there will not be this separation that people worry about today that there's a growing gulf between our military "elite" and our general society. So I think the standards are high, they should remain high.

A month later Secretary West addressed these new recruits and whether or not they were ready to perform their duties.

Now I've admitted this before today, so I'll admit it again. I'm aware that our recruits in America's Army these days probably know more about computers than they do about physical education. But we have been training Americans for two and a quarter centuries. We can handle that and we are handling that. We are producing trainees who can do America's job, and the proof is in the pudding.

READINESS

Many of the speakers discussed the readiness of the Army as they saw it at the time. General Johnson addressed equipment readiness in December 1967.

I was asked, in the Spring of 1965 by one of the congressional committees, what the biggest single problem confronting the Army was at that time. Well I hadn't prepared myself for that question...I suppose it was short-sighted of me not to have made some preparation but I hadn't. And my answer to the question after a moment's thought was knowing what we have and where it is. What we have and where it is. I would add to that now one other thing: and whether or not it works. [Laughter] Because we've got a lot of doggie stuff throughout the Army and we're not really sure we ought to send it off to war if this becomes necessary. Now we've been scrambling and scrambling hard to first get an inventory of everything we have, to relate the inventory to the jobs we have to do.

General Bruce Palmer, Jr., Commander of the U.S. Readiness Command (which eventually became U.S. Special Operations Command in 1987) discussed personnel readiness in 1974, one year into the AVF, as well as the need for a readiness mindset.

In terms of readiness, I think we have reached a plateau, and I'm sorry to say I think the Army will start coming down again this summer. Primarily manpower problems, and it's not only a question of quantity but distribution. [The] Air Force, I think we'll see them stay up a little better. The other services, that is Navy and Marines, are having their problems likewise. All of them are having funding problems. But readiness, more than just materiel and manpower, it's a state of mind. And in my view I think balance is the thing we've got to keep in mind. If you don't have balanced forces, I think we're in trouble. We don't know where we might fight. We don't know when. But I think we can be reasonably certain that you people here will be fighting someday somewhere. But when you're faced with that kind of uncertainty, you'd better have balance. And I mean by balance, balance in strategic thinking, strategic concepts, you can't afford to put all your eggs in one basket. And in terms of balanced forces. And Israel learned the hard way in this last war. An unbalanced force, and they damn near lost.

The next year, General DePuy spoke extensively about combat system readiness based on the lessons of the Arab-Israeli wars.

...The U.S. Army's not in good shape on its air defense weapons. The Vulcan is not a good weapon. And we're having an argument amongst ourselves in Washington about what ought to replace it. We have let a contract for a short-range air defense missile. Foreign made. Our Hawk is probably the best medium range missile in the world, it's slow to emplace. And we're trying to fix that up by putting radios in place where cables now exist. And SAM-D [development program that became the PATRIOT Missile], if it ever survives the vicissitudes of the Washington decision-making process, will be a pretty good weapon. It has flown its proof of principle test. I think there were some five or six rounds fired. And as you probably know that has a supremely sophisticated system where for the last 10 to 12 seconds tracking is done from the missile and the data is fed to the ground computer and back to the missile. The only one like that, and it flew, and it worked in all of its initial tests.

...All that lethality that I've been talking about is not automatic. The fact that a T-62 tank can do a certain thing at 2,000 meters doesn't mean that the Russian tank crew can achieve that. In almost every instance we buy a weapon system because the Army Materiel Systems Analysis Agency says that [pointing to capability chart] that red line is its performance *goal*, those are the performance specifications. And so when the decision is made to buy the weapon, back in Washington, spend millions of dollars on it, we buy it because it will do what the red line says, some probability of hit over some range. We put it out in the hands of our troops and what happens? It's down on the yellow lines. Now bringing the yellow line up to the red line is more than an academic exercise. The first thing that it is is training. So if you're going to spend hundreds of millions of dollars on a system, you've got to spend also hundreds of millions of dollars on training time, ammunition, simulators, and so on. Now that is a subject which is obvious, you know, once you think about it, but not always recognized.

...I talked about first-round hit. And there is probably the best way of pulling the performance characteristics of the T-62 and the M-60A1 apart. That slide was put together with research data here in the United States plus data from the Arab-Israeli war. A mixutre. But what it says is that if you fire first at the short ranges where you only get one round, and where you fire battle sights, and where the weapon is very accurate and very lethal, the fellow who fires first has got about an 8 to 1 advantage. Turning it around the fellow who fires second has had it. When you get out to the longer ranges, you might be able to get two rounds in, and the advantage narrows. Now you'll notice it doesn't add up to unity, because in some places, in some battles nobody wins, everybody misses. So we have changed at Fort Knox, we've changed our gunnery procedures because of that, because of that very consideration. Instead of starting from scratch and

225

letting a tank commander detect the target, tell the gunner where it is, call for a certain round, have the loader put it in the tube, finally get the thing laid on in 13, 15 seconds and fire, the doctrine now is you've got to carry a round in the tube. If you think you're going to run into infantry, why, put a high-explosive (HE)] round in the tube. If you think you're going to run into tanks at extended range, put an [armor-piercing (APDS)] in the tube. Set it on battle sights, train the crew so that when the tank cannon is on battle sights, and the tank appears close to you fire at where he meets the ground, and the super-elevation will nail him right in the middle. And if he's at what looks like a mile fire at him with cross hairs, and get it off in 5 to 7 seconds.

... The good old 82d Airborne division that almost gets sent here, there, and everywhere from time to time to go out there and wrestle with enemy tanks with their bare hands, I guess. Brave men in that division, always. But not fair to them to put them into battle that way, so we're putting lots of TOWs and Dragons in there [Anti-tank weapons]. We also want to give them an anti-tank round for their little 105mm cannons.

...Right now we have a national aversion to [Chemical, Biological, Radiological Defense] which permeates in a subtle way the decision making process and the appropriation process. The Soviet equipment, the sophistication of the filtering equipment on the tank, the T-62, and the BMP are kind of frightening just in terms of the extent to which they're willing to go and the money they're willing to spend. We're about to crank up more emphasis in training, all defensive because of national policy. But that national policy has spilled over into some apathy, one of the aspects with doing away with the Chemical Corps and combining it with the engineers and the ordnance. Who am I to say that was right or wrong? I won't. All I'm saying is it's a symptom of an attitude which up to now has made it difficult for us to meet head-on the problem of chemical warfare. I just have to say to you the legacy which the current high command of the Army is leaving you is not in my opinion a good one. We're trying to attack it, and we're trying to get the money to do something about it, and I would say up to now our efforts have not been blessed with much success.

In December 1975, General Weyand discussed the Army's readiness in terms of facing the Soviet Union in Europe.

...Can we whip the Soviets? And how do we go about doing that? What timeframe are you talking about? You think of the variables. You take something like our ability to get to NATO, and to establish a real conventional defense that can hold those guys, let's say at the Weser-Lech [River] line or something like that. Okay. [Consider] strategic lift, the amount of it, the amount that's going to be available to the Army. Have we got enough for everybody? No, we don't have, so I'm pushing on supporting the Air Force in getting more strategic lift in their Reserve Air Fleet, augmenting or modifying 747s and DC-10s. Warning time: You can take that same situation, achieve one result with a certain warning time, completely different with some other kind of a warning time. What does that mean? That means the validity, effectiveness of our intelligence in determining what's going on, and the effectiveness of our decision making process. Well, as you go through these things these are all variables, and what you're talking about is that same old hackneyed thing, you know, is it half empty or half full? As I say, I think you just state the facts. I like to tell the Army it's in good shape, because I want you to be proud of it.

I wouldn't tell you that if I didn't believe in it. I'd tell you what I thought we'd have to do to get it in good shape. It's too small, it isn't as ready as it should be, it isn't as capable of sustained combat as it should be.

And yet when I look back, I was in Japan [and] Korea [in] 1950. We sent the 24th Division into Korea the day or so after that war broke out, whatever it was, or a few days, snow had fallen and so forth. MacArthur testified when he came back that he sent that division into Korea even though it was about half equipped, untrained, manning about half to two-thirds of its manpower. He testified that he knew that that division would be destroyed. But he sent it in there because that's all he had, and he wanted to convince the enemy, as he reported, by the audacity of his action that he had more power at his disposal than he had. And it worked. Also that division was almost literally destroyed. Now it was reborn and it came back to fight, but it gave them time to get in the First Cav and the 25th Division and so on and so forth. Then again in Vietnam. I took the 25th Division into Vietnam. We had more than a year to prepare for that, and yet what did I take in there? A bob-tailed division: Two brigades. I formed the third brigade from odd-lot units from Alaska, and we did that on the run and we did it in four months, and that was the 25th Division that fought in South Vietnam. Those are the kind of experiences that I have in my mind. When I went into Korea I went in with the 3rd Infantry Division. I know that there's not one of you in this room that knows when that division went into Korea, an old line division, it had 7,900 U.S. in that division and 8,500 Koreans who had had 4 weeks of basic training, having been swept off the streets of Pusan and Seoul and elsewhere. I had two U.S. [soldiers] in most squads and eight Koreans who could not speak English or anything else. Now that's what we sent into war and called them 'divisions.'

And so I've got to be careful when I say that the 9th Division is ready for combat. It's not C1 [the highest readiness rating], but it is C2, maybe it's C3. It's operationally ready. And having said that, it is so much better than anything else that we ever sent into combat—it's no contest. And so there are no blacks and whites in this game you're playing. The only reason I'm telling you this, is not by way of apology by your Chief of Staff, but I want you to know that as you go through your career, you're not very often going to find the nice clean-cut decisions. If they are clean cut, you know what's going to happen? You're not going to hear about them. They're not going to come to you. So, yes, there's optimism, and there's pessimism, and you put it all together, and I'm more optimistic now in this total thing than I was a year ago. Why? Because I see, after I've looked at the Soviets and their weaknesses and their strengths, I see a chance. If we exploit missile technology, air defense and anti-tank missile technology, harden our TOW missiles, improve our armor, battlefield mobility, for the first time really develop the capability for night operations, and we know the potential for that in terms of equipment and we've talked about it all the 37 years I've been in the Army, but we never have really been an Army that could fight 24 hours a day, day in and day out, and yet that's our great forte compared to any other Army in the world. Flexibility, new tactics, new doctrine, get away from the linear defense, maximize these things that I see we can do better than anybody else. You know there's not another Army in the world has the capability of doing—those of you that served in Vietnam, I don't know how many of you there are, but if any of you had command, using close air support was automatic, it was no big thing. You kept the attack helicopters working, you kept your artillery and mortars working, you brought in the [Tactical] Air and it was all going on at the same time. Now that really takes guys who are true professionals, it takes equipment and all the rest. The Israelis can't do it, the Russians can't do it. And so we have got either capability or proven potential that is going to enable us, as Bill DePuy or somebody from his outfit I'm sure has told you their slogan is to win the first battle, and I accept that, although again, literally, what do you mean by battle? [Laughter] But we are going to be ready. And we can do it.

In 1976, General Rogers warned the students about post-war trends in the United States: "And then, here we are in a time of peace. It's always been true in this country during time of peace that we've always dreamed that peace is going to continue, and the wishful thinking that war will never come again. And we've always ended up being kind of flat on our ass when it did." General DePuy was back later that year to discuss the readiness aspects of training.

By about the middle of next calendar year, we will have a soldier's manual in the hand of every soldier that tells him what he's supposed to do at his grade. Isn't it strange that we've never had such a thing, ever before? You see, we've had an operator's manual for a platoon leader, but he's an officer. We had an operator's manual for company commander, troop commander, battery commander, but he's an officer. Told him how to run his, whatever it is, platoon, battery, troop. We've got one for our lieutenant colonels, how to run a battalion. We've even got a manual for division major generals, how to run a division. But we never had a manual that specifically told a sergeant squad leader what he had to do. Well, we have that.

…We talk readiness, but we don't practice readiness. Now this is a philosophic question that gets to the heart of officer education or training or whatever you want to call it. Because the question is if you really thought you were going to go to war tomorrow morning, or could, you know if you really believed that, then you would adopt a wartime training system in which you would train lieutenants as platoon leaders to go out and be a tank platoon leader tomorrow morning and fire and maneuver and hit the target and maintain tanks. On the other hand if you say, no we're not going to go to war for twenty years, we don't want to spend all of our time training platoon leaders, what we want to do is train generals. That's different. Now TRADOC, very clearly, is trying to move the Army toward training for an early war. We don't want an early war. Training against the contingency of an unexpected war, where we have to have an Army that can exploit all that firepower including tank gunnery and everything else, from the outset. Therefore, TRADOC is tending to go over towards train lieutenants to be platoon leaders first, and for higher things second. Now I happen to believe that a lieutenant trained to be a platoon leader, completely trained, will make a good battalion commander. And one who was never trained to be a platoon leader will never make a good battalion commander.

So the philosophy here is that in an army with high turbulence and turnover of the private soldier, in a volunteer army in which we get fine young men, but not the finest of the nation's young men, that more and more, the officer must be able, and the sergeant, to do everything from battalion on down. Every job. In other words an army in which the best tank gunner, the best tank commander, the best tank mechanic, the best tank driver, and the best tank loader in the 1st Battalion, 37th Armor is the battalion commander. The second is the battalion exec, the third, fourth, and fifth are A, B, and C company commanders, and so on. That is an Army which exploits the highest percentage of potential firepower made available to you to fight the first battle. That is not, gentlemen, the style with which we have pursued the last thirty years. So I submit to you you have to bite that bullet. You have to decide whether that's necessary or not. I'll tell you that it's necessary if you're going to exploit the capability of weapon systems. If you can prove to me or anybody else that there is something more important than that, for lieutenants and captains to do, then of course the Army should do whatever that is.

In 1978, General Trefrey briefed the students on the poor state of maintenance and equipment readiness in the Army, remarks which revealed little progress since General Johnson's similar concerns in 1967 at the beginning of this section.

I believe there is a tendency on the part of some of my contemporaries and some of my peers and O-6s that you guys are to blame. And the captains in the Army are to blame. Nothing could be further from the truth. The fact is the system is screwed up. We are all products, each and every one of us, of 15 years of a throw-away war. When we went to computers, and the printouts go from the [Division Support Command] to the company commander, we left out the brigade commander, we left out the battalion commander. That's a hell of a lot of battalion commanders, that's a hell of a lot of brigade commanders running around the army that don't know a damn thing about supply—not only accountability, but supply, or logistics. All they've ever got is what they got here [at CGSC]. [Pause and laughter] Boy I waited 16 years for that! [Big laugh]

… I'll give you an example of what we're trying to resolve on turn-in procedures. A unit commander was down in his supply room, supply sergeant says "We have got a problem." He said "What it is?" "We found this jeep on post." [Laughter] They found it on a range. They were out on a range, jeep was there. No bumper markings, they checked. They tried to turn that thing in. And what a real rat race that is. Had to have a complete [technical inspection]. Had to have all the equipment on it it was supposed to have. After three months of this, he took the damned thing back out to the range and left it. [Big laugh]

In 1979, General Meyer was asked to evaluate the United States' industrial base.

Well, I don't want to get sick to my stomach and throw up all over. That's about the way I would end up, if I gave you an honest answer, I'd have to stand up on the front here and wretch! We started about a year and a half ago, in the Army, to start focusing the Department of Commerce, the Department of Labor, industry and so on on the mobilization needs. We proposed for the [Joint Chiefs of Staff], and had the department at that particular point and time, we had the— GSA, the General Service Administration, had the federal preparedness agency under it, and got them involved in a mobilization exercise last fall. So that the industrial community could understand what their mobilization capability was. And it was a great eye opener…All the lessons learned in wars of the past, through World War II, are lessons that have to be relearned every time we go through a mobilization exercise. We have the capability of going back in history and being able to understand the basic premises we have to use in developing a mobilization capability for our country.

...The next thing I'd like to tell you about industrial mobilization is interesting. And that is that in the past we have always said that we needed to have cold lines out there that were available at wartime to be able to expand. There's another facet of industrial mobilization that is very interesting. We have the capacity currently in our industrial base out there, in all of the factories which are turning out guns and tanks and so on, to go out today and buy immediate expansion and elasticity in the production base—$21 billion worth of equipment that we need. So that tells you that there's $21 billion worth of elasticity in the base just the way it is. We have to somehow figure out through our [Research and Development] folks how to take advantage of that elasticity within the base itself and we don't know how to do that very well now. So that's an aspect of it that we've never taken into account before. We've always only taken into account what we had in cold storage in the way of ammo plants and so on. But clearly, as the half-life of technology gets shorter and shorter and shorter, we have to be beginning to build into the going industrial capability this elasticity and be able to take advantage of it. We may have to pay a price in buying stuff to be able to ensure the elasticity to expand.

General Sullivan gave students the bottom line on readiness in August 1992. "No "timeouts" from readiness. No time out. Ruck it up, move out, and draw fire. Don't stand around and tell me 'Well it's going to take me a week to get ready. We're going to take apart the Army today and be ready in 1996.' Not true."

INFORMATION OVERLOAD; COMPLEXITY; THE RATE OF CHANGE

Almost all of the speakers addressed the increasing complexity of the world situation, the information overload that accompanied new technology, and almost all noted that change and events had never moved at a faster pace. Field Marshall Montgomery implored the students to seek simplicity in 1953.

It's frightfully important these days to be simple. I think simplicity today is needed as it has never been needed before, because the tendency is for everything to become complicated. That's the tendency. And the amount of paper that people have to read today is frightful. [Laughter] I don't believe any sane man could read half the paper he's given to read. And I don't believe the other half's worth reading! [Laughter] It's frightful. I tell you in my organization, a NATO organization, I didn't know there was so much paper in the world. It's really frightful. And I think we must get back to simple ways of doing things, which in the end are the best. In the late war, when I was commanding some pretty big outfits, I never used any paper at all...not for that purpose I mean, I... [interrupted by laughter, 'paper' having the double meaning of 'toilet paper.']

General Decker told Associate Course graduates in December, 1960 that adaptation was crucial to survival, saying "Like any profession, the military profession must adapt itself to change if it is to retain its vitality and utility. This requirement poses a particular challenge today, for change is the basic characteristic of our time. Change world-wide, and in almost every aspect of man's existence." General Lemnitzer also warned the 1961 Regular Course graduates about the rate of change.

There never has been a time when events were moving at a faster pace. That is why the experience that you have gained here in solving problems is so important. The solutions you have found are less important than the methods of finding solutions that you have learned here at Leavenworth. Details are undergoing frequent change. But the fundamental principles you have practiced and the characteristics you have developed have an unchanging validity.

Two years later in December 1963, General Johnson sounded a similar alarm. "We must adapt ourselves to change if we are to retain our vitality. This poses a particular challenge now in our time, because the basic characteristic really of the era in which we live is change. And we're moving awfully fast." The following year General Bruce Clarke expressed his concern regarding the encroachment of technology into leadership.

Another thing that is coming into the picture a great deal is data processing, and we should worry about that in the Army too. Because that is pushing the individual, the blue collar people farther and farther away from the white collared people. And it will do it in the Army if we don't watch out. It will get us to the point where we don't get out as commanders and staff officers and visit the troops. We will glue ourselves to a display console. And I can point out to you that you can't command a division or corps or army by looking at a TV screen all your life. [Applause]

General Bradley addressed a similar topic during his 1966 visit: "I don't know how much you have to work with computers, but there seems to be a great tendency to solve everything by computers. Going around the classrooms yesterday I didn't see one." [Laughter] In 1967, Secretary Kissinger addressed the rate of change and pace of events as it related to the high-level decision-making process.

I think we are facing a serious problem. Until the beginning of World War II it would never have occurred to a top leader that he was less competent than his staffs in solving certain problems. Today we face a situation that the difference in the amount of attention that can be given to a problem between staffs and the leadership is fantastic. The staffs have months and years to give to a problem, where the leadership may have only days. Much of the communication in government now, as you know better than I do, takes place by means of briefings. Briefings represent the prepackaging of information to produce a desired effect. They reward theatrical qualities. They magnify the insecurities of top leaders in many ways, because the leaders know they are being taken but they don't know how. [Big laugh and applause]

...But the relationship between knowledge and action is a very serious one. And I feel unless we can do something about the style of life of the top personnel so that they become more reflective and so they have genuine time to think, there is no way of solving these problems. As long as they are so harassed, they are always going to pick the answers that seem most familiar to them, no matter where these answers come from.

...For the policy maker, the problems present themselves. There is an enormous pressure to deal with the day to day decisions. One reason, in my judgment, why it is always true that there is inadequate long-range planning, is that by definition, long-range is that you do not have to deal with today. And there are so many decisions that must be taken today, that the psychological pre-disposition is to emphasize the current, and let the future take care of itself. To be sure every agency has planning staffs. But in any large bureaucracy, it is less true of the military than any other bureaucracy, but in any large bureaucracy, I do not believe that it matters so much what the staffs do, unless the staffs can get the attention of senior personnel. If the top people do not believe that what the planning staff does is of significance to them, it does not really matter what is written down on paper.

In 1970, General Johnson addressed his concerns regarding the rate of change.

Now what are we confronted with? We are confronted with a rate of change that troubles me. It's troubled me particularly since I have retired. Because I'm not too sure that we, and by we I mean those of us in uniform, having had our nose so close to the grindstone, that we haven't been fully conscious of all that's going on around us. I think we're partially conscious of it in some cases, some of the activities on campus for example, some of the street demonstrations we resent. But are we fully conscious of the rate of change? Because rather than being even, I think that it's accelerating. We've been fortunate in the Army because we've been either abreast or in some cases even slightly ahead. Most cases where we've been behind we haven't been far enough behind where we haven't been able to catch up. Does this continue to be the case? I wonder. I wonder.

...Communications. Where were we at the end of World War II? Trying to get a telephone, because there was a pent up demand. Now we've got communications satellites. You can transmit volumes of data that we don't know what to do with. [Laughter] Well, this is too bad. This is too bad, and this is a symptom of what I was talking about. We knew we were going to be able to transmit volumes of data, we talked about handling the data, but what have we done about it? Well, I know one thing we did about it, we set up the TAIRS [acronym unknown] system in the Army, and now we've got rooms full of stuff, and we don't know what to do with it. [Laughter and applause] There's nothing wrong with collecting this if we'd projected it all the way on through. And I share the blame here.

TV. Now we've had TV for quite a while. But we haven't been lugging it to the beach, and the ski slopes, I guess in some cases even into our bathrooms, some of it ought to be I suppose, and flushed! [Laugh] We aren't conscious of what TV is doing to us. Now I've said this before [Vice President Spiro] Agnew came on the scene with some of his charges. You know, you sit in your living room, or wherever your TV happens to be located, and you see your screen filled, and over time there grows on you the idea that this is all really that's happening. We forget that out there, where this all starts, or started, because most of it is taped, you've got a little narrow lens, and you've got a fellow behind it, pointing it, and he's got a prejudice. He's one of these blind men. And alongside him is a fellow with a microphone, telling about what's happening. And he's got a prejudice. He's another blind man. And then behind them, 'cause this stuff is processed back, you've got somebody editing, an editor. And there are a whole succession of these, and every one of them has a prejudice. Every one of them a blind man looking at this elephant from a different direction. Until finally there comes on this screen in your living room a picture. And this is convincing you. Captives we are, captives! This is serious, this is really serious. I'm not talking from the point of view of censorship, we can't have censorship. I'm talking from the point of view of just molding opinions and molding viewpoints and getting shifted to certain values that we're unconsciously taking in, and we haven't really assessed. Somebody's going to have to do something about this. And I don't know how, I wish I did. I wish I did.

In 1974 General Abrams was asked if he would support the publication and distribution of the discussions between guest speakers at CGSC and the students.

I don't want to sound arbitrary, but the quick answer is I wouldn't, and I'll tell you why. [Applause] I have virtually no confidence in putting stuff out in pamphlets—I don't even like to send messages out. I'm always afraid that nobody will pay attention to it. [Laughter and applause] I'm really quite frank about that, and I'll tell you why. It's not because they don't give a damn. [Raising his voice] It's because of the damn flood of paper that's coming in there now, and the senior guys, and the responsible guys that you want to get to, they've got more to read every day that they ought to read and they should read in order to do their job well and by God they can't get it done now! [Huge round of applause]

The following year General Vessey had a different take on the dissemination of information.

When I [took command of] the 4th [Infantry] Division one of the first things I did was to go out and look at some training. Well, we got out there and I noticed that all the pistol holsters were empty. And I said "Why is that?" They said "Well, we don't carry pistols south of a given point, and that's a division policy. So those people that are armed with pistols don't carry them on training exercises." And I had lunch at a field mess that day and I asked the cooks where their rifles were. And the cooks said they didn't take their rifles to the field because that was a division policy. I went back and talked to the Chief of Staff, and I said "Gee I just heard about this policy on weapons, why do we have this policy?" And the Chief said "Well, because we lost a number of weapons, and it seemed the prudent thing to do, so that was put out as a policy." So I met with the major commanders the next day and I said "We've got a new policy on weapons. There are two parts to it." And I said "The first part is if you're going to take the troops out on a training exercise which they are doing what they're supposed to be doing on the battlefield, they will carry those weapons that they would normally carry with them on the battlefield in the training exercise. And there's a second part to this policy: You will not lose the weapons." [Laughter] Well, the next day I went out again, and I found empty pistol holders and I found cooks without muskets. I got the brigade commander of the brigade concerned and I said "Why do these people not have pistols and rifles?" and so forth. And the brigade commander said "We're waiting for the change in the policy." [Murmurs in the audience] I said "I announced the change in the policy yesterday. The policy I announced is the policy." Well he said "We have not yet seen it in writing." Well then I went back to the headquarters—well, after some consultation [laughter] with the brigade commander—I went back to the headquarters and said "What is this jazz about the policy in writing?" to the Chief of Staff. And he said "Well, we have a set of division policies, written policies." I said "Well, since I'm the division commander perhaps I ought to see these things."

Well he brought in this damn book about that thick [laughter] and I started thumbing through these things and policy number one was the assignment of quarters to full

233

colonels on post, and that seemed to make a lot of sense. And the next one had to do with parking in unit areas and it seemed to make a lot of sense. And I got through about 15 of these things and so we had another session with the commanders. And we got all of the major commanders in and I said "Okay, now I have the book of policies. There are some 200 and some of these things that are here, and I've taken a fairly good sample—20, 10 percent—and they all seem to make good sense. They seem to me to be what you as good commanders would do if I didn't say a damn thing about it." So I said "This is the end of the policy book. There are no more written policies. Now my policies are for you to do what makes sense in your outfits, and if you're going to look for written policies from me, you're not going to get them. Now you can divine or develop policies, my policies, from what I say and what I do or something like that, and if that's of interest to you, and you want to list those in your mind that's fine. But my policy is we want a good Army and a good division here and we want to do it at a reasonable cost to the taxpayer. And we don't want paper."

Well that was kind of hard for some of those guys to swallow, because if you live with this announced policies business—and it's alright, perfectly alright, and I'm sure there was a need for those written policies when they were put out. But I said we're [4th ID] a mechanized division. And mechanized warfare is not poop-sheet warfare. And if you're looking for a written field order to come out of division headquarters, I said, you're going to see one when we deploy to go off to fight the Russians, but that's the last one you're going to see. You'll see some overlays, you'll get some messages, but you're not going to see any great raft of poop-sheets coming out of here.

And that's my view of it, and God, the poor company commander. You know we've had a million studies over the last 35 years that I've been around about reducing the administrative work in the orderly room. And each study that we've run has added about 10% more work in the orderly room. And now we're talking about solving that problem by giving the guy a second clerk. Well that all sounds very good and everybody's for it except the [Army Deputy Chief of Staff for Operations (DSCOPS)] . And the DSCOPS is against it because it means taking two battalions out of the force structure in order to cough up the spaces to put that second clerk in the orderly room. And what I say is let's get rid of the damn paperwork that we're expecting that guy to do. [Applause]

In 1975, General Weyand described the very problem that Secretary Kissinger highlighted 8 years before: "Unfortunately, people like myself, the men who should be leading you, strongly, should be looking way out ahead, sometimes are caught up in the problems of the day, and fail to do that." General DePuy discussed the issue of "right now" in detail in 1976.

Sometimes when you've sort of been in the Army about ten years, and you look around at this great big green machine and it has a lot of good people in it, and a lot of mediocre people in it, and a lot of dubious people in it, it does a lot of strange things and it seems like it's kind of hard to get a handle on it. You get a little bit of a preoccupation with "right now." You know, you get worried about the colonel's wife, for example. You get worried about all the gossip that goes on in the Ladies' Aide Society in the Army and it kind of gets depressing. Then anyway when you take good, healthy soldiers and put them in a school for nine months, they think too much, and it's depressing too. [Laughter] So, it's a dangerous period in your life. But the worst thing you can do is to arrive at the erroneous conclusion that things are kind of stuck where they are. And that you're kind of stuck there too. The proposition that I want to put to you this morning is that all of you are being moved along on a great big wave that's really moving fast. No way to get off. It's going to keep moving. It may even get bigger. And you can kind of decide how you want to handle that wave. You can go buy yourself a surfboard and gracefully go along on the leading edge of it. You can let it break over your head. You can drown in it. You can try to ignore it. It's up to you individually how you handle that.

...Let me describe to you the United States Army as I see it, today, in units. I'm not talking about combat service support units now, I'm talking about divisions. The division commander and his staff is staggered with the number of things he has to do and the small amount of time he has to do it, with the resources he has, and the state of training of his officers, sergeants, and soldiers, and the—what he calls—the distracters from training, and so on. He looks at the world of training as a cyclical problem of successive peaks. He has to peak his division for general inspections, for ROTC camps, for ARTEP, for an FTX, for a REFORGER. Underneath all that he has to have some of his people going to school, got to comply with the race relations regulations, got to keep records on all the alcoholics. He's got all sorts of things to do, he hasn't got enough time to do them, and when he subtracts the Sundays and holidays and all of that, pretty soon his head is swimming and he's sort of depressed about the whole thing. His G-3 is frantic. Along comes TRADOC and says "Add the SQT" and "Oh my God! [Laughter] One more good idea will kill us." [Big laugh and applause]

Now the Brigade Commander, he's just about as bad. He's nervous; he's only going to be there a couple years. And he doesn't want any race riots or anything like that going on, and he does want to do what he's supposed to do, and some of them even want to feel strongly about training. [Laughter] The battalion commanders are sort of worried about the cycle too and they're overworked. And they tell you a lot of stories about how you can't afford to make a mistake or the Army will zap you if you do—none of them can ever give you an example of anybody who got zapped, but it's good talk at the bar. It's sort of hedging in case he gets fired. Because then he's explained the whole thing ahead of time.

DePuy was asked, in light of all the things commanders had to do and how complex and lethal the modern battlefield had become, whether the Army looking into harnessing technology to put order to confusion.

There was a period of time that lasted about 15 years in which people looked for the solution which you suggest, which was an automated control system. I myself am very happy that at no time in the last 15 years did we adopt any of those proposals. They all would have been a bad mistake. The battlefield systems have got to be more robust, than any high—you see, the strength of an army is its decentralization. Why is it decentralized? Because we fight in an environment which is infinitely varied, and the air force fights in an environment which is infinitely constant. What you are looking for is to try to optimize the exchange of combat information from the center to the operating systems and from the operating systems to the center. Because the intelligence people get a lot of combat information that you want to shoot at, but most of it comes from their own system.

But the biggest mistake you can ever make is to do what some intelligence people want to do, which is you visualize a great big vacuum cleaner, sucks in everything, it massages, collates, analyzes and regurgitates this in intelligence too late. Too late for any of the combat systems except maybe maneuver. So intelligence people must not be permitted to dominate or capture control of combat information. If you go to a naval ship you will find a thing called the combat information center. It's not intelligence. The radars say there are the enemy ships, there are the friendly ships, there are the enemy aircraft, and there are the friendly aircraft. And that is the universe of combat information, and they want to see it all, and they want to see it all at once. What that means is—all of that is made available to the fleet intelligence officer who says it must be that some element of the Russian fleet came out of the Black Sea, or something like that. That's intelligence. But the fact that there's an airplane up there, and you're either going to ignore it, send an F-4 after it, or launch a missile, that's operational combat information. And for a survivable, robust system to fight, the Army had better keep these two clearly separated.

General Vuono was still wrestling with the battlefield information overload problem in 1986.

The first thing we're trying to do is to reduce the amount of information that the battalion, brigade, division, and corps commander think they need. And that'll go a long way towards helping him, because it's too much of what we want, not what we need. So the first thing we are trying to do is to ensure that only the critical items are asked for and are being dealt with. The reason I say that is that the more information the commander has, the more time he is trying to spend sorting through all of that and the less time that his subordinate leaders have to receive the intent, plan their operation, and so forth. So that's kind of a doctrinal fix that we're working at. Trying to help the platoon leader in terms of what he can do to be more rapid [in his decision making], we've got a couple of things going. One is a thing called the electronic clipboard, which is a very small, hand-held digital business that the platoon leader and platoon sergeant can use for a variety of tasks, not the least of which is handling of orders, handling of plans and so forth. It's got a little storage capability there, only comes I guess about 5 by 8 or 6 by 10 [inches] and so forth. Matter of fact it's small enough it can fit in his [uniform] pocket, to assist him in doing that. But I believe the major step we can take is the screening through of information so that we give him the time necessary do what tasks he's required to do down at that level.

General Sullivan led the charge for the Army in the information age, and as such information flow and technology were a major part of his presentations, as in 1992.

What is the role of electronic media? When I can sit in my office as the DCSOPS and have some special forces guys in a hotel in San Salvador with their picture on TV as we're trying to get them out of that hotel, now that is something. 'Cause I was watching them on CNN at the same time we were trying to get them out of that hotel. That is big time stuff. There's probably somebody in this room who was going to the hotel down in Panama City to get the Eastern Airlines crew out of that hotel. And we were watching it on TV. What is the impact of all of that on doctrine and warfighting?

In December 1993, he addressed how technology had changed the speed at which commanders could influence operations.

> [*Shows A Revolution in Command slide describing speed of observation to action over history, compares commanders: Washington Yorktown 1781, Grant Vicksburg 1863, Patton Bastogne 1944, Schwarzkopf Kuwait/Iraq 1991, with tomorrow*] Look here. Norm Schwarzkopf could decide in hours, it took him about a day to act. Here, tomorrow, with JSTARS [Joint Surveillance Target Attack Radar System aircraft], with some of the Air Force platforms and Navy platforms which they are building now, we will be able to observe real-time and act in an hour or less. I'm not completely sure we understand what JSTARS is really going to do for us. And you here, at the Command and General Staff College, must be getting your head into that kind of an operation, because I can tell you, we're buying the equipment to do it. And that's going to require a lot of you. What we know is, when we digitized the tanks and the [M2] Bradleys and the artillery systems and the Apaches, is that the battalion commander and the company commander initially are overwhelmed with the speed of the fight. And it takes training and acclimatization to understand what happens, it gets going so quickly.

To the graduates of the class of 1995, General Sullivan spoke of the transition the Army was undergoing: "You are inheriting fundamentally different institutions than the one in which I served for 36 years. And it's fundamentally different in many respects than the one you joined 13 or 14 years ago. As we approach the future, we have one foot in the industrial age, one in the information age."

OPERATIONS TEMPO

General Sullivan led the Army at the start of the period of frequent deployments brought about by post-Desert Storm requirements and numerous peacekeeping operations, causing a dramatic increase in operations tempo (OPTEMPO) in many units and specialties. In December 1993, he showed the students that relative to history, they didn't have it too bad.

> [*Slide: A Message From Normandy which showed a World War II Operations Tempo of 6 campaigns in 20 months*]. Here's a message. Campaigns in Europe. November '42 we invaded North Africa, the United States Army and Navy and our Airmen. February '43 we were in Tunisia. July '43 we were in Sicily, September '43 we were in Italy, '44 we had Anzio, Normandy. And in the Pacific, by the way, we landed in the Philippines. Now look. That is 20 months. 20 months. [Points to 1st Infantry Division patch] North Africa and Sicily. [Points to 82nd Airborne Division patch] Sicily, they picked themselves up, went to the UK, and 24 days after this outfit was there and invaded Normandy...right. Right. There was a lot going on. Okay? They did it...Suck it up. Move out. Hooah.

One month later in January 1994, General Reimer provided the students some OPTEMPO statistics.

> We took a snapshot here, this happens to be the fourteenth of December [1993], we've got about 16,500 soldiers at FORSCOM installations deployed away from home station. They're not all in contingency operations, they're not all in harm's way. Many of those are in CTC rotations, JRTC, NTC [Army training centers]. Some of them are in counter-

drug operations. Some of them are in individual taskings. Some are in [contingency operations], most of those at that particular time were Somalia. So that's the type of thing that we look at on a daily basis, and that's pretty much an average snapshot. It'll vary between 10,000 and 20,000 but that's about what we've been running at here recently. Interesting to compare to before '89, before the Berlin Wall came down, with '93. I had them take a look at a day in June in '89 and compare it to a day in June in '93. What we found is we had twice as many soldiers deployed in '93 as we did in '89. So the pace is pretty fast.

General Sullivan gave the students an update in November 1994, and again he used history to demonstrate that a busy Army was nothing new.

Today we're in 74 countries, 36,000 of us....the only people in the Army now who don't move are those that are assigned to Korea. If you go to Korea I won't move you. But if you are anywhere else you are eligible to move somewhere to do something. This number has been as high as 105 countries, within the last six months. That's a relatively high number now because of Kuwait, and Saudi Arabia because of the Gulf, and what's going on Haiti. But the numbers are starting to come down, and they'll be down in the 20s here before too much longer.

...Now listen. There are some tough days ahead. Fine. Fine. Bring 'em on. Bring 'em on. Ruck it up. Tonight watch PBS. Battle of the Bulge on there. Right? Okay? Nobody knew, when the orders were issued in October to move out, nobody knew that the Battle of the Bulge was going to take place. Grant didn't know that Cold Harbor was going to take place. Look. We are not the first ones in the U.S. Army to face tough times. Suck it up. Suck it up. Move out.

The following month Representative Skelton discussed his concerns about the rising OPTEMPO of the armed forces.

Simply put, American forces are overextended, we've cut our forces too much, we've committed them to too many peacekeeping missions, and the crisis in the [Persian Gulf] not so many weeks ago confirms that. When Saddam Hussein made his move, our Army had more than 37,000 troops deployed in over 74 countries around the globe. We also had another 130,000 troops deployed in South Korea and Europe. At the same time, the Navy was engaged in five economic embargoes, two counterdrug operations, a support commitment to the Haitian operation. Our Air Force, the branch of service that gives us such quick reaction, was heavily engaged in Bosnia, Kurdistan, Southern Iraq, and Rwanda. Overextensions have long-term consequences. Once we get involved in a place like Haiti or Bosnia, this thing called mission creep can become real. I believe we need to exercise restraint and think twice often before we commit ourselves militarily.

General Reimer, then the Chief of Staff, discussed in 1995 how the immense drawdown undertaken by the military did not mean that missions would stop.

There have been no "closed for remodeling" signs that we have been able to put up for the United States Army. Our missions have expanded, and we not only have the traditional mission of providing regional security and stability, but we've also picked up additional missions. You're very familiar with those also. Haiti, Guantanamo Bay, Macedonia, places like that. Somalia, Rwanda, those types of places. In fact we say that there are about 20,000 soldiers deployed away from home station on a daily basis. Our soldiers spend, on average, about 138 days a year deployed from home station, and that varies by MOS. And you look at MOSs like Patriot [air defense batteries], and you look at MOSs in the [military police] and that type of thing. I said goodbye to a Patriot battalion going to Korea, and I talked to soldiers and families who were going on their seventh deployment since Operation Desert Storm. That's a lot of turbulence, that's a lot of moving out and picking up your rucksack and going for it.

300% increase in operational deployments. That's an important factor over there [pointing to *Global village, CNN factor* bullet on slide]. We truly do live in a global village, and if you watch CNN you find out what the Joint Chiefs are really spending their time doing. We're trying to find out what's going on in Bosnia, if [CNN is] over there. Wherever they are, chances are the military is working on that particular plan. So I just think it's something we're not going to change, we have to accept. We have to live with that, and that's kind of the environment we face right now, this environment all of us live in. And it's an environment you're going to live in for the rest of your Army career, I think. I don't see this changing dramatically.

Vice Chairman of the Joint Chiefs General Joseph Ralston told 1996 graduates just how busy the force had been.

It's no surprise to you. Contingencies are up 500% in the last five years. We have drawn down our military by a third, while demanding that we keep this smaller force fully ready. And with some 40 successful operations since the end of [Operation] Desert Storm, we've proven that this military and this Army is the best it's ever been. Capable and ready to respond wherever America's interests are at stake, and American leadership is needed.

In 1997, Secretary West relayed an interesting caution from a senior noncommissioned officer about categorizing the difficulties of the current OPTEMPO.

Deployments are up, as we have said time and again. Although I would caution us all, as recently I was cautioned by a very senior and very sage noncommissioned officer. He said to me "Sir, we need to be careful about how much we talk about how hard our job has become. About how much we tell each other about what a strain deployments are, and about what a tough load it is for us to bear." He said "Don't misunderstand me. It's useful for us to say it to Congress and the American people. They need to know what our soldiers are going through. But in terms of how we say it to each other," said this senior noncommissioned officer, "we need to be careful." Now I think I understand what he meant. Certainly some portions of it are clear to me. There are some things that aren't certain. For example, did he mean that we have to be careful about telling each other the truth? I think not. Did he mean we have to be careful about ignoring the obvious? That our soldiers are doing what they signed up to do? That they are doing it well, and that they, whenever you ask them about it, are prepared to sign up again? Did he mean that we have to remember that our soldiers are voting with their feet? And their feet are staying in Army shoes and boots? Possibly. The point is nonetheless, deployments are up. This means strains on our family; this means challenges to our Army generally.

The fact is, surely, we are asking more of our soldiers. And in the process we are asking more of those who lead our soldiers. But my sense is that is not where the real tension and the stress is, for whenever I talk to your soldiers and say "Hey, how are you doing here?" and "What about all these rotations?" I get the answer that I'll bet you get. Now maybe we need to go beneath it and see if those are just soldiers that are trying to sound good for the boss, but what they say is "Sir, this is what I signed up to do." The stress is on their families. The stress of OPTEMPO is directly felt by spouses, by youngsters who don't get to see their parents anywhere near as much as they should. By families who are essentially torn asunder every time someone deploys and goes off. The best I can say to you is that we in the leadership, including you, have to be sensitive to that. We have to do all we can to support our families. I think that the reason for the [training center] rotations, you know as well as I: We can run the risk of working our soldiers harder, or we can run the risk of sending them off less trained. I will take the [former]. Even as we do that, though, we have got to think, and plan, and be sensitive as to how we deal with that stress that we are increasing for the families.

Secretary Caldera outlined some of the costs of a high OPTEMPO in 1998.

Quite often from your perspective you look at "How is my unit doing? Am I going to the National Training Center, and do I have the ability to train my soldiers the way I would like to?" And sometimes the answer to that is "No." Not able to do all the things we would like to do. Why? Well, because we've got these missions that we're performing that mean that we have a high operating tempo, that many of our soldiers are in Bosnia or other parts of the world, so therefore our units don't have their fill of soldiers that we would like them to have, or some of the specialties. We've got to give people the opportunity to get back with their families, reconnect, to have some down time, so that we don't burn them out. And so we cut back a little bit on some of the other kind of training that we do.

That same year General Reimer discussed OPTEMPO and decisions to support operations in relation to the armed forces' ability to conduct two major theater wars (MTW) simultaneously.

Any time we commit troops to an operation like Bosnia for example, we get together as the Joint Chiefs and meet, and one of the things we talk about is what's the impact in terms of sending a unit over to Bosnia, what's the impact upon our war plans, on the two major theater wars. So that is something that we go through. Now the assumption that is associated with the two major theater war strategy is that you will pull back that force that you sent over there once the first MTW starts, because you need time to get that unit trained back up. You can probably get them ready for the second MTW; you can't get them ready for the first MTW. Now, don't ask me how comfortable I am with that assumption, because I'm not overly comfortable with that, but that is the assumption we have to work on. And I'll guarantee you, if an MTW starts they're going to have me hammering on the table, "You've got to pull the 1st Cav now" because you need that total force in order to be able to do that. [Referring to an earlier question about deploying the First Cavalry Division to Bosnia] The issue on two MTWs I think is an interesting one. What we have said and what I believe is that the risk of doing one is moderate, the risk of doing the second in 45 days bumps that up to high. The risk is not winning or losing, because we'll win. But the risk is in number of casualties that we will experience. And it's going to take a total Army effort; we're going to have to go deep into the Reserves, to include the [Individual Ready Reserve] which we're going to have to get access to…You're going to have to put in stop-loss. People that were going to be released from active duty will not to be released, they'll be sent on to do that type of thing.

…But when you stop and think about that…are we that scared of Iraq? Those guys aren't ten feet tall. We took them pretty well in '90, '91, and best I can tell they haven't done a whole lot to improve what they're doing. Now you throw weapons of mass destruction in there that's a big new ball game…You look at North Korea, and you look at the [intelligence] that's available there. Go back and tell me the last time they had a good training cycle…We have to be realistic about this thing. General Westmoreland told me one time after Operation Desert Storm, after I talked to him about it, he said "I think you made two mistakes. One is you underestimated your own ability, and two, you overestimated the ability of your enemy." Well, those are the errors that you want to make…you want to make them in that direction. [Laughter] But I think we also, amongst ourselves as professionals, we must be realistic. We can't convince ourselves that these guys are ten feet tall. They really are not. This is by far—our Army—the best Army in the world. Talk to your international officers. The Soviets—The Russians, for example, they want MREs. Now that's kind of funny that anybody would want MREs [laughter] but it also is an illustration of how bad things are over there, and I feel sorry for them, quite frankly, I feel sorry for any soldier that's in that situation. They haven't been paid in five months. But let's don't undersell ourselves either. Let's don't oversell it, but let's be realistic about this issue. And we should always err on the side of assuming that [enemy] capability is greater, but I think we can handle two MTWs.

General Shelton discussed the impacts of the high OPTEMPO and the procedures in place to keep it to a minimum in 1999.

OPTEMPO, [Personnel Tempo (PERSTEMO)]. Let me talk about that for a second. It's high. We have 33 [low-density, high-demand] types of equipment or types of units. You know them: Civil Affairs, [Psychological Operations], we've got almost every one of our sixteen [Special Operations Forces] units, we've got a large number of Air Force units, specifically in our intelligence, surveillance, and reconnaissance-type aircraft, things like U-2s, like AWACS [Airborne Warning and Control System], like Rivet-Joint, etcetera. We have got to fix that. And what we've tried to do is we've got a good tracking system in place now. If we're going to break the service-established standard for that particular aircraft or that particular unit or those people it will go all the way to the Secretary [of Defense]. And the first thing we're going to do is challenge the requirement, second we're going to look for a substitute, third we're going to look at what the impact would be if we didn't do it, how much the risk would be, and then finally, then and only then would we go forward to the secretary and recommend approval. So it is being scrutinized quite well right now.

In 2001, Senator Roberts addressed a different method for reducing OPTEMPO.

And right now, even as we speak, the Bush administration and some of us in Congress are carefully studying what really comprises our vital national security interest. Or put another way, where we send you. Some of us believe that we ought to be adopting a program of realistic restraint to slow down the PERSTEMPO, the OPTEMPO, and increase training to meet those vital national security interests. I mention these things because they are our obligation to you and to your families. And in return, I know you will continue to give us your commitment.

CURRENT EVENTS; SCANDALS

Hearing speakers discuss the events of their time—events that are now viewed through the lens of history—and discovering how they perceived them and dealt with them is an interesting aspect of reviewing this collection. A good example of this is the dichotomy of remarks made by General Decker in 1960 and Army Secretary Ailes in 1965. Decker warned against the trend of using mathematical methods to evaluate warfighting.

> ...Our philosophy and doctrine must be pragmatic and flexible. Army planning, by its nature, must be detailed and provide for various contingencies. We must exhibit a flexibility, a resiliency, and an adaptiveness to cope with the shifting tactics of an enemy always quick to probe any chink in our armor. Similarly, Army tactics and organization cannot be evaluated by mathematical methods alone. Always they must be evaluated in light of the wide experience which the Army has gained in the art of warfare in the land environment.

Ailes explained to the graduates in 1965 the benefits that Secretary of Defense McNamara and his "whiz kids" were bringing to the department with their highly analytical processes.

> On the Administrative side—the job of the officer is more complex, as the techniques employed in the Department of Defense become more advanced. I personally welcome this development and believe quite strongly that better decisions are made as a result of these improving methods of analysis. I do not believe that military judgment is degraded by these techniques, although I recognize that unexplained and unsupported military judgment has less force than it may have had in some periods in the past. Certainly military leadership is not degraded if the Secretary of Defense and his assistants ask that those judgments be explainable, if he asks that the basis of the judgment be articulated. That the process by which it was arrived at be described, that the alternatives that were considered be listed, the reasons for their rejection be explained. And that the relevance of cost be always kept in mind. Let me tell you that the Army is prospering in this environment, managing its affairs more effectively every day. Doing a better job in every way.

> And the military judgments which our military officers reach in this environment are constantly improving in quality, understandability, credibility, enhancing acceptance. In this connection, I would give one piece of advice. This is always a risky thing to do. There is a great premium in the Army today on the ability to express oneself clearly. The level of education of the officers and men around you goes up every day. The command structure to the contrary notwithstanding, the most effective leadership is the leadership of ideas. Clear thinking cannot exist apart from the ability to express ideas clearly. One

of the developments over the last four and a half years most pleasing to me personally has been the marked increase in the number of briefings given by the officer in charge of the program rather than by a briefer, and from notes, rather than from a manuscript, in clear, simple, direct, conversational English. Communication has benefitted tremendously from this development.

In 1967, Secretary Kissinger described the expectations of those individuals that were brought in to the Executive Branch with the Kennedy Administration.

Prior to 1961, it used to be axiomatic around Cambridge, Massachusetts that one of the difficulties with American foreign policy was the inadequate attention paid to the advice that originated in the major institutions of that locality. This—and a number of learned articles were written about the absence of national purpose, long-range planning, and other matters of this kind. In 1961 this condition was remedied, and a fair number of my colleagues went to Washington full time, and a number of others, including myself, went down part-time. And with the humility which is so characteristic of Harvard professors, [laughter] we were all wondering what might happen in the last two years of the Kennedy administration when we would have run out of problems to solve. I don't think I am revealing any state secrets if I point out that this condition did not exactly arise, and for very good reasons.

General Johnson made some eerily prescient comments in 1970 regarding the Middle East.

Have you ever stopped to think how tough it is to get into the Middle East in the absence of bases and over-flight rights? When the straits of Tehran were closed, there was a lot of discussion in the Joint Chiefs of Staff about what might be done, and there was a Navy carrier that had just passed through the Suez, heading for the Far East, and a lot of talk about what air could do there, particularly from carriers. But when you began asking the tough questions about time over target, ability to identify the kind of targets specific to the area, the prospects of the interferences and this type of thing, air alone wasn't going to cut it. I recognize what air did in the Six Day War, and the spectacular success during that period of time, when air was covering columns that were advancing pretty fast on the ground, we mustn't forget. What do you do without the ability to go into Turkey? What do you do with the loss of Wheelus [Air Force Base in Libya]? What do you do, when there's some differing kind of arrangement with Greece? Tough.

General Rogers described Army life at Fort Carson in 1971, a life that may seem quite foreign to today's Soldier.

The commanders in these areas where these [Enlisted Man] clubs were going were told "Find out from the soldiers what they want." And every time it came up beer, whiskey, some kind of short-order food, and go-go girls. Now, you go in the back of the club, and sit there and watch them. They're not really watching the go-go girls, they just like to know she's there. [Laughter] Except when Big Red was performing. Now when Big Red was on, that's something different. Everybody was watching her. Boy she was something. [Big laugh]

Rogers also described a visit from Jane Fonda in great detail, much to the delight of the students.

We knew that Jane Fonda was coming to Denver to take part in a rally in the middle of April, 1970. And we also knew that some soldiers had gotten in touch with her and asked her to come down to Carson to help support the 'sick call strike' of April 15th, which was going to be held in Carson. You know, some places have mess hall strikes, they're not going to eat in the mess hall, sick call strikes and so on. And I got a hold of this man Gottiola [spelling unknown], he was a member of the movement, he had been working for me in the stockade, and I said "Gottiola, I know you are going to see Jane Fonda" and he says "That's right." I said "Now when you see her, invite her to come in and talk to me. I'd like to find out lots of things about her." [Laughter] He said fine. When I was talking to him, interestingly enough, the ACLU lawyer in Denver who was going to bring her down had called my judge, and said "We'd like to come on post, and could we see the [Commanding General]?" So you see we're both thinking about the same thing. Well, maybe. [Laughter] So, she showed up. Man what a crew she had with her. She stopped by the downtown coffee house and picked up a group of people and also she had all the local TV cameras with her, and [correspondent] Ike Pappas from the CBS crew was along. Well I saw 'em coming from my window, and as we often do out there in the West, we cut them off at the pass, momentarily, and had all of them stay in the outer office, much to my aide's chagrin.

And we brought in Jane Fonda, a French lady who was accompanying her, who was the widow of a French writer named Valiare [spelling unknown], Gottiola, I wanted him there because he had credibility with the movement I didn't have, and I wanted him there sitting on the couch with Jane Fonda, confirming or denying the things I said. And then her ACLU lawyer came in and I brought my judge just to keep a hand on my wallet at the same time. [Laughter] First after the pleasantries, I welcomed her to Fort Carson and telling her I was always interested in having good looking gals show up anyplace we had soldiers, she's a nice looking gal, even though she was wrapped in her sweater and jeans, but all the finer points were there, [Big laugh] there to be seen. I asked her "Miss Fonda, I'm interested in knowing what you're interested in." And she says "Well I'm against war." And I said "Well, welcome to the club." But we discussed the fact that perhaps I had a little advantage on her because I'd been around for three of them, and I'd seen some of them, and it's a hell of a way to do business, and a waste and a folly and when our deterrence fails it means we'd failed. Well, we kicked that around for a little while and I said "What else are you interested in?" And she said "I want our soldiers back from Vietnam." And I said "Well, I welcome you again to the club Miss Fonda, because so do I. So does everybody else. But you got to start from where you are and not where you wish you were back in '62 or '63 where you might have done something different. We've got to start from where we are and how you get them out to the best of national interest" and so on. And that didn't make a believer out of her on those I can tell you, on that answer.

And then I said "What else are you interested in?" And she said "I'm interested in the welfare of the soldiers." Well, I thought I had a pretty good chance there...and we started talking about some of the things we were trying to do for soldiers at Carson. And I started ticking off these precepts, and when I got to the one about 'Give a Damn for your Soldier', or as the chaplains would say 'Love your soldier' she stopped me. And she said "General, you and I are talking about the same thing." I said "Hell, I know that. Why does that come as a surprise to you?" She says "I didn't know generals thought this way." I said "Have you ever talked to a general before?" She said "No." Well, we had a very interesting exchange. I learned some things from her and I hope she did from me.

But then she had to get back to Denver and I knew she was on a short schedule and I said "So while you're here Miss Fonda I want you to know that I have nothing to hide at Fort Carson, you can see anything that you want to see. And I'll go with you to be sure that there's no door closed." She said "I'd like to go to your stockade." "Great. But I want you to know you're not taking that crew with you outside." And she said "I'm not sure they'll let me go." I said "It's your option. Those of us in the office will go, they stay outside the gate." "Well," she said, "I'll go ask them." And she did and she came back and said "Yes, they think I ought to go." We had all kinds out there. Including a man, a Frenchman who had fought in the Korean war and become a prisoner and he was working against them, you see, he was on a hunger strike himself against the movement at that time, and I didn't know he was out there. [Big laugh] And he was out there stirring them up you know. I'd hear this rumble grow out there, and he stuck his head in a little later when we took a break and identified himself and he said, in his broken accent, he said "General this is what I'm trying to do." And I said "Well, I'd really appreciate it if you didn't get them too worked up. I appreciate your motives, I'm on your side, you understand, but don't get them too worked up."

We ended up heading out to the stockade, and I asked Miss Fonda "Now we worked long and hard to improve the conditions in that stockade and those soldiers belong to me and I don't want your rabble going out there and stirring them up and causing trouble for them." She says "I'll talk to them again," and she did and she came back and said "They'll be disciplined." Well we went in the stockade and showed her everything: Minimum custody to maximum custody with the soldiers in individual cells. The mess hall, the industrial area, the whole works. Minimum custody with a TV and a pool table and so on for the soldiers who are in that category. She turned to me one time and said "General, I didn't know a stockade could be so nice." And Madam Bayard [spelling unknown] said [imitating French accent] "I've been in many stockades in France, and I can tell you, some that I've seen, much worse than this." She said. And for you Frenchmen present I'm sure some much better than ours. [Laughter] So I said to her "What did you think we had, a black hole of Calcutta?" And she said "Yes, I did." And she said "I thought 99% of your soldiers would be black." And I said "Well, you can see for yourself." She was able to go anyplace and talk to anyone she wanted to, 25-30% at the most were black. And I said "Have you ever been in a stockade before?" And she said "No I haven't." Well, it was obvious she hadn't. Well we went outside and the media got to her. Of course, Ike Pappas was beside himself not being able to come in, but we weren't going to have him shooting the faces of the soldiers see, 'cause she was going all over the place. And so she started making some statements that were against the movement, like "I didn't know generals thought this way" and "I didn't know a stockade could be so nice" and some of them are standing there pulling on the back of her jeans, to say to hush up, some of the members of the movement.

And I asked for equal time, and didn't get it. [Laughter] As you would expect. But then a few months later she showed up in New York, and she said "You know that place Carson, man that stockade is really miserable. You know 98% of the soldiers there are black? And it's a lousy, miserable place." She finally got back on track and was coming back into the fold with her friends. But one of the interesting little sidelights that happened during that one, and she left after that and went on back to Denver to participate in a rally. And there's a sequel to that story. She came back to Carson, I suspect I'd better tell you this one too.

After that was over I got everybody together and said "Now look. We've had Jane Fonda day and you Mr. Provost Marshall, I don't want to see her on this post anymore, unless she comes in with my authority. Do you roger?" "Roger." Well, tough to be a provost marshall. Next night, she showed up, lying on the floor in the back of a Volkswagen van, driven by a soldier with an enlisted man's decal, who was being 212'd out of the service [Honorable wartime service subsequent to desertion]. And came driving and went right down to our coffee house. And there were about 40 men down there with the chaplain. We assigned a chaplain into that facility for six months. He had to get somebody to do his thing every night, five nights a week, you can only stand it for six months. The chaplain had about 40 men in there. And she went in and started doing her thing. Well I admired my chaplain. He could have put a hammer lock on her you know and tossed her out. But he let her do her thing. After she left at about 20 minutes, jumped in, went out to the MP gate, the little E4 stopped them and made them all get out and account for them, that's another story, and she ended up saying, well, using four letter words, "We can't get arrested here, let's get out of here."

But the chaplain, after she left, they had about two hours, those forty men, and one of them who was in the SPD [Special Processing Detachment], one of these deserters, got up and said "You know, I don't think there's anything wrong with being asked by your country to serve two years in the uniform." And of course he was one of our best deserters. [Laugh] And she had been maintaining a "What you have to do is you get a dishonorable discharge and hang it around your neck and wear it as a badge of honor" you see. That went over like a lead balloon with these fellas. Another young man got up and said "You know it's obvious she's dumb, 'cause she can't even explain the movement to you." So it had a salutary effect in letting her come in there. We didn't see her—let me rephrase that, we were not aware that she came back on post. I had a prayer meeting with my Provost Marshall, [laughter] and still haven't got a satisfactory answer. One of the little interesting things that happened though, [as] she was going around [the stockade], went by one group of soldiers, stood and talked to them, and I was coming along behind, and stopped and talked to them. And this one little soldier, who was AWOL, cause 89% of them were in there because of AWOL or desertion. He said "You know General, isn't it ironic, that I have to get in the stockade in order to meet Jane Fonda?" And you know, he's right.

Secretary Laird spoke extensively about the Nixon doctrine during his appearances in 1971, first in the Eisenhower Auditorium.

There is one thing we should understand, if history teaches us but one lesson, and that is to be successful in negotiations we must pursue those negotiations from a position of strength. We should not ever be in a position where we force our Commander in Chief, the President of the United States, to crawl to the negotiating table anyplace in the world. [Applause] And as long as I'm serving as Secretary of Defense, I will recommend to the

Congress, and through the Congress to the American people, the steps I believe are necessary to enter this era of negotiations in a position of strength, the steps that are necessary in order to adequately protect the national security interests of our country, and the safety of our people.

He elaborated later that evening at the Officer's Club.

The Nixon doctrine, which was first enunciated by President Nixon in Guam, was a policy that was based upon building a partnership between our allies and friends all over the world, and building at the same time the military strength that was needed and necessary for them to protect their own security. And at the same time showing a willingness, as far as the world was concerned, to negotiate at all levels. We then instituted a policy of Vietnamization. In this policy of Vietnamization was to instill in the South Vietnamese an awareness that we would no longer take over their responsibilities, but that we were willing and able to turn over those responsibilities to them, not only in the combat area, but in the artillery area and logistics area, in all phases, both political, economic and military, as far as South Vietnam was concerned. This was the first test of the so-called Nixon Doctrine. A test which showed the world that the United States would no longer be the policeman throughout the world, but that we were interested in developing a few patrolmen, or if you please, a few cops to assume the beats in their own neighborhoods. That we would give them the tools, and the equipment, the training and the know-how, but we felt that these countries and these individual citizens should be in a position where they took over this particular responsibility as far as the peace keeping responsibility, as far as the combat responsibility, as far as the security responsibility was concerned within their own country.

...Many countries that have looked to us for protection in the past have come of age through the help that the United States had given them through the various programs such as the Marshall Plan and many of the foreign aid programs that had been sponsored by our government. These nations have reached a stage of maturity and development at which they were capable of assuming more of the burden which we had been carrying. Most of them we believed were not only able, but willing to do more for their own defense in a new form of partnership for our country for the security of all. Under the strategy of realistic defense a new form of partnership is being created. Our partners are assuming increased responsibilities for providing conventional forces, and especially ground forces. The United States retains its preeminence and almost exclusive responsibility for providing strategic nuclear forces, for our country is the only country in the free world with sufficient nuclear power to furnish a credible deterrent to this form of warfare. To make this strategy work, other nations must do their utmost to build up their conventional forces to levels appropriate to counter all of the threats we face and which they face in the period of the 1970s and beyond.

This strategy permits us to reduce the size of our forces, and those forces have been reduced during the last two and half years. They have been reduced by 1 million men in the armed forces of the United States...But even though we can get along with smaller forces, we must maintain modern forces, we must upgrade those forces. It means more emphasis in the period of the 70s on our National Guard and on our Reserves, so that these elements of our defense force will be ready and be effective as far as action is concerned, should they be required.   And this is a part of our Total Force construct. [Applause] The new strategy lessens the strain on our country's resources, through more equitable burden sharing with other nations of the world. It puts within reach the day the draft can be ended for our regular forces. It raises the threshold at which the military power of the United States need be committed in future conflicts. It makes unlikely any future involvement of the type in which this nation was engaged in Vietnam. And it brings greater security by mustering the latent strength of nations that have made too little an effort to develop their capacity to defend themselves. This administration has thrown off the bureaucratic inertia that resulted in the continuous assumption by the United States of a disproportionate share of the burden of keeping peace in the world. It has called on other nations to do more. These other nations are responding.

General Taylor told the students not to be overly concerned with the post-Vietnam anti-military feeling in the country in 1973.

And then a final point resulting from Vietnam is simply the anti-military bias which is rife in our country today. I wouldn't take that in a tragic vein, because I've lived through several wars in the past, certainly after World War II, after Korea, there was a great deal of anti-military bias. Not as deep, not as vindictive as now, but nonetheless it was there. Inevitably the man in uniform symbolizes that past, bitter experience of the last war. But we have to take this as part of our business and shrug it off as best as we can. But nonetheless we must recognize that while it lasts, it does indeed affect military budgets, and it increases the need for a rational solution, a rational explanation of the need for national security.

In March 1974, General DePuy provided some insights from the Arab-Israeli war.

Now I have to warn you to be careful about what people say about the Arab-Israeli war. General [Orwin] Talbot has a very entertaining approach to this. He starts out his little talk and he has 19 lessons that everybody knows have been derived from the Arab-Israeli War. Like the Soviet Air Defense system drove the fighters out of the air, the Sagger [Soviet anti-tank missile] has made the tank obsolete, and all Israeli radios were jammed and so on and so forth. Then he goes on and points out they're all wrong. All 19 of them. Second thing you have to be careful about is that the big institutions of the U.S. military establishment have got to be watched carefully, they tend to be revisionist. They rewrite the lessons once they get thinking about the implications.   [Laughter and applause]

[Discussing the sophistication of the Soviet BMP] …Now I mentioned the [Soviet] BMP. And it is the kind of a weapon system that would never get through the OSD/congressional scrutiny. It would be called "gold plated." The Russian generals are doing better than the American generals with their civilian masters. That's not necessarily good, but it's a little bit worrisome. We'd never get a weapon system like that through.

…[Electronic Warfare/Electronic Countermeasures (EW/ECM)] That's a subject about which we, as a body, are neophytes. The Air Force and the Navy are not. The reason? It's never been a premium, as far as success of Army operations is concerned. But air attacks over North Vietnam depended utterly upon it. I'll tell you a little bit later about the Israeli experience with it, and if we plan to run air mobile operations, or use air mobile forces against the kind of air defenses that we've now seen, then EW becomes a necessity. It's no longer sort of an interesting sideline to be put over an ASA and left there and ignored.

General Palmer spoke to the students about the Department of Defense organization in 1974, specifically the way in which the globe was divided into commands in a process called the Unified Command Plan. He also emphasized the importance of an organization to oversee joint training and coordination.

[The Unified Command Plan] has some very major weaknesses in my view. First of all the Middle East. The Chiefs made a great mistake in my opinion when they assigned the Middle East to the European Command some years ago. As a matter of fact they took away the old MEASSSA area—and that stood for Middle East Africa South of the Sahara and South Asia—they took that area of responsibility away from my predecessor command which was known as Strike Command, and divided the area up. They gave the Middle East to Europe, they left Africa south of the Sahara unassigned to anybody, and that's another weakness. A planning vacuum. And they gave South Asia, that is India and Pakistan, to the Pacific Command, which was already over-extended in my view. But in my opinion they gave the Middle East away to Europe at precisely the wrong time in history. And the Army predicted what would happen, they said the first time you get in trouble in the Middle East you're going to find a conflict of interest between the NATO nations and our own interest in the Middle East, and you've got problems. And that's precisely what happened as you all know.

…The problem to me is I hate to see us reverse the trend towards unification. And I saw it very clearly in the beginning of this interservice fight in the joint arena over the Unified Command Plan. Some of the early proposals, all services were so parochial it sort of scared me. I'd thought we'd gotten over, and long since passed Pearl Harbor days, that we'd learned the lesson. But when I saw some of the earlier views I was kind of worried. And this often happens in the joint arena where the views sometimes are overstated just for tactical purposes. Nevertheless it told me something, that maybe we're not as grown up as we ought to be in terms of looking at things from the point of view of our country rather than our service. I think the hope lies with the younger people like yourselves that hopefully aren't as parochial as the older ones like myself. And that's what bothered me about this fight. On the other hand the split is clear-cut, and it's honest difference of opinion, which basically stems from difference of opinion in strategic concept rather than command arrangements.

But if we are going to have a decade of peace, and maintain the peace from the position of a strong central Reserve in the United States with fewer forces deployed in the forward areas—and this is precisely the concept this administration is moving towards—if we're going to do that it seems to me somebody has to perform the role of training and maintaining and readying that strategic reserve to perform in a joint way. You see the services, they're responsible for having the forces ready to fight as services, and I'm the first to admit that we still fight as a service. But there has to be an operational joint interface at certain levels between those headquarters that has to work. And as weapons get more lethal and ranges get greater, you have to have that joint interface, otherwise you've just got one big mess on your hands. And so to me the development of modern weapon systems tells me that we've got to have better joint interfaces than we certainly had yesterday, if we want to be able to fight successfully in a modern war. I see major weaknesses still in the joint arena in that interface that I am talking about.

General Abrams also discussed DoD organization in 1974.

I believe that there is an authentic and proper role for the Joint Staff and the Joint Chiefs of Staff. The problems I have with it is that I believe over the years the Joint Staff, the Joint Chiefs of Staff, the charter is really so fuzzy that they've gotten into business which they don't belong in, and still are. I must say that the Joint Chiefs today, when I think about it in comparison to when I was Vice Chief and General [Harold K.] Johnson was Chief of Staff, it's really quite different. For instance, and maybe some of it was the personality of General Johnson, but it was every morning at 0930 or something like that, General Johnson met with the [operations] people. I was present. And they went over the agenda and the papers connected with the agenda, really in most cases sentence by sentence, and it was maybe a one and a half, two hour affair. And that went on every JCS day, three days a week. Well then when the JCS meeting was over, there was a debrief by the Chief, and a debrief by the DCSOPS, and the whole thing started all over again. Now, well I just, quite frankly, I don't, and General Weyand doesn't, spend anywhere near that amount of time on JCS matters.

I think the members of the JCS should also be the service chief. Unless you've got hung around your neck the responsibility of your service, you're up there in the position of giving free advice. You know, you've got to beware of the guy who is giving advice and doesn't have any responsibility. It's really easy. But when you get talking about deployability or reaction time of forces, that sort of thing, I really think the service chief is the proper fellow to be there as a member because he should know that. He should know it factually, and he should be able to say what in fact they can do. And another fella wouldn't be able to do that, in my opinion.

That same year, Secretary Schlesinger was asked if the Watergate scandal was having any impact on the civilian leadership of the DoD.

I think basically the answer to that is very little. It has been my objective to keep the Department of Defense as far apart from these political problems, and incidentally, to develop as much as we can, or restore as much as we can, a sense of bi-partisanship in support of the defense and foreign policies of the United States, certainly the defense policies of the United States. I urge candor upon you, so you would probably feel it was not completely candid if I were to say there is not some distraction in Washington over that issue, and some of that distraction, needless to say, comes over to the Pentagon, but relatively little of it.

He also responded to a question about the Army's role with respect to the Nixon doctrine, his answer containing an accurate prediction.

As I indicated, a principal concern will remain Western Europe, the flanks of Western Europe. If you recall the crisis of last October [the 1973 Arab-Israeli War], at the time that [Soviet Premier Leonid] Brezhnev sent his note [to President Nixon complaining of cease-fire violations by the Israelis and possible Soviet unilateral response], there was at least the possibility that we would have to put forces into the Middle East, and a contingent possibility that we might have to reinforce Europe. That represents a major claimant on the forces for the foreseeable future. We shall have to maintain forces in the Far East, but as I read the attitude of the American public I would not expect extensive Army duty in the Far East in the immediate future. The Middle East constitutes the jugular vein, and if the Soviet Union were astride the oil tap that would result in a strangulation of Western Europe and perhaps Japan as well. It would certainly have major effects on the United States as well. I think that the events of last October demonstrated that the world, increasingly as we should have recognized, is becoming a single strategic theater. And the concept that underlies the NATO alliance, which is this alliance is defensive and therefore its responsibilities stop at the frontiers of the members of the alliance, is increasingly irrelevant. A principal, if not the principal, point of vulnerability for all of the developed world now lies in the Persian Gulf. And therefore, without making any predictions, I do not regard it as beyond the realm of possibility that US forces might at some point have to be introduced into that area of the world.

In 1986, General Max Thurman was asked about the war on drugs and the newly passed Goldwater-Nichols Act reorganization of DoD.

I think the drug suppression business will be a high interest item for the balance of the Reagan administration. Secondly, I think that the House, which as you know, and incidentally this is not in any way disparaging, the House, which is democratically controlled, has put up a bill which would say, among other things, that the military will seal the borders of the United States in 45 days after enactment of the bill. [Whistling and murmuring in audience] Now [Secretary of Defense Casper] Weinberger has come out and said that is not a reasonable deal.

…[Goldwater-Nichols] sort of empowers the Chairman at the expense of the corporate JCS. You know I spend about a third of the time that we have JCS meetings, I'm there, because we have to sit in the JCS when the Chief is gone. And I'd say to you that all this baloney you read in the paper about people, interservice bickering and rivalries, and all that stuff, I don't see that. The one thing you want to happen in the JCS is you want people who are knowledgeable about their service to come forward and be able to describe that which they are able to do if you have to do it on a moment's notice…you're really looking for payoff in people who know their business, not professional staff officers who have lost touch with reality by being in the head-shed for so long they don't know how to smell troops. So I'd just say to you I think we'll live with all that, I don't think it will be the end of the world, and manage our way through that. The bill probably will be signed by the President of the United States. So it's over and done with. Now all we have to do is implement it.

In 1995, General Downing spoke about the incursion of political considerations into military operations, especially during peacekeeping type missions.

Political considerations are going right down to tactical level. In many cases this gets translated into rules of engagement in operations other than war which are entirely appropriate, but they're very difficult to execute. Yet we expect our young American men and women in the armed forces on an operation to follow those rules of engagement. In fact not only do we expect it ladies and gentlemen, we demand it. And if they take actions which are not covered or exceed their rules of engagement, we throw [the Uniform Code of Military Justice (UCMJ)] at them. You know, look at Panama. We tried a First Sergeant in the 82nd Airborne Division for murder in Panama, for excessive violence.

One major topic of discussion in the mid-nineties was President Bill Clinton's much-publicized affair with Monica Lewinski and his subsequent impeachment proceedings. Clearly the students felt the Commander in Chief should be held to the same UCMJ standards that they were. In November, 1995 Secretary West was asked for his assessment of the level of trust between the officer corps and President Clinton, a question which elicited "oohs" and murmuring from the audience.

No, no, no, that's a good question. In a way—I want to ask you what your assessment is, but let me take the question first. [Laughter] No, let me tell you why I say that. Because it really doesn't matter what I think, does it? What matters is what you think. What matters is what your peers out there think. What matters is what every soldier, and for that matter, what every member of the armed forces thinks, because they are the ones that hold the perception. But let me tell you what I think anyway, because I've managed to get around a few places in two years. I managed to even be there when the Commander in Chief himself was there, and I've managed to be there when he wasn't. So I have about two or three reactions, I won't put a number on it, let me just tick them off for you. First of all, I am aware of the opening two years ago when there were pundits and all who predicted that this new president, who was new two years ago, would not be a great favorite of the soldiers. That there would be those who would not render him courtesies and who would not want to, I don't know, whatever it is they thought they would not want to do, these pundits. I thought at the time that I could understand why people would write that, but that I couldn't understand why anyone who knew our armed forces, the Army I grew up in years ago, the Army I now know today, or any of our services, why that would be a problem, because our soldiers serve their country.

They'll take an oath to serve those who are put in authority over them. They take an oath to faithfully follow the orders of their Commander in Chief. And I don't know a single officer worth his or her salt who doesn't believe that right down to the bottom of his or her shoes. My sense is that our armed forces respect their Commander in Chief, because that's what professionals do. My sense is that our president has no fear of going anywhere where there are men and women in uniform. I say that for a couple of reasons. One, for the ones I've advanced, two, because I've seen it. When he went up to the 10th Mountain Division up there, they mobbed him. It's a Commander in Chief who likes his soldiers, his individuals. In fact, the problem when the president shows up is that everybody knows they're not going to get to go away for a while because he likes to talk to everybody. And he'll stay and he'll talk until every last person has had his chance to talk to him. So my perception is I'm not worried. And I don't think anybody who is a professional in the United States Army is worried either.

Secretary Cohen brought up another wrinkle with the double-standard issue in 1997.

252

I went through a number of things picking a Chairman of the Joint Chiefs. And suddenly I was accused of having a double-standard, because of what took place in the Air Force versus what was taking place with [Air Force Lieutenant] Kelly Flynn and what was taking place with General [Joseph] Ralston. That you would have people in some service accused of fraternization that wouldn't apply in a different service. And so there has to be some regularization amongst the services in terms of standardization so people know exactly what's acceptable conduct and what isn't. So we don't have the constant drip, drip, drip of another story saying here's somebody else who's being prosecuted or persecuted over this issue. So it's complex, because people are complex. But what we don't want to do is lower the standards in the military. We want to insist upon high standards and make sure we measure up to them. And that we have as much uniformity as possible, understanding that different services will have some different rules, but as much uniformity as possible, as much uniform enforcement, so there's no selective enforcement. You eliminate discrimination as much as we possibly can as human beings, and that we have a fair system. That's what we need to have, and I believe that we will have.

Students were still talking about President Clinton in 1998, when General Reimer was asked to provide guidance to field grade officers in their role as citizen soldiers with regards to criticism of civilian leadership.

This is the way I believe. All of you have your personal views and opinions about what is happening to the President of the United States. And that's alright. I have mine, and you have yours, and all of that. But you know, all of us in the Army take an oath to support and defend the Constitution of the United States, and that's where our loyalty goes. That's why we don't have problems in terms of military coups and that type of thing, because the Constitution is the document. The Constitution says the president will be Commander in Chief, and until somebody removes him as Commander in Chief that's where our loyalty goes. But it's not a personal thing, it's a thing to the Constitution. That's the way our system works, and that's the way I kind of sort that out. The other thing I say is "Look, I've got enough things that I've got to worry about, and some things I can influence." [Applause] And I gotta tell you, I've got limited time and energy, and I'm not ready to give up my running time yet, so I'm not going to worry about things that I don't have any impact over. I'm very comfortable with the oath I took to support and defend the Constitution of the United States, and I think we have a great process to determine who is the President of the United States. So let's let that all work, and I don't spend a lot of time worrying about that cause I can't do anything about it anyway.

In 1999, Representative Skelton was asked about his vote against impeachment of the president, if he felt the military ethic and legal standards of behavior were too high, and if not, how he justified demanding a higher standard of military personnel than of the president.

How many times have I heard that from my military friends? You're right. The military is expected to have the highest standards, and if you don't there will be a penalty therefore. However the impeachment, as it was matter of fact I voted to extend the investigation, though I voted against the impeachment, I voted to extend the investigation which didn't sit well politically with me back home. But it was the right vote because I wanted all the cards on the table. It was a political decision as to whether you cripple the presidency or you go forward and put that very, very sad and unpleasant and unacceptable chapter behind us. I don't think you should ask for a lower standard for yourselves or your brothers and sisters in uniform. You are not elected. You choose to be where you are and your mission is to guard our interests or fight our wars. The presidency is of course the Commander in Chief. The presidency also is an elected office. And I would hope that we will never see that chapter in American history again. Never. I hope that we can get past it, not let it be an example for you or other Americans.

The services had many scandals and sensational items of their own to discuss, as General Reimer did in 1996 when he addressed a recent discovery of extremist behavior in the Army.

I would tell you also, on the extremist case, that it's a difficult situation. It's a prejudice issue; I don't think it was extremist as much as it was racial prejudice. I think it was also attributed to the fact that the Army is awful busy. The OPTEMPO had picked up so much that we had lost sight of the fact that soldiers were really our main responsibility and the chain of command—and I'm not being necessarily critical on the chain of command on this one, they were doing what they were asked to do. We were bouncing them around the world. [Fort Bragg] was a very busy installation, and they were going from contingency to contingency to contingency. And so we didn't know what was going on in the barracks, [the] fundamental place where our soldiers live.

We used to have a first-line leader rule where the first-line leader was required to visit the soldier wherever they lived, whether it was in the barracks, or whether it was off-post, to see how they were living. You have to be careful on that, because that's something that gets into somewhat invasion of privacy with families and that type of thing. There is no invasion of privacy in the barracks as far as I'm concerned. I told the chain of command I want the chain of command in those barracks. I don't want them to harass soldiers, I don't want them to pick on soldiers. I don't want "Hey You" details, but I want to know how our soldiers are living. Because that's fundamental to the way we do business. We don't run college dormitories, we run barracks. We want unit integrity. We operate as a unit. That's how we're going to go to war and that's how we're going to do it in peace. [Big applause]

In 1997, Secretary Cohen brought up the sexual assault scandal at Aberdeen Proving Grounds.

There was a press conference that took place today in Washington, Secretary Togo West and General Denny Reimer held a press conference to deal with the issue that the Army has been facing, that at Aberdeen, and throughout the Army itself. And one of the things that's most impressive to me is saying, well, isn't it a great sign of strength that you have an institution that is willing to look at itself, to find deficiencies, to point them out, and say "Here's the problem, and we're going to correct it?" And we ought to take great pride in the fact that we can correct it. In virtually every service we have experienced problems in the past. We had one with race earlier in our existence, we had one with drugs in the seventies, we're having one with sex in the nineties, but we will deal with all of them the same fashion that we've dealt with other problems. We faced up to it. We

254

have put our best minds to correcting the problem. And we have come back to the issue of leadership.

During the same appearance Cohen was asked about his decision regarding the commander responsible for the security of Khobar Towers at the time it was bombed by terrorists in June, 1996. The blast killed 19 airmen. Cohen had removed Air Force Brigadier General Terry Schwalier from the major general promotion list because of the attack (an Air Force board retroactively reinstated the promotion in 2008).

> ...My message is very simple: That force protection is part of every service. I've heard the argument made, and it was made to me by many, quietly, privately, it's really an institutional problem. If you talk to the Marines, they really know force protection. If you talk to the Army, they know force protection. But the Air Force, others, the Navy might not be as well-skilled in force protection as those who are on the ground. And if we're going to have a joint force, which we are, and that is what we're training for, jointness—that's going to be the fighting element of the future, then we have to have the same standard. One standard for all the forces. And that standard means force protection. We must take care and do what is reasonably necessary to protect the lives of those that you are charged with protecting. Not everything, not what is unreasonable, but what the reasonably prudent person, reasonably prudent military commander would say "This must be done to protect the people that I have under my charge." Commanders must take reasonably prudent actions.

Reimer also had to address the Aberdeen Proving Grounds sexual harassment scandal with students in 1998.

> I don't think we overreacted...The issue that I was solving was not just sexual harassment and sexual misconduct. The bigger issue for me was the issue of solving what was a betrayal of trust of leadership. We had leaders in one company that went bad...and they abused soldiers...I would have done the same thing if it had been physical abuse of some other sort, because you have to send a very strong message internally to the Army, and also externally to outside the Army, that this doesn't exist in the United States Army. Soldiers are our credentials, and we're not going to abuse them, we're not going to take advantage of them. And I think it was important for us to send a message here that this is not going to be condoned in the Army. If you're a leader in the Army, America has placed their most significant trust in you to take care of their most precious asset, their sons and daughters. We expect you to do that right and do that properly, and that's the message I was trying to send.

> I was not a proponent of the 1-800 number, I think that caused us a lot of pain. We were chasing cases that went back to 1954...I don't think you can make yesterday perfect, I think you ought to spend your energy trying to make tomorrow better. It was important for the Army to realize that we had a problem there, and we're not treating all soldiers, regardless of race and gender, with dignity and respect, and fairly. So, while I'm critical of the 1-800 thing, and I participated in that decision—it wasn't ultimately my decision, I do think that going through that, as painful as it was, was a healthy situation. From that came the focus on values. What we learned...was that we're not getting people, young men and women, from a homogenous values-base society...Leaders not only [must talk

about values], we have to exemplify it: Leadership from up front. If we're not willing to do that ourselves, then our words are going to be not credible.

TERRORISM

It is both interesting and heartbreaking to hear the guest speakers talk about the growing threat of terrorism and how well the government and the services were prepared to handle this threat given what occurred on September 11, 2001. Secretary West addressed the increasing power and reach of terrorists in 1997, and what the DoD could do in response.

> We face throughout the world...the fact that nations and individual groups can wage war now in small numbers. They call themselves terrorists. And they can reach almost any society that is as open as our societies. Any society that believes in relatively free movement, that believes in protecting the rights of individuals to live decent, peaceable lives...What can we do about terrorism? We can cooperate, we can share information, we can continue to work on technology that will deal with the weapons that they threaten to use. We can continue to try to deny them access to weapons of mass destruction, to chemical weapons, to nuclear weapons that can all too often be able to be purchased in inappropriate markets.

Just five months before the September 11th attacks, Senator Roberts gave a very detailed presentation on terrorism and how the government was addressing this threat.

> I have the privilege, as has been indicated, of serving as the chairman of a relatively new subcommittee of the Senate Armed Services Committee. It's called Merging Threats and Capabilities. And the topic of combatting terrorism falls under the jurisdiction of this committee—at least the Department of Defense portion of the national response to combatting terrorism. A little background. The Unites States has developed nine fundamental principles for combatting terrorism. One: Address terrorism both as a crime and a national security threat. The CSIS (Center for Strategic and International Studies) think-tank in Washington, Bremer commission, Gilmore commission, Hart-Rudman commission have all increased the focus on what we call homeland defense. I won't say it's number one, but it's damn close to every kind of index that these folks have recommended. Second principle: To protect U.S. personnel and facilities and interests. Third: To preempt threats and respond to attacks. Four: Bring the terrorists to justice for their crimes. Five: Support nations that cooperate in combatting terrorism. Six: Isolate and apply pressure on states that support and sponsor terrorism to force them to change their behavior. Seven: Make no concessions to terrorists and strike no deals. Eight, [and] here's the key in regards to emerging threats subcommittee: To prepare now to manage and mitigate the effects of a terrorist incident. And then nine, finally, focus on both state-sponsored and non-state actors in our analysis and our information gathering. My main concern and that of the committee is number eight, to prepare now to manage and mitigate the effects of a terrorist incident. That's one of the most difficult aspects of the national effort.

> President Clinton issued a Presidential Decision Directive, Combatting Terrorism—it's number 62—to focus and provide a more systematic approach to fighting the terrorist threat of the century. Within that document a national coordinator within the National

Security Council was established to try and integrate the actions and efforts of the various agencies and departments involved. The National Coordinator is Mr. Dick Clark. And he does not have an enviable job. The Bush administration is now taking a hard look at the terrorism issues. Senator Bob Bennett and others of us in the Senate met with the National Security Advisor, Condoleezza Rice basically about a month ago. "Where is the Bush administration?" we asked. "Why don't you give us another two months? We'll be back to you." Dick Clark is still in place. Through the Nunn-Lugar- and Domenici Act [the Defense Against Weapons of Mass Destruction Act of 1996] Congress has attempted to be supportive of this directive and provide money and training for first responders: Fire and police and medical in 120 American cities including Wichita and Kansas City. The intent is to provide the common equipment and training to ensure the capability of key equipments such as communications and detections and our decontamination gear.

Under the original provision, the Department of Defense was responsible for this program. And some say the Department of Defense made a mistake in not assuming its command of this program, but that decision has been made. 1 October, 2000 the responsibility transitioned to the Department of Justice, except for an annual exercise to be run by the Department of Defense. However, DoD does play an important part in accordance with legal constraints with providing unique resources and capabilities not found in other federal agencies. The Department however must remain sensitive to all sorts of concerns regarding a perceived increase in a military role in domestic law enforcement. That's the Posse Comitatus. The departments combatting terrorism activities are divided into four components: Anti-terrorism, counterterrorism, terrorism consequence management and intelligence support to combatting terrorism.

I'm just going to talk about that number three, and that is the terrorism in regards to consequence management. At the core of the department participation is the establishment of something called 32 weapons of mass destruction civil support teams (CST). Now they were first called the RAID teams, somebody in the Pentagon didn't like that acronym, so now it's the CST teams. I don't particularly like that either. We were trying to have an acronym that spelled out "TED," mainly because of Ted Stephens who was Chairman of the Appropriations Committee. You have to think about that a minute. These teams are comprised of 22, soon to be 32, highly skilled full-time well trained and equipped Army National Guard personnel. These are the teams that would deploy to assist the local first responders in trying to determine the precise nature of an attack, to provide medical and technical advice and to help pave the way for the identification and arrival of follow-on state and military response assets. They're unique because they are federal and state. And the Governor has to say "Okay, they're yours." Will the governor do that? They're under the command of the Adjutant General. We think they will. But there is some concern about that, so we may have to federalize part of that chain of command. We thought we should be in the business of accelerating the funding for the last two years. We went from 10 to 22 to the current level of 32. As I've indicated, I think it's not a matter of "if," but a matter of "when" and we'd better be ready.

What are some of the problems that I see for our ability to prepare and deal with the consequences of a terrorist strike with a weapon of mass destuction? And as I indicated we had the Bremer commission, the Gilmore Commission, CSIS, and Hart-Rudman.

Basically we have what I consider to be some confused organizational responsibilities and funding within the federal government, too many organizations, too little coordination, too little understanding of what the other guy is doing. By the way, the same problem exists in the Congress. 46 federal agencies have some role or some mission in regards to homeland defense and terrorism. 46! The task organization chart looks a lot like that health care plan that was first proposed by the junior senator from New York, [Laughter and applause] whose name will come to me in a minute. [Hillary Clinton] 46! On this task organization chart. My God! We are going to have a joint hearing, if it's a Joint Forces Command, I guess we're going to have a joint hearing. We're going to have the appropriators, we're going to have intel, we're going to have my subcommittee, and we're going to have the full Armed Services Committee. Supposed to be in April, it's going to be in May, because the administration had a little trouble getting their team all together to send somebody up.

We're going to ask them three questions: What's your mission, what do you do, and who do you report to? Three basic questions. Does the left hand know what the right hand is doing? And I can tell you I'm not sure of that to say the least. In the Congress we have seven committees and at least eleven sub-committees. And by Congress I'm talking about the Senate, let alone the House, that have jurisdiction over this. We're trying to get one belly button. Hopefully it will be the Emerging Threats Subcommittee, because sooner or later if there is some kind of a terrorist incident we know that the Department of Defense will be involved. Not the lead agency, that's the Department of Justice. But all the other agencies involved [Federal Emergency Management Agency, Centers for Disease Control, Health and Human Services], all of them. Now even the Department of Agriculture. Have you heard about a threat called Agri-terrorism? We have foot in mouth in the Senate, we have hoof and mouth here about ready to descend upon the country. Not to mention something called BSE [Bovine spongiform encephalopathy or mad cow disease]. I think it is possible, I hope to hell it's not really probable that agri-terrorism could decimate this country and cause panic. It's so easy to do.

The National-level organization is badly fragmented and not prepared to adequately respond to a WMD attack. Additionally the potential problem of cross-state sharing of the CST teams is also a problem. The U.S. medical system is not prepared to handle the consequences of such an attack, and they readily admit it.

Sadly, much of what concerned Senator Roberts came to fruition five months later. The attacks of September 11th led to a massive increase in budgets and resources for the Department of Defense. Near the end of the Global War on Terror, or at least the operations in Iraq and Afghanistan, these resources began a precipitous decline, as has happened after every major conflict. Budget and resource drawdowns were a constant topic of discussion by the speakers at CGSC.

10. Budgets and Drawdowns

Resource constraints and military drawdowns were a constant theme in Eisenhower Auditorium, especially in post-war eras. Many of the guest speakers included thoughts regarding the economy, the drawdown, and the budget during their remarks, often sounding very much like those that came before them, as well as those who would follow.

ECONOMY

In December, 1951 General Milton discussed the balance between the size of military required to confront the Soviet Union and the health of the nation's economy.

> It is totally impossible for this country to maintain a standing establishment large enough to meet a potential onslaught without endangering the economic structure of our nation. Now I know that some of you may say that other nations maintain relatively higher regular establishments than do we, but I would reply, and my repartee is: "But do they not do it by a form of slave labor and by an economic status which reduces their very existence to almost the barest existence?" I think unquestionably that is true. When you stop to consider that the funds which will be expended over a two year period for the maintenance of our establishment as it now is will reach something like 84 billions of dollars, you certainly must appreciate that the economies that are involved are of tremendous import.

Representative Short spoke of this balance in more urgent terms in 1953.

> Burdensome and onerous as is the heavy load we are carrying, the billions we are spending for our national defense are still much easier and better than defeat. The American people don't complain or crab or bellyache too much about the high taxes they pay as long as they feel they are getting their money's worth...Being chairman of the Armed Services Committee charged with the responsibilities of the security of this nation, I know how difficult it is for our citizenry to carry the heavy load of 40 to 50 billion dollars a year. Two-thirds of all the taxpayers' money today goes for our national defense...Even the Congress, or you men, or our people are not the ones who determine these vast expenditures. It's the potential powers, motives, purposes and actions of an enemy that stands diametrically opposed to practically everything we believe in. They're the ones who determine the size of our armed forces...And as long as these aggressors are loose, we must remain strong on the land, sea, and in the air. But in order to preserve military might we've got to maintain a sound domestic economy. We've got to have security with solvency. We must preserve not only our mighty military machine, we've got to preserve a strong domestic economy, a strong dollar, and financial solvency. You cannot have one without the other. Military might and economic strength go hand in hand. The battlefront can never be stronger than the home front.

> ...As we build up our mighty military machine, we must never for one moment forget to preserve our economic strength which is basic, because a bankrupt nation never lifts anybody, and it never will. While I am in favor, as I'm sure all of us are, in helping allies and the friends of freedom everywhere, ...even America, the United States, with all our wealth and resources, cannot forever siphon out welfare in foreign, economic, and military aid to all nations scattered all over the world. Our resources are not inexhaustible. There is a limit to our capacity. And for any individual or nation to

succeed ... in this world, he must recognize his limits and respect those limits…You can't fight two world wars as we have in our generation, sowing the bones of millions of men into the mud, and the billions upon billions of dollars of our wealth up in smoke and powder, without suffering serious economic consequences.

…Let's not bleed ourselves white! And that is the chief weapon and tool of the Soviets: Lenin and Stalin have both written in black and white. They stated in public addresses. Their one hope that the United States, like all capitalist countries, would spend itself into bankruptcy …We must be careful, my fellow countrymen, not to carry out the wishful thinking of the mad dogs in the Kremlin. We must not knock ourselves out by our own profligacy. We must as good soldiers do everything to eliminate waste, avoid overlapping and duplication of functions, and to give the maximum efficiency of our particular job, whether it be in Congress or in the Army or Air Force or Navy: To give the maximum efficiency in service at a minimum cost and expense. It may seem little and insignificant. Every paper clip or lead pencil you save, every telephone call you make you can get along without making, the more you can cut down on unnecessary transportation costs, the better are you serving your country and the stronger you are making it.

Army Secretary Robert T. Stevens discussed the importance of economic strength to the same class at their graduation ceremony in 1953.

We all know that our security requires a dynamic American economy. To strike a balance between our military security on the one hand, and our economic security on the other, is one of the most difficult problems of our times. Yet in my judgment, that is exactly what we must do for an indefinite period of years. President Eisenhower in his address to the nation last month pointed out that there is no such thing as maximum security short of total mobilization, of all of our resources. As the president stated, the military program that has been developed for this coming fiscal year is a sound and a sane one. It recognizes in each of the armed forces calculated risks which have been prudently reasoned. And, as the president said, it represents what, in his judgment, and I fully concur, what is best for our nation's permanent security.

…I am confident we will be successful in instituting new and better ways to accomplish our missions at less cost. That is the only way in which sizable savings can be made. And in this area, I believe we must look at our line operations as well as our administrative and technical procedures. An appropriate method must be found to reward accomplishment in the field of intelligent savings in all phases of Army operations. While it is essential that we devote continuous and serious consideration to the business and materiel side of the Army, there is a much more vital element in our national security that we are not overlooking. I refer to the fine men and women in the Army.

In 1969 Senator Miller spoke about the economy in a way that would sound familiar to anyone reading today.

Our national security of course is affected deeply by the state of our economy. Monetary and fiscal policy, tax policy, government spending policy, all of these have an impact on the economy. And actions taken by the Congress give meaning to these policies. For example, a policy for stimulating the economy by multi-billion dollar deficit spending may be recommended by the White House, as it has been for a number of years. But the responsibility for maintaining a balance in that budget and the accountability for the inflation that occurs when we don't get it, the responsibility cannot be placed on the executive branch [tapping the podium] in the final analysis. It must go on the backs of the majority of the members of Congress who vote that way.

Secretary West highlighted the importance of the economy to national security in 1994.

And the final security challenge in this new environment of course, is demonstrated just last week by the passage of [the updated General Agreement on Tariffs and Trade], the realization that our national security has as an essential component, the economic security of our nation.

DRAWDOWN

Economic considerations, especially in postwar periods, often led to a significant reduction in military structure. Many speakers addressed the reality of postwar drawdowns and the accompanying neglectful attitudes towards the military, especially the ground forces. On June 5th General Westmoreland warned the graduates of 1970 of this trend.

Traditionally after every war our Army has shrunk in size, its equipment needs have been neglected, and the professional has oftentimes been shunned. Our organization has been portrayed as a burden to the society that it has sworn to defend. Yet during these low periods the dedicated professional in our country has remained loyal to his obligation; preparing himself through education and training, knowing well that in time of war, the country turns to him to perform in the finest tradition that has typified the American soldier. Many of those who were marshaled and were embarking their commands 26 years ago today [referring to D-Day], and were about to write some of the proudest pages of American Military history, were products of this mold. They had seen their Army shrink to 136,000 officers and men during the 1930s. This is the Army that I joined. They had seen equipment grow obsolete. They had experienced stagnation in promotion, and they had been required to take furloughs without pay, for during those years of the Great Depression, the Nation could not meet the government payroll. Yet during those dark days the true professional responded to our country's call later on during World War II.

In September of that same year, Westmoreland spoke to the allied officers about burden sharing and the Nixon doctrine.

Now the Nixon doctrine reflects pressures in our country for reduction in the amount of money spent on defense. We're devoting 8% of our Gross National Product, and 38% of our federal budget to defense. Now you can relate this to your own country's expenditures, and I'm sure you will better appreciate our problems when you do. The Nixon doctrine also reflects American public opinion to the effect that our allies and friends should bear more of the burden of their own defense. The Nixon doctrine, however, in no way changes our resolve to meet our commitments. It means an emphasis on self-help, helping our friends help themselves. It also means a reduction of

United States presence overseas, and greater reliance on our strategic reserves, our troops stationed here in the United States. For the Army, the Nixon doctrine means a smaller Army, a smaller force structure. But as we grow smaller, we will retain a balanced force capable of meeting a wide range of contingencies. We will rely, however, increasingly on our Reserve components as a back-up force. Indeed some of these Reserve components will provide round-out units, elements of those units required to sustain us in combat.

Regarding post-war national defense, in 1973 General Haines remarked "Manifestly there is always a tendency between wars to sort of organize the Army for a generation of peace, to structure our organization on a cost-effectiveness basis without regard to its wartime mission. And I suppose this is inevitable." In December 1974, Army Secretary Callaway described working with the Congress in the face of the post-Vietnam drawdown.

What we are prepared to say to the Congress is if you will just give us a stable force, here is what we will do for you: We will come back today in a timeframe where we don't have the draft, which means we don't have cheap manpower; where we have a volunteer force, which means that we want to pay every single soldier what he's worth, and that's substantially more than we were paying in 1954; we will take the same amount of money that you gave us then [1954], just give us inflation, the value of inflation as it goes along, and here's what we'll get for you: We'll get you 16 divisions, better than you had then, better trained, better disciplined, better equipped, better prepared to fight. And we will do it with 200,000 less men. 25% less men. And we will do that by cutting down headquarters, by cutting down support, and just by plain making the people that are in there more effective, more efficient. Part of which comes from not standing the troops in the sun and hanging around the motor pool, but part of it comes just from treating a man as your most valuable asset, and we can't afford to have him doing anything other than his best all the time because he's too expensive. So we'll give you that with 200,000 less men. We'll give it to you at a cost of 2% of Gross National Product. And it cost 4% back in 1954. As a matter of fact, we'll give it to you at a cost of 7% of the federal revenues and it cost 18% back in 1954. I think that's a pretty exciting story. To say that we will come out of a situation when many people thought the volunteer force wouldn't even work, and we will come and build up to that kind of force with all of those efficiencies, all for the same money, it won't cost you anything, just what you planned to pay anyway.

Now, to do that we've got to do a lot of things that are going to hurt. We've got to do a lot of changes. [CGSC Commandant] General [John] Cushman spoke of the kind of attitude we must have, of innovation, and that's true. We've got to look at every way where the Army is not at maximum efficiency. And as Abe [General Abrams] used to say, we're not talking about something to help the Army, we're talking about something to save the Army. Because unless we're able to do such an outstanding job of selling this Congress to hold for a stable Army, the chances are that we're going to get in the habit of each Congress cutting another five or ten percent each year until we get to the point not only of disrupting the Army, but to the point where we cannot accomplish our mission. And when we're facing one other nation that is of the size and has the power to give a serious challenge, we've got to have something that's somewhat comparable to what that nation does to keep a balance of power and without that, we're in serious trouble throughout the world. And the danger is not that anyone in Congress will suddenly try to destroy the U.S. Army, the danger is that by attrition a little bit by a little bit each year we end up to where we suddenly don't have the Army.

General Rogers told the Combat Division Refresher Course students about the budget cuts in 1976.

> We're under resource constraints. The downward trend of federal expenditures in this environment, I can tell you, is disturbing to just a hell of a lot of us. And we never miss an opportunity to talk about it, whether it's to the choir, or those who don't sing, or to those who even don't show up for church. And we've got to get that message across, because I don't care how you measure it: You know whether you take percent of Gross National Product, or percent of the federal budget or percent of total public expenditures—that's local and state and federal—real buying power, compare us, what we're doing with the Soviet Union, any way you cut it. That downward trend is disturbing, and we've got to stop it. And those of us, you and I, that have the chance to get out in public in various type forums, we've got to get the word across. Now don't misunderstand me. I know and appreciate the desire to spend money for social services. But I always go back to what Sir John Slessor told us. And that is that it's customary in a democratic country to deplore expenditures on armament because they conflict with requirements of social services.

General Vuono was a bit more direct in 1988, when he talked about military reductions in light of the strategy they were asked to accomplish.

> We cannot afford any more major reductions within our military without an appropriate relook at the global strategy and the national security objectives of this country. You can't have it both ways. You can't draw down and apply resources to other programs and have a strong military. You just flat can't do that. And people who state that don't know what the hell they're talking about. That's as pure and simple as I can make it. [Applause]

> …We are the stewards of this military, we've got a responsibility to be efficient. But we also have the responsibility to stand up and say "Listen, you can't have it both ways." And I am convinced that we would not be having the arms control discussions that we have today, we would not be seeing the things happening today, if we didn't have the kind of strong defense that we have. And we simply cannot allow ourselves to get to the point where the risk becomes unacceptable. So to answer your question, I think we are going more than halfway in doing our share. But I tell you we've got a responsibility, you and I, to stand up and be counted, when it gets to the point where it's to the detriment of this country. And it's not very popular to do, but it's something we must do, because the country expects that from us.

Two years later Vuono was asked about Defense Secretary Dick Cheney's vision of the future of the Army's mission: "This weekend Secretary Cheney said that he is firmly committed to the pre-eminence of the Navy and the Strategic Air Command, and the Army's mission is up for grabs. How would you respond to that?"

[Interrupting] Did you read that in the newspaper, is that where you read that? [Yes Sir] See, you've got to be careful about what you read around here. [Laughter] I saw that this morning, as a matter of fact, flying out. And I don't know the source for that, or anything, but I know in my personal dealings with the Secretary, that's not his attitude at all. The fact of the matter is he understands the importance of ground forces—Army and Marine forces. He also has to strike a balance between conventional and strategic forces. He has to be aware of our newfound friends and what they're doing from a strategic modernization standpoint. [Audience chuckles] But I believe given the strategic environment and the level of resources that we have been asked—not just the Army, all the services—have been asked to work towards in the program years, over the next five years, I don't believe that that article accurately reflects his thinking.

Now having said that, we are going to have to restructure the Army...we're going to have a smaller Army. We're going to have a smaller Army. But let me tell you something: We're not going to have a smaller Army because somebody's going to dictate a smaller Army. We're going to have a smaller Army because we're going to shape it the way we think is right in order to meet our requirements. We're going to have a smaller Army, but the goddamn Army we have is going to be trained and ready...And so, read all you want by those who are responsible for nothing. [Laughter and applause] But those of us who are responsible for something are going to do it based on that.

Let me tell you something else, now that you've got me on the subject. We didn't just start thinking about the reshaping of the Army last month when it got everybody's attention. We've been working at reshaping the Army for 20 months. 20 months we've had people working on this subject. And so we've been through a great deal of analysis on what it is we ought to have. And we know what it is we want to have in order to meet our commitments. Now you see, the Sunday evening when President [George H.W.] Bush made the decision to go to Panama he didn't call me and say "Carl, is the Army ready?" He didn't do that. Now he called me later on in the week on the wounded and on how the operation went. But he never asked me if we were trained and ready. He just expected us to be trained and ready. So does the American people. And the way you stay trained and ready is by focusing on those imperatives. And if it means you've got a smaller force to do that, but it's got the right stuff in it, then that's what we're going to have. But that's going to be our choice. Not somebody dictating it to us. And what we've got to do is ensure people understand that we're not knee-jerking on this business and we're not just doing something in '90 and '91. You've got to understand the end-state of the Army by '95 or '96 and then you'll understand the glide path that we're using to get there. And it's a sound position, that we'll be able to accomplish—whether it's a Panama or whether it's something even more significant than Panama that involves a greater number of forces.

In 1992, General Sullivan framed the challenges the Army faced going into the massive drawdowns of the 1990s.

After every war the effectiveness of the United States Army is diminished, so that the next time we went out to fight we paid the price in blood. It happened in the War of 1812, when the White House and the Commandant of the Marine's Corps' quarters were burned to the ground, or almost. It happened in World War II, when we went off to

North Africa and were kicked all over the lot in Kasserine Pass. It happened in Korea, when we sent a task force there, Task Force Smith, and the North Koreans beat us up. Challenge? Challenge? Flatten the sine curve. Flatten it out. Keep the effectiveness of the organization up. Never again.

...Expectations slide. I'll let you read the bottom part of the slide. [*We must not hold slavishly to preconceived notions or plans developed during different times. We must move into the 21st Century*] Preconceived notions. We must not hold slavishly to what we thought would work two or three years ago, this is a different world. The Army will be smaller—smallest since '39—pretty small. We must maintain the institution as well as the divisions.

...[Slide: *Challenging issues: Zero Defect vs. Innovation; Personnel Policies; Managing Change (Big A...little a); Fiscal Realities*] Be very careful about [Zero Defect vs. Innovation]. As we get smaller there are more people telling me this is a zero-defect organization. You need to resist that. [Points to "Managing Change"] The Big A...can I keep the institution—Leavenworth, Carlisle, Walter Reed Institute of Research, Army Materiel Command—can I balance the needs of the institution and the fighting part of the Army? You can't have [the fighting part of the Army] without [the institution]. Fiscal realities play a big role here. But we will have to make some tough calls. You can't have an Army without this place [Leavenworth], and you have to stay focused on the requirement, which is a trained and ready Army.

Representative Skelton gave his thoughts on the drawdown in April 1994.

Let me for a few moments give you a historical perspective about where we are and where we're going, the ups and downs of the military in our country. I feel very strongly, as a footnote, that we are cutting too fast, too far, and we will regret it someday down the stream. That hasn't happened this time for the first time, it seems to be a regular American phenomenon...I gave a speech in 1990 down at TRADOC to all of the colonels and the generals. At that moment the United States Army had an endstrength soldier number of 750,000. I told them at that time there were people in Congress, to which I belonged, that would like to see the Army come down to some 300,000. I also pointed out at that speech that everyone was talking about Low Intensity Conflict; I urged them not to forget how to fight a major war. 1990 also saw [President] George [H.W.] Bush giving his speech in Colorado, a speech pointing toward the so-called "Base Force" that cut in the military of the United States. Ironically that was the same day that Saddam Hussein invaded Kuwait. The Base Force at that time was to be 12 divisions, U.S. Army Divisions, I'm talking about active divisions with a total endstrength of 536,000 soldiers.

Two years later he would elaborate on this, saying "My floor for the Army [is] 495,000. Too small. Too small. Can you do two major regional contingencies? I have it worked out on the back of an envelope. My staff's worked it out down to the soldier. You can't do it. Can't do it. But nevertheless, that will be the floor."

In September 1995, General Reimer spoke of the issues the drawdown and lack of resources were presenting the Army.

[Modernization] is a real challenge to Army. We've got to figure out a way to recapitalize our fleets, we've got to figure out a way to replace the old equipment, and also fill the shortages. One thing that's good about getting smaller is that you're able to cascade equipment down to some of the people that haven't had it. But that's not enough. We're not filling all the shortages, so we still have some shortages out there, and we certainly have got to make sure that those tanks, those great tanks we brought in, the M1s in the 80s, when they become 20 to 30 years old that we've upgraded those and made them even better. The same thing is true with all of our equipment. The "Big Five" is getting old, it's wearing out [M1 Abrams tank, M2 Bradley Infantry Fighting Vehicle, Patriot Missile, Apache and Blackhawk helicopters]. And what we've got to do is figure out a way to recapitalize on all of that. At the same time we've got to invest and leverage technology to make sure that we've got the right systems out there in the 21st century. And that of course, most of you know, is what Force XXI is all about. But this is the major challenge that we face in the Army today: How do we keep the training and readiness of today high, at the same time invest the right amount of resources in quality of life and the modernization program that we need for the 21st century?

The next year he gave an update on the drawdown.

A tremendous amount of people have left the Army. That's a tremendous impact on an institution. It does have a human dimension to it, and those human dimension problems and challenges have not been dealt with completely yet. We're still dealing with them. We closed over 600 bases throughout the world. Most have been in Europe. We've taken about 500 and some, 570 is about the right figure. And we basically have closed a large number in the United States also. As the FORSCOM commander before I came back to Washington I participated in three base closures, one in Fort Sheridan, one at the Presidio in San Francisco, and another one at Fort Ord, California. All of them totally different, all of them the reason they were done exactly right, in my opinion, but all of them very emotional. The people that lived around those bases did not want to see us leave.

At Fort Sheridan I talked to a man who had flown up from Green Bay, Wisconsin, to Fort Sheridan. And I asked him "What's your relationship with Fort Sheridan?" He said "Well I first started my—" He was drafted, World War II "and this is the first place that I came." And I said "Are you still in the military? Are you retired military?" And he said "No, I really only spent that time in the military, but this place has meant so much to me that I wanted to come back for that base closure." And that was the importance of all those bases, and every base we closed was kind of like that. So those were emotional experiences that changed fundamentally the way we do business in the Army.

If we looked back at what's happened to us since 1989, we have used our military 25 times, and you can compare that to the Cold War where we used it ten times. So there's been a 200% increase in the pace at the same time we're drawing down. Resources have come down about 40%, the infrastructure has come down about 35%. You don't have to be a laser-brain scientist to understand that in order to balance that equation you've got to do something differently because you haven't taken your infrastructure down as fast as your resources have come down.

...This is a challenge: Modern Equipment. What we did is we mortgaged the future. We basically took from the modernization account and moved it over to the personnel account. We wanted to make sure we took care of the people that remained in the Army and the people that left. That's why we did [the Basic Skills Education Program (BSEP)] and [the Bonus Extension and Retraining (BEAR)] programs and transition programs for those people that left. I participated in that decision, I would not have done it any differently with hindsight that I have right now. I think it was important to take care of the people, that's what we concentrated on doing. But in so doing, we took away from the modernization account. So now when you look at the budget for this year, you find about $10.6 billion going into modernization, and that's probably the lowest we've been in some time, and it's as low as we can possibly go. We've got to figure out how to rebalance that equation, that equation that talks about the size of the Army, the quality of life of our people, and the modernization program. And the way to do it is with a little more resources into modernization. We still have the best equipment in the world, but if we don't do something about that we'll run up against block obsolescence and we won't have enough in the 21st century.

In 1998, Secretary Caldera talked about the impact the drawdown had on readiness and soldiers.

I wanted to talk about two things with you today. One was readiness and the second one is taking care of soldiers. And I say that because of these different perspectives that you might have at the individual level of how we're doing, and the perspective that someone would have at a major Army command or in the Secretariat or in the Chief of Staff's office. Much has been said recently about our current state of readiness. I can tell you that as I have gone about making my own personal assessment of how we're doing and talking to our installation commanders, our brigade commanders, our battalion commanders, to ask them how they're doing. Are they ready? Are they able to go fight and win? I am assured that we are. I am assured that we can do that. We've taken a little bit of risk in many different areas, but we can accomplish what our nation would ask us to do to fight and win two major theater wars simultaneously.

Having said that, commanders will also tell you that they are stretched to the limit in trying to be able to balance their priorities: Having ready troops, and trying to take care of their soldiers by investing in quality of life programs, as well as the additional challenges that we sometimes place on them to be more efficient, more effective so that they can generate internal savings that then we are using to rededicate to our highest priorities. And those priorities are current readiness, modernization, and quality of life.

So our commanders have been under a tremendous challenge, responding to a tremendous challenge as we've gone through this post-cold war era of balancing these different priorities. Downsizing the force, and as we downsize the force, making sure that we still have the right capabilities and capacities that we need to be able to accomplish those missions; looking towards the future, conceptualizing the future, making sure that we're making the right kinds of investments; and taking care of soldiers so that we can keep good soldiers in our Army. Because this development process, of which you are part, means that we bring soldiers in, whether officer or enlisted, and we grow them throughout a career of developmental experiences that prepare them for the next level of

267

responsibility. And in that process we have to make sure that we keep good soldiers in our Army.

The assumptions that we were operating [under] in terms of how this downsizing would work, and where the resources were going to come from to make sure we were attending to all those imperatives is a process that constantly needs to be reassessed. Are we in fact generating the kinds of savings we thought we would generate, whether it was through BRAC and infrastructure reductions, or through business efficiencies, or through better acquisition methods that allow us to capitalize the force at lower cost, and to spend more of our money not in carrying programs but in actual acquisition of platforms? And given the high operating tempo that we've been operating under, and some of the missions that we've been asked to do, we've been showing strain, and that strain has been recognized. And we are now in a period where we are having discussions with the White House, with the administration, with our representatives in Congress, and within the Department of Defense about what it is that we need to do to make sure that we are doing all those things that we need to be able to do that. We are maintaining a high state of readiness.

BUDGET

Along with economic realities and military drawdowns came the inevitable reductions in budgets. In 1959, General Clarke warned the students to learn to operate using the currently available resources.

Before we go too far into the future, let's look a moment at the present. The important thing is the mission. And the Army's mission today is mobilization readiness. We must learn to use what we have, not what we're promised or hope to have. We must learn to live within our means. Achieve our objective without too much distraction from promises. We have the doctrine, the organization, and the equipment to get the essentials of the job done. Making time for highly specialized and over-expensive equipment is unrealistic and tantamount to arming yourselves with a blueprint. Anyone can do the job with the maximum facilities. A good commander and a good staff can do it with the minimum essentials. True, we need the ability to anticipate sudden breakthroughs in development or refinement. And Leavenworth instills these forward-looking qualities. But we must also use wisdom whenever the word 'anticipate' appears in our planning.

General Ridgway was asked to compare management and leadership in industry with that of the military in 1966, and ended up talking about training soldiers to maximize their resources.

I think it's become a far more complex problem than it ever was before. The great differences of course in industry are that the basic motive is profit, and in the military it's tactical success in war. And war is about the most uneconomical, most extravagant, and in some way the most inefficient activity that human beings have ever created. You can't make it cheap and you can't make it efficient from the industry's point of view, so all of that has to be balanced. When you're once at war, or at least it used to be in the past, I don't know now, the military man didn't have to worry much about cost—except to conserve your supplies. I may say this: I tried my best to use every means I had to get down to every man in the 8th Army there that everything he used, everything he shot, everything he ate practically, everything he wore came from about 9,000 miles away. And for him to waste it or destroy or damage it unnecessarily was a disservice to the whole Army. And in fact I had these replacements taken through the rebuild shops in Japan before they came to Korea so they could get some knowledge. These boys who'd never been in a factory, never seen industry at all would get some knowledge of the complexity of the equipment with which they were being furnished. Because as many of you know, somebody gets a—this one time when a grenade is a dud or he gets a misfire of a round of small-arms ammunition he says "the hell with it" and throws it away and "What the hell are those birds doing back in the United States?" and so forth. Well, if he gets to the extent that he appreciates all of the technology and the science and the skill that goes into the things that industry produces and gets across to him, the better man he'll be in his own little end of the game.

In March 1967, General Johnson gave a novel view of limited resources.

We never have really given the commander the resources they required. Because we're always a little bit limited—I won't use the word short, but we're a little bit limited in one pocket or another. It isn't in the right place. We may have it, but it may be halfway across the world, and it just isn't available at the moment. We're always in the business of redistributing shortages. [Slow laughter]

In December of that same year, Johnson spoke about the waste built into the Army's logistics system.

Where's another waste? In the logistics system. You know, we structure our whole Army on the basis of distrust. [Laughter] Did you ever stop to think of that? Squad leader doesn't trust the platoon leader, therefore, give him an automatic weapon in the squad. Platoon leader doesn't trust the company commander, give him an indirect fire weapon in the platoon. Company commander doesn't trust the battalion commander, give him a little heavier indirect fire weapon in the company. Right on back up the structure. I'm a great believer that the infantry should just do one thing: Be a master of maneuver. I trust the artillery. They spend their lives laying them down where they belong. Miss every once in a while, but basically they don't. [Laughter]

But in the logistics area it's worse. Everybody has to have a little pool of something to draw on in case he can't get it from somewhere back. We've been doing some comparisons of the things that people ask for, and the things that people use. And we find that what they ask for will range from about two and half to three times, up to about 15 times of what they use. Now in the event that what they ask for is available, it begins to go around this circle. And every time it moves somewhere, you see you ask for something you have to put a dollar bill on it, and it ties it up. So you can't use it for something else, in the event that something comes along later, and it always does. But we have an enormous amount of our resources tied up because people don't trust each other.

The Army's top logistician, General Heiser, addressed the efficient use of resources in 1971: "I hope I've made the point that we can spend our country into bankruptcy, and other countries allied with us into bankruptcy, or we can save billions of dollars by using intelligence and put those monies where they belong, where the president has indicated." General Max Taylor, in 1973, took issue with how the DoD justified the budgets it requested.

Now let me pass to the general purpose forces, which I imagine are of greater interest to this particular audience. It's a particularly difficult field to rationalize. There's been a major effort on the part of the spokesmen for general purpose forces, Army, Marines, also Air Forces and Navy, to justify, to determine how much is enough in these forces which are available not for general nuclear war but for all the little things which may occur, little or big, short of general nuclear war itself. In the past various devices have been used to justify the force structure. In the Army, at least, we for years, and to some extent today I think, used hypothetical cases. We would war game the requirements of putting a three division force in Southeast Asia let's say, or in the Middle East, let's say, and use that "You see by this study we've proved we need so many troops and so on, hence in our peacetime structure that justifies so-and-so." Well that's pretty logical, that sounds pretty good, but I don't know that it ever swung a dollar in the budget, not that I was ever aware of, at least. I would be listened to politely when I would give this kind of description to the National Security Council, but meanwhile the dollar ceiling had already been set, and all the eloquence of Demosthenes would not have swung anything, no matter how logical it might appear.

Also we've had in the last two administrations a tendency to use a two-and-a-half war or a one-and-a-half war measure. This has meant absolutely nothing except deception. It's been deceptive, not intentionally I would say, because the average citizen hearing that we are preparing forces so they can fight a two-and-a-half war or a one-and-a-half war rather naturally thinks "Well my goodness, one, either they're asking enormously too much, or if indeed we have got the means to do this, and we are indeed able to have a war and get it out of the way and never draft anybody, never disturb the life of the country because we have, in house, this ability to fight from A to Z in the course of other major military interventions." There again, I was never shown a budget which really seriously took into account of this alleged requirement and used it as a justification for forces asked by any of the services.

In 1973, Secretary Callaway demonstrated that Congress and the Department of Defense have been worried about being able to afford the retirement plan for the all-volunteer force since its inception.

As you know we're asking every year for more housing money. We're asking for, both in this budget and the '75 budget we're now beginning to prepare, we're asking all we think we can ask for in family housing and things of this kind. We're aware of the shortages on most of the posts. I just don't have a whole lot of encouragement for you, I'm going to have to tell you the way I see it. I don't think we're going to get a whole lot of extra money to improve much on family housing…[Regarding] non-disability retirement, the Congress has extreme concern about the size of retirement pay. It's going up enormously, and they're so concerned they're not sure if the money will even be there to pay the retirement commitment that we already have. As you know that retirement [is] not funded, it just will be appropriated the year you're due to get yours appropriated, and if they haven't got it appropriated you don't get it, you know, there's no money sitting up there waiting for you. And it's getting so big that it concerns them.

270

Now the new system—and I don't fully understand it and I'm not sure anybody does—but the new system is designed, and I think probably is designed not to hurt anybody who's already in, and not to go back on any commitments to anybody that's already in or what's already been promised. [Murmuring] I'm sure you don't agree with, as I said, the design. Now I'm not going to pass this around, I mean the Army takes its full share of responsibility. I'm not really up on all of the details of it. I know that it does not guarantee the 50% retirement, I know it talks in terms of dollars and not percentages, and as pay goes up, you may feel this is going back on a commitment. I know that the people who put it together think that those of you who are already in will live up to all of the commitments, and people who come after you won't get as much as you've got. These are realistic situations. The retirement pay is so high in trying to fund it right now that the Congress is going to do something about it. And they're going to do something about it whether you and I want them to or not. And the Department of Defense approach was one that the Defense Department thought they did the best they could do to live up to commitments that we have to.

General Abrams talked of the political pressures of operating within reduced resources in May 1974

In the pressure of money, we have got to make certain that we don't have anything in our base structure in the United States or overseas that really isn't essential. It's got to be critical, or we shouldn't be paying for it. So we're reducing our base structure, the last part of it, in honor of Thanksgiving Day, will be announced about the middle of November, and as a coincidence it also follows November 6th. [Referring to national elections—the audience chuckles] In other words it's an explosive political problem. But it's things that have to be done, and I think the case is good, and we'll be on with that. But we as professionals should work hard to make sure that every dollar we get in appropriations is a dollar well spent in defense of the country. And that's got to be overriding.

Defense Secretary Schlesinger gave his take on Army resource issues two days later.

General Abrams is proceeding to attempt to reduce areas of low productivity and waste of manpower and budgetary resources so as to build up the combat capability of the Army. The Army had 13 divisions, it is his intention to get up to 16 hopefully, with some integration of Reserve units. The budget this year contains an increasing force structure for the first time since FY68: A third of a division for the Army. But the main point is that in the past we have provided certain perverse incentives for the services with regard to the question of efficient use of resources. As the services have seen it, the reward for efficiency is the shrinkage of force structure. That is not necessarily the most appealing carrot to any institution. So the proposition that is now being made to the services is "You find waste, because you are really the only ones who can find it, and you convert that into combat capability, and you will have the complete support of the [Office of the Secretary of Defense (OSD)] and the administration. And you will have our powerful arguments, for whatever use they are to you, when you deal with the Congress." So far as I'm able to see, the Congress has responded quite well, at least to the Army's initiatives. So that I think we can look out to continued budget support for an expansion of the combat capability of the Army. The advantages I think are very clear in the area of manpower and budgetary stringency.

Let me say a few words on weapon system acquisition. I think that General Abrams talked to you about the [Army Materiel Acquisition Review Committee (AMARC)] study. The Army has not been extraordinarily effective in this area. That is the only euphemism I shall indulge in today. You should take an opportunity, while you are at the college, to read the report on the M-16 rifle or the report on the Sheridan Shillelagh [anti-tank missile] development that was done by the [House Armed Services] Stratton subcommittee [referring to subcommittee chair Samuel S. Stratton]. The Army felt under pressure to violate all of its own regulations. And the result was chaos. Those were extreme examples. But if one reflects on the last decade or more with regard to the development of tanks, while the Soviets have been producing T-62s at perhaps $300,000 a copy, the United States has been producing relatively few tanks in comparison. But it has spent $2 billion in research and development in the tank area, a substantial chunk of that went to the late-lamented MBT-70. [Tank under development to replace the M-60] If those $2 billion of resources had been applied to the acquisition instead of, more or less, being frittered away in the R&D area, the Army would have 10,000 additional tanks today, instead of an inventory situation which I think you will all regard as regrettable if not reprehensible.

Secretary Callaway returned in December 1974, and was again asked about the new retirement system proposal and how it might be breaking faith with those currently serving as well as those recruited under the guise of a 50% retirement. His remarks sound similar to those made during the debate about the retirement program in 2012.

No question there's a lot of inconsistency about that. Let me just give you a little bit of the background and I'm sure it won't satisfy everyone. One of the features of the current retirement system is that it's so simple, you can explain it in a sentence and everyone understands it. That's 50% in 20 years, and 75% in 30 years, period, you understand it. Now when you get into the new retirement system that is proposed, it is quite complicated, and you hand out a booklet and you read the booklet and then you read it again and you still sort of try to figure it out. That is of course going to hurt because as we try to explain it, everyone can understand the other one so easy that they don't particularly want to change, like yourself. The fact of the matter is that retirement costs are going up so enormously, and I don't have the figures in my head right now, but I've been told what they're going—exponentially, they're going up so fast. Congress has just made it clear to us that we're going to have to do something.

Now we, the Department of Defense, had two choices: One is to do nothing and let Congress just come and do what Congress wants to because they've made it very clear they're going to do something. The other one is for us to come up with a program that we think will be in the interests of our officers and soldiers, one that will be in the best interest of the Defense Department and will still fit within the congressional restraints. For example, if you had a private company with the Army's retirement system ... it would be clearly illegal. You could never get it qualified. One of the things that they would never let you do is to give no vesting until 20 years. They'd say, you know a guy's got to have vesting shorter than that. He's got to have his own part of it shorter than that. So one of the things this does is give earlier vesting. And that's all to the good. One of the problems that bothers me is you get a soldier or an officer who has served extremely well and for whatever reason it's necessary to have him out of the service and maybe he's served 15 years and he gets no retirement at all. How much better if he'd had some reasonable progression after 10 years? So this will do that, and hopefully everybody will agree.

It does cut back on the 50% and there [are] various formulas that go through it. It has some save pay provisions in it which at least protects those years you've already spent, it protects those at the 50% and 75% and that kind of thing. Very, very complicated. In most cases if you'll put it all together and try out your own system and whenever you think you'll retire, you'd be surprised to find that you're not really hurt substantially. In some cases it would be a lesser amount, there's no question about that. Here's sort of the way the Congress feels about this. When you came in the Army, however many years ago, 10 or 15 years ago, whatever time it was or less, you were paid substantially less in money, and the pay raise has gone up enormously since then. And at the time you came in the philosophy was we're going to pay you very little now, but we've got the best retirement game in town. And the Congress is saying you can't have it both ways. If you're going to raise the pay, you've got to quit having the best retirement plan in town. And if you look at your whole package of what you're getting now, even in what it will buy, and I know inflation, I know something about that too, but if you look at the whole package of what you're getting now, compared with the whole package at the time you came in, a person of your same rank that you now are, I think you'll find the total package compares very favorably. And if you look at it that way I think you'll see that the Army has kept faith. Other than that, you know the Army naturally would like to continue like it was. We'd just like to keep on going, but we're not going to be able to do that.

General Vessey expressed the importance of understanding financial management to the students in late 1975, and outlined a problem that has become all too familiar to those in today's military.

Now when I say to you as staff officers, and commanders to be, and potential installation and division commanders, is you've got to get a handle on the financial management. We have been for years in the Stone Age in costing our operations in the Army. We are now getting out of that and it's because of the sort of instruction you are now getting here at Leavenworth, and it's because you people are smarter and brighter, and the guys that are going to work for you are smarter and brighter that some of us old fuds who fudded along with the EARN [acronym unknown] system years ago. And we said "We don't have to worry about money. Somebody will give us tank track and [Petroleum, Oil, and Lubricants (POL)] and parts and so forth. And if they don't give it to us we'll whine and snivel about it until they give it to us or until they tell us to shut up."

…We're into a new fiscal year, we're going to a new fiscal year, and the whole object of the exercise was to catch up with the Congress, knowing that the Congress didn't pass the appropriations bill until late in the [previous fiscal] year. Well here the Congress has got their first whack at it, this year, and we're already into December and we've got no appropriations bill.

...You know when you finally figure out that it's going to cost you four and a half bucks to move that tank a mile, you're not going to just crank it up and move it a mile for laughs. You're going to get some training value out of starting the tank, moving it, shutting it down, and getting it back to the motor park, and that's the value of it...We're no longer in the business of firing nickel rifle rounds as the main bit of training ammunition that we use. It costs $23,000 in ammunition alone to get one tank crew through table eight. Now you've got to put some thought behind what you're doing. We've got to train for tomorrow's readiness.

As we were discussing in General Cushman's office a little while ago, when the clock struck midnight last night, the probability of our using yesterday's readiness in fighting the Russians on the 3rd of December has gone to zero. An absolute zero. All the money that we put into readiness for yesterday that can't be carried over into tomorrow is gone. And this Army is very, very expensive. And that's what the Chief is wrestling with the Secretary of Defense about today. And that's the debate that's going to be in the Congress this coming year on next year's budget. And that's the debate that's going on in every single nation that's represented in this room. Can we afford to spend what our military leaders are telling us we have to spend for a ready force?

In 1976, General Rogers discussed rising manpower costs and the issues of inflation with the Combat Division Refresher Course.

In the area of money, 66% in Fiscal '77 will go for manpower costs. That doesn't leave much for procurement, doesn't leave much research and development. Although in fiscal '77, the budget that is now being defended in Congress does have a greater percentage for procurement than the more recent budgets have had. Inflation, double-digit inflation, that's eating us up as it is everybody across the country.

General Meyer implored the students in 1979 not to be defeated by limited resources.

It would be great if we had a perfect Army, if we had all of our units at [Authorized Level of Organization (ALO)] 1, and at [Readiness Condition (REDCON)] 1...If we had all of our units with the newest equipment. If we had all of the individuals trained up to the ability to be able to handle that equipment. Then we would have a perfect Army. Clearly we don't. We don't have a perfect Army today, and I would be less than honest if I told you that during my tour as the Chief of Staff of the Army we will have a perfect Army, or an Army which I thought was perfect or an Army which you thought was perfect. Within the resources we have, within the energy, within the leadership, within the capabilities we have, we have to be able to bring the Army to as close to perfection as possible. And that requires, as I pointed out earlier, a re-ordering of priorities.

...We can't run around bad-mouthing the Army and saying "It's not good enough here. It's not"—we can say that, among one another, but we have to be able to look at it and determine what we can do with what we have, and that's the challenge to us. And there's opportunities there if we don't throw our shoulders up, if we don't give up on one another. And that's the great opportunity to exist for you, and the chance to prepare for it is now.

General Max Thurman gave the students a budget update in September 1986, once again sounding a familiar theme.

> Now as we proceed to think about where we're going with the support of the operational art and the equipments which make the operational art come to fruition, one of the things we must obviously take into consideration is what's the status of the budgetary process. You'll see here [pointing to chart] the halcyon days of the Reagan administration are essentially over. This is what we're executing this year, about 1% below what we did the previous year, and we'll be about 2% below this year in 1987, if and when we get a budget. I don't anticipate a budget, we'll operate under a continuing resolution authority I would suggest, because it's going to be very tough to come to grips with a budget, since there are only about 15 days left to go in the Congress, before it adjourns on the 3rd day of October to go home and get re-elected…But it's time for a little appetite suppressant here. But I would want to hasten to tell you that one of the line items in the budget is not the lined paper on which you must do your history project. So it will still be due in on the schedule intended.

General Vuono gave a very detailed resource update two years later, sounding very much like General Meyer nine years earlier.

> Now the other part of that environment we live in has to do with the resource issue. And we're going to go through a period of constrained resources, no doubt about it. We're in it right now, have been in it as a matter of fact the past three or four years. If you look at the defense budget it's been in negative real growth for about the last three or four years, and that's going to continue over the next several years. Now what we need to do is to make sure we go beyond the hand-wringing stage and say "Woe is me," because you don't accomplish anything when you do that. You get on with saying "Alright, I have a certain amount of resources that I can plan for over the program years. Now how best to use those resources, and still keep [my] eye on the ball of a trained and ready Army, and those global responsibilities?" What we've done in the army is very simple: We've prioritized. And we've made certain decisions on what we would and would not fund based on what gives us the greatest combat capability. We set those priorities last year when we had to go through a decrement for the '89 budget.

> …[One of these priorities is] the force structure of the Army. Are we structured properly to carry out our global responsibilities? Do we have the right mix? And what we do is have a mix. We have a mix of heavy forces, light forces, and special operations forces. We have a mix of Active and Reserve. We have a mix of forward deployed and forces that we can deploy from [the continental United States (CONUS)]. My view is you always can use more force structure, and we'd like to have more than we have right now. Because we don't have enough to meet completely, and to ensure that we don't have any risk, in terms of our strategic responsibilities. The fact of the matter is we've never had all the structure required to meet every possible contingency that we have. So what we do, we say we're willing to take a reasonable risk. And in my view the structure we have now allows us to do so.

> Now we had to take a structure cut in '89. We had to take about 8,000 out of the structure, simply driven by budgetary considerations. It had nothing to do with the

requirements. A budgetary requirement that we had to reduce to get to the dollar level based on the $33 billion cut the defense department took, and all the services took a cut. The Air Force took a sizable cut, the Marines took a cut, and the Navy took some. The Navy's was in their program growth, Air Force, Marines, and Army took some muscle out in terms of the force structure. My view is we can ill-afford to go any lower. And as we put together the '90 budget right now, we've been able to hold the line on further force structure cuts at least in the near-term, and we'll continue to fight so we don't take any more force structure cuts. Because, given our global responsibilities, we need that mix. We need to know how to deploy that mix, that's a different matter. But we need that mix of heavy, light, and special operations forces.

…We were mandated by Congress to take a sizable cut in the strength of the officer corps. It came out to be about 7-8,000. As it turned out we were successful in making a strong enough case over what was a very arbitrary and a very inappropriate number that they wanted us to produce, by the way. It was not tied to requirements, it wasn't tied to anything but the fact that some members of Congress thought we had too many officers. So we were able to get that down and we ended up with about a 3,000 cut in the officer corps. But when you take 3,000 out, and you already have [lower promotion rates and command selection cap] factors working, that causes you to say "How do I reduce without mortgaging my future in the officer corps?" And what we did was we held down the number—there was some pressure on us to take more out of accessions, in other words, bring in less officers. And I didn't want to do that, because if you do that it causes you problems in the future. So we took some out there, not many, and then we gave early release to certain officers, and then we had a Selective Early Release Board [SERB] for lieutenant colonels and colonels in '88. We're looking now to see whether we have to have that in '89 and '90, I'm not sure yet whether we'll have to have a SERB board in '89 or '90.

Vuono was asked about the Army's role in reducing the funds required for the defense establishment so they could be used for other national priorities.

We gave $33 billion to do that last year. So I've got some experience on how to do that. Not a very good experience, I might add. First of all, I think that the military has to take part in, and be responsible in trying to solve a tremendous problem that this country has today, and will continue to have, and that's the deficit problem. And how do you help solve that and still take care of other programs within the country? I think we've done our share and I think we're doing our share right now. Fact of the matter is that the real growth in the program that we have built is a 2% real growth. We have said that a 2% real growth will keep the momentum that we have going right now…But that's not what we *need*. We need to have a lot more than 2% real growth to achieve the kind of direction that we want to go, to keep abreast of the threat, and to take advantage of technology. So I'd say first of all we're doing our share right now. And we can ill-afford anything less. Because one of the responsibilities I have, and my colleagues in the Joint Chiefs have, is when that risk becomes unacceptable, we must stand up and so state that. That risk has not yet become unacceptable given our strategic responsibilities and the force levels that we have right now. And if we can keep a modest 2% real growth during the crunch years, then I think we'll be alright.

In November 1994, General Sullivan spoke of the frictions between reduced resources and unforecasted peacekeeping missions.

> This right here [points to *Reduced Resources* and *Increasing Number of Unresourced Missions* bullets on slide] is causing us problems. Because I was not funded up front for Haiti [Operation Uphold Democracy] and the [Persian] Gulf [Operation Vigilant Warrior] I had to take money away from 4th quarter training, and I paid a price. I must give [U.S. Transportation Command] a fund cite to get the ships and the planes to get to the fight. When I give them a fund cite I have to have money. So I am paying up front for ships and planes. And that means the 1st Infantry Division, 4th Infantry Division, and 2nd Armored Division don't do as much training as they should, and that causes me a problem here [points to *Lack of Funds for Repair Parts* and *Replacement of Aging Equipment* bullets]. Training is driven by repair parts.

A month later Secretary West elaborated on Sullivan's point.

> I must also say to you that it was I and the Chief of Staff who drafted the letter that the Secretary of Defense sent over to [House Appropriations Defense Subcommittee] Chairman [John] Murtha and others a couple of weeks ago that informed him that three of our divisions had C3 [readiness] ratings. By and large, the reason for that is a quite straightforward one. In the 4th Quarter, as we had to divert training funds to support our two deployments abroad, to pay for that, training opportunities were missed for those divisions. That will be made up—one of the encouraging things is the president's initiative, which I will talk about later, to provide additional money. We have a supplemental underway. The concern for me is the one that I think you already know of. Training opportunities, once missed, really can't be made up. And so that is what we will have to work with. In terms of funding, in terms of resources, the indications are we will have it. But the training opportunities now lost will be difficult to make up and it will take a while to do that.
>
> In terms of equipping our soldiers, about two months ago I received a memorandum from the Deputy Secretary of Defense—one was sent to all the service secretaries: [Air Force Secretary] Dr. [Shelia] Widnall, [Navy] Secretary [John] Dalton. It very helpfully identified for each of us our primary modernization programs, and said in my case "Mr. Secretary of the Army, I know that the Comanche [helicopter] is important to you, I know that [the Advanced Field Artillery System (Crusader)] is important to you." Well it is. I testified in the Spring along with General Sullivan that Comanche was our top modernization priority. And then it said this: "The Secretary of Defense is personally concerned, about readiness yes, but also about quality of life for our Soldiers and Marines, our Sailors, our Airmen, our Airwomen, and he's going to look for ways to do new initiatives to enhance that quality of life. The modernization accounts will pay for it if we cannot get additional money on the top line. Look at your two programs and send me plans for either terminating or stretching them out so that those accounts can produce the needed monies." I think you've heard about that memo, I think you've read about it. My report to you is I don't have the final results back on it. As you might expect I went back with our response on behalf of myself and General Sullivan that said "We recommend you not terminate either of the programs. They're both at the top of the Army's list. Whatever you can do that will enable us to save them, please do so." But

at the same time I must say to each of you as important as those programs are to us, I wholly endorse the initiative of the Secretary of Defense to put more emphasis on our soldiers and on our soldiers' families. That is especially important to us in the Army.

A year later in November 1995, West spoke of the challenges of modernization in an era of diminished resources.

> Equipping our force, modernization, is, as you know, a challenge for the United States Army. We have the lowest modernization budget of any of the services. And maybe that's understandable, since that things that we buy, the engines of war, somehow don't rival the cost of a B-2 [bomber] or a Seawolf [submarine]. Nonetheless they are every bit as important to our soldiers and the accomplishment of our soldiers' missions as any of those, and perhaps more so. Since the Army is the world's premiere ground force, it is also America's go-to force. The force which, when we go in on the ground, finally tells America that the objective has been achieved, that the results they'd hoped for are there, that we can actually begin to count on delivering the victory or the result that has been anticipated. So our modernization program is every bit as important, not just to us, not just to you the users, but to the country we defend.

That same visit he was asked about soldiers surviving on food stamps and when something would be done to address it.

> Right away, in fact I'm a little surprised at the question, first of all E-5 and E-6 is a fairly high level for that, but secondly I'm surprised that the results aren't beginning to be shown. One of the things we tried to do is simply get the pay raises in...One of the reasons I emphasized the president's commitment to the pay raise, every year, without question, to the fullest extent of the law is to put money in our soldiers' pockets. We are trying to make sure that our infrastructure at an installation or post is able to know about the families in these straits so that we can work with them and help them. But we've got a lot of concern, and the answer to the first question, the basic question "when?" is if we're not doing it now then we're already behind the curve. The key thing is pay. To lift our soldiers to where they are entitled to be. It's a funny notion, isn't it? That when a person decides to give himself or herself to his or her country that suddenly they find themselves living less well than if they had not been willing to serve. And it is precisely that thing that we wish to stop and we are trying to stop right now.

The next March, Representative Skelton was also asked about pay, this time tied to congressional cost-cutters looking at making changes to the retirement system. The questioner ended with "We take that oath, when we first come in, freely, voluntarily, and based on that oath, we expect Congress to take care of our families, and ourselves. There's some concern in the military that Congress is breaking the faith. Could you please respond to that?"

> You're right. You're absolutely right, sadly. [Applause] There was a revision of the pension system back in the middle/late eighties when Les Aspin was chairman. And we thought—it really did need some upgrading and we thought that was going to put it to bed forever...Pension, like end-strength, is a cash cow. You get immediate payoff, dollar for dollar. It's not like money you invest in a B-2 Bomber, or you cut a B-2 bomber or you cut a tank or you cut a ship, you're only going to get about 10 cents on the dollar this

year because that money is spread out over several years. You cut the endstrength, you cut something that pays out now and you get immediate dollars. I think you will see a continuous fight between those of us who understand from whence you come and those that don't. You see—I never served in the military, I got sick when I was in high school and was unable to do so, but I think I understand a little bit about what you do. Those who have served in the military are fewer and fewer in the Congress of the United States. That doesn't always mean they will understand and look at things through your eyes. But it's a pretty good guess that those who have worn the uniform understand pretty well your needs and your problems. I think this will be a year by year fight, sadly, and there are those of us who are determined to live up to our, and our predecessors' obligation to you. Stay tuned.

In 1997, Secretary Cohen gave highly detailed insight into the budget machinations of the Department of Defense.

The pressure coming on saying we're looking for balanced budgets, and with balanced budgets that means we have to start cutting down the size of our military and spend more on our social programs. That's always the pressure in a democratic society to cut spending for defense or military and put it into social programs, that's true of any society, but now especially, when we seem to be in an era of relative peace. So these are all the demands that are constantly placed upon elected officials in Washington. They are the people's representatives; they in fact reflect the country's sentiments. So that's the kind of pressure that's put upon elected officials. You have this tug of war, so to speak, in terms of where the ever-shrinking pie is going to be divided up, how it's going to be divided up, and where it's going to be going.

…We have to be able to prepare. And there comes the rub. We have to be able to prepare for the future. Now what is the problem? Every year when the Chairman of the Joint Chiefs would come to testify before the House and Senate, he would have a chart that he would point to. And it would show what we were allocating for our resources, how we were allocating our resources. And there was one chart that always stood out. And that was the chart on procurement, acquisition. And it showed that we were spending roughly about $42 billion a year on acquiring new technology for our forces. But we really had to get from $42 billion up to approximately $55 to $60 billion. And we kept falling short each year. Each year [General] John [Shalikashvili] came to testify, he'd say "Here's our goal, and here's where we expect to be next year." And the line was supposed to go up. But the line wasn't going up. It kept going down. And the reason it was going down or not moving was because we were always taking money out of procurement in order to shift it over to operations, and [operations and maintenance (O&M)] accounts.

And so we were not able to continue to prepare for the future. So that's where our strategy was. We were going to shape, we were going to be able to respond, and we were going to prepare. And the way we're going to prepare, we have several alternatives to do this. We had what we called three paths. We can stay with the status quo, exactly what we're doing today. We are shaping the environment in ways that are favorable to us. We are capable of responding across the full spectrum and we do it day in and day out. And we can, in fact, still prepare for the future. Not as much as we'd like, but we're still developing some systems. We're going to have some major shortfalls, but we're getting by, we can do it for the time being. Eventually we're going to run up against a wall, because if we don't put that investment into the procurement account, then by the year 2010, 15, and 20, when these new systems will have to come on line, we will not have made the investment for them. But we could maintain the status quo and stay exactly where we are and carry out our strategy.

There are others who felt we needed to be much more visionary, much more radical in our thinking, much more creative in our thinking. Some of the proposals said in order to achieve that kind of investment in the future, why don't we just cut out roughly a half a million people from our Active forces? Reduce the Active force by half a million, that will free up a lot of resources. You can get a lot of money by cutting out a half a million people of our force structure, and take that money that would otherwise go to pay for salaries and retirement, other types of benefits. Take that money and put it into acquisition, and then we can bring the future forward that much faster. That would allow you to do what? Could you shape the environment? The answer is yes, but not as well, because if you cut back a half a million people it means you're not going to be as forward deployed as you otherwise want to be. So you're not going to be able to shape the environment in the ways we are currently doing. Could you respond as well as we respond today? The answer is no. That by virtue of having that kind of a reduction you'd be less capable of responding to the full spectrum of threats. But what you would do is you would accelerate the future a lot faster by getting those kinds of systems which you need. So basically what you're doing is you're taking a short-term risk of not being able to shape as well, not being able to respond as well, but you'd get to the future a little bit faster.

But we decided that was too risky. Given the uncertainties of the world as it exists today, given the potential for conflict to erupt on a moment's notice, we decided that there was a better way, and that's what we came up with: A much more modest approach, an evolutionary approach rather than a revolutionary approach. And of course that was bound to produce criticism from both sides. By taking a much more modest approach, by saying we need to shape, respond, and prepare, and we can do that in a way by cutting back—more base closures, you've heard a lot of discussion about closing down more bases and how we can save money in doing that, and we need to close more bases. We can change the way in which we do business. We're going to have a revolution in military affairs, which we can talk about in a moment, but we need to have a revolution in business affairs. We waste a lot of money by still doing things the old way, with a lot of paper, a lot of bureaucracy, a lot of redundancy, things that are completely outmoded in the way that commercial enterprises in our country really operate today. So we can make some savings there and take those savings, and we can cut back somewhat on our investment in our acquisitions.

For example, tactical air. I assume, I can't quite see all of you, but I assume we have some Air Force people here today. We look at the TACAIR, that our Air Force—all of our air units wanted. For example, the Navy said we have to have the F-18 E&F. And those E & F models were rolling off the production lines. And the Air Force said we've got to have the F-22. And the Marines and the Air Force and the Navy said by the way we've got the Joint Strike Fighter. We need all three. And so we had to make some trade-offs, and what I did was to make some trade-offs by saying on the F18 E&F, the Navy's made a case. The older models don't give you the legs that you need. You're running out of space as far as the computer technology that has to fit into that aircraft because of the kind of threats they're going to continue to face. So you can make a pretty good case that we're going to need the E & F model. But instead of having 1000, I reduced the buy to 548 at a minimum, and then to use that buy to say we're going to use the F-18 E &F to offset the Joint Strike Fighter because we've had this problem in the past.

The easiest plane for me to have recommended to vote to cancel would be the Joint Strike Fighter. Why is that? It's a piece of paper. It doesn't exist. It's always easy to cancel something that doesn't exist except on paper. So that's the easy thing to do from a political point of view. You don't have an industry built up, you don't have the workers who are employed, you don't have metal being bent, you don't have the political kind of pressure being generated. But it would have been the wrong thing to do, to cancel the Joint Strike Fighter, because that is the fighter of the future.

But on the other hand we didn't want to be, and I didn't want to be, held hostage to the manufacturer of this aircraft if there is no competitor. And I went back and I drew upon my experience in dealing with the C-17 [cargo aircraft]. I know many of you are familiar with the C-17. When I first went on the Senate Armed Services Committee, the C-17 was also a piece of paper. And we didn't, couldn't decide at that time, it hadn't been decided by the Air Force exactly what the design should be. Should it be short legs, long legs, wide body, narrow, what should it carry, transport, etc.? Hadn't really decided that. It went on for several years, and finally what we found was the price was getting out of reach. And so there was a real effort underway to cancel the program. And thanks to former Deputy Secretary of Defense John Deutsch, he went and met with the manufactures, and we said "Look. Unless you can start measuring up to these standards here, we're going to go with an alternative. We're going to take a commercial, wide-bodied aircraft, and that will be our alternative." As a result of having that kind of competition, we were able to in fact agree to procure the C-17 which we're now using, which is an invaluable piece of equipment, which I've had the privilege of flying in on several occasions now. But that was started back in 1979, 1980. We're just now really getting them into the inventory in a significant way.

And so what I wanted to do with the F-18 E &F is to say we're going to build the F-18 E & F, and if the Joint Strike Fighter doesn't really come in at a level, and a price, and a production line that we can afford, we're going to build more F-18 E&Fs. And that will give us that kind of constructive tension and leverage so that we can have an affordable aircraft for the future. The Navy is satisfied with that. The Marines are somewhat satisfied with that. And the Air Force, ultimately, is satisfied with that.

F-22: Cut buy down from four to three wings. As a result of those kinds of tradeoffs and trimming back, we were able to present the [Quadrennial Defense Review] saying we have a strategy that's shaping, that can respond, and now we're preparing for the future with these other changes. And as I said before, it was met with criticisms on both sides. We had those who want more spending for defense that say it's too little for defense. We had those who want it to be more visionary saying you're just buying some of the same old systems. So I think we came out about right by being criticized by both from the right and the left. And it was quite interesting; when I went to testify on Capitol Hill I had one member who said "You know, we were hoping you would be more visionary." And I said "Well, I could have been visionary to cancel a Seawolf." And they said "Well, I don't mean *that* visionary." And someone else said "Well, you could have been more creative." And I said "Well I could have cancelled an aircraft carrier." And they said "Well, don't be *that* creative!" So I found out visionary means cutting someone else's program.

The next year Army Secretary Caldera talked about the impact that reduced resources were having on readiness, and he was once again asked about the Army's retirement plan, this time with regards to implementing a thrift savings or 401K plan.

As I've talked to junior officers, company grade officers, [their morale] has been positive. They have questions. Sometimes they don't understand. They say "Geez, I'm a company commander. I've got lieutenants, platoon leaders who have never been to the field. I don't think that's good for them developmentally because they may move on to the next job not having had the experience that they needed to have of actually taking their platoon to a rigorous exercise." So I think that there are concerns. And again, part of that is the challenge that we have at the Secretary, Chief of Staff level of balancing out all of the requirements that we have. Not just current readiness but also future readiness, so we haven't been able to do all the things that we've wanted to do. But I think the situation is going to improve. I think that should be a shot in the arm for those who are concerned about where it's been going and about whether our country supports a strong defense. I think it does, and we're going to work hard to show you that.

...I think we need a 401K kind of plan, and you can do two kinds, the kind where the organization contributes and matches what the soldier contributes, and you can do the kind that's simply based on soldier contributions. But the reason I think that that's important is one, because a lot of our soldiers understand that that is a benefit that virtually every other employee of great organizations has: a tax-advantage savings program; two, because they don't have as much confidence in social security, your generation and the generation below you, as others do. So this sort of notion of saving for your own future, and of building something for yourself for the future, I think is really something that speaks to our younger soldiers. So I think that it is something that we need to do. Now in terms of strategically how we're going to approach this, what we don't want, is we don't want someone to say well we gave you a 401K plan and therefore we don't have to fix the REDUX [Career Status Bonus with reduced retired pay] program or the current retirement programs.

So what we're going to do first of all is really talk about—have a very serious, hard look at the current retirement programs, the erosion of retirement benefits, the pay gap that exists, and what it is that we can do to improve that situation. We're going to work hard to do the right thing by our soldiers. I would ask you not to raise the expectations too high with your soldiers, because the cost of those changes, if you just went back and said we're going to buy back the changes in REDUX and we're going to put in the [Cost of Living Allowance], the full COLA, and give back the 10%, etcetera, it's about $8 billion per year, for all of the military departments. That's a lot of money. And it's probably not realistic that given our challenges—readiness, modernization, other things we want to do in quality of life, like improving family housing, improving barracks, improving medical care, you would have ended up putting all the money in one area and not attending to some of those other needs. But we are going to take a hard look at that. And I think it's important that we get to the 401K discussion.

In late November 1998, General Reimer made a startlingly prescient remark about the underfunding of the military in the 1990s and having to make up for it at a later date.

> You know, people will say "Well, what about the Peace Dividend?" We've got peace, and sometimes we very fliply say "Well, the Peace Dividend is Peace." Well, it's more than peace. For those of you interested in numbers and dollars, if you were to take the 1989 budget, the last budget of the Cold War, and if you were to draw a straight line, just draw it out there for inflation only. And if you then took that budget out to 1998, and if you then looked at the budgets we executed from 1989 to 1998, the area underneath the curve is equal to $757 billion. $757 billion. Now people will say "Gee, isn't it great that we now have a thriving economy, and a balanced budget, and a budget surplus?" I think it is. But I would say that defense contributed to that. $757 billion went into that, so if we don't have it quite right, why can't we get $30 billion more per year to get it back up where it needs to be? And so that's the resource issue that we face. The point we made, with both Congress and the President of the United States, was it's a "Pay me now, pay me later" thing. You either have to put enough money into maintaining the force that you need to do what you're asking to force to do, or else you're going to pay it later. And it's going to be a much steeper bill. World War II is a great example. We mobilized about 16 million men and women. We fought in World War II, and we won the greatest military battle, I think, in the history of warfare. The cost on that, as historians have analyzed that and put it into near-term dollars, was $4.3 trillion. $4.3 trillion. But that doesn't reflect the real cost of World War II. The real cost of World War II was the 405,000 Americans who paid with the last full measure of devotion. That's the issue of "Pay me now, or pay me later." And so $30 billion, while it might seem like a lot right now, is peanuts compared to what we might have to pay later on.

Predictions like this were commonplace, as each guest speaker tried to impart some of his vision of the future to the students. Unlike Reimer's, however, not all of them were correct.

11. Predictions of the Future

Many speakers made predictions during their appearances: the future of warfare, what the Army should or would look like, and what the future weapons would need to do. Some also predicted what the future would hold for the United States, with varying degrees of success.

FUTURE WARFARE

How warfare would look in the future was (and continues to be) a frequent topic at CGSC. In 1952, General Harmon warned the students against preparing for the future by leaning on the past, saying that officers had a responsibility

> ...to foresee the tactics and the military employment of the future. You have to look into space, you have to keep your feet on the ground, because of new inventions that are on the drawing board but still won't be ready to use maybe even in your lifetime. So here it is tremendously important that you keep abreast, at the same time keep your feet on the ground with respect to military tactics and future development...I was on a board about 1947...in selecting the colonels for the Army. I think we went down into the lieutenant colonels list also. And in looking over the cards of the officers, I was struck by the very limited battle experience of the average officer, the average colonel. There were some who had been all through the war, maybe three years, four years in combat. But there were many who just were in at the so-called tail end of the war, who maybe had a month. I'd say the average all told was less than two months. It was astounding to me. And our tactics are often based on this very limited experience. We were in one little show, and we do all of our thinking based on that one little show that we were in, and we're apt to become too set.

> True flexibility of tactical ideas comes from successful experience on battlefield. And the more experience you have, the more tolerant you are of the other fella's views, because you realize that anything can happen, and therefore it might happen his way. And the less experience you have the more dogmatic you are apt to become. You're very fortunate in having instructors at this time who are rich in battle experience. Obviously 20 years ago it was all theoretical. All of your instructors have had some experience under fire here and therefore can give you first hand ideas of the battlefield.

> ...I want to say a word or two about "normal employment." There was a statement in my day that "Regulations were made for second lieutenants and damn fools!" Now the idea of that homely statement was that the second lieutenant needed the advice of the regulations because he was new and had to have something to rely on. And the damn fool of course had to have it because he'd wreck himself and the outfit if he didn't. Actually we teach normal methods, particularly here at school—you have to because you not only have officers of all degrees of experience, but you have to give them a mark, you have to grade them so they can take their place among themselves. And if you let them go wild, all kind of solutions, you can't control it, you can't bring out the principles. But I wanted to warn you against normal employment actually, because there is nothing normal that ever happens on the battlefield that I know of except you get scared to death—that's very normal. Sometimes you have to accept improper missions or be used improperly.

In his 1956 graduation address, General Gavin tried to put nuclear weapons in perspective.

> And gunpowder originally was as dangerous to the men who used it as it was to those against whom it was used. And the object was to create a greater risk on the other side rather than on this side. And finally through years of use it was brought down into refined form. There are those who felt right along that it would be destructive to the entire human race, and you remember the writer of the Middle Ages who wrote: "O cursed device, base implement of death, by Beelzebub's malicious art to bring an end to the race of human kind." Actually the military too opposed its use. Now you are of a young coming generation. Now I must impress upon you the fact that atomic weapons are here to stay. They will be refined in size and delivery systems until they will serve in every echelon of the military establishment. This is the inevitable course of the present development programs of all nations concerned with atomic energy.

> Actually I would like to quote you but one line on the use of gunpowder that must have bearing on the attitude of a staff officer. At the time, when gunpowder was first used, and the military opposed it's use, the senior staff officers of the variety such as I represent in the Pentagon, just wouldn't accept it. And in Shakespeare's Henry IV, you remember he tells the story of the senior staff officer going to the field of battle where Hotspur was leaning on his sword just having finished a heavy day's fighting in which gunpowder had been used and in which he had been wounded. And this staff officer, quite irked by the attitude of this junior commander in the field, said "Ah, but for that accursed salt Peter dug out of the vile bowels of the earth, I too would be a soldier." Well now, you are soldiers, and you must learn to live with atomic weapons. This is not a case of whether or not atomic weapons will be used. Make up your minds they will be used. And they will be developed, I know they will, by your Army to where they can be brought down in very small size, very precise yields, to where they will be indistinguishable from high explosives, I can assure you of this. And the economics of it alone will push people into their use. This is a certain course you must adjust your thinking to.

General Johnson continued discussing the realities of the nuclear battlefield in 1962.

> Some units must stand and fight. Now it's my conviction that the type of disposition [on the nuclear battlefield] that we've made here give a division commander more than a reasonable chance of accomplishing a mission that may be assigned to him. The proposition of spreading out too wide, the proposition of keeping everybody moving doesn't give him this capability, in my humble opinion, because war is fighting. Some of us are going to have to stand and fight, regardless of how mobile we would like to be. Everybody likes to be mobile, because nobody likes to get shot at. But it's imperative that we recognize the necessity of standing and fighting when this is required. I'm going to change the normal mode of operation here. I'll let you stand up so those that have fallen asleep will be awakened...

Army Secretary Ailes prepared the 1965 graduating class for a different kind of warfare.

> The job which lies ahead of you is an unusually demanding one. Professionally, in the area of purely military skills, the Army officer's job becomes increasingly complex by the very necessity of coping with all conceivable levels of conflict. Mass movement of

troops, massive confrontations may indeed happen again, but the conflicts that are more likely in the immediate future are at a much lower level—not of intensity, but of sophistication. Yet they require all the traditional skills of the officer, and other talents besides: The ability to guide and encourage, rather than to command; the ability to improvise and to make do, to meet situations with something less that our traditional quantities of equipment and supplies; and to persevere in the most trying of circumstances and conditions.

In December 1967, General Johnson spoke of the difficulties of this less sophisticated form of warfare.

> We added this third principal mission of focusing on, not a general war, which we define as one in which nuclear weapons are exchanged—here we get back to absolutes of destruction again; not a conventional war, which we define as one in which major forces are engaged but nuclear weapons are not employed; but in countering this lower spectrum of violence, from the single assassin up to the sapper companies consisting of cells of assassins. Now just the day before yesterday, as a matter of fact, I sat down for a couple of hours with General [Harry] Kinnard and General [John M.] Wright from [Fort] Benning because what we have promulgated in 1964 ostensively we are practicing to a degree in Vietnam and some other places in the world today. But I'm not satisfied that we really have gotten down into the very heart of the problem. These answers are going to have to come from you, because we're not going to get them quickly. How do you cope with this lesser level of violence and suppress it, so that you restore this climate of order that I've alluded to? How do you cope with this?

In March 1974, General DePuy described his theory of developing the Army of the future, using an example that Army Chief of Staff General Eric Shinseki would also use in congressional testimony in 2000.

> Before TRADOC was formed, the combat development command at Fort Belvoir, with its agencies here and at all of the schools, concentrated on studies primarily out in the future, like maybe 10 to 15 years out, on the premise that you had to look out there and put a mark on the wall or you'd never get there. TRADOC doesn't believe that. We don't think you get out into the future by looking out 15 years and programming your way there. We think you get out into the future the same way you walk, one step at a time. So we're not making any studies of the Army in 1980, or 1990, or the year 2000. We are however, right here, looking at what would have happened to the 82d [Airborne] division had it gone into the Middle East. Well, it might not have been the right outfit to send. In any event, it wouldn't have survived without the TOW [wire-guided anti-tank missile]. It just wouldn't have survived. Even then it would have exhausted itself, even with the TOW, in stopping a Syrian attack of one division. It's that kind of work, done jointly by TRADOC and FORSCOM, and the 82d, and the XVIII Airborne Corps, and Fort Leavenworth, that means something now to the Army, because we could go tomorrow.

> The American public doesn't want us to match rusty bayonets with Mongolian recruits. They want us to do better than that, 'cause that way you kind of kill 100 of them and lose 100. They want us to do better with less. So it's not at all clear that that's the right way to go. However, the 82d Airborne Division is the most nimble division we have. And it

may have to go. But if it does, it has got to take with it more combat power than it has right now, or you're not going to like the results.

In 1975, General Weyand gave the same warning that General Harmon delivered 23 years earlier, that of not preparing to fight the last war.

> I have had reservations about the balance in the Army, because as many of you know, we have moved more sharply away from a balance that's overwhelmingly one of support to one of a cutting edge. Now we've not tried to do anything dramatic, but we've shifted that balance because we've felt that we had to have visible combat power. By visible, where it could be seen by potential adversaries, a measure of capability. Also at the same time recognizing "Well I'm not about to buy into any short war concept." The next conflict is going to be very intense and lethal right from the beginning. And it's not going to be one of these things where you can trade a lot of space for time and so on and so forth. It's going to be one of these affairs where we're going to be in it right up to our necks, and we're going to win it, and I know that we can win it. There's all sorts of reasons I can give you that will bear that out.

> And we want to be ready too, the programs we've had in mind that we've been working on, so that we fight—whatever we do, if we're unable to deter conflict—that we fight that war or that conflict or that action the way we perceive the future battlefield to be, not the way it was the last time. We are simply not going to be caught in the trap that we're preparing to fight the next war the way we fought the last one, because we have had enough experience looking out around us to know that it's going to be different. And so we've got to keep innovation going, we've got to keep TRADOC going, we have to keep this college going, and [the Combined Arms Center] and all the rest of it, because it's from there that the new doctrine, the new tactics, putting weapon systems together, changing linear defense to something else, giving up on a highly fluid, mobile defense, still retaining flexibility so that we can deal with the enemy main effort properly and all of that.

General Rogers spoke of this different fight in 1976.

> The Training and Doctrine Command has done a tremendous amount of work in describing for us what the modern battlefield's going to look like. And we need to be realistic about how we fight out there, because it's going to be different from any war we've had before in that environment in Europe. And the [1973 Arab-Israeli] Yom Kippur War taught us that. So understand what the modern battlefield is going to be like and be realistic in your training.

"Win the first battle" was one of the catch phrases of the Army doctrine being developed in the 70s. In 1976, a German international officer asked General DePuy "What does [win the first battle] really mean? Does it mean you only can win the first battle? The first battle will be the total war? The enemy will start negotiations after the first battle? Wouldn't it be better to win the last battle, or the first and all subsequent battles to win the war?" His question elicited laughter and applause from his classmates. DePuy responded:

If you read [FM] 100-5 [Operations] it says win the first, second, third, all the rest, and last battle. That's what it says, so there isn't any question about that. The question is whether the United States Army is going to get ready to win the first one. You know, it's like a prize fight: You don't win the first one, you don't get to fight the second one. We've been, historically, preparing to win the last battle. If there's one group of people in the world who ought to be interested in our winning the first battle it's German officers, for several reasons. One is so the battle can be fought forward successfully. You know, for years we expected in Germany to fall back to the Rhine River, wait for reinforcements from the United States and counter-attack. That is politically and militarily unattractive to the West German government. [Laughter] It gets back to just such questions, are we going to train our officers to be platoon leaders tomorrow morning or generals twenty years from now? The business of winning first, second, third, and last battles is obvious.

You know, that raises some very interesting questions in NATO, and that is: Do your NATO allies have enough ammunition to fight the last battle? And how long from the first battle could the last battle be? You know a lot of people like to play with things like that, and say it's a mistake to talk about the first battle. Sure, it's a mistake to talk about anything. Because everything you say is an oversimplification. Talking about the first battle is poignantly important to the United States Army. And it's very important to your country and your army too, because if our tank crews are operating at 20% effectiveness, then instead of being outnumbered 6 to 1, we're outnumbered 30 to 1. So we use that in order to excite discussion, and even controversy, in order to highlight the important aspects of the problem to our Army—meaning real readiness now, not mobilization readiness sometime in the future.

In December 1993, General Sullivan spoke about the challenges of being ready to fight two different styles of warfare.

[Slide: Today's Twin Challenges] This is a problem for us. Third Wave, [futurists Alvin and Heidi] Toffler, and First Wave. Prepare an Army to fight in the third wave [information age]—we don't quite understand everything about the third wave—while you are fighting people who find themselves back here [points to first wave, pre-industrial]. That's a real challenge for us. Some of [the first wave] is people intensive [and] some of [the third wave] is equipment intensive. Balance it out, and do [the third wave] at a time of declining resources. There's a lot you could say about that, I'm not going to say much.

[Slide: George Crook's Army] The Army's been in this before, by the way. George Crook was a Civil War officer who went out West to fight the Indians. While he was out there taking these kinds of casualties [from slide: 1866-98 Indian Wars: 943 engagements, 948 KIA, 1058 WIA], they were eating their boots, and you can see some of their names up in the Leavenworth Chapel. The Congress of the United States spent that kind of money to defend against Britain and Germany [from slide: $127 million coastal defense program vs. Britain and Germany--other bullet on slide refers to Crooks Army: 1877, 1879 No Pay authorized by Congress], Fort Monroe was kept safe from whatever. It's still there. General Franks is very secure. [Laughter] General Crook and his troopers out there were in bad shape. [from slide: Best and Brightest: George Crook—early death. George Custer—killed in action. Ranald Mackenzie—insane. Emory Upton—suicide.] Fight today's wars, get ready for tomorrow's. Don't forget the troops out there who are fighting today's wars. The United

289

States Army has been through a lot of this...and [pointing to slide] we weren't ready to fight Spain in 1898.

[British military historian] Michael Howard said our challenge is to get it sort of right so if we have to fight we can fix it. [*Quote on slide: Whatever doctrine the Armed Forces are working on now, they have got it wrong ...It does not matter that they have got it wrong. What does matter is their capacity to get it right quickly...it is the task of military science in an age of peace to prevent the doctrines from being too badly wrong. Michael Howard 1973*]

General McCaffrey spoke of the difficulty of "getting it right" in 1994.

We've got a structure, we've got a dream, we're writing the doctrine, we're moving forward. It's going to be as painful as operating on your own body. There is no blueprint. We're trying to anticipate situations that face us ten, twenty years out. We know it takes us five years to get an idea out into the United States Army. And that's not a sarcastic comment, it's a recognition that until the majors of the Army have come to Leavenworth and encompassed the reality of a new concept and gone out to the divisions and corps, it doesn't really exist as a doctrine, as a practice, as a way of life.

General Downing elaborated on this in 1995, and gave students a preview of what they would face in the next decade.

[*Slide: 3d Generation Maneuver Warfare in the information age: conventional, high-tech, precise, short, inter-state, low casualties*] All this leads to the two views of warfare, or two requirements I should say. And to me this is the crux of the challenge that faces us for the next five to ten to fifteen years. We must create a military which is first class and which can take on any potential adversary and decisively defeat them on a field of battle. Hopefully we can deter anybody from fighting us. But if we can't we've got to be able to decisively defeat them. Right now we probably are the most powerful military nation. That's not the largest army, the largest air force, the largest navy, but the most powerful. So we've got to maintain that, and that of course is what we as an institution have been trained and conditioned to do—that is, not fight the last war but project ourselves into the future, develop the weapon systems that are going to enable us to remain preeminent on the battlefield. That's the bottom line. That's what we get paid for in this country: To create a force like this and to keep it on top.

[*Slide: 4th Generation Regional & Niche Warfare: unconventional, low-tech, protracted, intra-state, bloody*] The problem that we're facing, ladies and gentlemen, the challenges we are facing right now are not [3d Generation Warfare] kind of challenges. The problem we're facing is with this new Operations Other Than War, these new non-traditional threats to our national interests. And how do you take this [3d Generation Conventional Force] here, and apply it to these [4th generation] kinds of situations? Sometimes the forces over here [3rd Generation] are not appropriate to be used over here [4th Generation]. Sometimes the forces over here [3rd] are not only not appropriate, they're going to get you in trouble if you use them for something like [4th Generation Warfare]. So the question is how do you get at that, and how do you make that happen? How do you maintain the capability to fight [the 3rd Generation] kind of war, when many of your day to day challenges are over here [in the 4th Generation]? And by the way, just to set your mind at ease, I'm not going to tell you that special operations forces are the answer to your problems, because we're not. We've got a role to play, a role to play here [3rd Generation], and a role to play here [4th generation]. But the entire armed forces have a role to play here [3rd generation], and portions of our armed forces certainly have a role to play here [4th generation]. And we've got to sort out how it is we're all going to play these roles. And to me, that's the challenge that's before us today, 1995, as we're going in and building this force for the 21st century.

In 1996, General Reimer warned students about one particular vision of future warfare.

We want the doctrine to reflect that world that we live in, not the world as we wish it to be...I think there's a hope out there, maybe a belief, that you can, through precision engagement, do all of these things and make this a kind of a computer game in terms of warfare. I would just simply say to you that [author T.R.] Fehrenbach's quote about—you can bomb the land into the stone age, and atomize it and pulverize it, but if you really want to save it and preserve it for civilization you have to do like the old Romans did and put your soldiers in the mud. I think that's always going to be true as long as people live on the land. We've got to have boots on the ground in some cases. I don't understand how precision strike alone could save the oil wells in Saudi Arabia. And I'm not arguing against precision strike, believe me. I think what I'm arguing for is the balance that needs to be there.

When we were facing a threat-based force, the Soviets, we spent a lot of time on precision strike because we were on the defense, and I think that precision strike in that particular case was terribly important. And you have to be able to tell the enemy that you hold them at risk. You've got the [intelligence] capability to know where they are, you've got the [intelligence] capability to identify those targets, to detect them, and destroy those that are most important to you. Precision strike gives you that capability. But if you're looking at a different type of operation than defense, I think you've got to have dominant maneuver and precision strike in balance. And so that's kind of where we're moving. There is a tendency for people, I think it's sometimes wishful thinking, to want to emphasize, too much in my opinion, precision strike. And basically what we've got to be able to do is to maneuver and control that ground and make sure that we occupy it and be able to preserve it for civilization...I think it's one of the issues to be discussed in the Quadrennial Defense Review, I think it will be one of the major points of debate in the next year or so.

When Air Force General Richard B. Myers was the commander of U.S. Space Command, much of his mission dealt with the future of warfare, and during his 1999 visit he offered students a glimpse.

The last item we are responsible for is force application, and that is the application of force from space. Clearly today we have no capability in that area. Obviously very politically sensitive. [Force application], in the future, would have to be a decision by our national command authorities and the Congress, and the will of the American people if we're ever going to go to force application. What we have been asked to do at Space Command is to be thinking about force application, and to be looking at concepts of operation and so forth, if we're ever called upon to do that. Again we have no capability today in force application. And if there's one thing to take out of these couple of slides I would focus on the space control. We surveil pretty well, but we don't do very well in protection, prevention, or negation. We have virtually no capability there today. And that's going to become more and more important as we have our commercial assets up there, they're unprotected. We have a lot of our military assets up there, and they're somewhat unprotected.

The example I would give you would be the Hughes Galaxy 4 commercial satellite that, it was just a little less than a year ago, went haywire. A lot of pagers, ATM machines and things stopped working, probably the first time at least the American people found out how dependent we were on some of those space assets when they couldn't fill up at the gas pumps. When they swiped their card there was no satellite to transmit that data back to the clearing house so they could get approval to go do that. The big thing was for about a week we didn't know why that satellite wasn't doing what it was supposed to be doing. We didn't know if that was adversary action, weather phenomenon, space weather phenomenon, or what it was, or just a malfunction on the satellite bus. It turned out it was a satellite bus problem that was later rectified, but that's what I am getting to when I say we're not very good at protection and prevention because we don't have things like— most of us flyers are used to operating with some sort of radar warning receiver so we know when enemy radars are painting our aircraft. There's nothing like that on spacecraft. We don't know if they're getting lased, we don't know if there are other phenomenon up there that's impacting their capability.

… More on communications. The only thing I would point out here is for our military satellites, [Defense Satellite Communications System (DSCS)], Milstar, and [Ultra-High Frequency Follow-On (UFO)], we have some protection on most of those. You can see they have low and different types of data rates depending on the system. But when you get to commercial, where we have 60% of our military [communications] now going over commercial [satellites], you can see that we've got no protection. We pay a pretty good [operations and maintenance] cost, we fight some landing rights—what the [combatant commanders] worry about is "can I get a terminal in places like"—the two places where we're having issues right now are Japan and Saudi Arabia. If you want to put a terminal there you've got to get host government approval for that, and sometimes that's more difficult than other times. That's an issue with the commercial side of it. Like I said we have about 60% of our comms in commercial today. My view would be as we go into the future we will have more and more of our communications on the commercial side of the house. If you were to ask General [Anthony] Zinni, CENTCOM commander, how important commercial is to him, he would tell you it's very important, because it is what gives him a lot of his primary communications capability in Southwest Asia today.

And what's the future? Well the future is this chart on the right. And that shows our legacy [satellite] systems, those first three on the chart over there, here's their capacity. And you can see where their capacity is with respect to demand [well short of demand]. And I would say we're going to fill that [shortfall] with commercial satellites in the comms, with the kind of issues we're talking about right there. We had one of our industrial associations do a study for us in space comms. They spent a year doing this study to look at—and this was a partnership with industry, so these were the commercial satellite builders and operators. Our question to them was "Are you interested in protecting your commercial satellites?" And the answer was after a year of study "No, we're not interested. There is no business case for us to worry about protecting our satellites." Which ought to give us great angst in the military if we're going to put a lot of our comms on them. I've never seen an issue where there were two sides to it like there was on this one. The commercial folks on the one hand saying there's no threat, don't worry about this, and the military on the other hand saying, you know we think there's a threat, certainly in the future, and we've got to be taking steps to fix it. That's something we'll continue to work, because if we're going to migrate a lot of our comms to commercial, we've got to figure out a way to protect those and make sure they're secure and they're there when you want them. But that's the only way we're going to meet that growing demand, and most of you understand that chart very well.

… It was a couple years ago that there was a big push to make space an area of responsibility (AOR). There was a lot of pushback at the time for that, and in the end I don't think that argument is all that pertinent. What happened was out of that argument these responsibilities were given to U.S. Space Command. They look an awful lot like the responsibilities that a Regional Commander in Chief has as well. So we're absolutely delighted with the responsibilities we have. We think we have the wherewithal, given that direction, that we can go do what we need to do to support the warfighter. And this whole AOR issue, as far as I'm concerned that will happen someday but it doesn't have to be actively pushed. If it's appropriate, it will happen, and it will happen at the right time. [It] does not need to be actively solved right now

1999 Unified Command Plan. One of the big things that's going to come out of this will be impetus for the United States Space Command to become responsible for what we called information operations. And I apologize for using information operations because that's going to mean something different to everybody in this audience. The thing that's important about it is computer network defense, or computer network attack. And if you just take the computer word off and say network defense, network attack I think you're a lot closer to what we're talking about. This is a responsibility that's coming our way, and coming our way very, very soon. In October of '99, if the president signs this out, we will have responsibility for network defense. The new Joint Task Force Computer Network Defense set up under [the Defense Information Systems Agency] will come under U.S. Space Command. And then in October of 2000 we'll have the responsibility for the attack side of that house as well. You know, if you've dealt much in this at all I think you think this is probably a huge growth area. It makes our head hurt sometimes at Peterson [Air Force Base] to get our arms around this. This is a very large issue. All the services treat both the things I talked about, defense and attack, in the United States anyway, we all treat them a little bit differently, with different pockets of expertise spread around. Our job is going to be to try and leverage all that that's already been done, bring it together, integrate it, and then again, provide the warfighter what they need in terms of defense and in terms of attack capability

…The reason we're doing this, by the way, the reason that information operations is coming to US Space Command is not because we said we wanted it. In fact I went to my first [Commander in Chief (CinC)] conference this last September, and I'm sitting around all these tables, and this is one where we had the president, we were able to talk to the president about our readiness needs. But after he left we talked about the Unified

Command Plan and it was all the other CinCs who said "Somebody's got to get a hold of this and we think it ought to be Space Command." [Laughter] I was a very silent—I mean, I'm the new guy, right? I've been on thirty days, right? What do I know about— All I knew was it sounded like a lot of work. So I was very quiet, and I said I think it's probably the right thing to do, and space is probably the right place to put it. So we didn't ask—this isn't one of those things we went out and asked for.

In the question and answer period, General Myers was asked about an article written by New Hampshire Senator Bob Smith calling for a separate space force.

We were in Boston in November at a—I think it was the Fletcher School of Diplomacy symposium where Senator Smith first made this speech and rolled this out. And we were at dinner with him. In fact I was sitting right next to Senator Smith and I had my wife on the right side, and the Senator came in to give this speech. And we had this delightful dinner conversation, and then he gets up to speak and boy he's throwing barbs and darts at us about everything, and how the Air Force has been a poor steward of space and all this stuff. And my wife's sitting next to me and she says "How many knives do I have to pull out of your back before this is over?" And then when he came back we had this nice discussion again. [Laughter] Senator Smith is a great advocate for space and for what space can bring to the fight. And he understands that probably as well as anyone on the hill. On this one issue of a separate space force, I guess you have to ask yourself what's the objective? What are we trying to accomplish here?

…We've got to make this part of our operational lexicon, this system has to be as natural to us as other things that I talked about in terms of employing ships or tanks or airplanes or whatever it is—we've got to know this business. And my fear is that if you take it off and make a space force, or the other paradigm is another major force program like [Special Operations Command], that that's probably the wrong thing to do. I don't think that meets any of the objectives that I think we have for it. The issue is not so much how we organize for it, I think we're organized fairly well. The issue is the commitment of resources. And that's, of course, given our defense budget, even with the small increases that we think we're going to see over the next few years, that will be the issue. The issue will be technology and resources and policies, and it won't be so much how we're organized. I think we are organized fine. I think any effort we spend, intellectual effort, on trying to reorganize, or any other layer of overhead we want to put on this is not going to help the fundamental problem of resources and technology. I think we're working that pretty well…My vision is for space to be integrated, not to be separate, stand-alone, [where] you've got to have a thousand clearances before you can figure out what the hell's happening. That's not what we're about.

… In terms of weaponizing space: My crystal ball is not all that clear in that particular area about weapons in space. There is a lot of debate in this country and I assume in other countries about the peaceful uses of space. We have some folks that are very adamant that if the U.S. were ever to put weapons in space that would just create this huge space arms race, which would be in nobody's interest. There's others in our country that are very vocal and say we ought to put weapons in space as soon as we can. That will not be our decision in the military of course, that will be for our political masters to decide. In any case I think weapons in space is probably—to be able to physically do it you're probably talking two decades away. We have some time to go through the debate, and we should go through this debate, I think. I think it's very conceivable in the future to have maybe a space arms limitation treaty, you can visualize that sort of thing. That's probably not ruled out. Where we're going in that area—that's one of the areas we worked on some concepts, and we think about it, and we've got a few technologies, but that's about it. Again, we're decades away from having any real capability, at least in this country. I don't know about other countries.

FUTURE ARMY

Many speakers shared their thoughts on how the Army would need to organize for the future, and what that fight would look like. In 1959, General Clarke offered to the graduating class an opinion on force structure and missions that has been reiterated (and contradicted) throughout the years.

> Our defense posture requires that we maintain strong deterrent forces, prepared for a general war. But we must maintain adequate forces and means to cope with limited war. Two forces, not the same force. This is the point we must get over to the public, and to ourselves. Preparedness for general war does not necessarily include preparedness for several types of limited war. This is a popular complacency. This is ipso facto reasoning. This is reasoning from the Land of Nod.

> Let me quote something from another land. These are the words of the Communist China Defense Minister: "Ours is a policy of fight fight, stop stop, half fight, half stop. There's no trick to this, but it is a normal thing." To contain limited war, to control the communists' perimeter nibbling, we cannot use a general war force. This would enlarge, and not reduce, the size of the conflict. We're asking a lot of our forces and our people in preparing for two wars, two different types of wars, at the same time. The communist block seems to lull us into complacency by admitting nuclear war is oblivion for all civilizations. But they have other plans while they seek international respectability by appearing at respectable conference tables. This is status seeking on a global scale, and most people are aware of it.

In March 1967, General Johnson spoke of the impacts of the future strategic mobility of the force, as well as his understanding of the second and third order effects of making changes to the organization.

> You all know that we have in programs for future years the C5A aircraft and a concept for marrying some equipment, prepositioned on the fast-deployment ship, or the FDL, with some people flown in by aircraft…this capability of being able to move, and being able to project force suddenly is going to cause you, in the years ahead, to view, first the composition of our force, and secondly the extent to which it's prepared to move at any given time, significantly differently than it's been viewed in the past.

> …It takes a long time to make significant changes in the numbers of officers by branch that you have in the structure, and I am very conservative in the personnel area from a personal point of view because any change that I make I am inflicting on some successor

295

of mine about 25 years from now. And I'm hesitant to give him that cross to bear. I'm bearing some from 1945 [Laughter] that I wish I didn't have. [Applause]

In December of that same year, Johnson alluded to similar force structure questions that General Clarke raised eight years prior.

> All over the face of this globe, with the improvements in communications, with the improvements in travel, with the speed with which we can go, people who haven't known are aspiring to something better for themselves. And what does this mean? Unrest, turbulence. And what does that mean to us, as the most affluent of them all, and with the kind of consciences that we have, and the kind of national conscience that we have? That we're going to be concerned, not necessarily that we're coming in, but there's going to be a concern with some kind of assistance to maintain a reasonable order so that the larger violence can be avoided. Now the analogy is very simple. It's easier to put out a little fire than a big one. But it doesn't necessarily take a barrel of water to put it out when it's little. And all I'm saying is what kind of a glass might we need? That's the only question I'm asking. This is what will face you, and these are the kinds of questions you'll have to answer, looking out ahead.

In 1973, General Max Taylor had much to say about the reasoning behind U.S. force structure and composition.

> It worries me to see the fact that we are giving the primary basis for our general purpose force requirement is the Soviet threat. That's not going to work, it's getting weaker every day—and that includes of course the NATO collective. If that's the only reason we have an Army of the size we have we're going to lose it. I would say that the future is so filled, so fraught with obvious causes for conflict and war growing out of environmental factors, population growth, the have-nots versus the haves, which is going to be the new ideological sizzle, red button. There's the place you ought to be looking. And your answer will not come up in a single commitment, but rather a rational and convincing presentation of the uncertainties of the world and the obvious need for general purpose forces...Even at best the NATO commitment has been wearing thin over the years as those who testify Army budgets have discovered. Now living in the present climate it's going to go—might not be this year, not next year, but fairly soon. So you'd better have something better.

> ... When I say let's go down to a small, hardcore excellent force, it seems to me we outgrew our ability to have a "good" Army under the conditions of Vietnam. They were special conditions, but nonetheless, under those terms we didn't end up with a good Army. We started off with a good Army, but the "pollution" of the draft, if that's what you want to call it, certainly wreaked a heavy toll, and you gentlemen have seen it more closely than I. So that I would say what we need now is to get back to where we're sure of ourselves, confident of ourselves, know what we've got, and be sure that we're building on something sound. Then let's experiment with other combinations. If indeed size becomes a factor, if it is determined that we cannot have a big enough force to meet the requirements which our civil masters tell us we should be able to do, then by that time, having built soundly on a fairly narrow base, then we can branch out. Then we can expand with some safety. Until we get to that point I'd feel uneasy about it.

Taylor was asked about the logic of a "one-and-a-half war" strategy, as well as for which types of wars the Army should be organized.

> [The one-and-a-half war strategy] is nonsense. Of all the cock-eyed things, two and a half wars, one and a half wars, what does that mean, by the way? How are you going to interpret that? What is a one and half war preparation? That means to the average citizen, now this is the other thing, two and a half wars just happens to be twice as bad as one and a half wars. It really gives the intelligent citizen a [mindset] that assumes the Army, the armed forces, are going to Congress to get money to have in their pocket, to have troops and equipment to go out and fight two and a half wars or one and a half wars. It's obviously never—I never saw a nickel in the budget change on the basis of that one and a half war, two and a half war [strategy]. It changed on a lot of other causes, but not that. And it's misleading, misguiding, and furthermore gives you a bad defense and one that you will pay for later.

> …I would say, as I view it, we have a core function, a core function of [the] ability to present military force of limited size into the various areas of plausible threat and not concentrate on one. The reason costs are high is all you gentlemen, you tankers, and artillerymen and so on, and certainly the Navy and the Air Force, go out and ask for the most expensive equipment in the world because they think we're going to fight the Soviet Union, and that they will have the best and we must have the best. Well that's nice if we can afford it, but we're running out of money very fast. But the concept of having a core capability to go any place with limited strength, and then to have pooled equipment, and specialized tactics, if you will, oriented toward special theaters. Some concept like that, I think it'd be—we tried that outward of World War I, we were developing certain units that were specialized in desert training, not that they would be the ones we'd send to the desert, but at least you had centers of some expertise, some experts that could be then infused into those areas where they were required.

Secretary Schlesinger summed up the problem nicely in 1974, stating "The future is contingent, and one cannot predict the contingencies, and consequently we need an additional reserve of forces to deal with what we cannot anticipate. How you structure your forces for that is a little bit difficult for the analytical mind to grapple with. The analytical mind likes to plan its contingencies, rather than to adapt to the contingencies when they develop." In December of that year, a student asked Secretary Callaway about the 16 Division force and quoted a fellow student, saying that "The Army has been asked to do so much with so little for so long that it believes it can do everything with nothing forever." [Laughter and applause]

> That's the spirit alright! [Big laugh] Well, you know, to answer in a serious vein, you've got to live in the real world. If you and I were emperor and we could wave our magic wand, we might have 100 divisions all equipped at full [Authorized Level of Organization] and everything would just be wonderful and the rest of the world would quake when we dared to give a suggestion to the world. But that's not the real world. The real world of most democracies—matter of fact most countries, but most democracies—is in times of peace the soldier is not treated with the same kind of interest as he is in a time of war. What's changed now is we're talking about short wars rather than long wars. General DePuy was talking yesterday and he's got a saying—you may

297

have heard it here at Leavenworth I don't know, but his point is what we really need to do is be prepared to win the first battle. Now why is that so important? It's important because our thinking has always been, as Eisenhower emphasized all through World War II, you've got to be prepared to win the last battle. Very different situation now. Not many wars you can conceive of, not many scenarios you can conceive of, that would go through a four-year war like World War II, of continuing on for four years where you've got to win that last battle. Almost any scenario you come up with is a very short war where in the first two or three days you set the political climate under which the UN is operating and all this is going on, and you'd better win that first battle. So that being the case we've got to have a ready Army now.

...So we've got a situation that is far different from any time we've ever had in our history: A volunteer force, hopefully a long period of peace, with an enormous challenge to be ready at a moment's notice. And I think that gives the climate under which you can have a damn fine Army. And you say too little and all that, and yeah, we'd like more. But if we get this Congress—when we get this Congress to give us 16 divisions and we trim out some of the things we're doing, we're going to have a mighty fine Army. And as Abe used to say, anybody that wants to take us on, you'd better bring your lunch. [Laughter and applause]

...If you take any kind of scenario that lasts—we'll say take a NATO scenario that lasts more than a few days. The Reserves would certainly be involved in a great way. It's just impossible for us to economically justify having all of that support in the Active Army. The kinds of support that you don't need except when you're in combat. And the kinds of support the Reserves can fill quite well. And we have a proposal before Congress that will go before the next Congress asking for authority for the Secretary of Defense, on his own initiative without declaring any kind of emergency, just on his own initiative to call up 50,000 Reserves for—I've forgotten what the period of time is, maybe six months but I'm not sure. The purpose of that is to let the Army know and to let the Reserves know and let the world know that we're serious about making Reserves part of the total force. There is great concern—the Active army doesn't—they've got nothing against the Reserves, they want to work with the Reserves. But the biggest hang-up the Active Army has got is "Yes, but we start counting on those Reserves, and we cut the Active structure counting on those Reserves, and we'll have another period like Vietnam where we don't have the national will to call the Reserves and then where are we? So we can't rely on them." And that's a valid, you know, whatever your opinion on Reserves is, that's valid. So we're trying to say, so let's get that 50,000 call up, everybody knows, they understand that if we get in a tight spot we're going to call them, because the Secretary of Defense will call them, if he's got that authority, if he needs them, it's his discretion, obviously. Now that's a kind of thing that we're looking toward. I think the biggest problem that the Active Army has as we're moving now in so many ways to closer integration with the Reserve components is that there's still that feeling back in the background of every officer "Yes, but we might not be allowed to call them and then where are we?" So I think if we pass that legislation you'll see a very different attitude on the part of the Active forces. They'll really believe that they really are available in event of an emergency and then they get a whole lot better.

298

In 1976, General DePuy spoke about organization as it related to the company commander.

Now what we see here is more and more combat power resides in systems that are back behind the line, and that's good because you don't have to cart a lot of heavy tonnage around on the front line. But now the problem is how do you exploit all of that? That's one busy company commander, if he's the guy who's doing it all. He's forward on the battlefield in his M113, or hopefully in a better vehicle in the future, being shot at, issuing instructions to tank and infantry, trying to manage some mortars if he has them, then somebody suggests that he used artillery. Which kind? Oh, three or four kinds. And here comes some attack helicopters and the battalion commander says that there are some A-10s above. And now, can we depend on our company commander, who since Vietnam has been the key to our tactical employment and application of weapon systems? Can that man do it? Can he exploit all of that?

The German Army tells us that in their opinion he cannot, when they have looked at our organization. There are other armies, the Israeli Army, for example, both the German and Israeli armies have small companies and small battalions, we have big companies and big battalions...But the real question is not whether which one of those countries is right, the real question is how do we organize ourselves to use all that combat power and get it applied on the battlefield at the right place when we need it? Now our army has not fought a modern mechanized battle, and has not effectively and successfully done all of this, and so we don't have any experts.

But we know by inspection it's a hell of a big problem. Now one of the things that we have suggested in TRADOC to the Chief of Staff of the Army is let's examine an alternative to our current organization and see if it's better. Logic tells us that the company commander is overloaded. For example, if a Soviet tank attack is mounted in Germany where the average intervisability is only about 1,200 meters, sometimes longer, sometimes—lots of the time much shorter, and if they mass and move fast the company commander only has seven, eight, ten minutes with his twelve tanks to knock out sixty. Now while he's doing that and being shot at and maneuvering his people, can he handle all the rest of this? We say probably not. So we're going to propose for test and study and evaluation and analysis and all that—meaning, try it out—a small platoon of three tanks, a small company of 11 tanks, a small battalion of 33 tanks, but more tank battalions. Infantry companies of 100 men, and more battalions—like 5 battalions in a brigade, and that's a problem. Same number of tanks in the division, more officers required, more officers required to help us supply the combat power to the enemy under difficult circumstances. That wil be a problem to get more officers. More artillery tubes per battery, eight instead of six. Two platoons of four each. One [fire direction center], radio communication within the battery, rather than a battery of six. We're gonna try that.

...We're gonna take all administration out of the company. In fact, the Vice Chief of Staff directed the Army by message last week to remove the administration from the companies Army-wide. All the tests have been sufficiently impressive and successful, so that it's going to be removed. We intend to remove supply, mess, and make some kind of an accommodation with maintenance. We want the company still involved in maintenance, but we don't want a lot of people down in the motorpool bored to death, pulling all the battery cables off out of sheer frustration. [Laughter and applause]

... So for your lifetime in the Army, for all your remaining years, your principle problem is going to be how can the Army organize, train, and equip itself to focus this enormously effective combat power on that part of the battlefield where you wish to attack and break through, or on that part of the battlefield where you wish utterly to destroy an enemy attack? Gentlemen and ladies the combat power is there today. It's there today and its gonna get more and more and better and better, and I would rate the ability of the United States Army to apply it, under pressure, on the battlefield again, somewhere around 25% of its potential. So you've got 75% to work on for the next 20 years in the Army. I'll be watching.

He also talked about treating Army weapons as systems as opposed to individual pieces of equipment.

... What did we do in Vietnam with helicopters? In Vietnam the helicopter was very important. In fact it's hard to imagine anything that was more important than the helicopter. The helicopter is not easy to maintain, but they were maintained. Why? Because we cut through the middle of the logistics system and set a separate one up for helicopters. That's what happened in Vietnam. They called it a closed-loop logistic support system. Every spare part that went on a [Military Airlift Command] charter flight was recorded and the people at the other end knew exactly which airplane to go meet and get the [ball spline?] that you needed. It cut through the system. The replacement of pilots, the supply parts, the positioning of mechanics, all was a single system, management by exception. And the operational ready rate, 10,000 miles away from St. Louis, [Army Service Command (ASCOM)], was phenomenally high. Had the general purpose logistics system tried to handle that, the operational ready rate would have been 50% instead of 80%. I'm not anti-logistics, but I want to say that generalized logistics will not support systems.

...Let's compare for a minute the tank with the helicopter. Right now today, the helicopter and the tank cost the same. And I'm talking about lift helicopters. Right now, today, in Europe, the tank is more important than the lift helicopter. Right now, today, we have either two warrant officers, one warrant and an officer, or two officers flying the helicopter. What have we got in the tank? E-3? E-4? E-5? Hardly ever an E-6. Do they get any special pay? No. Do they get a separate physical examination every year? No. Eyesight checked? Nope. 24% of them can't correct their eyes to 20/20. Is there a separate training system that puts a crew chief and a master mechanic in the loop? Nope. Why? How'd we get all mixed up like that? Why have we got Hueys, you know, that aren't as important as tanks, in Europe at least, being taken care of in a closed loop system and high-quality personnel but the tank, which is more important to the outcome of the battle, we don't do much about it? The answer is, gentlemen, we haven't started to think systems yet. Now I'm telling you that you have to do that.

We're making a proposal that goes side-by-side, cheek-by-jowl with the reorganizations of the divisions, to go to a system approach for the following: These are separate: Aircraft, missiles, communication electronics, tracked fighting vehicles, maybe artillery, and we don't know how far we can go. Now the logistics system must continue for everything else, which is the bulk of the line items in the system. Out of 140 line items, these discrete systems will only take part. Will this be expensive in duplication and personnel? Yes. Is it justified? I say it is. Because the generalized logistics system won't keep the equipment going. It's not keeping the equipment going.

In 1987, Representative Gingrich took this systems approach even farther.

The Army fundamentally procures wrong. The Army procures weapons, the Navy procures systems. The Navy's right. The Navy would never walk in and ask for an Aegis-class cruiser, but accept half the radar. The Army accepts an armored division that's not an armored division, it's a collection of weapon systems. And one of the things the Army needs to study is, should we, in fact, go to the Congress and say "How many divisions do you want, here's what a division looks like." And then buy the division, not buy the weapons. Now there's a very powerful side-effect to that. First of all you get a synergistic division, and all of you understand, like the M1, M113 match-up that's nuts. Second you end up having to force the congressman to learn to think in division bites rather than to think in weapon systems.

In 1986, General Vuono spoke about the students' role in modernizing the force, and gave an example from his own past in answer to a question about the numerous different division structures in the Army.

Many of you will find yourself in jobs where you are intimately involved in the force modernization business. You will be on a staff somewhere where that will be your lifeblood. I would maintain that everybody in this audience will be involved in force modernization in some fashion. Whether you are in the business of writing requirements in the materiel development business, or whether you're down in an organization somewhere on the receiving end of all this modernization, we're all into it. And so the implications for all of us, wherever we're at, is to understand that we're going to be in a high/low mix for a significant period of time. We're going to have a combination of new and old. Now the organizations will be designed and changed, but they will only be changed as we modernize the force with the various systems. So we've got to be prepared to fight with a high/low mix, and then we've got to be prepared to do that during a period of change. Now we all like to plan for change, but very few of us like to be on the receiving end and have to execute the change. Why is that? Because we get comfortable with doing things today.

…There's a place for the 9th Division in a motorized role. What we've got to do is be smart in the areas of the world that we want to deploy the motorized division. It's just like a number of years ago—a little history—when General Shy Meyer was Chief of Staff. I was a combat developer at Fort Monroe. [Deputy CGSC Commandant, General] Fred Franks was working for me down there as a colonel. [Meyer] had said to us "I want you to design a light infantry division." This was what, Fred, about '79 or so? He says "I want you to design a light infantry division." We said "Fine." And we started to work on it. And one of the concepts was that it had to defeat enemy armor in open terrain. [Laughter] Well now, we had a great challenge on our hands. And so what you ended up with was not a light division, but you ended up with a much heavier division which you couldn't move anywhere, because you wanted to defeat enemy armor in open terrain. You're not going to do that with a light division as itself, you're going to have to augment it in some cases.

And so, same thing with a motorized division. You've got to make sure that you know where you're going to employ it, how you're going to employ it, and then it's got tremendous capabilities to do that. Now, there's been a great deal of discussion about what design are we in for the light division, for the motorized division, is it here to stay and so forth. As much as anything is firm in this business, the motorized division is here to stay. It is not in any state of flux. It's in transition to a design which supports the concept of a motorized division. Now what the division does not have is what those who worked on it, of which I happened to be one of them among others, said it needed was some kind of an armored gun system that gave it a [kinetic energy] capability. We have not yet produced that. And so we have interim systems in there, which is the HMMWV TOW [Wire-guided anti-tank missile on an unarmored troop carrying vehicle].

I might tell you on the Armored Gun System just as an aside, even though you didn't ask, we've commissioned about January, General [Robert J.] Sunell to head up an armored family of vehicles task force, and his job is to look at the requirement and come up with a family of vehicles, both heavy and light, that give us some commonality and some supportability opportunities, so we no longer in the future have the mobility differential we have say between the M1 and some of our support vehicles. And a role out here being played by [TRADOC Deputy Commanding General] General [Towle] Bartlett and his crew, so that we look at commonality for an armor, infantry, engineer, artillery, and combat service support system. And he's putting all that together because if you go back to the force [modernization] business that I talked about, commonality in terms of combined arms is going to be essential. His major task, Sunell's priority task right now is to define for us the armored gun system that we can develop and get it on the books for not just the motorized division, but for other elements of the light force. Not necessarily that they would go in organic to the light division, but they would be available let's say at the corps level as a corps package in terms of task organization if you went somewhere where you needed them. And they would be the armored gun system for the motorized division. And he's a few years away from that, and in the meantime it would be the HMMWV-TOW business for them. But the motorized concept is here, the division is a valuable division.

General Reimer told the students about a new concept in strategic mobility efficiencies in 1994.

We've come up with a system or a concept called Adaptive Force Packaging, and I want to talk just a little bit about Adaptive Force Packaging, because I think there's a lot of potential there. First of all, Adaptive Force Packaging is very complimentary to what we do in power projection. It's absolutely the point of the spear as I see it. What we've done is take the factors of [mission, enemy, terrain, time, and troops available (METT-T)] and put together a package, primarily a naval package, to be able to deploy it to certain points of the world. And we've tailored that package, it'll never be the same, it'll be different based upon the METT-T factors, and we deploy that for a certain period of time. It complements the forward deployed forces that are out there. Now to be very honest about this, this is not a concept that is chiseled in stone. We've still got some refinements. This is not totally accepted throughout the world. There are other [Regional Commanders in Chief] that have different ideas about that. But I think the Adaptive Force Packaging from the Army standpoint, certainly from FORSCOM's standpoint, has a great deal of potential, particularly if you look at the flexibility that's involved there, and the potential to save money, and still provide capability.

In 1994, General Sullivan described a technique for determining the Army of the future that was quite different from the one General DePuy outlined twenty years earlier.

[*Slide: Create a vision and pull the Army to it*] Get out here, get out here in the 21st century, look back, and bring this great organization into the 21st century. I believe that we are now able, through the use of synthetic theaters of war and simulations, we are now able to get out here and see not only what the next Army looks like, but what the army after that looks like. Now you may think that's Zen-like—I told you I was going to let you in my head and it's not necessarily neat and orderly, okay? I believe that we are now able to see the Army After Next, and the Army After Next will be much different, but if you can see that, you will enable yourself to build Force XXI, the next one, better.

What does it mean when you can put a mortar round on the target—the first one—on the target within three minutes? And that includes 64 seconds time of flight? It means that you have fewer ships. It means that the Rangers, who are carrying their 60 mortar rounds, don't have to carry as many 'cause it's not taking them four rounds to adjust. It means you lase to the target, you know where the mortar is, so you're already solving the equation. Boom. Three minutes. It means the enemy's going to act differently. And you're not going to send 40,000 containers, so you reduce the number of ships. We can do that with World War II mortars. Hmmm. Bonk. Hey wait a minute. I can now do the same thing with the M1A2 [tank]. I now have 58 lasers. I can't handle it—the doctrine won't handle 58 tanks—you can't handle 58 forward observers. We can't figure it out yet. But that's what synthetic theaters of war enable us to do. And why do you have 58 tanks in the tank battalion, when with the M60 you only had 54? How come you've got more? Hmmm. Get out here [points to Vision portion of slide], get out here, way out, and build [Force XXI].

Two years later General Reimer elaborated on Force XXI.

If you go to Fort Hood Texas today, as I did about three weeks ago, you'll find Task Force XXI forming up. Task Force XXI is basically a product-improved Army. It's taking the equipment suite that we have in the Army today, and it's basically putting in all the information-age technology that we can get our hands on, to figure out how to achieve not only situational awareness, but situational understanding. To be able to know where all the friendlies are, all the time, a large percentage of the enemy is all the time, and to be able to pass that information from place to place and level to level. It's a tremendous power in that particular potential, in that particular technology. It's also very hard. The soldiers there today when you look them in the eye will tell you: "This is tough. This is hard work." But the potential is so great, that we've got to stay the course. When I was there in the division [tactical operations center (TOC)], they showed me an icon, it was a fuel tanker and they knew exactly where it was. And they were able to send that fuel tanker a message that said don't go to C company, go to D company and top them off instead of C company. Now I've been in a lot of TOCs in my life, and most of the time we had no idea where the fuel tanker was. We always said—the question was do we send the first-sergeant and a party out to try and find the fuel tanker or not? Just think about the power of that single event and how that changes how you do business. It's like football and having someone in the enemy's huddle. You know what play they're going to run, what defense they're going to run. You can do things vastly different. There is tremendous power in information-age technology.

What we have to do is develop that with Task Force XXI. We don't have the organization right. We don't yet really know how to train it. We don't know the tactics, techniques, and procedures that we'll need for that. And we don't really know how to leverage that technology, because what I don't want to have happen is for everybody to just pile on more information at every level. That would be the worst thing we can do with that. So we've got to sort all that out, and Task Force XXI is doing a great job doing just that. I am convinced that there is enough potential in there that we'll stay the course. We need to test it and we will. We'll take it to the National Training Center in March and April of [1997], run it up against the opposing force, get beat a couple times, learn our lessons, and we'll learn what the potential is and then we'll invest in those technologies that provide us the best payback as quickly as we possibly can.

At the same time we formed that Task Force XXI, the intellectual focus of the Army is focusing on something called the Army After Next. The Army After Next is a different type of force. It's not a product-improved force, and I can't tell you the details of it. I can tell you certain characteristics about it. And it's going to be totally different than what the Army XXI is all about. I'll talk to that in just a minute, but we need to continue to develop that objective force, the Army After Next, but we cannot lose focus on Army XXI, because there's so much we don't know about information technology. And the only way we're going to find that out, is to be able to test it on Fort Hood and throughout the United States Army.

... [The Army After Next] is, as I said, a different type of Army. We don't know how it will be configured, or how it will be organized yet. We do know that we want greater lethality in this Army. Much more lethal. We want to make sure that we have greater strategic and operational mobility to be able to move this Army around the world, get it into the global village as quickly as possible and move it on the battlefield, wherever it needs to be very quickly. We want it logistically unencumbered. We know that we cannot continue to have the iron-mountain behind each unit. We have to break that cycle and we have to move from a supply-based logistical system where we build up the iron mountain and everybody had lots of supplies, to a transportation-based logistical system which means we're going to move equipment there when you need it but you're not going to get a whole lot more than you need. There are some fundamental changes in our culture that have to take place before that can happen.

And so that's why you have to go through Army XXI to do that type of thing. But I will tell you that unless we're able to solve this problem we're not going to be able to come up with the Army After Next model that we would want. It's got to have greater versatility [than Army XXI]. We want it to narrow the gap between heavy and light. We're interested in any technology that makes the light more lethal, and makes the heavy forces more strategically mobile. We're interested in any technology that helps us in terms of lethality, and non-lethal means. We see a need to be able to go quickly between non-lethal and lethal means in the global village. When you look at the projections in terms of organizations and that type of thing, you're going to have to have non-lethal means available to you, and of course it's got to have expansibility, and that means better use of America's Army. The total integration, the seamless blend of Active component, United States Army Reserve, and Army National Guard.

FUTURE WEAPONS

Developing the weapons of the future was a frequent topic of discussion and some speculation. Secretary Pace devoted a large portion of his comments to the graduates of 1952 to materiel development.

In the field of materiel the Army today is facing some of the greatest problems which have ever confronted it in its history. A single look at the enormous and complex task which we have and will have in the area of procurement and supply is enough to prove the fact that in this field we need special leadership, and to an extent which has never been equaled in the past. In making this statement I am not thinking of our current needs for this year or next year. But for the long pull which lies ahead of us in the period in which we must bear the responsibility for leadership in a world threatened by communism. This continuing responsibility will demand that Army personnel who are engaged in the work of logistics have the best training and experience that we can possibly give them. It will demand that they become much more familiar with the capacities and techniques of American industry and labor than is the case at present.

The Army of the future will have to develop soldiers who can present the Army's needs to industry and labor, and who at the same time will have an appreciation for industry's problems in meeting these needs. We will have to develop more leaders, who know where to look for help we will need from production men. And just as important, will know how to use that help intelligently and effectively when it is given to us. For this reason, I feel that it is just as important for us to arrange for many of our future leaders to get training from firms such as General Electric, Dupont, or General Motors as it is to ensure they serve tours of duty in Europe or the Far East. Compare for a moment the responsibility that is bore by the G-4 of the Department of the Army with that of an executive of private industry. The job that he handles cannot be compared exactly with any which is done in private industry. However in sheer size alone it is apparent that the work he supervises is equal to that done by three or four of the largest private corporations in America. This alone should make it apparent that in this type of work we need a man of outstanding competence. Training this kind of man and all of the men that will work with him in positions requiring great responsibility and great skill is a problem to which the Army must devote much more time, attention, and work in the future than it has in the past.

... In an attempt to reduce even further the number of men who die from wounds, the Army and the other services in Korea have been experimenting with an idea that is almost as old as warfare itself: Body armor. As you know this armor consists of a light vest, made of nylon layers. It is designed primarily to stop shell and grenade fragments from causing serious wounds in the chest and stomach, where more than half of the fatal battlefield wounds occur. Experiments in Korea indicate the vest is more than worth the extra eight pounds which the soldier wears when he carries it. As one infantryman put it "I'd rather wipe sweat than blood."

General Johnson highlighted one of the difficulties of developing future weapons in December 1967.

> And we're always confronted with lead times. The fact that we get something into an appropriations bill doesn't help us very much, because we're still two and a half, to three, to four, and even five years away from something with which to work. So the man—and this will be you—the man who has to make forecasts needs a good database from which to operate, and he needs a very clear crystal ball, just as clear as he can make it, to visualize what might confront us in the years ahead.

In March 1974, General DePuy used the lessons learned from the Arab-Israeli wars to discuss Army equipping and modernization.

> For the next 10 years, the second ten years of your Army life, or approximate, you're going to be equipped with M-60 tanks. If we go to war that's what you're going to fight with. Maybe M-60 A3s but they'll still be M-60s. And if you fight Syrians, Egyptians, Russians, you name it, Rumanians, Bulgarians, Germans, East Germans, they're all going to have T-55s and T-62s. So you're not going to have any advantage. So the difference is going to be training. It's going to be: Who are the best gunners? Who's got the best tank commanders? Whose platoons are trained best?

> …We say that we are not willing to advocate buying for the United States Army a mechanized infantry combat vehicle that can be destroyed by the [Soviet] BMP [infantry fighting vehicle] alone, because psychologically it would drive it from the battlefield. Psychologically it would change our tactics. What it would do is it would force us to dismount, and use the mechanized infantry combat vehicle as a truck, the way we've used the M113 [armored personnel carrier] in mechanized infantry divisions for years. We have had to agree [at Fort Knox and Fort Benning] on the doctrine and the concept, on the tactics and techniques. And having done that, then we can say that what we want is the smallest caliber weapon that can fire an [armor piercing] round that will outrange the BMP so that it will not be driven from the battlefield, so that it can perform its primary mission. And we want the smallest round, because every time you go up 5mm you double the bulk. It's an exponential increase in size and weight. So we want the smallest one we can get. Down around 25mm if we can get it, because that means we can have twice as much ammunition stored in that combat vehicle.

> …I think that the extensive enemy air defense system revealed in the Arab-Israeli war has had many effects on the Army in its thinking already. One that I know it has already had, is it has resurrected the long dormant interest in drones, now called RPVs…We're several years, I think, from drones. Some of the drones are intelligence collectors. Some of the drones, the artillery hope, for example, can be also target locators and laser target designators. And if you could combine that with the cannon-launched guided projectile, which is a laser seeker with a high first-round hit probability you've probably got a very

interesting weapon system. The expense is going to be high, and that cost-effectiveness analysis that I talked about is going to show you that for a while you probably can't prove cost-effectiveness.

DePuy returned in 1975, still discussing modernization.

Air Defense: Well, we just need a lot more of it and we need it fast. And we need it mobile, and we're working on that and we're way behind power curve. I would say of all the areas of vulnerability we have, that is the most serious. For years air defense in the United States Army languished in the background. Only some zealots down at Fort Bliss were interested. Why? Because the United States Air Force had provided us in three wars in a row total air superiority. We didn't need air defense. There isn't a man in this room that's probably been bombed. Not a man out there has probably ever been strafed. May even be people out here who have never seen an enemy aircraft. You're going to see a lot of them. And we're not equipped to cope with them. So if there's one thing you'd better pay attention to fellas, is this.

…We're working on RPVs, Remotely Piloted Vehicles. We went at it by saying "We don't know anything about them, we want to play with some and learn about them." We were very wise because the first ones we bought flew upside-down. You know if we'd written the specifications right off the bat that's what we would have gotten.

…I think what we may find, is if XM-1[tank] costs as much as it undoubtedly will, a million dollars in the dollars of the year in which we buy it, which will be about $500,000 in the money of the year we started developing it, we may have to train and handle tank crews almost like we handle air crews. I have a feeling we're getting close to that point. Whether we're there or not, well obviously we're not there, we're not doing it. I think the Army has to seriously consider that. I think the power of the weapon, the intricacy, the skill required, the maintenance required for the fire direction equipment in it, fire control equipment, may require a dedicated crew, somewhat along the lines that the Air Force for example, or the Navy, have for fighters. Now that sounds like a long way out, we're probably not going to get there for a while. We're not going to have XM-1s for a while. But don't you young fellas discard the possibility that you may have to do that. That's going to be after my time. But it's not going to be after your time, so keep that one in mind.

The next year DePuy looked even farther into the future.

You know, you can turn a radar up in the air and you can see both your friendly aircraft and your enemy aircraft. So why not fight the battle that way? Why not cause collisions at the right place? We not only can't see the enemy, we can't see ourselves, you know, most of the time. You ask a corps commander or a division commander where the platoons of his unit are and where the enemy is right there on the front and nobody knows, except the guy right there. Now, given jamming and given long-range direction finding and given long-range weapons that are pretty accurate and [Soviet] FROGs [rocket artillery] and you name it, the one thing we can't afford is to have that great pulsating electric brain somewhere upon which everything depends. Sometimes the battle goes a lot better because they don't know what's going on at corps. [Laughter]

That's not that that's what we want. But what we have is a highly decentralized series of what I like to call combat systems: [Command Posts], artillery systems, air defense systems, electronic warfare systems. All systems use combat information, and all that combat information should be given to intelligence folks to assemble and figure out what is going on.

…The two highest priority requirements for a modern army that has to fight against a superior enemy is to be able to see over behind the enemy front lines far enough so you're never surprised. So when he moves a large force to some part of the battlefront you will be there. That's first priority, and second priority, and I would even say of equal priority, is secure, unjamable communications so that you can move your units to that point. I would bet you that if you had a seminar with the leaders of any modern army they would say those two things have just got to be on top. This is assuming, of course, that you've got tank battalions, artillery, and so on to fight. But the things we don't—we have those, but we don't have those other two. We have got to get them. All the discussions I've had with the German army, the British army, the Israeli army they all agree that that is the biggest problem we have. Where is the enemy—what's he going to do next and where? And how can we command and control not only our fast-moving maneuver units, but how can we bring to the battlefield all the combat power that I talk about in an environment of mutual interference and jamming and security?

Technically speaking both are receiving heavy attention. The Air Force has got drones, we've got satellite capabilities, the Army's working on RPVs, unfortunately our RPVs don't fly, which is the first requirement. [Laughter] But we'll get them to fly. They have lovely sensor packages inside, but they fly upside-down, crash into the ground can't be recovered. We also have in the [Single Channel Ground and Airborne Radio System (SINCGARS)] radios, essentially non-jamable secure communications, and about 1982, it's that far away, you young fellers will find it coming into your Army, both of those capabilities. Until then, you've got a problem to try to do both of those things with the equipment we've got, and that's tough.

…I will venture a prediction that 15 years from now there will be mechanized infantry fighting vehicles, probably called armored infantry fighting vehicles or even tank infantry or something we haven't thought of yet, in tank battalions that have the same vulnerability, no more no less, than the tank itself, that can accompany tanks across the open to the objective. And that there will also be mechanized infantry, for the other purposes I described, with slightly less armored vehicles, slightly less expensive, to do the other things I mentioned. And that the cross-reinforcement will probably then not take place so much at the tank battalion level, if you follow.

At their commencement, General DePuy spoke about the dramatic changes the Army would undergo during the careers of the graduating class of 1977.

Now you've been studying a lot of the weapons that we don't yet have but have talked about endlessly. But they really are going to arrive during this next chapter of your life. Many of them will arrive while you're in command. All of them will arrive by the time you go to the War College. Now, you've heard me before, saying that this is going to change things, not just in degree, but in kind. And that's true. There's no way I can put an exact number on what's going to happen, but surely your War College Army is going to have a potential on the battlefield at least twice that of the Leavenworth Army. And that is true whether you're in the artillery and all of a sudden you're dealing with computers at the fire direction center, computers at the battery, eight-gun batteries, artillery locating radars, laser designators, and all of that. Or whether you're in the XM-1 tank, or whether you're in the business of repairing all that, or new sets of communication, it doesn't matter, it applies to every branch. It applies to every family of weapon systems, and in some cases the order of increase is more than two. More than a factor of two.

...We no longer have the Army that the public thinks we have which is typified by the infantry battalion walking down the dusty road with rifles slung. But we have an Army, and we will have it in spades by the time you have your War College Army, that, like the Air Force and the Navy, can't fight without its machinery, and machinery that won't work without its men. Now our army doesn't know how to handle all of that. And when I say our Army I really mean your Army. In the next seven years that chapter of your life on which you are about to embark, your Army is going to try to learn what to do about all of that. I think we already know some of the implications, but we certainly don't know all because we've never been there. We've never had a weapons intensive army, except in narrow sectors of it.

...An Army is a strange beast, as you know. It's hard to describe, hard to manage. A multi-purpose, multi-cellular organization. It lives by adapting. And it dies by failing to do so.

General Vessey implored the 1981 graduating class not to fight change, citing an historical example to make his point.

You finish the CGSC course at an exciting time in the Army's history. There's more going on out there today in the terms of doctrinal development, equipment changes and modernization, organizational changes, training refinements, than I've seen in my forty-plus years of service. You have a great opportunity to participate in moving the Nation's armed forces forward into the future. As you do it, preserve what is important and useful from the past, but move confidently into the future. You'll find yourselves perhaps in a similar position to a naval board, when they reviewed the qualifications of a new warship over one hundred years ago.

The warship was the Wampanoag. She was commissioned in 1868. It was a steam ship. 4,200 tons, 355 feet long, very narrow of beam, heavy armor, heavy arms, and at 17 knots was the fastest warship in the world. But the naval board reviewing it, after a great success in its sea trials, decided it should be disposed of. And as I read one passage from the board's report, you can see what I'm talking about: "Lounging through the watches of a steamer, or acting as firemen or coal-bearers will not produce a seaman, that combination of boldness, strength, and skill, which characterized the sailor of an elder day. And a habitual exercise by an officer of the command, the execution of which is not under his direct eye, is a poor substitute for the school of observation, promptness, and command found only on the deck of a sailing ship." Now I'm sure that we could find the same sort of report about why we should not have gotten rid of horses and substituted trucks in the annals of the United States Army. But I hope as you go on to your service in the future you don't find yourself throwing out the baby with the bathwater, as did that board.

In 1986, General Vuono talked about the discipline of prioritization in the modernization business of the Army.

> What are some of the challenges of modernization? In my view one of the greatest challenges is to discipline the system. We must discipline it ourselves, or others will discipline it for us. It's a look at the battlefield from a combined arms standpoint, both jointly and a combined perspective, do a thorough analysis, and prioritize. The business that TRADOC's in, and my business, is laying out requirements. But it's also prioritizing those requirements. And it's making the tough choices between three or four competitive systems that you'd like to have. You'd like to have all three or four of them. The tough choice is which gives you the greatest payoff on the battlefield from a combined and joint perspective? That's the tough call, because there's a lot of folks who become disciples for a system. And it's a great system. But unless we not only lay out the requirement in terms of making sense, and then prioritizing that requirement, making the tough choices, the tough trade-offs and then sticking with that, we're not going to discipline the system. And that's part of the challenge, but the biggest difficulty is we're not going to get in the hands of the force what they need to fight on the battlefield. So that's a major effort, and has tremendous implications for the Army.

That same year, Vice Chief General Max Thurman channeled General DePuy as he discussed modernization in great detail with the students.

> Now people ask us "What did you do with the trillion dollars we gave you in the Reagan administration?" And I always say "Well, look, I'm the impoverished third service, the Navy and the Air Force got all the money, but with the small amount we did get we've been able to make some improvements." In 1980 we had zero M1 tanks in the field. And today we have 3,800 M1 tanks in the field. World's greatest tank, sees at night better than you and I see in the daytime. I took one of those tanks downrange at Knox about a year ago, shot four out of five rounds into a 2 meter by 2 meter target at two clicks downrange. That's not bad, 45 kilometers over rough terrain, that's not bad for a one-eyed, 55 year-old field artillery officer. If I can do that, think of what some 19 year-old kid can do with that hummer. Bradley Fighting Vehicle, we've got 2,500 of those in the field, we didn't have them in 1980. 790 Blackhawk [helicopters] in the field, didn't have those in 1980. 300 [Mulitple-Launch Rocket Systems (MLRS)], didn't have those in the field in 1980. And when you poop out two of these six-packs here 30 kilometers downrange, that's the equivalent of three battalions of eight-inch artillery arriving [time-on-target]. One of those [MLRSs]. And it's a three-man crew in there, and it takes 1,500 people to operate three battalions of eight-inch artillery. And for all you Ranger Infantryman, we'd like to get you in the follow shot of that and see how you like it. [Big laugh and applause]

> ... Now one of the fights we've had this year to sustain ourselves is the famous Bradley Fighting Vehicle fight. I was over in Germany on REFORGER and I got a call. I'd just happened to end up at Garmisch on a Friday night, [laughter] arduous duties required

that I go down and dissect the Armed Forces Recreational Center Project on foreign ground. Just happened to stop by the ski shop the night before and see whether or not the lifts were going to operate the next day. And there's the nice gentle falling of snow, and my horse holder [aide] came in the next morning at 6:30 and said "Hey, boss, we're going back to Washington." I said "Is that right?" That's Saturday morning. I said "Is that right, we're going to do that right after a ski?" He said "No, you're going to testify on Tuesday." And I said "What am I testifying on?" He said "Well, you're testifying on the Bradley." And I said "In that case get the car." So the car rolled up and Saturday morning I pulled out and bade fond farewell to the falling snow at Garmisch, and I headed back to go over and testify about the Bradley.

Here's the Bradley Fighting Vehicle. It has a range, with the 25mm down here all the way to the ellipse [using a map of Washington D.C. to describe capabilities-garnering laughter from audience]. Read that 2,000 meters against the Soviet BMP, and it has a range all the way down to Memorial Bridge with the TOW, 3,750 meters. Meanwhile there are people telling us we have to go back to the M113. Which has a range of a .50 caliber against a BMP of all of 300 meters, and with a Dragon on board it's got the capability to go all the way here to the L'Enfant plaza. Now I thought for a moment of putting the Bradley over here [putting Congress in the Bradley's firing range fan], but the better part of valor told me no, I'll leave it on this side. The argument is this: We built the Bradley to sustain a shot profile of 14.5mm bullets, 155mm overhead ammunition, and land mines. And then the question came up is "Listen. What we'd like for you to do is take the Bradley and we would like for you to fire a 120mm tank round at it and see whether or not anything would be damaged." [Laughter] And we said "Yeah, sure enough, it would probably deadline it." [Laughter] And they said "Well, let's actually see that happen." So we're actually doing that.

Now you may think that's a little bit far-fetched, but I'm telling you that's what the issue is. And when I got over to Congress on the second three-hour testimony that I gave there, I suggested that I would like to be present when they put an F-16 at the end of the runway at Andrews Air Force Base and take a Sidewinder at it. [Laughter] Do I have any Air Force officers in the crowd? Is there a chance that a sidewinder is liable to deadline an F-16 parked at the end of the Andrews Air base runway with the engines running? Okay. Don't laugh now, any Navy guys in here? I asked to be invited to witness the firing of torpedoes at the Ticonderoga-class cruiser that would be an event on Chesapeake Bay and see whether or not it would do any damage. Chances are it would. Now that is the argument, troops. That is the argument. And so what I'm telling you is, we tried to make horse sense out of all of that. Now let's take another look at the shot lines. We tried to make some horse sense out of it, and the Senate has ratified 720 and the House has ratified 593 of those, so we will be perfectly alright. Meanwhile we will continue to shoot 120mm rounds at the front end, RPG-7s at the side and the rear, and we'll shoot TOWs through the rear door, and we'll shoot TOWs in the side, right in the chops here on the Bradley sights there for the TOW.

It's exciting stuff. What I'm telling you is that stuff is here to stay, so all you Navyphiles and Air Forcephiles get used to it, because we'll do more of the same. Now have we learned anything in all of this? Yeah we have. We really have learned a lot about it, and we will do better. And it's amazing if you go through this process will we be able to have a more survivability-related vehicle than we had before and the answer is yes. But I want to tell you this is the world's finest fighting vehicle today. Because I'll tell you what. It follows maxim number one, which is kill the other S.O.B. before he kills you. Okay? And this thing operates at 3,750 meters with a TOW. And no other vehicle in the U.S. inventory, or anybody else's inventory, operates with that with the level of protection that it already has. But we'll continue to do that. But I'm just telling you you have to continue the fight in order to get the resources in order to have the operational art come alive.

In looking at bringing on the new equipment, we also had the problem of sustaining it once we bring it in, so that we can make sure we get the very best out of our sustainment capabilities. And that includes host nation support in our lines of communication-based development and the like, all these things get into how do we sustain our equipment not only with people but with spare parts.

To give you some notion about that, in fielding our equipments we had to stop the fielding of the Squad Automatic Weapon, for example, because we didn't have enough ammunition. I was chairing one of these Functional Area Analyses and I said "How much ammo have we got for the SAW?" And they said "Well, we've got three days worth." Now can you imagine all the troops going into a contingency situation, 82d or 101st or whatever, and saying, three days after we go into the fight, they say "Gee whiz, throw down your weapons and bring in M-16s"? Because you don't have enough ammo. So we had to stop fielding until we could ratchet up the ammo…On the M1A1 tank we were taking a review of that about a year and a half ago, and I said "Tell me how many days of ammo you'll have when the first tank battalion reaches the field?" Answer is 54 days. "What happens when get the second battalion in the field?" Answer was 32 days. "What about the third battalion?" "Well, then you're down to 17 days." So we said turn up the Bunsen burner underneath the production base. We want 60 days' worth of ammo, 120[mm], for each one of the tank battalions when it's fielded, so that we have a substantial amount of ammunition on site. Because obviously shooting the 105 ammo in a 120[mm] tank gun causes a great deal of clatter as it goes down the gun barrel. [Big laugh]

… So sustainment is one of our critical ingredients, but that has also brought up a very interesting dichotomy. The M1 tank, we've said look, we'd like to have a goal of 320 hours mean miles between failure, and we're actually demonstrating 400 miles on mean miles between failure. And we want a gun tube that will fire 1,000 rounds, and we've demonstrated that. And we said "look, we'd like to have a goal of 2,000 miles of track, and we've only demonstrated that. And that is a heavy O&S cost burden during peacetime. But then you say "But the wartime life is how many miles?" Substantially less than that. So we've sort of uncovered a dichotomy between peacetime O&S rates and wartime survival rates. What should the power pack look like for wartime replenishment? It should look like a 500-hour throw-away, right? Then you take it out and throw it away, because there's no sense repairing that hummer because the tank isn't going to last that long anyway. So I'm just saying to you that we've uncovered some things here, and we're beginning now to take stock of, in our production base support business, how can we look at, for example, surging production from 24 months to 6 or 7 months so we can create new battalions, given the fact that all of our plant facilities may not be exactly right, may be short some component parts. We may have overseas some sub-tier vendors that produce parts that are in there. And the question is can we reduce our specifications based on predicted battle life in order to speed up production when we want to turn up the Bunsen burner as we have to mobilize for full production? So we're working hard at understanding that better.

In 1988, General Vuono described his recipe for modernization.

Another priority is modernization of the force. In an era of resource challenges probably the toughest priority to meet. How do you modernize a force so that you've got a capable Army today and a capable Army tomorrow? And why do you modernize a force? Well, you modernize it to improve combat capability, that's why you modernize. And in my view you're never going to stop modernizing. You're always going to modernize a force, because you always want to get that edge over a potential enemy, and you always want to take advantage of technological opportunities. And they're going to be there. And as we looked out and said how do you continue to modernize given resource challenges? Well first of all, you've got to have a modernization strategy. You've got to have a plan for modernization, and it's got to be tied to what gives you the best return for your dollar in terms of combat capability. Then we said the first point on that modernization strategy has got to be a concept. A concept of what it is you want the particular system that you're trying to develop to do on battlefield. So that's tied to your long-range plan and looking out into the future as you develop your concept.

Then it says your modernization strategy has to have about three ingredients. First is, you've got to ensure that you're taking care of near-term requirements, that you're providing systems on the battlefield for today. Secondly it says that you have to product-improve those systems, that you can't just field a system and not continue to improve it. Thirdly it says that you've got to reach out and push the research and development tech base, so that you are stretching them so they can produce for you the system that you need based on how you see yourself fighting fifteen years from now. And then you have to do that with the resource available, and you've got to make some tough calls on that. One of the things you do is say "Alright, I'm going to prioritize my fielding. And everybody is not going to get everything." And you're going to do it based on who is going to the fight first. And then it says that you're going to make some tough choices on exchange of equipment. And you're going to retire and get out of the force some of the older things that don't give you quite the payoff that the new equipment does. Those are tough decisions that you have to make, but those are decisions you must make if you want to modernize the force.

Which programs do you prioritize and which do you do first? And you do that based on where your capabilities are most limited, and where your enemy's vulnerabilities are the greatest. Now what are the challenges in that? The challenge, I think first of all, is to stay the course with that kind of strategy. Second challenge is make sure you are making the right decisions on where you're putting your dollars. That you've done the work and everybody's focused on combat capability. And then thirdly, that you are pushing not only near-term capability, but you have set the course for the research and development community on where they ought to be putting their efforts. Not all over the map sheet, but a focused effort. And then finally that you do all you can to push 'O.P.M.' Which is use 'Other People's Money,' because the opportunities to do that are there. The opportunities to use other people's money who are working other research programs that you can piggy-back on, both within the government and out in industry. And it says you make industry full partner in all of this. And you don't stand back from industry because we've had a little problem on some alleged fraud within government. And you don't stiff-arm industry. You bring them in. And you say to industry as we have said, "Listen. We owe you the requirement, we owe you the very clear articulation of what we expect from that requirement, and then we owe you a dialogue of how you best can meet it. And then you owe us something, industry. You owe us a) A system that meets that requirement, b) You owe it to us on time, and c) You owe it to us at the reasonable price that we agreed upon." By the way, industry is very willing to sign up on that. But that's the challenge that we have in modernization. If we want to have the kind of trained and ready army tomorrow that we have today.

General Sullivan described the trade-offs to modernization in 1992.

Can we digitize the battlefield to put all of that [points at slide *Shaping the Future/Horizontal Integration*] together in a synchronized and focused way? Yes. Will it take resources? Yes. Sell off the World War III stocks. Get money from management efficiencies.

[*Slide: Modernization initiatives*] You're going to see a lot less modern equipment, although you wouldn't know that down at Fort Hood, Texas if you were down there with me last week. The tanks that the 1st Cavalry Division were issued in the Gulf are now being given to the 5th [Mechanized Division]. The troops are now working out with the M1A2. Kill 4 targets in 30 seconds. 4 targets in 30 seconds! That's sixteen tanks in 30 seconds. The problem is the targets don't recycle fast enough. Can we run simulations and reduce risk? About all you're going to see in the Army now, and I need your support on this, is—well you're going to see the AWS-M, a shoulder fired anti-tank weapon, focal plane array, the Comanche [helicopter], digitized tank, M1A2, we'll go for the M1A2. And the Armored Gun System, it's a 105mm gun on a tracked vehicle. And we'll do some other stuff. But we are trying to reduce the functional requirements, and we're trying to get out of this Mil-Spec business that has bedeviled us for years. [Points to *commercial vice military specification unless justified* bullet on slide]

That same year, retired General Thurman spoke about modernization through the example of the Army's unified support of the Big Five in the 1970s.

[*Slide: The Big Five...Cast in Stone Early 1970s*] And the last of these items that gave us the undergirding for providing the platform on which intelligent leadership can carry the fight was the bringing up of modernization of equipment. You see it proceeded on the grounds that good men needed great equipment in order to prosecute war swiftly and to truncate the duration of war. In 1978, The Big Five weapon system [M1 Abrams tank, M2 Bradley Infantry Fighting Vehicle, Patriot Missile, Apache and Blackhawk helicopters] was written down on a piece of paper as part of the strategic vision of the Army. It was signed out by the Chief of Staff of the Army and the Secretary of the Army, and low and behold the low-life major general or lieutenant general or assistant secretary of the service who tried to low-rate these five items...you were, on pain of death, executed.

Now, you say, "Well why did you have to write that down? Why didn't you just tell people to do that?" And the answer is, you see, we all change our jobs every couple years. Secretaries come and go. Officers come and go. Staff officers come and go. Secretaries of Defense come and go. Congressional people come and go. Staffers on the Congress side come and go. And if you're not careful, you'll look around and say "What are the equipments [sic] we're going to bring in in the next five years?" Ponder that for a minute. Let me ask you a question. Would you write down on a sheet of paper—this is a rhetorical question—would you write down on a sheet of paper and tell me what five items of equipment are going to be brought into the United States Army between now and 1999? The answer is there's no such list.

And therefore, when Congress goes around and asks people about various and sundry items of equipment, people say "Geez, I like the Comanche." Another guy says "No, I don't. I like the Apache upgraded." The next guy says "I like an M1A2 tank." "No," he said. "I like the M1A1, it's fine." Next guy comes in and says "Gee whiz, I'd like to get a PAC 3 missile." "No, no, we don't want a PAC3 missile, we want an [Extended Range Interceptor missile (ERINT)] and a [Terminal High-Altitude Air Defense missile (THAAD)]." Therefore, you come to grips with: You don't know what you're going to get. If you don't have this boiler-plated, and this is a deficiency at the moment in the Army, then you're liable to get NOTHING. Because the Congress is going to play both ends off against the middle, and you get nothing out of the schluss after five years of working on it. So these five things that I've just described to you were the strategic vision in the 1970s. Everybody under pain of death was sworn to get with it and ratify it. We all got with it willingly because the leaders at that time—Creighton Abrams and others— had passed out of their stewardship and others were taking on the mantle—but we all fell in behind these five items. To create a volunteer force, a total force policy, change the doctrinal set of the Army, bring on a whole new training paradigm, and to bring in modern equipment. And you saw the result of that, when we used all that on the desert floor.

General Sullivan painted a bleak picture of modernization in 1994.

[*Slide: 1988: We Began Process of Change*] We actually started back in '88. We saw Conventional Forces Europe and Conventional Forces Europe II and we began this drawdown. These divisions [slide shows seven] have gone away, I've got to take two more out—don't ask me [laughter]...'cause I can't tell you, although I'm about to announce them now that the election is over. But apropos of the election, now that we've got that out of the way, we'll get on with some stuff here. We have traded force structure for readiness, so I'm going to give you my assessment of readiness now before we're done here. Cancel the World War III modernization. We have essentially taken most modernization in the Army off the table. The only thing we'll get hopefully will be the Comanche—as a minimum I would like to get two flyable prototypes; the advanced field artillery system—need that, we're outranged by almost every gun that anyone makes, we need a new artillery piece in the United States Army; and a shoulder fired anti-tank weapon, product-improved existing capital goods is essentially what you would get from us. And we're taking no time out from readiness, although there are some real problems, and I'll show you my assessment in a minute.

In 1998, General Reimer explained the risk involved in modernizing the Army during the constrained resources of the nineties.

> ...we realized that somewhere along the line you've got to put money in the modernization account. If you don't do that, and somebody here in 20 years or 25 years will be the Chief of Staff of the Army and he'll say "Why didn't Reimer make that tough call over there to put more money into modernization so I'm not dealing with block obsolescence over here? So I have better weapon systems and better trucks, and I've got installations that run properly and that the infrastructure is in a little bit better shape?" So you've got to make the transfer. How do you do that? 14 years of declining buying power. The only way that we were able to do that was to take some risk. Take a little bit of risk in current readiness and move some money into future readiness to try and get the balance about right. Maybe we don't have it right. Maybe we've taken a little bit too much out of current readiness and we've got to go about and fix that. And that's what the September session in the [Senate Armed Services Committee (SASC)] was all about.
>
> It was important to go to the president first, before we went to the SASC, and talk about the readiness, because you always, I think, have to tell your boss what you're going to tell Congress before you go. And so we went to the president and we told him, basically, this is what we're going to tell Congress. All the Chiefs were there, all the Commanders in Chief, it was a very unified effort. We basically had the same thing to say. The different services had different viewpoints on it, but basically the thrust line was straight down the middle. And what we said is that we've gone about as far as we can with what we've got available. We've got too many requirements and too few resources. And we've got to plus it up. And so we went through that with the president. The president said "You make a compelling case. What you're saying is absolutely correct." He said "You've also got to understand that I've got to look at this from the viewpoint of what takes place in the total picture. There are some people that are talking about the global economy going south and we may need to do tax cuts. There are other people talking about improving education, improving social security." The point I'm trying to make here is that national security is a part of the overall issues that we deal with as a nation. And again, to get the balance right from his perspective and from Congress' perspective is very, very important. We then went to Congress, we told them, and basically I think you've seen the first part of the results. About $9 billion has been added to the defense budget in '99. Now I don't want anybody to think that solves our problem. This is not a one-year problem. This is a problem that we're going to have to have additional resources for some time.

General Wesley Clark relayed an allied opinion on Army modernization in 1999.

> At one of my conferences in [Supreme Headquarters Allied Powers Europe (SHAPE)] last year, an admiral from a navy that will remain unnamed stood up and asked a very pertinent question after he heard a U.S. Army TRADOC brief on Force XXI. He said "Why do you Americans keep bringing in all this new technology and forcing us to keep up? Why don't you just stay where you are, you're plenty good enough now?" It's a very important question. But of course, technology keeps moving. And I think it took us over a year, but I think we won that dialogue inside the alliance, and everybody understands it.

FUTURE PREDICTIONS

Many of the speakers made general predictions about the future, some coming eerily close to what would actually occur. Future Undersecretary of the Army, General Hugh Milton, provided a prediction of the length of the Cold War in 1951.

> No man can tell you what tomorrow's sun will bring forth. No man. At the same time we may remain in this state of suspense for one, two, or possibly three decades. And we must be ready to meet those opposing forces. Whether they move in upon us with the speed of light, or whether they are delayed through the thirty years, which General Eisenhower has mentioned. And the only way that our military commanders and leaders can see that we can possibly meet both of these demands is as I said before to have a strong, technically trained nucleus of a regular establishment, and with a mass of Reservists ready to step into the breach when and if that challenge comes.

In 1959, General Bruce Clarke predicted the type of wars the Army would face in the future.

> In regard to our concepts of security, we all, U.S. and allied officers, have a mission of informing our armies and our public of a current new danger: This is the danger of overemphasis on nuclear deterrence alone. It is a case of public attitude. An increasing number of our national leaders are becoming convinced that the foreseeable future will call upon us to fight limited, rather than general war.

General DePuy, in March, 1974 predicted a war against the Soviets, stating "In your lifetime in the Army, it's not going to be like that [referring to the U.S. ability to field massive armies]. You're going to fight outnumbered, in all probability, and maybe outgunned as well."

In 1994, General McCaffrey made some predictions about the future, one more accurate than the other.

> Let me mention Nuclear weapons. It's a subject that those of us in Army uniforms frequently forget to acknowledge as the principal defense responsibility of those of us in uniform is the deterrence of nuclear conflict. And I would argue that in the coming twenty years the principal threat facing all of our peoples, and I include the allied officers in the room, the principal threat is to in some way manage the proliferation of Weapons of Mass Destruction (WMD), whether they be chemical or biological or nuclear. That is the single central challenge to the security of our grandchildren. We're not doing too bad. It's a very unsettling era. It comes as a surprise to American civilian audiences when I talk to them, but we have already walked out of—the U.S. Army and Marine Corps—all of our tactical nuclear weapons. They are gone. They're back in the United States and will never reappear.

> Problems facing our regional partners are incredible. Latin American/South American partners don't face these threats. Essentially, with the exception of Cuba—which is on its final months or years of an implosion of a failed system—with the exception of Cuba, as you look towards the Americas you see unbroken political democracy.

In 1999, General Schoomaker came very close to predicting the events of September, 2001.

> [*Slide: Compelling reasons for change: Future Operating Environment, Impact of Technology, Changing Conventional Force Capabilities, Wild Cards*] I want to transition now a little bit and talk about something I think is very, very important, not only from the [Special Operations Forces] perspective, but from your perspective as we go forward. And I would venture to say that most of what I would say about this puzzle chart here is not news to the people that are in this room. But it is difficult, in most cases, for senior leadership to come to grips with it. Because it is so different from the way most of us grew up. My early days in the Army, not unlike the early days of most of the senior leadership, was all focused on things like the former Soviet Union. And I happened to be an armored cavalryman when I first entered the Army, and I did tours on the border over there in Germany with the 2nd Armored Cavalry Regiment. Did two of them over there, looking over at Russians, looking at East Germans, looking at Czechoslovakians, and waiting for the big one. Same thing in Korea on our deals over there, same thing all around the world.
>
> That world is blown apart now. It's become trite to say but the two kind of poles of the superpowers and all of the controls and all of the certainty that existed with that tension that existed between those two poles is now gone. And the kinds of things that we are seeing now in the world are becoming less and less certain and more and more troublesome. So the future operating environment that we are in is a challenge. And it is highly unlikely that there are too many people out there that are dumb enough that want to go carrier to carrier, tank to tank, bomber to bomber, etc. against the United States, from the standpoint of the kinds of things that we used to think about. They are thinking about how to work against some very, very real kinds of problems that exist in a nation like ours, and like the coalitions and the societies that we represent in the developed world. And they are developing the wherewithal to make it very, very difficult.
>
> The fact is that our homeland, the continental United States, is becoming less and less of a sanctuary. And it is highly likely that we're going to see serious problems and threats to the homeland that are not going to end up coming on ICBMs and in armored formations. And there are many, many things that we're now having to deal with, with our military, with our national defense structure, that is not as easy to deal with, and is not as clear cut and certain as it used to be. So this future operating environment we're talking about here probably is going to involve a lot more conflict—a lot more of the conflicts that we're least comfortable in dealing with. The kinds of things you see on the streets of Somalia, the kinds of things you've seen in some of the small wars and dust-ups that we've been involved in, as well as the kinds of things you see in the Balkans. And probably not things in the main that are associated with what we would define as real war.
>
> ...Wild Cards: One of the realities of military organizations is that it strives to define itself in ways that in many respects are searching for a sense of certainty. And if you take a look at the way, just throughout history, the military organizations have operated, we are constantly writing doctrine, tactics, techniques, and procedures. There's nobody better than the United States Army at printing [Standard Operating Procedures] and printing books out of TRADOC that fit in [Battle Dress Uniform (BDU)] pockets with checklists and all kinds of rules and all kinds of things to help you. They're supposed to

be guides, but in many respects they become prisons. The problem is that as we drive ourselves towards excellence in that regard, we tend to lose the ability to see the broader, the peripheral vision kinds of things, and to lose some of the flexibility of thought that's required in this world we're moving into here.

And I would challenge you—and in fact I'll tell you something that [Army Chief of Staff] Shy Meyer—when I sat in this auditorium back in '82-'83, General Meyer, Shy Meyer, came up here and he challenged us when we were sitting out there to challenge the system. If you don't think it's right, or you don't agree, or you think it's dumb, you've got a responsibility to challenge it. The truth is, there's more knowledge sitting in these seats out here about this future operating environment in many cases than exists in the more senior leadership of our organization. And you have a responsibility to challenge, challenge, challenge, and ask why. And not to follow blindly and not to beat yourself to death to try and fit into paradigms that people want to put in little books that fit in BDU pockets. And that's just the personal little advice I have for you, you can take it or leave it.

There's some of you that won't agree with me and you're very comfortable with the status quo and kind of the convenience of it all. But I'm telling you, to be successful in the future operating areas and battlefields of this thing you're going to have to be very inquisitive. You're going to have to ask and challenge and do some things that are different, because we are going to be surprised. There are wild cards out there that we will not see through our intelligence, that we will not anticipate, and that will surprise us. And it's going to be our ability to be adaptable and flexible to apply broader principles to the solutions to these things that are going to be important to us. The challenge we have is not to be surprised by surprise. Sounds like a play on words, but not to be surprised by the fact that surprises are going to occur. And for us to make sure that we've got our feet up under us and are capable of dealing with it.

…We are very engaged all around the world, and we're very engaged and very proud of the degree with which we've developed our tactics, techniques and procedures and all the rest of it. One of the things that we shouldn't be surprised about is that there are a lot of people out there that are potential threats to us that are reading our books fast. And they're on the distribution list. And they're studying them. And it always reminds me of that scene in the movie Patton. Remember Patton at the battle of Kasserine and he hollered "Rommel, I read your book!" So it shouldn't be surprising when a force that is executing its doctrine to a 'T,' [trained rating] is operating in an environment, when somebody that's got less resources and less training and everything else, outmaneuvers and outsmarts and tears it to pieces. Even though we're executing it to a 'T.' It's just a little challenge we were talking about, you know you've got to be careful here, because this is a thinking person's game. And you may get credit in [the Battle Command Training Program] and [the National Training Centre] or some place for the perfect plan, for the perfect execution, but on the battlefield you've got to earn it. And the other guy's reading our books.

General Schoomaker was proven right in many ways on September 11, 2001, and in the years that followed. The United States and its Army changed dramatically, and a chapter in its history closed. As the country emerges from the wars in Iraq and Afghanistan, the Army will once again find itself in situations very similar to those that occurred between 1949 and 2001: drawdowns, constrained resources, dynamic social change, and mission uncertainty. Understanding how their predecessors dealt with these issues will help future military leadership successfully navigate these types of problems.

Epilogue

Remarks delivered by Secretary of the Army Thomas White to the CGSC class of 2002 on November 5, 2001

Let me first say that it is wonderful to be back at Leavenworth. And I have to ask, how's the best year of your life unfolding? [Laughter] I suppose the answer to that question depends on what the rest of your life looks like. [Laughter] But for us in the class of '78-'79—we were just over talking to the charm class, the new Brigadier selectees, and [General] Roger Schultz was there, who is the director of the [National] Guard Bureau, and he and I were in the same section. And we played on the soccer team together, which—we were called the Killer Bees. Didn't win a game. Not one. [Laughter] And they had just changed the intramural curriculum the previous year because too many people were getting hurt playing flag football. And so they decided the violence level would be lower if we played soccer, which meant that there would be this ball on the field, and none of us knew how to kick and we would just go around colliding with each other in front of our children and wives, and fights would break out, and we'd ultimately lose the game.

…About two weeks ago we had a ceremony at Fort Meyer at which I presented Purple Hearts to members of the Army General Staff. That hasn't happened in 226 years, I don't think. I also presented Soldiers Medals, and I presented valorous decorations to civilians for acts of heroism on the 11th of September. I also had the misfortune of standing by the bed of a grandmother who worked in our administrative operation on the Army Staff and she died of her burns, with her only sin being that she happened to work in the Pentagon. So that says—if you don't think about anything more than that—that says this is a different environment going forward than in the past.

…People. We are and did recruit to our 480,000 number at the end of last year. We had that number locked up before the 11th of September. We are off to a great start this year, but in my opinion the Army is not big enough. If you look at the Personnel Tempo, and you are all experts at this because you've been through the rotations, you've been in the trenches, you served as company-grade officers through the nineties, through the Bosnias and the Kosovos and the Sinais and the Koreas and the Somalias and everything else that went on in that decade. You know exactly what I'm talking about. I have built a case and the Chief has built a case that the Army of 480,000 end strength is not big enough to meet all these requirements that don't seem to be going away anytime soon, and keep us on a reasonable personnel tempo as we go forward. So the first challenge that we have to deal with is to make sure that we've got enough bodies to support this in a reasonable way.

The second thing in "people" to recognize, I think, is that we're in a bit of an improved position in looking at what's going on in the civilian economy these days with the biggest jump in unemployment the last 21 years. We are in a less competitive situation than we were, and that's a fact of life, it all comes out of the same personnel pool. So that is favorable. We are also doing things in the business of "Army of One" [new recruiting slogan] which seems to work. I will tell you I was the resident skeptic. I knew General Max Thurman very well, who had created the old jingle, the "Be All You Can Be" stuff, I grew up with that, but the times have changed. And I am absolutely convinced looking at the data we have on "Army of One" that that is serving a purpose, that people understand it. When I enlisted the last person that we needed to make our number last [fiscal] year, on the 1st of September, as a matter of fact, and we did a press conference in the Pentagon. A reporter asked this young lad what an "Army of One" meant to him. And of course we all held our breath to see what he was going to say. [Laughter] One of those Kodak moments was upon us. And he said "It means the Army values me as an individual but I have to work as a part of a team." I said "Yes! That's it!" [Laughter] That's it! So that's the people piece. The retention numbers are good. The Reserve components are doing well. But a lot of that has to do with how long this accelerated [Operations Tempo (OPTEMPO)] lasts, how long the duration of this campaign, particularly with the activation, the wholesale mobilization of both Reserve and National Guard components. And so this is something that we've got to be tremendously concerned about, and we are.

The other thing that helps us in the people business, and I'll talk about this a lot, is the Leadership that you bring. And I know a lot of people talk about that, but to me the clearest indicator is whether leaders are actually participating in leading, and whether they have degenerated into a bunch of spectators. Now you have now arrived at the rank, as most of you are majors, when the spectator disease sets in full force. And by that I mean when I go to a range in Germany, as I did a couple of months ago at [Grafenwohr], where I fired many times during my active days, and I find the tank battalion commander, guess what the first question I ask the tank battalion commander? "What score did you shoot on table 8?" And if what I get back was or is "Well, we didn't quite have enough ammunition" or "We didn't have enough range time" and consequently I was not the first tank down table 8, so that I would demonstrate to my people in addition to the fact that I'm a Lieutenant Colonel why I am in charge of this battalion, and that is I'm a competent tank commander. If I don't establish those credentials I guarantee you the gunnery in that battalion will suck, no question about it. Alright? So I am telling you, that as you get to be more senior, you go out as S-3s, XOs, and the typical things that majors do in our Army, and then you'll be battalion commanders, you've got to participate. That's the cornerstone of leadership. That's the simplest rule I know of, and every time I see it violated for whatever wonderful—I mean, I never missed a target while I was sitting in the range tower. I always saw it clearly come up, I always had the perfect fire command, and I always hit it square inside six seconds, no question about it. It's a little bit different when you're down range. And that happens to be why this business is fun. I mean, God knows we're not getting paid very much, so it's got to be fun, right? Otherwise, we wouldn't do it. We're all dedicated to our country, but we have to enjoy what we're doing if we're going to be any good at it. And the way that you enjoy what you're doing is you become a participant. And you lead from the front. And you establish for people why you're in charge.

Let's talk about readiness for a minute. Readiness is challenging, because I'll tell you right now we have a legacy force that is out there, we've got an interim force that we're bringing along, and ultimately all of you in this room that stay with it will see the objective force fielded. And we have to keep all three of those things going. And that means we will not spend a tremendous amount of money on modernizing and upgrading the legacy force. That's just the facts of life. And you have to figure out a way to sustain the readiness of those organizations, you have to figure out a way to sustain combat capability of those organizations, because in the interim period they are the bedrock of our capability.

Second readiness challenge: Homeland Security. I am the executive agent for Homeland Security for the Department of Defense. As I've always said, that must mean that Don Rumsfeld didn't think I had a full-time job. But, be that as it may, and I also do the Special Ops/Low Intensity Conflict only because there is a portion of that business that has to do with Homeland Security. So let's focus on Homeland Security. The way I divide Homeland Security up is two major tasks. The first is homeland defense. Homeland defense are those areas in which DoD, the department has unique capabilities to be brought to the table, where we lead the effort. And a great example of that is combat air patrols (CAP). And fighter CAPs, which [the North American Aerospace Defense Command (NORAD)] is running, over the last weekend because of the heightened awareness of possible attacks, over ten cities in the United States. Imagine the level of commitment from the Air Force Active and Guard components to support that. There are others, obviously maritime in conjunction with the Coast Guard. Those are unique capabilities that we bring to the table.

The second piece is all other that has to do with homeland security and that is what I call civil support to other agencies. Like support to Health and Human Services on biological attacks. And so as you take a look at that and you organize it that way, you come up with three principle tasks that must be done. Task one: Get the DoD house in order and organized to do this. I held meetings when I got the rose pinned on to work on this. I held meetings and sent out a broad-based email that said "Anybody that thinks they have anything to do with Homeland Security show up in room x and we'll talk about it." Well, only if room x was this room would we have had enough seats and spaces for everybody who thought they had a piece of this thing. So there is a real need to bring policy, to bring budget, to bring R & D, to bring health affairs, Reserve affairs, and roll that all up under what I have proposed to be a dedicated undersecretary for Homeland Security in the department. That's task one. And we're hard at work on that, that's going to require some legislation to get the undersecretary piece of it done. But you're going to need a person of that seniority because of the interagency activities associated with it. So that's step one. Step two is the war planning. We said in early September when the [Quadrennial Defense Review (QDR)] was published that Homeland Security was the Department of Defense's number one challenge and number one mission. And yet there were at least, when the QDR was published, four different CinCs that had a piece of this: [Joint Forces Command (JFCOM)] had the Atlantic Coast and the continental United States, Pacific Command had the West Coast, NORAD had aerospace defense, SPACECOM had cyber and info network, [U.S. Transportation Command (TRANSCOM)] had the transportation support of casualties and that sort of thing, on and on and on and on.

So there are two fixes to this. The first fix is to say on an interim basis we're going to tidy this up and pin the rose on people. JFCOM, for example, has responsibilities for both coasts now, and the continental United States for planning purposes. But we still have the split between NORAD and JFCOM between air and land. And this is the only AOR on the face of the earth where we do it, and I don't see any point in why we would do it, because it just creates a lot of complications. For example, 11th of September, we are dealing with the crisis on the ground, recovering bodies and trying to save people. There are helicopters overhead and on top of that there is a fighter CAP. The fighter CAP is under NORADs control, all these helicopters floating around are under God knows whose control, and there we are on the ground, and the question is "Who's the airspace manager?" Right? Classic question to be asked. We are sorting out on an interim basis that, but the real fix will be the Unified Command Plan. Changes to the Unified Command Plan that put somebody in charge. And I think that will be done by December.

Because once you put somebody in charge we can deal with a really hard question, and that is will we apportion dedicated forces for homeland security? We have never done that before. We have biological detection units in the Army, because the Soviets 20 years ago had biological detection capability and we thought we needed that capability on the battlefield so we stood up the units. That's why we have two of them in the entire structure. Two companies. We have never stood them up because we felt we faced an anthrax threat in the greater New York City area, or 50 other cities across the—so we have to do a threat analysis as a part of the planning process, and then we have to figure out what we're going to apportion and who it is going to be, because we have run into conflicts already. General [Tommy] Franks running the war, at least the international war, the war in CENTCOM, has a troop list and force requirements and obviously these get greater and greater as the campaign plays out. The same troop list is sitting there with state governors, under Title 32, activating certain portions of their Guard for state-level purposes. Good and valid security purposes, like security of their airports. Well, all of that stuff comes out of the one Army force pool. And the question is who makes the decisions, and who apportions, and given that we're going to apportion for homeland security, what should the structure look like? An interesting thing for all of you to think of. You see the Guard is already—and Reserves—is already heavily committed on the Title 10 [federal] side. As we speak, the force in Bosnia is the 29th Division, Guard unit from Virginia and Maryland. So they are not available, obviously, to Governor [Jim] Gilmore in Virginia to accomplish Title 32 responsibilities within the state. And now you get the feel for the complexities and the rub associated with it.

So that's Homeland Security, and as you spend this year out here and have a little time to think about difficult challenges, that is a difficult relevant security challenge that some of you might want to think about. That's readiness. And we have to do both. You see the rub is that we've never thought about these things concurrently before. It was always "Well, what's Homeland Security?" That means a forest fire in the summertime, so we send a couple of battalions to help out that. Or that's a flood on the upper Missouri, and so the Guard gets activated to go help state and local officials there. But we have never looked at particularly low-density, high-demand units and the fact that there would be a call on those resources at the same time. That's the challenge that we have to get after.

Last topic: Transformation. We are in an interesting position. If you were sitting here in 1973, you would have very clearly recognized the need to transform the United States Army as it staggered out of the Vietnam experience. And being a company commander during that period, I do mean staggered. We had a horribly low state of readiness, and we were retooling ourselves to say "The principle threat to the United States is no longer counterinsurgency. It's the Soviet Union, Central Europe, the NATO-classic: Central Fulda Gap battle." And having spent six years in Fulda, I was a product of that twenty years' worth of intellectual process in the Army. A lot of which was done right here. So compared to today there was an advantage and a disadvantage as we looked to the need to transform. The advantage that they had back in '73 was they knew precisely who they had to prepare for. And consequently battle-books and highly precise planning and the kinds of stylized decision-making cycles were classic to the National Training Center (NTC). And all of that highly detailed staff process was a product of that. The disadvantage was the Army started at an absolutely horrible state of readiness. And so we had to do little minor things like retake control of the barracks, because there were certain parts of the Army where the leadership was not in charge of the barracks in that period of our history. And get back to basic leadership. We had no [noncommissioned officer education system] whatsoever. We had no professional development for noncommissioned officers. Nothing. And so on and so on. So that was rebuilt.

The advantage that you have today as we launch into the transformation that [Army Chief of Staff General Eric Shinseki] put out two years ago, and thank God he did, is that we start from a much higher level of readiness than the Army of the 70s. We are the dominant player in the world in land power, number one. That's the good news. The bad news is the threat is far more ambiguous and far more asymmetric than we ever dealt with before. And that is the challenge we must address. And the 11 September attack brought that home in brutal fashion. We are talking about it a lot, thinking about it, but that has forced us to action.

In my opinion, the transformation course that we have laid down, to significantly enhance the strategic mobility, to beef up the firepower and the survivability on the light side, to make the heavy side much more transportable, and bring that together on an interim basis, and then use that interim basis not only to solve the near-term warfighting challenge of the [combatant commanders], but also as a stepping stone to the objective force. Because for the first time in our lives we will have something we can experiment with, so as bits and pieces come out of the tech base that we're going to want in the objective force, we can glue them on to an interim brigade, we can take it into the NTC, and we can sort out the [doctrine, training, leadership, organization, materiel, and soldier] piece before and we can use that to shape what the objective force finally looks like. All of that, and the objective force that we have fully funded in the tech phase, I think is dead-on with the security environment that confronts us.

And because we have the vehicle out there [the Stryker infantry fighting vehicle], we can add an extra interim brigade if we want because we've got strong congressional support, and we're going to do that, we're going to add a seventh [Stryker brigade]. You know we've got two at Lewis, four more are coming, we're going to tag a seventh on the end of it. And we can get support for that, we've got the tech base cooking, and so we can get more money for that to support that activity. We have a vehicle out there people can support.

And that brings me to you. We have no choice but to transform the Army, period. What made the last transformation work, what made it work, was that all of us who came out of Vietnam and were sticking around for the long haul, knew that it had to be done. And we were absolutely committed to getting it done. And that's what made it work. It was either transform or die, one of the two. Well, I suggest to all of you in this room that while we will have our normal lively debates about exactly how the interim brigade should fight and how it should work and what the right technologies are to pull out of the tech base, and all of those very healthy debates we classically have in our Army, [striking hand in palm for emphasis] you must absolutely support transformation as we have laid it down. And you must be advocates and disciples of that, and you must bring your intellectual abilities to it to make sure we get it right, period. And that means fielding the interim brigades on time, that means secondly getting this thing out of the tech phase and getting this fielded before the end of this decade. So as you look at the next seven or eight years of your careers you will be dead in the middle of this, and maybe the first objective force brigade commander is sitting in this room. And I will bet you a month of your pay [Laughter]— I'm hedging my bets obviously, right? But I will bet you that the first objective force brigade commander is taken on as a second command and was an interim brigade commander on the way up, because the style of fighting is going to be very similar. So that's my thesis.

Let me end by saying that we have an Army that is at war. We are at war. Think about that. And think about it in the following context as you go to school for this year. Project yourself forward a year from right now. November of 2002. And hypothesize that in November of 2002 there is another event, like the 11 September. Only this time it's not 5 or 6,000 Americans, this time it is 100,000 Americans. And think about the year leading up to that event, and ask yourself if you did everything you could, in what you were thinking about, in what you were organizing yourself, and the ideas you were putting on the table and the energy that you brought to the game and the discipline and all the rest of that, to mitigate somehow what had happened, and ask yourself if you're doing enough and if you're focused enough. The Chief and I ask that question every day, and every day we find a new raft of stupid things that don't matter one way or the other to achieving that goal of deterring that event a year from now, and we kill them when we find them. You do the same. I think that's the focus, and that's the mindset that we have to bring to these very challenging times that we're a part of.

...If I could change I would change places with any of one of you in this room and start it all over again. And go back and be a major and look forward to a squadron command and a regimental command, it was the finest time in my life. God Bless You from the Army.

End Notes

Introduction:

3: General Creighton Abrams was a 1949 graduate of CGSC and would have almost certainly been in attendance at this speech. Harold K. Johnson was an instructor at the college from 1947 to 1949 and might have been present as well.

Chapter 1: The Army

11: President Eisenhower, in developing a new strategy for the post-World War II world, wanted to balance a strong defense and a strong economy. He felt that the previous administration's budget deficits were largely due to military spending, and felt the Joint Chiefs were obstacles to obtaining a balanced program. He directed a high-level study known as Project SOLARIUM which eventually led to his "New Look" strategy. This strategy relied heavily on a nuclear deterrent and what some called "massive retaliation," and resulted in dramatic reductions in the size and budget of the Army and the Navy, and increases in the Air Force. (Rearden, 140-6)

18: The Army designed the Pentomic Division as a way to fight in a war in which nuclear weapons were used at the tactical level (as opposed to an all-out nuclear war). The design was based on greater depth and dispersion, and the division consisted of 5 Battle Groups (somewhere between the modern battalion and regiment in size), each consisting of 5 companies, with an incredibly robust complement of indirect fire units. Ultimately the design never became operational due to artillery and communications shortfalls. (Combat Studies Institute, 20)

21: According to Albright's memoir, she once argued with Chairman of the Joint Chiefs General Colin Powell during the lead-up to NATO intervention in the Balkans in mid-1993, asking, "What are you saving this superb military for if we can't use it?" (Albright, 182)

28: Douhet's quote from Command of the Air reads: "Nothing man can do on the surface of the Earth can interfere with a plane in flight, moving freely in the third dimension. All the influences which have conditioned and characterized warfare from the beginning are powerless to affect aerial action." (Douhet)

Chapter 2: Leadership and Values

53: Bradley's memoir, *A General's Life*, doesn't refer to a gap in the line at Mortain, but instead a weakness owing to the fact that it was the hinge of the advance. Upon receipt of intelligence of an impending German assault in that location, he moved the 35th Division and "called Patton to explain the transfer." (Bradley, 291-2) In a different account, Bradley is told about the weakness and vulnerability of the line at Mortain by Patton's VIII Corps commander, General Troy H. Middleton. According to this account, Bradley ordered the 79th Infantry Division into the open flank, and drove to Patton's command post that same day. (Whiting, 32-3)

59: These are the two follow-up questions to Secretary Caldera referenced on page 59:

> Q: Sir, you made a statement in your remarks concerning the perception that officers are always kind of looking toward their next job. And I guess my question was is that from the enlisted soldiers that have that perception? What is your perception of officer morale? A: I wanted to raise that topic with you of taking care of soldiers but I was

concerned about raising it because I didn't want to leave the wrong impression, that I think that officers are always looking towards the next job. The perception was, from enlisted soldiers, that sometimes they perceive that the officers are looking toward the next promotion or the next job. So it is really a cautionary, but I don't want to overdo it, just a cautionary note. Which is, you are all talented, able people and everyone has the responsibility of managing their own career and there's nothing wrong with aspiring to get promoted and be able to move up. But the challenge is really do your job well. And get promoted on the basis that you did your current job well, and that you took care of your soldiers as part of that job so that they had the resources and your support that they needed to be able to do that job, so I don't want to overdo it.

Q: When you tell us that some of their officers are thinking about their next job, what does that mean? Does that mean that they perceive that we are unwilling to take certain risks? And if that's the case, what risks do they perceive that we're unwilling to take? A: I don't think it is a question of risks. In fact, I met with a group of young company commanders recently and just asked the open ended question "What's the key to success in your current job?" The first answer was taking care of soldiers. I think the danger— and it's true not just in the military, it's true in every kind of profession—is thinking about the next rung on the ladder: How do I line myself up to be the guy who gets picked for that? Who do I please? Those kind of things where the energy is going in to thinking about the next thing, rather than the energy going in to "What have I got to get done in my current job to fill the expectations that I have of those above me?"...It's really a question of being focused on doing your current job well, including saying "These are my people. They are entrusted to my care. What are the challenges that they face? What are the problems that they face that I've got to draw out of them, because they're troubling them and making it harder for them to stay focused on their job during the course of the day." And I think that is a challenge, that this is a people service and you've got to be people oriented, and if you're not, maybe you've got to ask yourself whether it's really the right place for you.

63: Navy Secretary Jim Webb resigned in February 1988, stating that he could not support the proposed budget cutbacks of Secretary of Defense Jim Carlucci's plan to decommission 16 ships. (Healy)

63: Lewis Sorley describes a JCS meeting on 25 August 1967 where, due to recent testimony by Secretary of Defense McNamara, Chairman of the Joint Chiefs Wheeler proposed a mass resignation at a press conference the following morning. After a lengthy discussion all other service chiefs agreed. The next morning, however, Wheeler had reconsidered and talked the chiefs out of resigning. (Sorley, 285-6)

72: Lewis Sorley covers Johnson's son's West Point dismissal in detail. (Sorley, 245-6)

72-73: According to Section II of a 1976 special commission report on West Point to the Secretary of the Army, "19 cadets resigned or were dismissed for cheating or toleration of cheating in Physics and Chemistry" in 1966-67. 152 cadets of the West Point class of 1977 were dismissed for honor code violations related to an electrical-engineering take home exam issued in 1976. Not all were directly involved in the exam violation, but were implicated for other violations in the ensuing investigation. After much publicity and review at higher and higher levels, all were invited to reapply if they made it through the screening process of a selected committee, and 92 of them did, graduating with the 1978 class. (Hansen, 60)

Chapter 3: The Army in Action

78: The Siegfried Line refers to the fortifications constructed by the Germans opposite the French Maginot Line.

79: The Remagen Bridge was a railway bridge over the Rhine River 10 miles south of Bonn, Germany, that was seized mostly intact by the Allied Forces on March 7, 1945. It enabled the establishment of a bridgehead and the crossing of multiple divisions before collapsing March 17, having four days earlier been closed to all but foot traffic. Tragically, engineers were conducting repairs at the time, resulting in 28 dead and 93 injured. (Collins, 304-8)

81: Potsdam, in what would become East Germany, was the third and final meeting of allied leaders Churchill, Stalin, and in this case Truman, in July, 1945 (Truman having become the president three months earlier). During the meeting Churchill would lose an election and be replaced by Clement Attlee (both as Prime Minister and at the conference itself). (McCullough, 446)

97: The Gulf of Tonkin Resolution was initiated by the Johnson administration in response to a supposed attack on the Navy destroyer *Maddox* by three torpedo boats in the Gulf of Tonkin on August 2nd, 1964. The resolution from Congress gave the president authority to "take all necessary measures to repel any armed attack against the forces of the United States and to prevent further aggression." (McMaster, 121, 133)

123: General Shelton used to say some variation of "The military is the hammer in America's foreign policy tool box, and it is a very powerful hammer. But not every problem we face is a nail," which is itself a variation of an old proverb "When all you have is a hammer, every problem looks like a nail." (Marano)

Chapter 4 The Buck Stops at Fort Leavenworth: Harry S. Truman Addresses the Command and General Staff College

129: Truman's reply to Johnson's invitation to the January 1961 event states that Truman had spoken at CGSC before. There is no record of such a visit, however. (Truman, *Harry S. Truman to Major General Harold K. Johnson*)

129-132: All Truman quotes from the first portion of this chapter (up to the Korean Decision filming session) are taken from sound recordings of President Truman's 15JAN61 and 15FEB64 appearances at CGSC. These recordings are held by the Combined Arms Research Library archives at Fort Leavenworth.

131: For more on how Truman hated to profit from his association with the Presidency, see Miller, *Plain Speaking*, p. 201.

131-132: Johnson enclosed the money in a letter thanking the president for his appearance. (Johnson)

132: The Spouses Club President was Mrs. Robert C. Works. (Works)

132: The Spouses Club Program Chairman was Mrs. Betty F. Harris. (Harris)

132: Letters regarding Truman's acceptance of this invitation and subsequent cancellation can be found at the Truman Library. (Truman, *Harry S. Truman to Major General Harry Lemley*, September 30, and November 27, 1963)

132: Miller sheds light on Truman's aversion to backing out of commitments in *Plain Speaking* on page 41.

132: Details about this appearance can be found at the Truman Library. (Bland, Lemley, and Editor, "16-hour day…")

132: According to the Fort Leavenworth Information Office, the military members present at the Korea discussion were: Major (MAJ) William S. Fulton Jr., Lieutenant Colonel (LTC) Norman H. Wampler, MAJ Philip D. Fischer, MAJ George M. Shuffer Jr., Captain Boyd W. Leer, MAJ John H. Houghen, LTC Mack J. McCaughey (faculty), MAJ Lewis A. Pick Jr., Colonel Augustus T. Terry (faculty), MAJ Lewis L. Millet, MAJ Jack J. Isler, MAJ Dwayne A. Panzer, MAJ Fank D. Proctor (faculty), MAJ Karl F. Bennet, MAJ Jerome M. McCabe, MAJ William P. Junk, Jr. (faculty), MAJ Phelps R. Womple, and MAJ Lawrence V. Hoyt (faculty). (Information Office)

132: Background for the Korea discussion at Fort Leavenworth can be found at the Truman Library. (Unknown, *The Korean Decision* Schedule for Filming and Notes on Filming)

132-135: All quotes and content from the December 15, 1961 Question & Answer regarding Korea come from two recordings located in the Truman Library. (Truman, Korea Decision Sound recording excerpts)

134: Secretary of Defense Donald Rumsfeld in 2004 told a U.S. Military audience in Iraq that ""You go to war with the Army you have." (Ricks)

134: "Questions seemed to irk the president:" The existing recording excerpts have been reordered, and portions have been omitted, so it is difficult to assemble these questions in the order they were asked. It appears these questions regarding support and restrictions occurred primarily during the first half of the questioning.

134: "Ask him if he's still alive:" This line of questioning was pieced together from excerpts. The portion starting "I was not the commanding general in the field and that's his business" actually appeared on the tapes earlier than the portion that begins with the officer asking why his division was stopped at the 38th parallel. As the earlier portion was edited, it is not known with certainty if that portion of the answer goes with this question, but the author is reasonably certain that it does.

135: Merle Miller chronicled the morning of the Korean Decision taping in a possible draft page from his Truman biography. (Miller, *Possible draft page of Preface from "Plain Speaking"*)

135: Robert Aurthur gave his own report of the Korea Decision taping in Esquire magazine. This is a highly interesting and colorful account of the filming. There are issues with the timeline outlined in the article, as it doesn't mention the graduation address, and actually discusses some filming said to have taken place in the morning at the same time as the graduation ceremony. (Aurthur, *The Wit and Sass of Harry Truman*)

135: For more on Truman's fall and declining health, see McCullough, 983.

135: Davison's open invite is available at the Truman Library. (Davision)

Chapter 5 Photos

140: The 1972 cartoons were drawn by then-student Major Robert R. Matlick.

Chapter 6 Civil-Military Relations

141: The article Bradley refers to states that in 1961 Secretary of Defense Robert McNamara had about 1,500 DoD civilians under his direct control. Through organizational changes, the article contends that six years later McNamara had 67,000 under his control. (Stockstill)

146: Bradley told Johnson if he resigned he'd be "a disgruntled general, you'll be a headline for one day, and then you'll be forgotten. What you do is you stay and you fight your battle and you continue to fight it to the best of your ability inside." (Sorley, 182)

146: Louis Johnson's manner and the way he dealt with people troubled Truman and all who worked with Johnson. He shouted at generals, admirals, and other cabinet members, and was determined to reduce Secretary of State Dean Acheson's influence with Truman (both Acheson and Truman later concluded Johnson was mentally unbalanced). On September 11, 1950, Truman told Johnson that Johnson would resign and would recommend George Marshall as his successor. Johnson asked for a day to think it over, and then next day begged Truman to reconsider. He broke down and wept when Truman refused. (McCullough, 741-2, 798)

146-147: The Navy was angered over the cancellation of the Navy's new super carrier and their marginalization in post-war military planning that was focused on strategic bombing. They turned their wrath on the Air Force's new long-range B-36 bomber, as well as the integrity and qualifications of everyone (including the newly-installed Chairman of the Joint Chiefs, General Bradley, and the Secretary of Defense, Louis Johnson). In testimony before an investigative committee of the House Armed Services Committee on October 19, 1949, General Bradley refuted the Navy point by point and took them to task, causing one reporter to call it "one of the most extraordinary tongue lashings ever given to high military officers in such a forum." (Bradley, 507-512)

149: In May, 1971 Major General Carl Turner was sentenced to three years in prison for selling guns confiscated by the Chicago Police Department for his own profit. The former U.S. Army Provost Marshall and former Chief U.S. Marshall had 13 charges against him involving weapons sales, possession, and income tax evasion.

152: The Army, Navy, Air Force Journal article in question highlighted numerous areas reducing the attractiveness of a military career: "Lowered comparative standard of living…Lack of housing…Reduced commissary and post exchange benefits…Increased instability of assignment…Reduced medical and dental care for dependents…Violation of "contracts" by the Government…Blunderbuss attacks by Congress and the press…Indications of spite legislation." The [Representative James] Van Zandt amendment is described in Chapters 3 (page 84) and 6 (page 152). The Davis Amendment aimed to reduce rank in the Armed Forces, and would have the effect of slowing promotions. It is unclear whether this amendment was referring to Clifford or James C. Davis. (Editor, "Confronted With Critical Need…")

153: Saudi Arabian King Faisal bin Abdulaziz Al Saud was assassinated during a reception in his palace on March 25th, 1975 by his nephew, Prince Faisal bin Musaid Abdul Aziz. (Onis)

156: General Shelton used to say some variation of ""The military is the hammer in America's foreign policy tool box, and it is a very powerful hammer. But not every problem we face is a nail," which is itself a variation of an old proverb "When all you have is a hammer, every problem looks like a nail." (Marano)

159: President Harry S. Truman relieved General Douglas MacArthur as Commander of U.N. Forces, Korea on April 11, 1951. Among the oft-cited reasons are MacArthur's ultimatum to the Chinese, and his correspondence to the opposition party criticizing Truman's policies, some of which was read on the House of Representatives floor.

160: In the late 1960s, the United States Army began forming requirements for a helicopter to replace the UH-1 Iroquois, and designated the program as the Utility Tactical Transport Aircraft System (UTTAS).

Chapter 7 Politicians

171: Air-Land Battle was the name given to the updated U.S. Army operational concept first introduced by the 1976 edition of FM 100-5, *Operations of Army Forces in the Field*. This concept was the brainchild of the Army's first Training and Doctrine Command commander, General William E. DePuy, and was based in large parts on the lessons of the 1973 Arab-Israeli war. Along with the concept came new equipment, known as the "Big Five:" the M1 Abrams tank, M2 Bradley Infantry Fighting Vehicle, Patriot Missile system, and the Apache and Blackhawk helicopters. At its core, Air-Land battle represented a closer relationship between Army and Air Force (specifically the Tactical Air Command) operations and doctrine. (Herbert, 8-9, 68)

173: The Somme was a disastrous World War I offensive undertaken by the French and British against the German lines in July, 1916. British casualties on the first day alone were 57,470, including 19,240 killed. This battle is often held up as a prime example of a failure of planning and leadership. (Hart, 528)

185: In 1803, the Supreme Court ruling in the case of *Marbury vs Madison* asserted the power of judicial review, where federal courts could strike down unconstitutional laws. Judicial review had been increasingly accepted up to this point, but its status as the foundation of the Supreme Court's power was uncertain. (Rosen, 30-31)

186: The Marine Battalion Landing Team Headquarters in Beirut, Lebannon was attacked by a man driving an explosives-laden truck on October 23, 1983. The truck breached several security measures, entered the lobby of the building, and detonated, killing 241 Americans: 220 Marines and 21 Navy medical personnel. (Frank, 1-3)

188: On April 1, 2001, a United States EP-3A surveillance aircraft collided with a Chinese fighter jet over the South China Sea. The EP-3A was able to make an emergency landing on China's Hainan Island. The Chinese pilot and his jet crashed into the sea. The EP-3As 24-man crew was detained for 11 days before being allowed to return home. The disassembled plane was returned to the U.S. in July. (Editor, Current Events)

Chapter 9 Events of the Day

203: Schuman Plan for steel and coal: In 1950 French Foreign Minister Robert Schuman hoped to reduce tensions and build a partnership between France and West Germany following World War II with a plan for joint administration of French and German coal and steel production. (Corum, 63-64)

206: Lisbon force goals of 1952 were an attempt by NATO to establish the conventional force requirements to defend Western Europe. Although there was a great deal of economic friction and the NATO members never achieved the goals, this agreement was an important step for strengthening the alliance and allowing West Germany to rearm. (Kugler, 56-59)

213: In 1975 President Ford signed into law a measure that required the service academies to admit women beginning in 1976.

213: Don't Ask, Don't Tell (DADT) grew out of a 1992 campaign promise made by then-candidate Bill Clinton when he pledged to lift the ban on homosexuals serving in the armed forces. What emerged from his efforts in 1994 was a kind of compromise, where applicants for military service were no longer asked whether they had homosexual tendencies, but if such tendencies came to light or were demonstrated following entrance into the military, the individual would be subject to removal from the service. DADT was repealed in September, 2011, and gays were allowed to openly serve in the military.

220: Although it wouldn't prove terribly effective, the 1973 War Powers Act (or War Powers Resolution) was an attempt by Congress to reaffirm its (and *not* the president's) constitutional authority to declare war. It required the president to consult Congress within 48 hours of troop deployments, and obtain congressional authorization for troops in combat longer than 60 days. This resolution was voted into law by the legislative branch over a presidential veto. (Zelizer, 254)

223: In 1996 a major sex abuse scandal occurred at the Aberdeen Proving Grounds where drill sergeants and officers in charge of trainees were accused of inappropriate sexual conduct, up to and including rape. At least three were convicted and given prison sentences.

232: Spiro Agnew delivered a speech against television news in Des Moines, Iowa, on November 13, 1969. The focus of his comments was the negative ("hostile" in his words) reaction to a major address on Vietnam delivered by President Nixon:

The audience of 70 million Americans gathered to hear the President of the United States was inherited by a small band of network commentators and self-appointed analysts, the majority of whom expressed in one way or another their hostility to what he had to say.
It was obvious that their minds were made up in advance. Those who recall the fumbling and groping that followed President Johnson's dramatic disclosure of his intention not to seek another term have seen these men in a genuine state of non-preparedness. This was not it. One commentator twice contradicted the president's statement about the exchange of correspondence with Ho Chi Minh. Another challenged the president's abilities as a politician. A third asserted that the president was following a Pentagon line. Others, by the expressions on their faces, the tone of their questions, and the sarcasm of their responses, made clear their sharp disapproval.

Agnew continued for some time outlining his charges against the television news media, questioning their credibility, and challenging Americans to "press for responsible news presentation." (Agnew)

235: General DePuy is referring to the Reserve Officers Training Program, the Army Training and Evaluation Program, a Field Training Exercise, and the Return of Forces to Germany, an annual NATO exercise to ensure rapid deployability and readiness of units into the European Theater.

238: In October, 1994 two Iraqi Republican Guard units' rapid movements into Southern Iraq caused additional U.S. units to be alerted to deploy to Kuwait, but most of these units stood down when the Republican Guard redeployed north of Baghdad.

252: Master Sergeant Roberto E. Bryan was charged (and later acquitted) with executing a wounded Panamanian during Operation Enduring Freedom. (Savage)

253: In 1997 Air Force Lieutenant and B-52 pilot Kelly Flynn was threatened with a court-martial over circumstances surrounding an adulterous affair. That same year General Joseph Ralston had to withdraw his name from the short list of those considered to be the next Chairman, Joint Chiefs of Staff when he admitted he had had an affair 13 years earlier while he and his wife were separated. (Raddatz, 16)

254: The effort to root-out extremist behavior in the Army was prompted by the murder of two African-American civilians by two soldiers, both members of the 82nd Airborne Division at Fort Bragg, NC, who belonged to a Neo-Nazi group.

Chapter 10 Budgets and Drawdown

282: The Military Reform Act of 1986 created the REDUX retirement system as a way to encourage service members to stay in longer than twenty years by using a percentage system. This percentage began at 40% of base pay for those getting out at twenty years (instead of the normal 50%) and increased up to 75% for those staying in for thirty years. This system was amended in 2000, allowing those affected by it to change back to what was known as the High-3 system, or to stay in REDUX and receive a $30,000 Career Status Bonus at their 15th year of service. (Office of the Secretary of Defense)

Chapter 11 Predictions of the Future

287: In 2000, testifying to the Senate Appropriations Sub-Committee, GEN Shinseki stated:

> There is a shortfall today in our formation... And the shortfall I can best describe to you as in Desert Storm, 10 years ago, as Saddam began to move south; overran Kuwait City and moved to the Kuwaiti border; this Army deployed what it had and it was a brigade out of the 82nd Airborne Division. We flew them in there and put them astride a high speed avenue of approach that moves south into Saudi Arabia. We got them in there and frankly all of us held our breaths...because if the movement south by Saddam's forces continued we knew that the arrangement of war-fighting is not one we would have chosen—heavy formations fighting light infantry. For reasons we don't know, Saddam stopped. He stopped at the border and he stayed there for 6 months and that gave us time to reposition our heavy forces out of CONUS and out of Europe. And the rest of it is history. My operational requirement in describing the need for the interim brigades is to fix the problem that occurred 10 years ago [during Desert Shield, Desert Storm]. Today, if we were called upon to go anywhere else other than Kuwait, where we have pre-positioned significant resources, or Korea... we would be in the same situation in a break-away crisis. And that is, we would fly the 82nd light infantry assets in and then we would wait for the first heavies to arrive... These interim brigades are the bridge between the light infantry and the arrival of those heavy forces. To provide what the 82nd does not have today, mounted weapons platforms; the ability to move infantry tactically;... also to provide them a modest amount of assault weaponry;...This interim brigade will provide to the 82nd Div, or any light division that goes in first, that added war-fighting capability that fills the gap between the initial light infantry going in and the arrival, about 30 days later, of the first heavy elements. That's the pressure on getting a [sic] interim force stood up. (Shinseki)

Epilogue

325: The objective force that Secretary White refers to was the Future Combat Systems concept, which was cancelled in 2009.

Appendix A: Guest Speaker Listing

Speaker appearance dates are listed below. If the chapter text says a speaker appeared in a certain year, this appendix will provide the exact date. Speaking dates in italics were consulted but not used.

Abrams, Creighton 17 Dec 1965, 1 May 1974.
Ailes, Stephen 11 Jun 1965.
Bradley, Omar N. 1 Jul 1949, 27 April 1966, 16 May 1967.
Caldera, Louis 26 Oct 1998.
Callaway, Howard 8 Sep 1973, 16 May 1974, 6 Dec 1974.
Clark, Wesley 7 Dec 1999.
Clarke, Bruce C. 19 June 1959, 9 June 1964, *11 May 1972.*
Cohen, William S. 11 Sep 1997.
Collins, J. Lawton 17 May 1983.
Dean, William F. 2 Jun 1964.
Decker, George H. 16 Dec 1960.
DePuy, William 12 March 1974, 7 Jun 1974, 25 Mar 1975, 1 Sep 1976, 10 Jun 1977.
Downing, Wayne A. 24 Jan 1995.
Gavin, James M 15 Jun 1956.
Gingrich, Newt *11 Jan 1985*, 1 May 1987.
Haines, Jr. Ralph E. 4 Jan 1973.
Harmon, Ernest 26 Feb 1952.
Heiser, Jr. Joseph M. 24 Feb 1971.
Ignatius, Paul 12 Jun 1964.
Johnson, Harold K., 28 Nov 1961, 10 Apr 1962, 7 Jan 1963, 20 Dec 1963, *18 Dec 1964, 23 Mar 1965*, 22 Mar 1966, 13 May 1966, 21 May 1966, 16 Dec 1966, 21 Mar 1967, 14 Dec 1967, 12 Jan 1970.
Kerwin, Walter T. 11 Jun 1976.
Kissinger, Henry 17 Feb 1967.
Laird, Melvin 23 Nov 1971 (spoke at the college and at a dinner at the Officer's Club that evening).
Lemnitzer, Lyman 16 Jun 1961.
Marsh, John 7 Oct 1986.
Marshall, S.L.A. 18 Nov 1953, 3 Dec 1962.
McAuliffe, Anthony C 6 Jun 52.
McCaffrey, Barry R. 25 Oct 1994.
Meyer, E.C. 9 Aug 1979.
Miller, Jack 10 Jan 1969.
Millton, Hugh M. 14 Dec 1951, *21 Dec 1956.*
Montgomery, Bernard Law 8 Apr 1953.
Myers, Richard B. 10 Mar 1999
Pace, Frank, Jr. 27 Jun 1952.
Palmer, Bruce 18 Apr 1974.
Ralston, Joseph W. 7 Jun 1996.
Roberts, Pat 17 Apr 2001.
Reimer, Dennis J. 5 Jan 1994, 13 Sep 1995, 25 Oct 1996, 6 Nov 1998.
Ridgway, Matthew B. 19 May 1966.
Rogers, Bernard 3 May 1971, 13 Feb 1976.
Schlesinger, James 2 May 1974.

Schoomaker, Peter J. 6 Aug 1999.

Shalikashvili, John 29 Apr 1992.

Shelton, Henry H. 28 Oct 1999.

Short, Dewey 8 Oct 1953.

Skelton, Ike 16 Apr 1993, 7 Apr 1994, 9 Dec 1994, 4 Mar 1996, 12 Nov 1999.

Stevens, Robert T. 12 Jun 1953.

Stillwell, Richard 6 Jun 1975.

Sullivan, Gordon R. 26 Aug 1992, Jan 1993 (day unknown), 8 Dec 1993, 9 Nov 1994,
    2 Jun 1995.

Taylor, Max 24 May 1973.

Thurman, Maxwell R. 19 Dec 1986, 23 Sep 1992.

Trefry, Richard 2 May 1978.

Truman, Harry S. 13 Jan 1961, 15 Dec 1961, 15 Feb 1964.

Van Fleet, James 24 Mar 1953.

Vessey, John Jr. 4 Dec 1975, 5 Jun 1981.

Vuono, Carl E 3 Sep 1986, *24 Sep 1987*, 27 Oct 1988, 8 Jan 1990.

West, Togo D. 7 Dec 1994, 2 Nov 1995, 27 Oct 1997.

Westmoreland, William 9 Apr 1969, 4 Jun 1970, 5 Jun 1970, 24 Sep 1970.

Weyand, Frederick 10 Dec 1975.

White, Thomas 5 Nov 2001.

Zumwalt, Elmo 13 Mar 1973.

Appenix B: Speakers as Students: Who They Heard

The chart below attempts to show the cyclic nature of CGSC students being influenced by (and becoming) CGSC guest speakers. It depicts when some of the speakers highlighted in this book attended CGSC, and which speakers they heard as students. Contemporary Army leadership is included to demonstrate that the cycle continues unabated. For example, assuming General Johnson heard Omar Bradley speak in 1949, one can draw a line from General Daniel Allyn to Max Thurman to Johnson and back to Bradley. This list in not all-encompassing, as not all speakers from the book who attended CGSC are shown.

Student	CGSC Dates From	To	Speakers they heard
Johnson, Harold K. (also CGSC Instructor, 1947-49)	Jun 46	Jun 47	Bradley (as instructor)
Abrams, Creighton	Aug 48	Jun 49	Bradley
Rogers, Bernard	Aug 54	Jun 55	Palmer
Thurman, Maxwell	Aug 66	Jun 67	Johnson (twice), Kissinger, Bradley
Sullivan, Gordon R.	Aug 68	Jun 69	Miller, Westmoreland
Reimer, Dennis J. (also Aide to Abrams 1972-74)	Aug 70	Jun 71	Westmoreland, Heiser, Rogers, Abrams (74)
Clark, Wesley	Aug 74	Jun 75	Callaway, DePuy
McCaffrey, Barry & Ralston, Joseph	Aug 75	Jun 76	Vessey, Weyand, Rogers, Kerwin
Schoomaker, Peter J.	Aug 82	Jun 83	Meyer
Dunwoody, Ann (CG, AMC, 1st female 4-star general)	Aug 86	Jun 87	Thurman, Marsh, Gingrich
Dempsey, Martin (former CJCS)	Aug 87	Jun 88	Vuono
Allyn, Daniel (U.S. Army Vice Chief of Staff)	Jun 92	Jun 93	Sullivan (twice), Thurman
Ierardi, Anthony (Deputy Chief of Staff, G-8)	Aug 93	May 94	Sullivan, Reimer, Skelton
Piatt, Walter (Director of Ops, Readiness, and Mobilization)	Aug 97	May 99	Cohen, Caldera, West, Reimer, Myers

Appendix C: Speaker Biographies

William Gardner Bell's. *Commanding Generals and Chiefs of Staff: Portraits & Biographical Sketches of the United States Army's Senior Officer* (Washington, D.C.: Center of Military History, United States Army, 2010) was consulted for some of the information below.

Abrams, Creighton (1914-1974): Army Chief of Staff, 1972-1974; Deputy Commander and Commander, U.S. Military Assistance Command, Vietnam, 1967-1972; Army Vice Chief of Staff, 1964-1967; Deputy Chief of Staff for Operations, 1962-1963; Commander, 3rd Armored Division, 1960-1962; Commander, 2nd Armored Cavalry Regiment, 1951-1952; Commander, 37th Tank Battalion and Combat Command B during Allied operations across Europe in World War II; graduated U.S. Military Academy in 1936.

Ailes, Stephen (1912-2001): Secretary of the Army, 1964-1965; Under Secretary of the Army, 1961-1964; legal consultant, Office of Price Stabilization, 1951; legal counsel to American Economic Mission to Greece, 1947.

Bradley, Omar N. (1893-1981): Chairman, Military Staff Committee, North Atlantic Treaty Organization, 1949-1950; Chairman, Joint Chiefs of Staff, 1949-1953; Army Chief of Staff, 1948-1949; during World War II commanded the 82nd and 28th Infantry Divisions, II Corps in North Africa and Sicily, and First Army and the 12th Army Group in Western Europe; Commandant of the Infantry School, 1941-1942; instructor, tactics and plans at the United States Military Academy, 1934-1938, and the Infantry School, 1929-1933; graduated from the U.S. Military Academy in 1915.

Caldera, Louis (b. 1956): Secretary of the Army, 1998-2001; presidential appointment as Managing Director, Corporation for National and Community Service 1997; State Assemblyman, California Legislature 1992-1997; Officer, United States Army, 1978-1983; graduate of U.S. Military Academy, 1978.

Callaway, Howard (1927-2014): Secretary of the Army, 1973-1975; U.S. House of Representatives 1965-1967; instructor, Infantry School, 1951-1952; platoon leader, 17th Infantry Regiment, 7th Division in Korea, 1949-1950; graduate of U.S. Military Academy, 1949.

Clark, Wesley (b. 1944): Supreme Allied Commander, Europe, 1997-2000; Commander, U.S. Southern Command, 1996-1997; Commander, 1st Cavalry Division, 1992-1994; Commander, National Training Center, 1989-1991; Commander, 3rd Brigade, 4th Infantry Division, 1986-1988; White House Fellow, Office of the Director of Management and Budget, 1975-1976; During Vietnam, served as assistant operations officer and company commander, 1st Infantry Division; student, Oxford University, England, 1966-1968; graduated United States Military Academy, 1966.

Clarke, Bruce C. (1901-1988): Commander, U.S. Army Europe, 1960-1962; Commander, Continental Army Command, 1958-1960; Commander, U.S. Army Pacific, 1954-1956; Commander, I Corps and X Corps, Korea, 1953-1954; during World War II commanded Combat Command A, 4th Armored Division, Combat Command B, 7th Armored Division, and commanded 4th Armored Division; graduated from the U.S. Military Academy, 1925; enlisted in the Army in 1917.

Cohen, William S. (b. 1940): Secretary of Defense, 1997-2001; U.S. Senator (Republican from Maine), 1979-1997; U.S. Representative, 1972-1978; Mayor of Bangor, Maine, 1971-1972; graduated Bowdoin College, 1962, law degree from Boston University, 1965.

Collins, J. Lawton (1896-1987): Special Representative of the United States in Vietnam, 1954-1955; representative of the United States to the Military Staff Committee and the Standing Group of NATO, 1953-1954; Army Chief of Staff, 1949-1953; Army Vice Chief of Staff, 1947-1949; Chief of Public Information of the Army, 1945-1947; during World War II commanded the 25th Infantry Division in the Pacific Theater and VII Corps in the Normandy invasion and operations in Western Europe; instructed at the Army War College from 1930 to 1940, the Infantry School from 1927 to 1931, and West Point from 1921 to 1925); during World War I commanded the 3d Battalion, 22d Infantry in France; graduated from the U.S. Military Academy in 1917.

Dean, William F. (1899-1981): Deputy Commander, 6th Army, 1953-1955; during Korean War commanded the 24th Infantry Division and subsequently all U.S. Forces in Korea (1949-1950), captured during defense of Taejon and was a POW from 1950 to 1953, was awarded the Medal of Honor in 1951; Assistant Division Commander and Commander, 44th Infantry Division during World War II, 1944-1945; commissioned through ROTC at the University of California, Berkeley, 1923.

Decker, George H. (1902-1980): Army Chief of Staff, 1960-1962; Army Vice Chief of Staff, 1959-1960; Commander, U.S. Forces and 8th Army, Korea, 1957-1959; Commander, VII Corps, 1955-1956; Commander, 5th Infantry Division, 1948-1950; during World War II was the deputy chief of staff and chief of staff of the Sixth Army in the Pacific Theater of operations; graduated from Lafayette College, Pennsylvania, 1924.

DePuy, William (1919-1992): Commander, U.S. Army Training and Doctrine Command, 1973-1977; Assistant Vice Chief of Staff of the Army, 1969-1973; during the Vietnam War he was Assistant Chief of Staff for Operations, Military Assistance Command Vietnam and Commander, 1st Infantry Division; China operations officer, Central Intelligence Agency, 1950-1953; during World War II he rose through the ranks from lieutenant to colonel with the 90th Infantry Division, fighting in the European Theater, 1942-1945; commissioned through ROTC at South Dakota State University, 1941.

Downing, Wayne A. (1940-2007): Commander, U.S. Special Operations Command, 1993-1996; Commander, U.S. Army Special Operations Command, 1991-1993, Commander, Joint Special Operations Command, 1989-1991; Commander, 75th Ranger Regiment, 1984-1985; Commander, 3rd Brigade, 1st Armored Division, 1982-1984; during Vietnam was an Aide-de-Camp and intelligence officer with the 173rd Airborne Brigade from 1964 to 1966, and a company commander, battalion and brigade operations officer with the 25th Infantry Division from 1968 to 1969; graduated from the U.S. Military Academy in 1962.

Gavin, James M (1907-1990): Ambassador to France, 1961-1962; Army Deputy Chief of Staff, Research and Development 1955-1958; Commanding General, VII Corps, 1952-1954; during World War II commanded the 82nd Airborne Division from 1944 to 1948 and the 505th Parachute Infantry Regiment from 1942 to 1943; enlisted in the Army in 1924, graduated from the U.S. Military Academy, 1929.

Gingrich, Newt (b. 1943): U.S. Representative (Republican, Georgia), 1979-1999, where he served as minority whip and Speaker of the House; teacher, West Georgia College, 1970-1978.

Haines, Jr. Ralph E. (1913-2011): Commander, U.S. Continental Army Command, 1970-1973; Commander, U.S. Army Pacific, 1968-1970; Army Vice Chief of Staff, 1967-1968; Commander, 1st Armored Division, 1962-1963; Deputy Chief of Staff, Operations, U.S. Army Europe, 1955-1957; during World War II he commanded an armored reconnaissance squadron and served as the operations officer for the 8th Armored Division and as Assistant Chief of Staff, Operations, for II Corps in the Mediterranean Theater; graduated from the U.S. Military Academy, 1935.

Harmon, Ernest (1894-1979): Deputy Commander, U.S. Army Ground Forces, Germany, 1947-1948; Commander, XXII Corps, 1945-1946; Commander, 2nd Armored Division in operations in North Africa and Western Europe, 1942-1943, 1944-1945; Commander, 1st Armored Division, 1944; during World War I fought in the Saint Mihiel and Meuse-Argonne Offensives, 1918; graduated U.S. Military Academy, 1917.

Heiser, Jr. Joseph M. (1914-1994): Deputy Chief of Staff, Logistics, 1969-1973; Commander, 1st Logistical Command, Vietnam, 1968-1969; Assistant Deputy Chief of Staff, Logistics, 1966-1968; Chief of Staff and Commander, U.S. Army Communications Zone, Europe, 1963-1965; Executive Officer to the Chief of Ordnance, 1956-1960; Ammunition Supply Officer, Pusan Base Command, Korea, 1950-1951; during World War II enlisted as a private in 1942, was a First Sergeant from 1942 to 1943, and was commissioned as a Second Lieutenant in 1943.

Ignatius, Paul (b. 1920): Secretary of the Navy, 1967-1969; Assistant Secretary of Defense, Installations and Logistics, 1964-1967; Under Secretary of the Army, 1964; Assistant Secretary of the Army, Installations and Logistics, 1961-1964; during World War II served as an officer with carrier duty in the Pacific from 1944 to 1945; received commission through Harvard Business School Naval program, 1942.

Johnson, Harold K. (1912-1983): Army Chief of Staff, 1964-1968; Deputy Chief of Staff for Operations, 1963-1964; Commandant, Command and General Staff College, 1960-1963; Chief of Staff, 7th Army, 1957-1959; battalion commander and commander of 5th and 8th Cavalry during the Korean War, 1950-1951; battalion commander during the defense of the Philippines in World War II, was taken prisoner and survived the Bataan "Death March," 1942-1945; graduated from the United States Military Academy, 1933.

Kerwin, Walter T. (1917-2008): Army Vice Chief of Staff, 1974-1978; Deputy Chief of Staff, Personnel, 1970-1974; during the Vietnam War he commanded II Field Force and was Chief of Staff, Military Assistance Command, 1967-1969; Commander, 3rd Armored Division Artillery, 1961-1963; served as an artillery officer during World War II in Italy, North Africa, and France; graduated U.S. Military Academy, 1939.

Kissinger, Henry (b. 1923): Secretary of State, 1973-1977; Assistant to the President for National Security Affairs, 1969-1975; faculty, Harvard University, 1954-1971, where he served as Study Director, Nuclear Weapons and Foreign Policy, and Director of the Harvard's International Seminar and Defense Studies Program.

Laird, Melvin (b. 1922): Secretary of Defense, 1969-1973; U.S. Representative (Republican from Wisconsin), 1952-1969; State Senator, 1946-1952; enlisted in Navy in 1942, received commission in 1944, served on destroyer in Pacific during World War II; graduated Carleton College, 1942.

Lemnitzer, Lyman (1899-1988): Supreme Allied Commander, Europe, 1963-1969; Chairman, Joint Chiefs of Staff, 1960-1962; Army Chief of Staff, 1959-1960; Army Vice Chief of Staff, 1957-1959; Commander, 7th Infantry Division in Korea, 1951-1952; Deputy Chief of Staff of Fifth Army in North Africa during World War II, 1942-1943; plans and operations officer on the General Staff and at Army Ground Forces Headquarters, 1941-1942; instructor of natural and experimental philosophy at the United States Military Academy, 1926-1930 and 1934-1935; graduated from the United States Military Academy, 1920.

Marsh, John O. (b. 1926): Secretary of the Army, 1981-1989, holding the office longer than any previous secretary; counselor to President Gerald Ford, 1974-1977; Assistant Secretary of Defense for Legal Affairs, 1973-1974; U.S. Representative from Virginia, 1963-1971; commissioned through Officer Candidate School, 1945. Following his duties as Secretary of the Army, he served as the chairman for the Reserve Forces Policy Board from 1989 to 1994 and the DOD Quality of Life Panel from 1994 to 1995.

Marshall, S.L.A. (1900-1977): During the Vietnam war, as a private citizen, he participated in an Army sponsored tour teaching his after-action review techniques to field commanders; retired from the Army Reserve as a Brigadier General, 1960; during the Korean War he served a three-month tour as a historian for the Eighth Army; during World War II was an official Army combat historian, including chief historian of the European Theater of Operations; journalist, Detroit News, 1927-1967; during World War I served as an enlisted soldier with the 90th Infantry Division, and received an officer's commission in 1919.

McAuliffe, Anthony C (1898-1975): Commander, U.S. Army Europe, 1955-1956; Commander, 7th Army, 1953-1955; Deputy Chief of Staff, Personnel (later Operations), 1951-1953; Chief, Army Chemical Corps, 1947-1953; during World War II commanded 101st Airborne Division Artillery (1942-1944), acting commander, 101st Airborne during Battle of the Bulge when he responded "Nuts" to a demand by the Germans to surrender, commanded 103rd Division and 79th Division (1945); graduated from the U.S. Military Academy, 1918.

McCaffrey, Barry R. (b. 1942): Commander, U.S. Southern Command, 1994-1996; Director, Strategic Plans and Policy (J-5), The Joint Staff, 1993-1994; Commander, 24th Infantry Division during Gulf War, 1990-1992; Commander, 3rd Brigade, 9th Infantry Division, 1984-1986; Commander, 2d Battalion, 30th Infantry, 3rd Infantry Division, 1979-1981; during Vietnam, battalion advisor, Vietnamese Airborne Division (1966-1967), Company Commander, 2nd Battalion, 7th Cavalry, 1st Cavalry Division (1968-1969); graduated U.S. Military Academy, 1964.

Meyer, Edward C. (b. 1928): Army Chief of Staff, 1979-1983; Deputy Chief of Staff for Operations and Plans, 1975-1979; Commander, 3rd Infantry Division, 1974-1975; federal executive fellow at the Brookings Institution, 1970-1971; during operations in Vietnam he was Commander, 2nd Brigade, 1st Cavalry Division (Airmobile) and division Chief of Staff from 1969 to 1970, Commander, 2nd Battalion, 5th Cavalry from 1965 to 1966, and Deputy Commander, 3rd Brigade, 1st Cavalry Division in 1965; during Korean conflict he was a platoon leader, company commander, and battalion staff officer, 224th Infantry from 1952 to 1953, and platoon leader, Company C, 25th Armored Infantry Battalion from 1951 to 1952; graduated from the United States Military Academy, 1951.

Miller, Jack (1916-1994): Circuit Judge, U.S. Court of Appeals, 1982-1994; Judge, United States Court of Customs and patent Appeals, 1973-1982; Senator (Republican, Iowa), 1960-1973; State Senator, 1957-1960; State Representative, 1955-1956; during World War II served in Army Air Corps in China-Burma-India theater, attained rank of lieutenant colonel (later brigadier general in Air Force Reserve).

Milton, Hugh M. (1897-1987): Undersecretary of the Army, 1958-1961; Assistant Secretary of the Army for Manpower and Reserve Affairs, 1953-1958; Executive, Reserve and ROTC Affairs, Department of the Army, 1951-1953; President, New Mexico State University, 1938-1941, 1947; recalled to Army during World War II, G-4 then Chief of Staff, XIV Corps, action in Pacific Theater from 1943 to 1944, eventually achieving the rank of Major General; commissioned in the Field Artillery, 1918; enlisted 1918.

Montgomery, Bernard Law (1887-1976): Commander, NATO Forces in Europe and Deputy Supreme Allied Commander, 1951-1958; Chief, Imperial General Staff, 1946-1948; during World War II commanded Eighth Army from 1942 to 1943, and commanded all land forces during the Normandy Invasion in 1944; Commander, 8th Division, Palestine, 1938-1939; during World War I, with the Royal Warwickshire Regiment, was badly wounded in the First Battle of Ypres, 1914; graduated from Sandhurst, 1908.

Myers, Richard B. (b. 1942): Chairman, Joint Chiefs of Staff, 2001-2005; Vice Chairman, Joint Chiefs of Staff, 2000-2001; Commander, North American Aerospace Defense Command and U.S. Space Command, 1998-2000; Commander, U.S. Forces Japan and 5th Air Force, 1993-1996; Director of Fighter, Command and Control, and Weapons Programs, 1991-1993; Operations Officer and Commander, 335th Tactical Fighter Wing, 1981-1983; instructor pilot and flight commander, 414th Fighter Weapons Squadron, 1973-1976; F-4D pilot, 13th Tactical Fighter Squadron, Thailand, 1969-1970; commissioned through ROTC at Kansas State University, 1965.

Pace, Frank, Jr. (1912-1988): Secretary of the Army, 1950-1953; director, Bureau of the Budget, 1949-1950; during World War II he entered the Army as a second lieutenant in 1942 and served in the Air Transport Command, exiting the service as a major in 1945; graduated from Princeton University, 1933. Following his time as Secretary of the Army, he was chairman of the American Council of NATO from 1957 to 1960, Vice Chairman, President's Commission on National Goals from 1959 to 1960, and a member of the President's Foreign Intelligence Advisory Board from 1961 to 1973.

Palmer, Bruce (1913-2000): Commander, U.S. Army Readiness Command, 1972-1974; Acting Army Chief of Staff, 1972; Army Vice Chief of Staff, 1968-1972; Deputy Commanding General of Army Forces in Vietnam, 1967-1968; Commander, II Field Force, Vietnam, 1967; Commander, XVIII Airborne Corps, 1965-1967; instructor, Infantry School, 1949-1951; during World War II was Chief of Staff, 6th Infantry Division, Pacific Theater, 1944-1945; graduated from the U.S. Military Academy, 1936.

Ralston, Joseph W (b. 1943): Supreme Allied Commander, Europe, 2000-2003, Vice Chairman of the Joint Chiefs of Staff, 1996-2000, Commander, Alaskan Command, 11th Air Force, 1992-1994;

Commander, 56th Tactical Training Wing, 1986-1987; Operations officer and Commander, 68th Tactical Fighter Squadron, 1979-1980; Student, Army Command and General Staff College, 1975-1976; Fighter Requirements Officer and Project Officer for F-15 and lightweight fighter programs, 1971-1973; F-105 combat crew member, 67th (later 12th) Tactical Fighter Squadron, Japan, 1967-1969; commissioned through ROTC at Miami University of Ohio, 1965.

Reimer, Dennis J. (b. 1939): Army Chief of Staff, 1995-1999; Commanding General, U.S. Army Forces Command, 1993-1995; Army Vice Chief of Staff, 1991-1993; Commander, 4th Infantry Division, 1988-1990; Commanding General, III Corps Artillery, 1984-1986; Commander, 1st Battalion, 27th Artillery, 4th Infantry Division, 1976-1978, assistant executive officer and aide to then-Army Chief of Staff, General Creighton Abrams, 1972-1974; executive officer and S-3 (Operations), 2d Battalion, 4th Artillery, 9th Infantry Division in Vietnam, 1968-1970; graduated from the United States Military Academy, 1962.

Ridgway, Matthew B. (1895-1993): Army Chief of Staff, 1953-1955; Supreme Allied Commander, Europe, 1952-1953; Supreme Allied Commander in the Far East, 1951-1952; Commander, 8th Army in Korean operations, 1950-1951; during World War II he served in the War Plans Division of the General Staff from 1939 to 1942, commanded the 82d Airborne Division from 1942 to 1944 and the XVIII Airborne Corps from 1944 to 1945; technical adviser to the Governor General of the Philippines, 1932-1933; served on the American Electoral Commission in Nicaragua and the Bolivia-Paraguay Commission of Inquiry and Conciliation, 1927-1929; graduated from the United States Military Academy, 1917.

Roberts, Pat (b. 1936): U.S. Senator (Republican, Kansas), 1997-present, with service on the Ethics and Intelligence committees; U.S. Representative, 1981-1997; administrative assistant to various U.S. Congressmen, 1967 -1980; Captain, U.S. Marine Corps, 1958-1962.

Rogers, Bernard (1921-2008): Supreme Allied Commander, NATO, 1979-1987; Army Chief of Staff, 1976-1979; Commanding General, U.S. Army Forces Command, 1974-1976; Chief of Legislative Liaison, 1971-1972; Deputy Chief of Staff for Personnel, 1972-1974; Commander, 5th Infantry Division and Fort Carson, 1969-1970; Commandant of Cadets, West Point, 1967-1969; Assistant Division Commander, 1st Infantry Division, Vietnam, 1966-1967; military assistant and executive officer to the Chairman of the Joint Chiefs of Staff, 1962-1966; Commander, 3d Battalion, 9th Infantry in Korean operations, 1952-1953; attended Oxford University, England, as a Rhodes Scholar, 1947-1950; graduated from the United States Military Academy, 1943.

Schlesinger, James (b. 1929): Secretary, Department of Energy, 1977-1979; Secretary of Defense, 1973-1975; Director, Central Intelligence Agency, 1973; Chairman, Atomic Energy Commission, 1971-1973; Assistant Director, Bureau of the Budget, 1969-1971; teacher of economics, University of Virginia, 1955-1963; graduated Harvard, 1950, received Ph.D. in Economics, 1956.

Schoomaker, Peter J. (b. 1946): Army Chief of Staff, 2003-2007; Commander, U.S. Special Operations Command, 1997-2000; Commander, U.S. Army Special Operations Command, 1996-1997; Commander, Joint Special Operations Command, 1994-1996; served in various command positions (1978-1981, 1985-1988), and eventually commanded 1st Special Forces Operational Detachment D, 1989-1992; S-3 and S-4, 1st Squadron, 2nd Armored Cavalry, 1972-1973; commissioned through ROTC at the University of Wyoming, 1969.

Shalikashvili, John (1936-2011): Chairman, Joint Chiefs of Staff, 1993-1997; Supreme Allied Commander, Europe, 1992-1993; Commander, Joint Task Force Provide Comfort, Northern Iraq, 1991-1992; Commander, 9th Infantry Division, 1987-1989 ; Commander, 1st Armored Division Artillery, 1979-1981; senior district advisor, Vietnam, 1968-1969; drafted into Army, receives commission through Officer Candidate School, 1959; received American citizenship, 1958; graduated Bradley University, 1958;

Shelton, Henry H. (b. 1942): Chairman, Joint Chiefs of Staff, 1997-2001; Commander, U.S. Special Operations Command, 1996-1997; Commander, XVIII Airborne Corps, 1993-1996; Commander, 82nd Airborne Division, 1991-1993; Assistant Division Commander, 101st Airborne Division, Gulf War, 1989-1991; Commander, 1st Brigade, 82nd Airborne Division, 1983-1985; Commander, 3rd Battalion, 60th Infantry, 9th Infantry Division, 1979-1981; during Vietnam, Intelligence officer, Commander, and operations officer, 4th Battalion, 503rd Infantry, 173rd Airborne Brigade, 1969-1970; commissioned through ROTC at North Carolina State University, 1964.

Short, Dewey (1898-1979): Assistant Secretary of the Army, 1957-1961; U.S. Representative (Republican, Missouri), 1929-1931, 1935-1957, with service as chairman, Committee on Armed Services.

Skelton, Ike (1931-2013): U.S. Representative (Democrat, Missouri), 1977-2011, with service as chair, Committee on Armed Services; State Senator, 1971-1977; special assistant attorney general, Missouri State Attorney General, 1961-1963.

Stevens, Robert T. (1899-1983): Secretary of the Amy, 1953-1955; chairman of the Business Advisory Council, U.S. Department of Commerce, 1951-1952; President (1929-1942) and then Chairman of the Board of the J.P. Stevens textile company, 1945-1953; during World War II served in the Office of the Quartermaster General's procurement division, spending some time in the European Theater; served as a second lieutenant of artillery during World War I, 1918.

Stillwell, Richard (1917-1991): Deputy Under Secretary of Defense for Policy, 1981-1985; Commander, U.S. Forces Korea and Eighth Army, 1973-1976; Commander, Sixth Army, 1972-1973; Commander, Provisional Corps Vietnam/XXIV Corps, 1968-1969; Chief of Operations and Chief of Staff, U.S. Military Assistance Command, Vietnam, 1963-1965; Commander, Cadet Regiment, Deputy Commandant, and Commandant of Cadets, 1959-1963; Commander, 15th Infantry Regiment, 3rd Infantry Division, Korea, 1952-1953; during World War II he was an operations officer, 90th Infantry Division, and Assistant Chief of Staff, Operations, XXII Corps from 1943 to 1945; graduated United States Military Academy, 1938.

Sullivan, Gordon R. (b. 1937): Army Chief of Staff, 1991-1995; Army Vice Chief of Staff, 1990-1991; Deputy Chief of Staff for Operations and Plans, 1989-1990; Commander, 1st Infantry Division, 1988-1989; Commander, 1st Brigade, 3rd Armored Division, 1981-1983; Commander, 4th Battalion, 73rd Armor, 1st Infantry Division, 1980-1981; personnel services officer, Headquarters, I Field Force, Vietnam, 1969-1970; assistant chief of staff, J-2 (Intelligence), Military Assistance Command, Vietnam, 1963-1964; assistant Civil Guard/Self-Defense Corps adviser, 21st infantry Division, Military Assistance Advisory Group, Vietnam, 1962-1963; commissioned through ROTC at Norwich University, 1959.

Taylor, Maxwell D. (1901-1987): Chairman, Joint Chiefs of Staff, 1962-1964; Army Chief of Staff, 1955-1959; Commander, U.S. Forces Far East, and Eighth Army, 1954-1955; commanded Eighth Army in the final operations of the Korean War, 1953; Commander, U.S. Forces in Berlin, 1949-1951; during World War II was Chief of Staff and Artillery Commander of 82nd Airborne Division from 1942 to 1944, and commanded the 101st Airborne Division in the Normandy invasion and follow-on operations from 1944 to 1945; student of Japanese at the American embassy in Tokyo, 1935-1939; taught French and Spanish at West Point, 1927-1932; graduated from the United States Military Academy, 1922. After his military service, he served as Ambassador to South Vietnam from 1964 to 1965 and special consultant to the president and Chairman of the Foreign Intelligence Advisory Board from 1965 to 1969.

Thurman, Maxwell R. (1931-1995): Commander, U.S. Southern Command, 1989-1991; Commander, Training and Doctrine Command, 1987-1989, Army Vice Chief of Staff, 1983-1987; Deputy Chief of Staff, Personnel, 1981-1983; Commander, U.S. Army Recruiting Command, 1979-1981, Commander, 2nd Howitzer Battalion, 35th Artillery Regiment, Vietnam, 1968-1969; Intelligence Officer, I Vietnamese Corps, 1961-1963; commissioned through ROTC at North Carolina State University, 1953.

Trefry, Richard (b.1928): Military Assistant to the President of the United States, 1990-1992; Inspector General of the Army, 1977-1983; Assistant Deputy Chief of Staff, Personnel, 1975-1976; Commander, Joint United States Military Advisory Group to Laos/Defense Attaché to Laos, 1973; Commander, 1st Armored Division Artillery; during Vietnam commanded an artillery battalion, 1966-1967; "Honest John" battery commander in demilitarized zone in Korea; graduated from the United States Military Academy, 1950; enlisted in Army Air Corps, 1943.

Truman, Harry S. (1884-1972): President of the United States, 1945-1953; Vice President, 1945; United States Senator (Democrat, Missouri), 1934-1945; judge and presiding judge, Jackson County Court, 1922-1924 and 1926-1934; during World War I was a field artillery officer, serving with Battery D, 129th Field Artillery in combat as a first lieutenant and captain, eventually achieved the rank of colonel in the U.S. Army Reserves.

Van Fleet, James (1892-1992): Commander, Eighth Army, Korea, 1950-1953; during World War II commanded the 8th Infantry Regiment, 4th Infantry Division from 1941 to 1944, the 90th Division in 1944, and the III Corps in operations in Western Europe from 1944 to 1945; during World War I commanded a machine gun battalion in the Meuse Argonne offensive, 1918; graduated from the United States Military Academy, 1915.

Vessey, John Jr. (b. 1922): Chairman, Joint Chiefs of Staff, 1982-1985; Commander, 8th Army and United Nations Command, Korea, 1976-1979; Deputy Chief of Staff, Operations and Plans, 1975-1976; Commander, 4th Infantry Division, 1974-1975; Commander, U.S. Army Support Command, Thailand, 1970-1971; Commander, 3rd Armored Division Artillery, 1967-1969; Executive Officer, 25th Infantry Division Artillery, Vietnam, 1966-1967; Commander, 2nd Battalion, 73rd Artillery, 3rd Armored Division, 1963-1965; Chief, Operations Branch, Artillery Section, 8th Army Korea, 1958-1959; during World War II served with the 34th Division as a First Sergeant from 1942-1944, received battlefield commission in 1944.

Vuono, Carl E (b. 1934): Army Chief of Staff, 1987-1991; Commander, U.S. Army Training and Doctrine Command, 1986-1987; Deputy Chief of Staff for Operations and Plans, 1985-1986;

Commanding General, U.S. Army Combined Arms Center, 1983-1985; Commander, 8th Infantry Division, 1981-1983; executive to the Army Chief of Staff, 1976-1977; Commander, 1st Battalion, 77th Artillery, 1st Cavalry Division, Vietnam, 1970-1971; Executive Officer, 1st Cavalry Division Artillery, Vietnam, 1970; exchange officer, British 7th Royal Horse Artillery, England, 1963-1965; graduated from the United States Military Academy, 1957.

West, Togo D. (b. 1942): Secretary of Veteran's Affairs, 1998-2000; Secretary of the Army, 1993-1998; general counsel of the Department of Defense, 1980-1981; special assistant to the Secretary and Deputy Secretary of Defense, 1979-1980; general counsel of the Department of the Navy, 1977-1979; judge advocate in the Office of the Assistant Secretary of the Army (Manpower and Reserve Affairs), 1969-1973; commissioned in the U.S. Army Judge Advocate General Corps, 1969.

Westmoreland, William (1914-2005): Army Chief of Staff, 1968-1972; Commander, U.S. Military Assistance Command, Vietnam, 1964-1968; Commander, Strategic Army Corps and XVIII Airborne Corps, 1963-1964; superintendent, U.S. Military Academy, 1960-1963; Commander, 187th Regimental Combat Team, Korea, 1952-1953; during World War II Chief of Staff, 9th Infantry Division from 1944 to 1945, Executive Officer of the 9th Division of Artillery in Western Europe in 1944, operations officer of the 34th Field Artillery Battalion, 9th Infantry Division in North Africa and a battalion commander during operations in Tunisia and Sicily from 1942 to 1944; graduated from the United States Military Academy, 1936.

Weyand, Frederick (1916-2010): Army Chief of Staff, 1974-1976; Army Vice Chief of Staff, 1973-1974; Commander, U.S. Army Pacific, 1973; Deputy Commander and Commander of U.S. Military Assistance Command, Vietnam, 1970-1973; Commander, II Field Force, Vietnam, 1967-1968; Commander, 25th Infantry Division, Hawaii and Vietnam, 1964-1967; Military Assistant and Executive Officer to the Secretary of the Army, 1954-1957; battalion commander in 7th Infantry and Assistant Chief of Staff, G-3, 3rd Infantry Division, Korea, 1950-1951; Assistant Chief of Staff for Intelligence, China-Burma-India Theater, 1944-1945; commissioned through ROTC at the University of California, Berkeley, 1938.

White, Thomas (b. 1943): Secretary of the Army, 2001-2003; retired from Army as a brigadier general, 1990; executive assistant to the Chairman, Joint Chiefs of Staff, 1989-1990; Commander, 11th Armored Cavalry Regiment (ACR), 1986-1988; Commander, 1st Squadron, 11th ACR, 1981-1983; served in Vietnam as a platoon leader with the 11th ACR (1968, 1969) and as an air cavalry aviation officer in 1972; graduated from the United States Military Academy, 1967.

Zumwalt, Elmo (1920-2000): Chief of Naval Operations, 1970-1974; Commander, Naval Forces Vietnam, 1968-1970; aide to Assistant Secretary of Defense and assistant to Secretary of the Navy, 1962-1963; Navigator, USS Wisconsin, during operations in Korea, 1951-1952; duty aboard USS Robinson in the Pacific during World War II, 1944-1945; graduated from U.S. Naval Academy, 1942.

Works Cited

Agnew, Spiro. *Speech on Television News Coverage.* November 13, 1969, Des Moines, IA. American Rhetoric, Top 100 Speeches website, accessed March 21, 2014. http://www.americanrhetoric.com/speeches/spiroagnewtvnewscoverage.htm

Albright, Madeline. *Madam Secretary.* New York: Miramax Books, 2003.

Aurthur, Robert Alan. "Harry Truman Chuckles Dryly." *Esquire,* September 1971: 134-137, 256-262.

---. "The Wit and Sass of Harry S. Truman." *Esquire,* August 1971: 62-67, 115-118.

Bland, Theodoric C., Col. *Colonel Theodoric C. Bland to Harry S. Truman.* January 8, 1964; PPP 840, Truman Papers, Truman Library.

Borman, Frank. "Report to the Secretary of the Army by the Special Commission on the United States Military Academy." Department of the Army, December 15, 1976. http://www.west-point.org/publications/borman.html, accessed on March 17, 2013.

Bradley, Omar N. *A General's Life.* New York: Simon and Schuster, 1983.

Clines, Francis X. "Drill Sergeant Gets 6 Months For Sex Abuse at Army Post." *The New York Times,* May 31, 1997, accessed March 19, 2014. http://www.nytimes.com/1997/05/31/us/drill-sergeant-gets-6-months-for-sex-abuse-at-army-post.html

Collins, J. Lawton. *Lightning Joe: An Autobiography.* Baton Rouge: Louisiana State University Press, 1979.

Combat Studies Institute. "History of Transformation." *Military Review,* May-June 2000: 17-29.

Corum, James S. *Rearming Germany.* Boston: Brill, 2011.

Davison, Michael J. *Major General Michael J. Davison to Harry S. Truman.* July 5, 1968; PPP 840, Truman Papers, Truman Library.

Douhet, Giulio, *Command of the Air.* Translated by Dino Ferrari, New Imprint by Office of Air Force History, Washington D.C., 1983, accessed November 21, 2015. https://archive.org/stream/dominiodellariae00unse/dominiodellariae00unse_djvu.txt

Editor. "16-Hour Day Not Enough Says Truman." *The Leavenworth Times* February 16, 1964, sec. 1: 1.

Editor. "Confronted With Critical Need, Services Feel Effects of Actions Against Career Officers." *Army, Navy, Air Force Journal,* May 17, 1952, 1138, 1158, 1164.

Editor. "Saving Face." *Current Events*, May 4, 2001, Vol. 100, Issue 25, 1. Accessed March 19, 2014, http://web.b.ebscohost.com.lumen.cgsccarl.com/ehost/detail?sid=ece0adfc-b16c-4299-8f1a-fff8a20b94c6%40sessionmgr114&vid=1&hid=124&bdata=JnNpdGU9ZWhvc3QtbGl2ZQ%3d%3d#db=a9h&AN=4422077

Frank, Benis M. *U.S. Marines in Lebanon, 1982-1984*. Washington, D.C.: History and Museums Divison, Headquarters, U.S. Marine Corps, U.S. G.P.O., 1987.

Hansen, Richard P. "The Crisis of the West Point Honor Code." *Military Affairs*, April 1985, 57-62.

Harris, Betty F. *Mrs. Betty F. Harris to Harry S. Truman*. Undated (c. 1961); PPP 766, Truman Papers, Truman Library.

Hart, Peter. *The Somme: the Darkest Hour on the Western Front*. New York: Pegasus Books, 2008.

Healy, Melissa. "Navy Secretary Resigns Over Budget Cutbacks: Webb Says He Can't Back Carlucci, Plan to Mothball 16 Ships." *Los Angeles Times*, February 23, 1988.

Herbert, Paul H. *Deciding What Has to Be Done: General William E. DePuy and the 1976 Edition of FM 100-5, Operations*. Fort Leavenworth, KS: Combat Studies Institute, 1988.

Information Office, Fort Leavenworth. *News Release, Caption 14-021-4428/AL 61*. News Release ed., 1962.

Johnson, Harold K. *Major General Harold K. Johsnon to Harry S. Truman*. January 14, 1961; PPP 840, Truman Papers, Truman Library.

Kugler, Richard L. "Laying the Foundations: The Evolution of NATO in the 1950s." Santa Monica: Rand, 1990. Accessed at www.dtic.mil/cgi-bin/GetTRDoc?AD=ADA257664 on March 3, 2014.

Lemley, Harry J., Jr. *Major General Harry J. Lemley Jr. to Harry S. Truman*. February 7, 1964; PPP 840, Truman Papers, Truman Library.

Marano, Lou. "Top General Cautious About Overseas Interventions." United Press International, June 15, 2000. http://www.balkanpeace.org/index.php?index=article&articleid=10382, accessed March 17, 2013.

McCullough, David G. *Truman*. New York: Simon & Schuster, 1992.

McMaster, H.R. *Dereliction of Duty*. New York: HarperCollins, 1997.

Miller, Merle. *Plain Speaking: An Oral Biography of Harry S. Truman*. New York: Berkley Pub., 1974.

Works Cited

Miller, Merle. <u>Possible Draft Page of Preface from "Plain Speaking"</u>. Undated; Papers of Merle Miller Box 6, Truman Library.

Office of the Secretary of Defense. Military Compensation web page, accessed March 20, 2014. http://militarypay.defense.gov/retirement/ad/04_REDUX.html

Onis, Juan de. "Motive Unknown." *New York Times*, March 26, 1975, 1.

Raddatz, Martha. "Uniform Complaint." *New Republic*, November 30, 1998, 16-18.

Rearden, Steven. *Council of War*. Washington D.C.: NDU Press, 2012.

Ricks, Thomas E. "Rumsfeld Gets Earful from Troops." *The Washington Post*, December 9, 2004, sec. A: 1.

Rosen, Jeffrey. *The Supreme Court: the Personalities and Rivalries That Defined America*. New York: Times Books, 2007.

Savage, David G. "Veteran Army Sergeant Acquitted in Shooting Death of Panamanian." *The Los Angeles Times*, September 1, 1990. Accessed November 21, 2015. http://articles.latimes.com/1990-09-01/news/mn-197_1_vietnam-war

Shinseki, Eric. *Prepared Statement of Gen. Eric K. Shinseki*. United States Senate, Committee on Appropriations, Subcommittee on Defense, Hearings Before A Subcommittee of the Committee on Appropriations, United States Senate, (Washington, DC: GPO, 2000): 406-407, accessed 2011. http://frwebgate4.access.gpo.gov/cgi-bin/PDFgate.cgi?WAISdocID=658239255280+0+2+0&WAISaction=retrieve

Sorley, Lewis. *Honorable Warrior*. Kansas: University Press, 1998.

Stockstill, Louis. "The Big DOD Build-Up." *Journal of the Armed Forces*, May 6, 1967, 1, 3, 31.

Truman, Harry S. *Harry S. Truman to Major General Harold K. Johnson*. October 12, 1960; PPP 840, Truman Papers, Truman Library.

---. *Harry S. Truman to Major General Harry Lemley*. September 30, 1963; PPP 840, Truman Papers, Truman Library.

---. *Harry S. Truman to Major General Harry Lemley*. November 27, 1963; PPP 840, Truman Papers, Truman Library.

---. Korea Decision Sound Recording Excerpts from 15DEC61 Truman Session at Fort Leavenworth: Compact Disc MP2002-86 and MP2002-87, Screen Gems Collection, and Reel Tapes SR94-9, 1961; Merle Miller Papers, Truman Library.

Unknown. *Truman at Fort Leavenworth: The Korean Decision. Notes on Filming*. 1961; PPP 768, Truman Papers, Truman Library.

---. *Truman at Fort Leavenworth: The Korean Decision. Schedule for Filming.* 1961; PPP 768, Truman Papers, Truman Library.

Whiting, Charles. *Bradley.* New York: Ballantine Books Inc., 1971.

Works, Robert C., Mrs. *Mrs. Robert C. Works to Harry S. Truman.* January 16, 1961; PPP 766, Truman Papers, Truman Library.

Zelizer, Julian E. *Aresnal of Democracy.* New York: Basic Books, 2010.

Index

D

E

Z

Made in the USA
Las Vegas, NV
20 November 2023

81206426R00203